COUNSELING FOR WELLNESS

Theory, Research, and Practice

Edited by
Jane E. Myers
Thomas J. Sweeney

AMERICAN COUNSELING ASSOCIATION
5999 Stevenson Avenue
Alexandria, VA 22304
www.counseling.org

COUNSELING
FOR
WELLNESS

Theory, Research, and Practice

10 9 8 7 6 5 4 3 2 1

American Counseling Association
5999 Stevenson Avenue
Alexandria, VA 22304

Director of Publications
Carolyn C. Baker

Production Manager
Bonny E. Gaston

Copy Editor
Elaine Dunn

Cover design by Bonny E. Gaston

Library of Congress Cataloging-in-Publication Data
Counseling for wellness: theory, research, and practice/Jane E. Myers & Thomas J. Sweeney, editors.
    p. cm.
Includes bibliographical references and index.
ISBN 1-55620-252-0 (alk. paper)
1. Counseling. I. Myers, Jane, E. II. Sweeney, Thomas, J., 1936–

BF637.C6C6374 2005   2004022820
158'.3—dc22

To all who would like to live long and live well:
We hope that this book can help uncover the secrets to doing so.

Acknowledgments

Jane E. Myers and Thomas J. Sweeney
Editors

We might never have considered wellness as an integral part of professional counseling were it not for the early 20th-century pioneers of what was then guidance and counseling. Beginning with Arthur Jones's *Principles of Guidance* in the 1930s right through to the present day, professional counselors have a heritage of and commitment to optimizing human development over the life span. Wellness, then, is not new per se. Our work simply extends and defines it more specifically through research and methods designed to help practitioners be more effective.

We also have current leaders in counseling to thank for their inspiration and encouragement. Professor Emeritus Dr. Melvin Witmer of Ohio University is foremost as our colleague and collaborator in the search for defining and explaining the elements of a first model and assessment of wellness suitable for use by practitioners and researchers alike. Pennsylvania State University's Distinguished Professor Dr. Edwin L. Herr's encouragement spurred us to conceptualize this work and see it to completion.

While not of the profession of counseling, we wish to acknowledge the leadership, inspiration, and example set by the Honorable Tommy Thompson, U.S. Secretary of Health and Human Services. There is no better spokesperson or advocate for a wellness approach to solving a broad range of problems in our society. His message is compelling in its substance and breadth.

The support of Dr. Robert Most of MindGarden, Inc. deserves special mention as one who believed that our first measure of wellness (the Wellness Evaluation of Lifestyle, or WEL Inventory) deserved to be available to others for use in research and practice.

Our students, workshop participants, and those who have taken and used our instruments and models over the years have our most sincere gratitude. Their feedback and encouragement have been invaluable. Several are among the authors of this book.

Of particular importance in furthering both wellness research and applications are the many scholars who, through their doctoral dissertations and related studies, helped to extend our knowledge of the meaning, scope, applications, and implications of a wellness philosophy. Those individuals, many of whom are authors for chapters in this book, included researchers from the University of North Carolina at Greensboro (Catherine Chang, Kathleen Connolly, Brian Dew, Caroline Booth, Carol Dice, Michael Garrett, Carman Gill, Holly Hartwig Moorhead, Gerald Hutchinson, Jayamala Madathil, Linda Makinson, Natasha Mitchell, Keith Mobley, Anne Powers, Andrea Dixon Rayle, Matthew Shurts, Stacey Sinclair, Shawn Spurgeon, and Suzanne Degges-White), Ohio University (Paul Granello, David Hermon, Fran Steigerwald, and Tom Vecchione), the University of New Orleans (Holly Tanigoshi), University of Florida (Stephanie Webster), the University of Arkansas (Wendy Enochs), and Haceteppe University in Ankara, Turkey (Turkan Dogan). At the time of this writing, additional studies are being conducted at the University of Technology, Sydney, Australia (Kerrie Wilson), The Nelson Mandela University in Port Elizabeth, South Africa (Sharon Amery), the University of Central Florida (Linda Roach and Linda Vanderbleek), San Jose State University (Kathryn Casey), Arizona State University (Tiffany Rice), the University of North Carolina at Greensboro (Mike Pisarchik and Derick Williams), and the University of Maryland (Dwayne Eugene Ham). These ongoing studies are among those that will further extend the knowledge base of wellness concepts and constructs.

For assistance in collecting data and literature for a review of wellness preparation in counselor education at institutions with honor society chapters of Chi Sigma Iota, Philip Clarke deserves special recognition. Likewise, for assistance with final editing of references, we want to thank Sweety Patel. Both are students at the University of North Carolina at Greensboro.

Finally, we wish to thank the reviewers for this work and their helpful insights and suggestions. In addition, Carolyn Baker of the American Counseling Association is especially deserving of mention for her thorough, timely, and incisive final editing and preparation of this book.

Table of Contents

Part III

WELLNESS APPLICATIONS IN COUNSELING: PROFESSIONAL PRACTICE

Part IV

WELLNESS APPLICATIONS IN COUNSELING SETTINGS
AND COUNSELOR EDUCATION

Foreword

A. Scott McGowan
Editor, Journal of Counseling & Development

The therapeutic benefits of a counseling approach that encompasses wellness as a key, critical ingredient have been well documented and empirically researched throughout the years. I personally follow a developmental, wellness model in terms of my own counseling practice and counseling philosophy. As a counselor educator, I am reinforced in this perspective by my own Department of Counseling and Development at Long Island University, C.W. Post that follows a wellness/developmental model. As such, Myers and Sweeney's *Counseling for Wellness: Theory, Research, and Practice* provides both the theoretical foundations and practical application for those of us who adhere to this point of view. The book will also open wide the doors of exploration for those seeking a fresh, cutting-edge counseling perspective and techniques that are theoretically sound, evidenced based, and practical in their application.

This book by Myers and Sweeney is divided into four parts. Part I: Wellness Theory and Measurement informs the reader in terms of the theoretical foundations of wellness and describes several wellness models, as well as providing both formal and informal approaches to assessing wellness. Part II: Wellness Research is both comprehensive and specific in terms of various populations (children, adults, etc.) and in terms of such variables as gender and sexual orientation, disabilities, and ethnicity. It concludes with an integrative chapter on wellness research by Earl J. Ginter, my predecessor as editor of the *Journal of Counseling & Development*. Part III: Wellness Applications in Counseling: Professional Practice moves through the stages of change and wellness and covers such topics as stress management and wellness interventions, spirituality in the counseling process, and habits and behavior change. Part IV: Wellness Applications in Counseling Settings and Counselor Education directly addresses practical implications for counseling in the major settings in which professional counselors work with clients and students, to wit: schools, community mental health agencies, colleges and universities, and business and industry. This section also covers wellness in counselor education and supervision.

In a National Public Radio address to the National Press Club (November 20, 2003), the Honorable Tommy G. Thompson, Secretary of the U.S.

Department of Health and Human Services, himself an avid advocate for wellness, addressed the high cost of health care and lamented the lack of prevention, which can lead to chronic diseases:

> The recently passed Medicare law also moves our health care system from a focus on treating disease to a focus on preventing disease. Our doctors will not be satisfied just to keep people alive; they will also keep them well. *From now on, we will measure success not by the absence of illness, but in the quality of life.*

Professional counselors, of course, deal not only with clients who suffer from chronic illnesses, many of which are preventable or treatable, but also with clients who experience psychological, emotional, and spiritual stress, as well as healthy, balanced human beings who seek to obtain even more fulfilling lives. Following a wellness model, counselors can be instrumental in helping clients and students in assessing and creating a healthy lifestyle that is holistic and "quality-of-life" enhancing. This book leads the way to life span wellness through a "best practices" approach that rests on sound research. Professional counselors are in a unique position of challenging clients to introspectively and reflectively look at their lives and life choices, as well as their basic living habits and behaviors that need to be changed to achieve balance and wellness. One of the goals of the counselor is to enable clients to clearly define what they want and to question the effectiveness of their current lifestyle in achieving wellness, and then to change what needs to be changed.

The purpose of the book is to provide the knowledge and means for professional counselors to help individuals across the life span to answer these questions with specific, positive, life-enhancing declarations. It is clear that children need to learn as early as possible how to make healthy choices and develop lifelong habits in all aspects of their lives. No less important are older persons and the opportunities they have to change old habits and improve the quality of their lives. In short, wellness should be a priority for everyone.

Counseling for Wellness: Theory, Research, and Practice is a solid, innovative, and state-of-the-art addition to the scholarly base of the profession and a model "best practices" tool for practicing counselors in all areas, counselor educators, and graduate students who aspire to become effective and competent professional counselors. I believe that readers will find this book to be relevant, not only in their professional lives but in their own personal lives as well.

About the Editors

Jane E. Myers, PhD, LPC, NCC, is a professor of counselor education at the University of North Carolina at Greensboro. She earned her bachelor's degree from the University of California, Berkeley, and her master's educational specialist and doctorate in counselor education from the University of Florida in Gainesville. She is a Fellow of the Gerontological Society of America, the Association for Gerontology in Higher Education, and the National Rehabilitation Counseling Association, and a Charter Fellow of the Chi Sigma Iota Academy of Leaders for Excellence.

A past president of the American Counseling Association (ACA) and two of its divisions, the Association for Assessment in Counseling and the Association for Adult Development and Aging for which she was founding president, Dr. Myers also served as chair of the Council for Accreditation of Counseling and Related Educational Programs (CACREP). In 2003, she was selected for inclusion in *Leaders and Legacies in Counseling*, a book that chronicles the contributions of the 25 individuals selected as among the most significant leaders in the counseling profession over the last century. She is twice recipient of the ACA Research Award in addition to ACA's most prestigious award, the Gilbert and Kathleen Wrenn Caring Person Award. She has been nominated by students three times for the University of North Carolina Teaching Excellence Award.

Dr. Myers developed a model and curriculum resources for infusion of gerontological counseling into counselor education, and coauthored (with Dr. Sweeney) the national competencies for training gerontological counselors. They coproduced seven training videotapes to promote counselor competence in this specialty. She has written and edited numerous publications, including 16 books and monographs and over 120 refereed journal articles, and she was noted as being in the top 1% of contributors to the *Journal of Counseling & Development*, ACA's flagship journal. Her books include *Adult Children and Aging Parents, Empowerment for Later Life, Developmental Counseling and Therapy: Promoting Wellness Over the Lifespan* (coauthored with Allen and Mary Bradford Ivey and Thomas J. Sweeney), and *The Handbook of Counseling* (coedited with Don C. Locke and Edwin L. Herr).

Thomas J. Sweeney, PhD, LPC, is a professor emeritus in counselor education in the College of Education at Ohio University in Athens, Ohio, and executive director of Chi Sigma Iota, International. He earned his bachelor's degree in social studies from the University of Akron, his master's degree in school counseling from the University of Wisconsin–Madison, and his PhD in counselor education from The Ohio State University.

Dr. Sweeney's scholarship, leadership, and service reflect a long and distinguished career. He has been national president of the Association of Counselor Educators and Supervisors (ACES) and president of ACA (formerly the American Personnel and Guidance Association, APGA). He served as the founding chair of CACREP and helped shepherd the Council to national acceptance and recognition among accrediting agencies. He wrote the ACA-adopted position on licensure that spearheaded ACA's state-by-state efforts for counselor licensure and remains the foundation of licensure efforts nationally. He served as founding president of the International Association for Marriage and Family Counseling prior to its becoming a division of ACA, and he was an elected board member of the Association for Adult Development and Aging and the National Association for Career Development. He also was the founding president of Chi Sigma Iota (CSI) Counseling Academic and Professional Honor Society International and is a charter member of the CSI Academy of Leaders for Excellence.

He has received numerous awards for leadership and service, including two national awards each from ACA and ACES. He also has the distinction of two awards associated with his name. In addition to books, monographs, chapters in books, research reports, and articles, Dr. Sweeney has had both training videos and an award-winning telecourse, Coping With Kids, distributed worldwide and broadcast on state and regional television. His book on *Adlerian Counseling* is in its fourth edition. He was noted as being in the top 5% of contributors to the *Journal of Counseling & Development* and selected for inclusion in *Leaders and Legacies in Counseling*, a book that identified 25 people as among the most significant leaders in the counseling profession over the last century. His most recent book, *Developmental Counseling and Therapy: Promoting Wellness Over the Lifespan*, was coauthored with Allen and Mary Bradford Ivey and Jane E. Myers.

Drs. Myers and Sweeney are coauthors of one theoretical (with Melvin Witmer) and two evidence-based models of wellness and assessment instruments based on these models. They are advocates for wellness lifestyles for people of all ages across the life span, including their 10 grandchildren and 85-year-old uncle and his fiancé (also 85). They share a love of flying, gardening, boating, exercise, healthy eating, reading, quality time with family and friends, watching sunsets, and Princess, their lab/Australian Shepherd dog.

About the Contributors

L. DiAnne Borders, PhD, LPC, NCC, ACS, is a professor and chair of the Department of Counseling and Educational Development at the University of North Carolina at Greensboro. Coauthor of the *Handbook of Counseling Supervision* and its upcoming revision, she has published numerous conceptual and empirical works on supervision practice and supervisor training and has received several awards for her work. She also has written extensively on school counseling and adopted children and their families.

JoLynn V. Carney, PhD, PCC, is an associate professor of Counselor Education at Penn State University. She is the author of numerous articles on counseling, suicide, and prevention of youth violence. Her clinical work has included agency counseling and also work in the schools emphasizing creative and wellness-based approaches.

Craig S. Cashwell, PhD, LPC, is a professor in the Department of Counseling and Educational Development at the University of North Carolina at Greensboro. He is coeditor of *Integrating Spirituality in Counseling: A Guide to Competent Practice* (American Counseling Association, 2005) and has published numerous conceptual and empirical articles on spirituality in counseling. He is a previous president of the Association for Spiritual, Ethical, and Religious Values in Counseling.

Catherine Y. Chang, PhD, LPC, NCC, is an assistant professor at Georgia State University. Her research interests include multicultural issues in counselor education and supervision, Asian American and Korean American concerns, and multicultural issues in assessment. She is a recent recipient of the ACA Research Award.

Kathleen M. Connolly, PhD, LPC, is the founder of Acumeans, Inc., a professional counseling and organizational consulting practice in Charlotte, North Carolina. She is an adjunct instructor in the Department of Counseling, Special Education and Child Development at the University of North Carolina at Charlotte and a career counselor at Central Piedmont Community College.

Suzanne E. Degges-White, PhD, LPC, NCC, is an assistant professor at Purdue University Calumet. She has published empirical and conceptual works on wellness, adult development in women, and sexual identity formation. Her research interests include the transitions experienced by contemporary midlife women, the lesbian midlife experience, and women's wellness throughout the life span. She has received a number of grants and awards for her research.

Brian J. Dew, PhD, is an assistant professor in The Department of Counseling and Psychological Services at Georgia State University. His primary research interests include wellness issues with gay, lesbian, bisexual, and transgendered (GLBT) populations. His research and publications have focused on such issues as coming out, sexual compulsivity, substance abuse, at-risk sexual behavior, and GLBT parenting. He is a recent recipient of the ACES Research Award.

Earl J. Ginter, PhD, LPC, LMFT, is a professor at the University of Georgia. He is a former editor of both the *Journal of Counseling & Development* and the *Journal of Mental Health Counseling*. His publications focus on issues that comprise the theoretical and practice base of counseling. His research and assessment interests pertain to the application of developmental-based approaches to working with individuals, couples, families, and groups.

Paul F. Granello, PhD, LPCC, is an associate professor at The Ohio State University. He is interested in researching the psychological and social mediators of individual wellness and has written several articles and presented numerous workshops in this area. Dr. Granello currently teaches a graduate-level counseling course on wellness and prevention. He has also written on psychotherapy outcome research, technology for counselors, and counseling at-risk children and adolescents.

Danica G. Hays, MS, NCC, is a doctoral student at Georgia State University. Her research interests include multicultural issues in counselor education and supervision with an emphasis on racial identity development and privilege and oppression issues, and multicultural competency assessment.

Richard J. Hazler, PhD, PCC, NCC, is an associate professor of Counselor Education and coordinator of Elementary School Counseling at Penn State University. He has published several books and numerous articles on the developmental nature of youth violence and humanistic approaches to counseling and counselor education.

David A. Hermon, PhD, LPC, is a professor of Counseling and coordinator of the College Student Affairs track at Marshall University. He has published on wellness, psychological well-being, and college student development. His research interests focus on the use of positive psychology and wellness strategies to promote community and student development in higher education.

Cheryl Holcomb-McCoy, PhD, NCC, is an assistant professor at the University of Maryland, College Park. She is the author of numerous journal articles and book chapters related to school counseling and multicultural issues. She is a former Secretary of Chi Sigma Iota International and is currently the American School Counselor Association Diversity Professional Network Chairperson.

Allen E. Ivey, EdD, ABPP, is Distinguished University Professor (Emeritus) at the University of Massachusetts, Amherst; president of Microtraining Associates, an educational publishing firm; and member of the board of the National Institute for Multicultural Competence. He developed the microskills approach to training and has authored or coauthored over 30 books and 200 articles and chapters, including *Developmental Counseling and Therapy: Promoting Wellness Over the Lifespan,* coauthored with Mary Bradford Ivey, Jane E. Myers, and Thomas J. Sweeney.

Mary Bradford Ivey, EdD, NCC, LMHC, is vice president of Microtraining Associates, an educational publishing firm, and on the board of directors of the National Institute for Multicultural Competence. Her school guidance program in Massachusetts was named one of the 10 best in the nation, and her multicultural work has brought her the ACA 'Ohana Award. She has coauthored 10 books, several articles, and produced several videotapes, among them *Counseling Children, Counseling Latina/o Children,* and many microskill video demonstrations. Her most recent book is *Developmental Counseling and Therapy: Promoting Wellness Over the Lifespan,* coauthored with Allen E. Ivey, Jane E. Myers, and Thomas J. Sweeney.

Courtland C. Lee, PhD, is a professor and director of the Counselor Education Program at the University of Maryland, College Park. He is the author, editor, or coeditor of four books on multicultural counseling and has published numerous articles and book chapters on counseling across cultures. His primary research interest is the psychosocial development of African American males. He is a past president of the Association of Multicultural Counseling and Development, ACA, and Chi Sigma Iota.

A. Scott McGowan, PhD, NCC, ACS, is a professor and chair of the Department of Counseling and Development, Long Island University, C.W. Post. He is past editor of the *Journal for the Professional Counselor* and the *Journal of Humanistic Counseling and Development,* and has just been appointed for a second term as the editor of the *Journal of Counseling & Development.* Past president of the Counseling Association for Humanistic Education and Development, he has received numerous professional awards, including ACA's Hitchcock Distinguished Professional Service Award.

Holly J. Hartwig Moorhead, PhD, LPCC, is an assistant professor in Counseling and Human Development at Walsh University. Her research interests include integrating wellness approaches in working with individuals across the life span, specifically, promoting wellness-based treatment interventions with adolescents and at-risk youths. She was selected as a Chi Sigma Iota (CSI) intern from among nominees in over 200 chapters of CSI.

Kathryn S. Newton, MS, LAPC, is currently a doctoral student in the Department of Counseling and Psychological Services at Georgia State University. She is a certified yoga instructor and yoga therapist and has extensive experience training individuals and primary providers in self-care techniques. Her research interests include identifying and providing effective wellness interventions, particularly for substance abuse populations.

Margaret A. Nosek, PhD, is a professor in the Department of Physical Medicine and Rehabilitation and founder and executive director of the

Center for Research on Women With Disabilities at Baylor College of Medicine. Her publications have focused on psychosocial and physical health, secondary conditions, health promotion, reproductive health care, sexuality, self-esteem, and violence against women with disabilities. As a person with a severe physical disability, she has been a pioneer and activist in the disability rights movement.

Cynthia J. Osborn, PhD, LPCC, is an associate professor in the Counseling and Human Development Services Program at Kent State University. Her teaching and research concentrations are in the areas of substance abuse counseling, solution-focused counseling, and counseling supervision. In addition, she is one of three editors (along with John D. West and Donald L. Bubenzer) of *Leaders and Legacies: Contributions to the Profession of Counseling*. She is currently president of the Ohio Counseling Association.

Andrea Dixon Rayle, PhD, NCC, is an assistant professor in Counseling and Counseling Psychology at Arizona State University. Her research interests include adolescents, wellness, mattering, meaning making, school counseling, school counselor education, and multicultural counseling with racially/ethnically diverse individuals. She has published in the areas of spirituality and mattering, racial/ethnic minority adolescents, and multicultural counseling.

W. Matthew Shurts, PhD, NCC, is an assistant professor at Montclair State University. He recently completed his dissertation titled, "The Relationships Among Marital Messages Received, Marital Attitudes, Relationship Self-Efficacy, and Wellness Among Traditional-Aged, Never-Married Undergraduate Students." Dr. Shurts has published numerous articles in peer-reviewed journals, and his research interests include the promotion of healthy romantic relationships and premarital counseling.

Moshe I. Tatar, PhD, is a senior lecturer and head of the Division of Educational Counseling at the School of Education, the Hebrew University of Jerusalem, Israel. He has published many articles in national and international journals. His major research interests focus on school counseling and psychology and include counseling immigrant populations, adolescent help-seeking behaviors and attitudes, diversity and multicultural education, and parental perceptions of schools.

José A. Villalba, PhD, NCC, is an assistant professor in the Department of Counseling and Educational Development at the University of North Carolina at Greensboro. His research interests include the academic and personal/social development of Latino children and adolescents and related school counseling services. He has published articles and chapters related to working with diverse and multicultural individuals.

J. Melvin Witmer, PhD, is Professor Emeritus, Counselor Education, Ohio University, where he taught for 32 years. He is author of the book, *Pathways to Personal Growth*, a holistic education approach for counselors and teachers, and codeveloper of the Wheel of Wellness, a holistic model for counseling and human development. His professional presentations and publications have focused on counselor credentialing, stress management, ethical issues, wellness, and leaders in the field of counselor education.

J. Scott Young, PhD, NCC, LPC, is an associate professor in the Department of Counseling, Educational Psychology and Special Education at Mississippi State University. He is coeditor of *Integrating Spirituality Into Counseling: A Guide to Competent Practice* (American Counseling Association, 2005), has published numerous works on the interface of clinical practice with spirituality and religion, and has received awards for his work. He is past president of the Association for Spiritual, Ethical, and Religious Values in Counseling.

1

Introduction

Jane E. Myers and Thomas J. Sweeney

Fully one-half of all causes of death in the United States are due to lifestyle and behavioral factors (U.S. Department of Health and Human Services [U.S. DHHS], Centers for Disease Control, 2004), which can be modified through conscious choice. Although people can choose not to engage in negative lifestyle behaviors, such choices apparently are difficult to make, as reflected, for example, in the increasing incidence of obesity and obesity-related diseases such as diabetes among Americans. Such diseases are epidemic, with an estimated two-thirds of adults being overweight or obese and one-third of children being similarly at risk (Centers for Disease Control and Prevention, 2002; U.S. DHHS, National Institutes of Health, 2003). In fact, obesity will soon surpass smoking as the leading preventable cause of premature death in the United States (Mokdad, Marks, Stroup, & Gerberding, 2004).

The total costs of illness are enormous, increasing from 5% to almost 16% of the gross national product in the period from 1960 to 2000 (U.S. DHHS, Substance Abuse and Mental Health Services Administration [SAMHSA], 1999). Interestingly, although more than 75% of health care dollars are spent to treat people with chronic diseases, less than 1% of federal funds and 2% of state funds are spent to prevent these diseases from occurring (National Association of Social Workers, 1995). It is widely recognized that health care cost containment will be most effective when the focus is on prevention rather than treatment (U.S. DHHS, SAMHSA, 1999). Thus, developmentally oriented professions such as counseling, which focus on prevention and the optimization of human potential, have a vital role to play in terms of both economic and human costs.

The history of our profession in relation to wellness is anything but new. Both Myers (1992) and Sweeney (1995a, 2001) provided historical perspectives and detailed descriptions of the developmental roots of counseling. They underscored the proactive role taken by the American Counseling Association in 1989 when the resolution shown in Exhibit 1.1 was adopted by the Governing Council. This resolution clearly establishes the role of counselors as advocates for optimum health and wellness for all persons across the life span, consistent with the developmental underpinnings of the

Exhibit 1.1

American Counseling Association Governing Council Wellness Resolution

The Counseling Profession as Advocates for Optimum Health and Wellness

WHEREAS, optimum physical, intellectual, social, occupational, emotional, and spiritual development are worthy goals for all individuals within our society; and

WHEREAS, research in virtually every discipline concerned with human development supports the benefits of wellness for both longevity and quality of life over the life span; and

WHEREAS, the AACD (ACA) membership subscribe to values which promote optimum health and wellness;

THEREFORE BE IT RESOLVED that the Governing Council of AACD (ACA) declare a position for the profession as advocates for policies and programs in all segments of our society which promote and support optimum health and wellness; and

BE IT FURTHER RESOLVED that AACD (ACA) support the counseling and development professions' position as an advocate toward a goal of optimum health and wellness within our society.

Note. Adopted by the Governing Council of the American Association for Counseling and Development (AACD), now the American Counseling Association (ACA), July 13, 1989.

counseling profession in which wellness is and has been historically viewed as a goal of helping (Witmer & Sweeney, 1998). The purpose of the present book is to provide a knowledge base for the profession to enable and support this advocacy role.

In Part I, the authors provide an introduction to wellness theory, beginning with a historical and multidisciplinary perspective spanning not just decades but centuries. Definitions of wellness and early models of wellness that emerged from physical health sciences and the public health area are described. Two comprehensive wellness models based in counseling, the Wheel of Wellness (Witmer, Sweeney, & Myers, 1998) and the Indivisible Self Model of Wellness (Myers & Sweeney, 2004b; Sweeney & Myers, 2005), are described in detail and provide the foundation for the remaining chapters in the book. Mention is made of the positive psychology movement, which emphasizes emotions and which emerged pursuant to the more holistic wellness models described in this section. The final chapter in Part I provides an overview of strategies for wellness assessment, with specific attention to the Wellness Evaluation of Lifestyle created by Witmer, Sweeney, and Myers (1993) and subsequently revised (e.g., Myers, Sweeney, & Witmer, 2000a) and the Five Factor Wellness Inventory (Myers & Sweeney, 2004a).

Wellness research is the focus of Part II, with an emphasis on research in counseling. Our dual purpose in this entire section is to establish the state of the art in relation to wellness research and to establish a long-range research agenda. Each chapter provides an overview of available research, an indepth analysis of studies, and a research agenda for the future that will provide a knowledge base for counselors to help promote wellness for all persons and groups. Each chapter has a specific focus on a segment of the life span or a particular and important population. Life span wellness is reviewed in chapters on children (Holcomb-McCoy), adolescents (Dixon Rayle & Hartwig Moorhead), college students (Osborn), adults (Degges-White & Shurts), and later life (Myers). Special populations include ethnic minorities (Lee), cross-cultural populations (Chang, Hays, & Tatar), gender and sexual orientation (Dew & Newton), and people with disabilities (Nosek). Earl Ginter, former editor of the *Journal of Counseling & Development*, concludes this section with an integrative summary of wellness research and a cogent analysis of future wellness research needs.

The application of wellness models in professional counseling practice is addressed in Part III. The authors present a model for evaluating and promoting personal change and apply this model in connection with a wellness approach to interventions. Strategies for counseling clients from a wellness perspective are considered and case examples included to underscore the effectiveness of this strength-based approach. Of particular importance are chapters that address strategies for integrating spirituality in a wellness-based practice (Cashwell) and the application of stress management interventions from a holistic wellness perspective (Young). The section concludes with a chapter on the *Diagnostic and Statistical Manual of Mental Disorders* (4th ed., Text Revision [*DSM-IV-TR*]) and wellness, underscoring the positive outcomes that can result when clients in severe distress are approached from a positive, developmental perspective (Ivey & Ivey).

In Part IV, the application of wellness principles and roles for wellness counselors in various settings are considered. The vital role of school counselors in promoting wellness of children is addressed in the first chapter (Villalba & Borders). Wellness in community mental health agencies is discussed and innovative strategies for infusing wellness in these settings are described (Carney & Hazler). The potential for infusing wellness in colleges and universities (Hermon) and business and industry (Connolly) is given in-depth consideration, and again potential roles for counselors in these settings are explored. In the final chapter, the importance of a broad-based wellness perspective as the foundation for counselor preparation is presented (Witmer & Granello).

Future directions in wellness counseling are considered in a final chapter. Our intent is to issue a challenge to the profession to reclaim our development roots, clearly articulate our commitment to prevention and optimum development, and affirm professional counselors as prime advocates for wellness. We welcome feedback from readers and are always happy to hear from others who are actively working to create greater quality of life, life satisfaction, and longevity for all individuals. We are confident that a wellness orientation is the shortest route to these goals.

Jane E. Myers (jemyers@uncg.edu)
Tom Sweeney (tjsweeney@csi-net.org)

WEB RESOURCES

- **The Centers for Disease Control and Prevention (CDC), http://www.cdc.gov/,** is the federal agency charged to promote and protect the health and safety of the people of the United States. The CDC helps to develop programs for disease control and prevention, environmental health, and health education.
- **Healthy People 2010, http://www.healthypeople.gov/,** is the national prevention plan created to recognize the major health dangers to the people of the United States and construct national goals to decrease these risks.
- **The Office of Disease Prevention and Health Promotion, http://odphp.osophs.dhhs.gov/,** works toward fortifying disease prevention and health endorsement activities in partnership with the other agencies of the U.S. Department of Health and Human Services.
- **Dr. Jane E. Myers's home page, http://www.uncg.edu/~jemyers/,** includes her biographical sketch and professional interests, and information on wellness and gerontological counseling.

PART I

WELLNESS THEORY
AND
MEASUREMENT

Sexton (2001) cogently argued the need for evidence-based models to inform clinical practice in counseling. In this section, we present wellness as an important evidence-based philosophy and paradigm on which to base effective counseling assessment and interventions. The four chapters of this section provide an important foundation of wellness counseling models and assessment strategies that are integral to the research and practice chapters throughout the remainder of the book.

In the first chapter, we review historical and multidisciplinary perspectives on wellness. This includes a discussion of varying definitions and models of wellness. Our intent is not to critique prior work so much as to explain how counseling-based wellness models differ from models arising in other physical and mental health professions.

The focus of the second chapter is the Wheel of Wellness, a theoretical model that evolved from extensive reviews of cross-disciplinary research on the characteristics of people who live long and live well. This model has been used for almost two decades in clinical practice, counselor education, and research to further understanding of healthy behaviors and functioning from a holistic perspective.

Over a decade of research using the Wheel of Wellness model resulted in a large database gathered from wellness assessments with people across the life span. Examination of this database using exploratory and confirmatory factor analyses resulted in the creation of a new, evidence-based model for clinical practice. The Indivisible Self model is described in detail in chapter 4. Readers are encouraged to study this chapter and will find it a useful resource throughout the book as the components of the model are referenced in chapters dealing with research, clinical applications, and applications of the wellness philosophy in various counseling settings.

The final chapter in this section provides an overview of practical strategies for using the wellness models to assess individuals and groups to provide tangible information on which people can base lifestyle choices. Both informal and formal assessment methods are included. Formal assessments include paper-and-pencil measures based on the wellness models described in chapters 3 and 4. These include the Wellness Evaluation of Lifestyle and its successor, the Five Factor Wellness Inventory.

2

Introduction to Wellness Theory

Jane E. Myers and Thomas J. Sweeney

Aesculapias, the ancient Greek god of healing, had two daughters who established separate ways of approaching health and illness. One daughter, Panacea, promoted the idea that healing meant approaching people to treat existing illness. Hygeia, his other daughter, believed that the best way to approach healing would be to teach people ways of living so that they would not become sick. Panacea was the forerunner of modern medicine, whereas Hygeia may be credited with initiating the wellness movement more than 2,000 years ago. It is interesting that the evolution of the medical perspective, or medical model, has been steady and based in scientific knowledge. The growth of wellness, on the other hand, has been sporadic, often viewed as "outside" of the scientific realm and relegated to the status of "alternative medicine," yet remains a foundation of healthful practice, particularly in Eastern philosophical and religious traditions.

The Greek philosopher Aristotle, writing in the fifth-century B.C., is credited with being the first to write about wellness. His scientific attempts to explain health and illness resulted in a model of good health as one in which humans avoid the extremes of excess and deficiency. Stated succinctly, this philosophy is expressed as "nothing in excess." The son of a physician, Aristotle identified *eudaemonia*, a state of happiness or flourishing, as the ultimate expression of a person's ability to live and fare well.

The health of body and mind were linked until some centuries later when Descartes (1596–1650), credited as being the father of modern philosophy, explained human functioning based on scientific reasoning. He believed that the mind and body were two separate entities that worked together in a mechanistic manner. This philosophy resulted in a reductionist and fragmented approach to human functioning, with illness viewed as being only in the mind. Fortunately, solid research in medicine as well as health-related professions is rapidly creating a new paradigm wherein not only are the mind and body viewed as inseparable, but the spirit is also seen as integral to understanding health and illness (Larson, 1999).

In this chapter, modern definitions of wellness are reviewed, and models of wellness arising from these definitions are briefly described. Most of the early models evolved from the health sciences professions, and while holistic in concept, in application the focus has remained on physical aspects of functioning and how physical change affects other components of well-being. In contrast, counseling-based models of wellness that emerged over the past two decades, while also holistic in nature, have a strong foundation in psychological theory as an organizing and integrative focus. The recent emergence of positive psychology, with emotion as the central and perhaps sole focus of efforts to understand well-being, is yet another attempt to determine how people can live in an optimal manner. This chapter concludes with a reminder from Sexton (2001) of the urgent need for evidence-based models to inform clinical practice in counseling. We believe the most useful models will incorporate the entire scope of human functioning and provide guidance for understanding the holistic needs and strengths of diverse individuals across the life span.

MODERN DEFINITIONS OF WELLNESS

Understanding wellness requires an understanding of health and how the two concepts differ. The World Health Organization (WHO) as early as 1947 defined health as "physical, mental, and social well-being, not merely the absence of disease" (WHO, 1958, p. 1) and later provided a definition of optimal health as "a state of complete physical, mental, and social well-being and not merely the absence of disease or infirmity" (WHO, 1964, p. 1). The *American Heritage Dictionary of the English Language* (2000) defines wellness as "the condition of good physical and mental health, especially when maintained by proper diet, exercise, and habits" (retrieved May 15, 2004, from http://dictionary.reference.com/search?q=wellness). Both of these definitions imply a static state of existence. In contrast, in the modern wellness movement, wellness is widely viewed as a dynamic process and not a static state.

Halbert Dunn (1961, 1977) is widely credited with being the architect of the modern wellness movement. Writing more than 40 years ago, he defined wellness as "an integrated method of functioning which is oriented toward maximizing the potential of which the individual is capable. It requires that the individual maintain a continuum of balance and purposeful direction within the environment where he is functioning" (Dunn, 1961, p. 4). Dunn's work was presented in a series of 29 short radio talks on wellness that are reprinted in his book, *High Level Wellness*.

If Dunn was the architect, many would argue that Bill Hettler, a public health physician, was the father of wellness as we now know it. Hettler established the National Wellness Institute (NWI) in the 1970s, and since 1977 the Institute has conducted an annual conference on wellness in Stevens Point, Wisconsin, which attracts speakers and participants from a variety of professions who meet to share perspectives on well-being. The NWI maintains a Wellness Speakers Bureau and provides resources for health promotion and wellness professionals to promote both personal and professional growth. Hettler (1984, p. 14) defined wellness as "an active process through which people become aware of, and make choices toward, a more successful existence."

Another person whose early and sustained work has done much to stimulate and maintain the wellness movement is Don Ardell. Ardell's 1977 book, *High Level Wellness: An Alternative to Doctors, Drugs, and Disease,* was the first of 15 books written on various aspects of well-being. His definition of wellness has evolved continually and includes topics ranging from self-responsibility to global healing (see http://www.seekwellness.com/).

John Travis, another physician, discriminated health and wellness by defining health as a neutral point on a continuum that ranges from illness on one end to high-level wellness at the other (Travis & Ryan, 1981, 1988). "High-level wellness involves giving good care to your physical self, using your mind constructively, expressing your emotions effectively, being creatively involved with those around you, and being concerned about your physical, psychological and spiritual environments" (retrieved May 15, 2004, from http://thewellspring.com/pubs/iw_cont.html). Building on the work of these early authors, psychologists Archer, Probert, and Gage (1987) conducted an extensive literature review on wellness and concluded that wellness is "the process and state of a quest for maximum human functioning that involves the body, mind, and spirit" (p. 311).

Wellness has also been defined from a counseling perspective. Myers, Sweeney, and Witmer (2000b), after reviewing literature from multiple disciplines, concluded that wellness is

> a way of life oriented toward optimal health and well-being, in which body, mind, and spirit are integrated by the individual to live life more fully within the human and natural community. Ideally, it is the optimum state of health and well-being that each individual is capable of achieving. (p. 252)

From the perspective of multiple authors, we can conclude that wellness is both an outcome and a process, at once an overarching goal for living and a day-by-day, minute-by-minute way of being. This global concept is multifaceted and hence has given rise to a variety of models that purport to explain both the process and goal of optimum human functioning that we call wellness.

MODELS OF WELLNESS

Early models of wellness, as noted earlier, evolved from physical health sciences and medicine. Notable among these are Dunn's model of high-level wellness, Hettler's hexagon model, and Travis and Ryan's illness/wellness continuum. Don Ardell developed a series of three models to describe wellness. From a chronological perspective, wellness models in counseling, notably the early model by Sweeney and Witmer (1991) and Witmer and Sweeney (1992) and the revision of this model by Myers, Sweeney, and Witmer (2000b), were the first models to emerge in the mental health professions. Early writings by authors such as Ryff and Keyes (1995) led to the emergence of the positive psychology movement that does not claim an emphasis on holistic wellness but rather is considered to be the "scientific study of ordinary human strengths and virtues" (Sheldon & King, 2001, p. 216). Each of these models and perspectives is described briefly in this section.

Dunn's High-Level Wellness

Dunn (1961) described high-level wellness in terms of a symbol. Three interlocking circles, or orbits, "represent the human body as a manifestation of organized energy, and also symbolize the body, mind, and spirit of man as an interrelated and integrated whole" (p. vi). A vertical arrow, or dart, driving upward through the center of the three circles is intended to symbolize the individual's life cycle as he or she strives to achieve and actualize a purpose in living. Growing toward wholeness, maturity, and self-fulfillment is the goal of the well person.

Hettler's Hexagon

Hettler (1984) described six components of wellness that are presented graphically in a hexagon: physical, emotional, occupational, social, intellectual, and spiritual. Hettler suggested that balanced time and energy be devoted to each of these components. He also developed equipment for fitness scanning and has been an active advocate for medical self-care. Hettler's model has been widely used in business, industry, and community settings. Hettler and his wife Carol presented their model during a week-long series on *Good Morning America* and were instrumental in helping the YMCA develop wellness programs.

The hexagon model is the foundation for several assessment measures, including Testwell (National Wellness Institute, 1983); the Lifestyle Assessment Questionnaire (LAQ; National Wellness Institute, 1983); LifeScan, a health risk appraisal; and LiveWell, a wellness appraisal. The latter two measures are available free through Hettler's Web site (http://www.hettler.com/). Although widely used and disseminated, empirical research using these assessments is scarce. In one factor-analytic study of the LAQ, only two dimensions of wellness were identified, termed *cognitive* and *behavioral* (Cooper, 1990).

Travis and Ryan's Illness/Wellness Continuum

In their *Wellness Workbook*, Travis and Ryan (1981, 1988) challenged the idea that the absence of illness was an indicator of wellness. Instead, they presented a wellness model depicted graphically as a continuum (Travis, 1972). On one end is illness, treated using a medical model that is initiated with signs and symptoms of illness and that progresses through increasingly worsening health, increasing disability, and eventually premature death. On the other end is high-level wellness, reached by an awareness of health needs, education, and growth in positive ways. The midpoint of this continuum health, is a neutral state wherein illness is absent—and so is wellness. Travis was convinced that "it's not where you are but where you're headed" that is essential (see http://thewellspring.com/pubs/iw_revisit.html), thus the dynamic nature of wellness and the importance of lifestyle choices were emphasized in his model.

Travis also proposed an Iceberg Model of Health in which one's current state of health is depicted as merely the top of the iceberg. Underlying current functioning are three levels under the surface, each of which contributes greater proportions to the nature of current health. In increasing order of importance, these are the lifestyle and behavioral level, the cultural/psychological/motivational level, and the spiritual/meaning/"being" realm (http://thewellspring.com/pubs/iceberg.html). Travis also proposed a 12-part wellness energy system. Although descriptions of his models are easily available, research support for them is difficult to locate.

Ardell's Components of Wellness

Ardell's (1977) original wellness model was depicted as a simple circle with self-responsibility in the center. Four characteristics surrounded the center and contributed equal proportions to wellness: nutritional awareness, stress management, physical fitness, and environmental sensitivity. A decade later he revised his model, leaving self-responsibility in the center and changing the four components to nutritional awareness and physical fitness, meaning and purpose, relationship dynamics, and emotional intelligence. More recently, Ardell redefined his wellness circle as consisting of three equal parts: the physical domain, mental domain, and meaning and purpose. Within the physical domain are the components of exercise and nutrition, appearance, adaptations/challenges, and lifestyle habits. The mental domain includes emotional intelligence, effective decisions, stress management, factual knowledge, and mental health. Meaning and purpose includes a meaning and purpose subcomponent, relationships, humor, and play (http://www. seekwellness.com/wellness/articles/wellness_models.htm/). Again, Ardell's models emphasized the dissemination and use of his models rather than studies to provide empirical support for the hypothesized components and their relationships.

Witmer, Sweeney, and Myers's Wheel of Wellness

Sweeney and Witmer (1991) and Witmer and Sweeney (1992) conducted cross-disciplinary studies to identify correlates of health, quality of life, and longevity. Using Adlerian Individual Psychology (Adler, 1927/1954; Ansbacher & Ansbacher, 1967; Sweeney, 1998) as an organizing system, they proposed relationships among 12 components of wellness depicted graphically in a wheel (see chapter 3, Figure 3.1). Following early research with this model, it was expanded and refined, with 17 components depicted in the Wheel of Wellness (see chapter 3, Figure 3.2; Myers et al., 2000b) that interact with contextual and global forces to affect holistic well-being.

Spirituality is depicted as the center of the Wheel and its most important characteristic of well-being by relating to meaning and purpose in life. Surrounding the center is a series of 12 spokes in the life task of self-direction: sense of worth, sense of control, realistic beliefs, emotional awareness and coping, problem solving and creativity, sense of humor, nutrition, exercise, self-care, stress management, gender identity, and cultural identity.

These spokes help to regulate or direct the self as we respond to the Adlerian life tasks of work and leisure, friendship, love, and spirit. This model is the basis of an assessment instrument, the Wellness Evaluation of Lifestyle (WEL; Myers, Sweeney, & Witmer, 2000a), and has been widely used in workshops, seminars, and empirical research. An extensive description of this model is the subject of chapter 3.

Sweeney and Myers's Indivisible Self Evidence-Based Model of Wellness

Use of the Wheel of Wellness model and the WEL over a decade led to the development of a large empirical database from which a manual and norms were developed (see chapter 4). Subsequently, these data were analyzed using structural equation modeling (Hattie, Myers, & Sweeney, 2004). The outcome of exploratory and confirmatory factor analyses resulted in a clearly defined structural model, described in detail in chapter 4 (see Figure 4.1), and led to a new, evidence-based model called the Indivisible Self Model of Wellness (IS-Wel; see chapter 4, Figure 4.2). In this model, consistent with Adlerian principles, the self is the central and indivisible core of wellness, represented by a single, higher order factor called Wellness. Surrounding this core are five second-order factors: the Creative Self, Coping Self, Social Self, Essential Self, and Physical Self.

Although one result of the factor analysis was that the circumplex structure hypothesized in the theoretical Wheel model was not supported, each of the original 17 components of wellness was confirmed as distinct third-order factors. In the IS-Wel model, these factors are grouped within the five second-order factors of the self. Contextual variables compose an important part of this model and include local, institutional, global, and chronometrical variables. Numerous studies using this model, reviewed and analyzed in Part II, support the factor structure as presented.

Positive Psychology

Ryff and Keyes (1995) observed that existing models of human functioning based on the psychology literature were grounded in the deficit-based medical model, in contrast to "abundant accounts of positive functioning in subfields of psychology" (p. 720). Building on the earlier work of theorists such as Abraham Maslow, Carl Jung, Carl Rogers, and Erik Erikson, all of whom depicted healthy adult development as a trajectory of expanded personal growth and fulfillment, Ryff and Keyes defined well-being in terms of affective elements of happiness and a cognitive component that emphasizes life satisfaction. They also developed a multidimensional model of well-being comprising six distinct components—autonomy, environmental mastery, personal growth, positive relations with others, purpose in life, and self-acceptance—which are widely reflected in emerging models of positive psychology that emphasize the central role of emotion in psychological health.

Positive psychology was first defined by Martin Seligman in his 1998 address as president of the American Psychological Association. The goal of research in this area is to understand optimal human functioning by discovering and promoting the factors that allow individuals and communities to thrive (Sheldon, Frederickson, Rathunde, Csikszentmihalyi, & Haidt, 2000; Snyder & Lopez, 2001). Sheldon et al. stated that, to meet the goals of positive psychology,

> we must consider optimal functioning at multiple levels, including biological, experiential, personal, relational, institutional, cultural, and global. It is necessary to study (a) the dynamic relations between processes at these levels, (b) the human capacity to create order and meaning in response to inevitable adversity, and (c) the means by which "the good life," in its many manifestations, may emerge from these processes. (http://www.psych.upenn.edu/seligman/akumalmanifesto.htm)

Seligman and Csikszentmihalyi (2000) considered positive psychology to be the "science of positive subjective experience, positive individual traits, and positive institutions" (p. 5). Positive psychologists are working to create a classification of human strengths that will function as a counterpart to the *Diagnostic and Statistical Manual of Mental Disorders* (*DSM*) published by the American Psychiatric Association. Called the *Values in Action (VIA) Classification of Strengths Manual* (Peterson & Seligman, 2004), the goal is to identify core virtues consistently valued across cultures and time. The main virtues identified are wisdom, courage, humanity, justice, temperance, and transcendence. We believe these goals are important to further a paradigm shift from illness to wellness as a means of promoting healthful living. To date, we have been unable to find citations of the counseling wellness literature among the work of the psychologists in this new tradition. Our hope is that they will integrate the vast body of knowledge and research, described in detail in Part II of this book, which provides a solid foundation for both understanding and promoting optimum human functioning based on comprehensive models of holistic wellness.

SUMMARY

Wellness is not a new concept; in fact, it dates back thousands of years to the earliest recorded civilizations. In the last half century, a renewed emphasis on well-being as an alternative to the illness-based, medical model has emerged. Definitions of wellness cited in this chapter share a holistic view of human functioning as incorporating aspects of body, mind, and spirit. These definitions are reflected in a variety of wellness models, all of which are holistic in intent, yet in application (especially in business and industry, as described by Connolly in chapter 25) the physical components often are the predominant or exclusive focus. We believe that the self is indivisible, hence attention to healthy functioning in any aspect of these models will contribute to greater functioning overall. At the same time, high-level wellness cannot be achieved in the absence of deliberate, conscious choices, made on a daily basis, to seek a lifestyle wherein wellness of body, mind, and spirit is an overarching goal.

Sexton (2001) argued the need for evidence-based models to inform clinical practice. Although each of the models described in this chapter has intuitive appeal, and clearly all are based on a wide body of knowledge concerning healthy lifestyles, empirical support for most of the models is limited. The preponderance of studies appears in the counseling literature or in the positive psychology literature. In the case of positive psychology, there is an almost exclusive focus on emotions and coping (Lazarus, 2003). The theoretical Wheel of Wellness model has stimulated both clinical applications and much research, to the point that a new, evidence-based model of wellness has been identified. The Indivisible Self model also is the impetus for recent and ongoing research that is helping to refine our understanding of high-level wellness. This new understanding is helping to inform clinical practice and allows practitioners to create new, strength-based approaches to helping clients change in positive, healthful directions. The goal of wellness is to help people take responsibility for the choices in their lives, and to choose healthy lifestyles that promote not only a better quality of life but happiness, life satisfaction, and longevity as well.

DISCUSSION QUESTIONS

1. How has the concept of wellness evolved over time? How has this evolution affected the way in which health and illness is conceptualized?
2. Review the models of wellness described earlier. What are the commonalities among these models? How is each unique?
3. Discuss the importance of research in wellness as a foundation for evidence-based, effective practices.

WEB RESOURCES

- **Don Ardell's Seek Wellness page, http://www.seekwellness.com/,** provides information on ways to increase wellness, with respect to fitness, mental health, nutrition, weight control, and health consumerism. This Web site also contains information on pelvic health, arthritis, eating disorders, Addison's disease, gout, heart disease, and other conditions as they affect one's wellness. The subpage, /wellness/articles/ wellness_models.htm, includes a summary and graphics for several wellness models.
- **Positive Psychology.net., http://www.positivepsychology.net/,** was designed to create an interdisciplinary, interactive forum that will include instruments, technologies, and methods to study and encourage human optimism and happiness.
- **Jane E. Myers's home page, http://www.uncg.edu/~jemyers/,** includes descriptions of the Wheel of Wellness and the Indivisible Self models, lists of dissertations and publications using the models, and an overview of the Wellness Evaluation of Lifestyle and Five Factor Wellness Inventory.

The Wheel of Wellness

Jane E. Myers and Thomas J. Sweeney

Sweeney and Witmer (1991) and Witmer and Sweeney (1992) reviewed literature across disciplines in an attempt to discover the characteristics of healthy people over the life span. The results of research and theoretical perspectives from personality, social, clinical, health, and developmental psychology were examined, as well as stress management, behavioral medicine, psychoneuroimmunology, ecology, and contextualism. Empirical correlates of health, quality of life, and longevity were identified as the foundation for the first wellness model based in counseling, the Wheel of Wellness. This theoretical model provides a holistic understanding of wellness and prevention over the life span, which can serve as the basis of assessments and helping interventions.

An organizing schema to explain relationships among the various correlates of well-being was readily available through Adler's Individual Psychology (Adler, 1927/1954), which was totally consistent with a wellness paradigm. In fact, an examination of Adler's writings reveals his orientation to positive human development long before others discovered holistic, positive approaches to growth (Sweeney, 1998). In this chapter, the Adlerian foundation for the model is briefly presented. Although summaries of research for each component as related to wellness are readily available (e.g., Myers, Sweeney, & Witmer, 2000b) and in fact are voluminous for virtually all of the components, these studies are not repeated here. Rather, the evolution of the model, the meaning of each component, and the relationships among the components are explored and discussed.

ADLER'S INDIVIDUAL PSYCHOLOGY

Adler (1927/1954) proposed a theory of holism, or indivisibility of the individual. Work, friendship, love, self, and spirit are life tasks central to understanding human growth and development (Sweeney, 1995b, 1998).

Portions of this chapter appeared in Myers, J. E., Sweeney, T. J., & Witmer, J. M. (2000b). The Wheel of Wellness counseling for wellness: A holistic model for treatment planning. *Journal of Counseling & Development, 78,* 251–266.

Adler's theory espouses three major constructs that help us understand individuals, their connections with others, and their relationships to the world around them. These three dimensions can be organized as *socio-teleo-analytic* in nature. *Holism*, a fourth concept, provides the foundation for the wellness models described throughout this book.

Socio

Socio refers to the proposition that humans have a social need for connectedness and belonging. Adler believed that human beings have a basic inclination toward *Gemeinschaftsgefuhl*—a striving to feel belongingness, a willingness to serve the greater good for the betterment of mankind (Dreikurs, 1967, 1971). The closest interpretation of this German word in English is *social interest*. An expression of this inclination is observed in each person's striving to feel a sense of belonging. Everyone wants to be of significance to others, to experience respect and worth. Behavior, indeed one's entire life striving, can be understood in the context of this motivation. From infancy in the family throughout later life, each person seeks to fulfill this goal through either socially "useful" means or socially "useless," self-defeating discouragement.

Teleo

Adlerians use the term *teleo* to denote the human tendency to be goal oriented in thoughts, feelings, and behavior. There is a private reason and a purpose for what we do. In fact, behavior is purposive even though the "why" and "what" we are striving for may be obscure to both the individual and the observer. Individuals choose to act or not act because it is useful to them in coping with their life's tasks. As Ansbacher (1969) noted:

> The science of Individual Psychology developed out of the effort to understand that mysterious creative power of life—that power which expresses itself in the desire to develop, to strive and to achieve—and even to compensate for defeats in one direction by striving for success in another. This power is teleological—it expresses itself in the striving after a goal. (p. 1)

This teleological orientation has an optimistic and encouraging nature. As Rudolf Dreikurs (personal communication, June 1970) once said, "Tell a person what they are, schizophrenic, so what? Tell a person how they feel, sad or bad, so what? But, tell a person what they intend! Now that is something they can change!" Because the goals of behavior can be understood and anticipated, they can be changed. Individuals may choose to change their goals or the behavior they use in attempting to reach their goals; thus we are not victims of circumstances beyond our control in any absolute way.

Analytic

Analytic as used in Adlerian terms means that human behavior is predicated on much that is not understood or conscious. Individuals frequently report that they do not understand their behavior or motives. Adler was a phenomenologist who believed that the social motivation to belong was understood best through the eyes of the beholder. He referred to the basic notions that guide us through life as our style of life, or *lifestyle*. He characterized lifestyle as "unity in each individual in his thinking, feeling, acting; in his so-called conscious and unconscious, in every expression of his personality. This (self-consistent) unity we call the style of life of the individual" (Ansbacher & Ansbacher, 1967, p. 175). Lifestyle is not determined by heredity or environment, though both are important antecedents. Individuals decide how they think, value, and feel about their gender, ethnicity, or family position. When unexamined, one's motivation may seem to result in random, even contradictory behavior. On closer inspection, however, the unity of purpose can be revealed.

Each lifestyle is unique and is developed in accordance to its usefulness in helping individuals make their place and cope with their life tasks. Through an understanding of their unique perceptions, individuals can come to understand the consistency in their behavior. Adler believed this consistency resulted from the *private logic* of the individual, including what is commonly referred to as one's *self-talk*. Given the opportunity to understand their private logic and the unconscious goals toward which they strive, individuals can choose to modify their self-defeating behaviors or to reorient their striving for a place among others through new life goals. Equally important, therefore, a deliberate choice to develop greater social interest and to pursue a goal of better health and wellness is within the capability of every person.

Holism

Traditional views of human functioning, described in chapter 2, have resulted in a tendency to objectify and dichotomize the human condition. Individuals are seen as a combination of parts that work in concert. When a part is diseased or damaged, it is removed or repaired. Hence, the person is once again "whole" or healthy. This tendency to conceptualize human nature as divisible and even at odds with its parts might be illustrated best by Freud's conceptualization of personality development. Certainly no personality theory has had more influence or notoriety than Freud's psychoanalysis. His contemporary, Alfred Adler (1927/1954), took exception to Freud's theory and its portrayal of human beings as parts at odds with one another (i.e., id, ego, and superego). Instead, Adler taught that individuals are mind, body, and spirit, indivisible, unique, creative, and purposeful. Equally important, whether for good or bad, one aspect of self affects the other aspects of self within this holistic interaction.

Adler (1927/1954), in writing about Individual Psychology, noted the importance of holism in understanding the individual. Further, he noted that "it is always necessary to look for . . . reciprocal actions of the mind on the body, for both of them are parts of the whole with which we should be concerned" (Ansbacher & Ansbacher, 1967, p. 255). Similarly, Maslow (1970, 1971), in studying characteristics of healthy people, concluded that a striving toward self-actualization, growth, and excellence is a universal human tendency and overarching life purpose. Thus, while the various components of wellness models may be discussed as discrete phenomena, it is the inter-action of these components, for better or worse, that influences our efforts to be well.

THE WHEEL OF WELLNESS

As originally presented, the Wheel of Wellness included the three basic life tasks defined by Adler (1954)—work, friendship, and love—and the two additional tasks—self and spirit—explicated by later writers as being central components of the Adlerian model (Mosak & Dreikurs, 1967, 1973). In this conceptually circumplex model (see Figure 3.1), spirituality was seen as at the core, and work, love, and friendship are seen as the rims of the Wheel. Self-regulation included seven components that defined the spokes of the Wheel: sense of worth; sense of control; realistic beliefs; spontaneous and emotional response; intellectual stimulation, problem solving, and creativity; sense of humor; and physical fitness and nutrition. A variety of life forces and global events provided the context for the Wheel.

The authors presented the Wheel as a sphere, or ball, such that deficiency or deficit in any component can affect the others in negative ways, causing the ball to collapse or "roll" unevenly like a wheel out of round. Moreover, there is evidence that different components of wellness are more or less salient at different points in the life span. Healthy functioning occurs on a developmental continuum, and healthy behaviors at one point in life affect

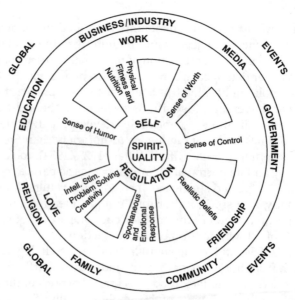

Figure 3.1

The Original Wheel of Wellness

subsequent development and functioning as well. Both gender and cultural differences have been identified in many of the components of wellness and are important considerations when conceptualizing individual well-being. The increasing salience of these differences, in concert with early analyses of our database on wellness of individuals across the life span, led to the evolution of the model and the resulting Wheel depicted in Figure 3.2.

The most recent Wheel of Wellness is conceptually identical to the earlier model, in that a three-dimensional model provides the most accurate explanation of human wellness. This model includes five major life tasks. Spirituality remains the center of the Wheel and is hypothesized to be the core and most important characteristic of healthy people. The spokes of the Wheel are shown as 12 subtasks of *self-direction*, a more active and empowering term than *self-regulation*, which was used in the earlier model. These 12 subtasks are: (a) sense of worth, (b) sense of control, (c) realistic beliefs, (d) emotional awareness and coping, (e) problem solving and creativity, (f), sense of humor, (g) nutrition, (h) exercise, (i) self-care, (j) stress management, (k) gender identity, and (l) cultural identity. Work, friendship, and love are life tasks met effectively through the self-direction subtasks, or not met, as the case may be.

As shown in Figure 3.2, the theoretical Wheel of Wellness model is contextual and hypothesizes a dynamic interaction between the individual and a variety of life forces, including but not limited to family, community, religion, education, government, media, and business/industry. Global events,

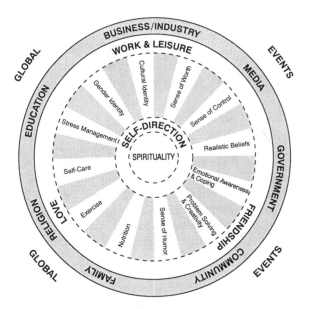

Figure 3.2
The Wheel of Wellness

whether of natural (e.g., floods, famines) or human (e.g., wars) origin, have an impact on the life forces and life tasks depicted in the model. In the sections that follow, the life tasks are discussed, and summary definitions are included in Table 3.1.

Life Task #1: Spirituality

Spirituality is defined as an awareness of a being or force that transcends the material aspects of life and gives a deep sense of wholeness or connectedness to the universe. A distinction is made between spirituality, a broad concept representing one's personal beliefs and values, and religiosity, a narrower concept that refers to institutional beliefs and behaviors that are a part of the broader concept of spirituality. Religiosity is a public matter, often expressed in group religious participation, whereas spirituality is more of a private issue that may or may not be expressed publicly. The dimensions of spirituality, or spiritual wellness (Ingersoll, 1998), include attitudes, beliefs, and practices such as a belief in a higher power; hope and optimism; practice of worship, prayer, and/or meditation; purpose in life; compassion for others; moral values; and transcendence (a sense of oneness with the universe).

Spirituality is conceptualized in the Wheel as the core characteristic of healthy people that helps to fortify the other components. The results of numerous studies reveal a strong relationship between spirituality and other aspects of wellness; for example, spiritual support, similar to social support, may have a stress-buffering effect due both to cognitive mediation of stressful events and to emotional support through organized religious or spiritual practices with others. Recent studies suggest that there is a significant, positive relationship between spirituality, mental health, physical health, life satisfaction, and holistic well-being or wellness.

Life Task #2: Self-Direction

Self-direction is the manner in which an individual regulates, disciplines, and directs the self in daily activities and in pursuit of long-range goals. It refers to a sense of mindfulness and intentionality in meeting the major tasks of life. The patterns of behavior and methods of adjustment to life that make up self-direction are sometimes referred to as positive personality traits that give one a stress-resistant personality.

Sense of Worth. Sense of worth is variously referred to in the literature as self-concept, self-esteem, and self-worth (Cooper, 1967). A person with high self-esteem is excited by new challenges and seeks self-actualization. Positive self-esteem is a preventive factor for illness, enhances recovery from illness, and enhances overall well-being. In virtually all studies of positive mental health, the key factors that emerge include a positive self-concept, sense of autonomy, social support, and an internal locus of control or sense of self-efficacy. Self-esteem is a more significant predictor of life satisfaction in individualist countries, such as the United States, than in those

Table 3.1

Definitions of Components in the Wheel of Wellness

SPIRITUALITY	Personal, private beliefs that enhance one's life; hope and optimism, purpose in life, moral values, transcendence, overall spiritual well-being.
SELF-DIRECTION	Process by which one directs, controls, manages the self in ways that are self-enhancing, within societal norms, through the following 12 subtasks:
Sense of Worth	Satisfaction with self, acceptance of self with one's imperfections, acceptance of one's physical appearance, valuing oneself as a unique, worthwhile person.
Sense of Control	Beliefs about mastery, competence, self-confidence, locus of control, self-efficacy, presentation of oneself as having influence through exercise of imagination, knowledge, skill, and choice; sense of planfulness in life; ability to be direct in expressing one's needs (assertiveness).
Realistic Beliefs	Ability to perceive truth/reality accurately (i.e., accurate information processing), lack of unrealistic expectations/wishful thinking.
Emotional Awareness and Coping	Being in touch with feelings, being able to express/disclose feelings appropriately, ability to respond spontaneously and appropriately to life experiences from the full range of possible human emotional responses, enjoying positive emotions, coping with negative emotions, lack of chronic negative emotional states (e.g., anger), sense of energy (vs. depression).
Problem Solving and Creativity	Being mentally active, open minded, ability and desire to be creative, curiosity, need to know, need to learn, capacity to collect data, analyze, synthesize, choose and evaluate consequences of outcomes (i.e., divergent and convergent thinking), capacity to change one's thinking to manage stress (cognitive restructuring), capacity to apply the above characteristics in resolving social conflicts.
Sense of Humor	Ability to laugh appropriately at oneself, ability to laugh appropriately at others, having the capacity to see contradictions and predicaments of life in an objective manner such that one can gain new perspectives, ability to use humor to cope with one's own difficulties, enjoying inconsistencies and idiosyncrasies of life.
Exercise	Leading an active rather than sedentary lifestyle, exercising 20–30 minutes three times a week, stretching regularly.
Nutrition	Eating breakfast regularly, daily variety in diet of healthful foods, maintaining one's ideal weight.
Self-Care	Not abusing substances, using seat belts, getting adequate sleep, obtaining preventive medical and dental care.
Stress Management	General perceptions of one's own self-regulation, seeing change as an opportunity for growth rather than as a threat to one's security, ongoing self-monitoring and assessment of one's coping resources, structuring—ability to organize and manage resources (e.g., time, energy, setting limits, scheduling); need for structure, satisfaction with one's stress management abilities.
Gender Identity	Satisfaction with one's gender identity, feeling supported in one's gender, valuing relationships with people of both genders, transcendence of gender identity, competency to cope with stress of gender identity.

(Continued next page)

Table 3.1 (Continued)
Definitions of Components in the Wheel of Wellness

Cultural Identity	Satisfaction with one's cultural identity, feeling supported in one's culture, valuing relationships with people of many cultures, transcendence of cultural identity, competency to cope with stress of cultural identity.
WORK AND LEISURE	Activities and tasks essential to personal well-being and social living, including:
Work	Activity that contributes to the well-being of self and others: perception of adequacy of financial resources (financial freedom), job satisfaction, feeling that one's skills are used, perception of work overload, role conflict, role ambiguity (i.e., psychological job security), participation in decision making (i.e., feeling appreciated), satisfaction with relationships in the job setting; and
Leisure	Activities done in one's free time: satisfaction with one's leisure activities, importance of leisure, positive feelings associated with leisure, having at least one activity in which "I lose myself and time stands still," ability to approach tasks from a playful point of view, ability to put work aside for leisure without feeling guilty.
FRIENDSHIP	Connectedness with others in a nonsexual manner; having social support when needed; having a confidant for tangible, emotional, and informational support; being able to give social support; not feeling lonely because of lack of friends, sense of comfort in social situations (social ease).
LOVE	Concern for the life and growth of that which is loved; having faith that one's well-being will be respected; reciprocating by respecting the well-being of another (i.e., trust); ability to be intimate, trusting, self-disclosing with another person; ability to receive as well as express affection with a significant other; capacity to experience or convey nonpossessive caring that respects the uniqueness of another; presence of enduring, stable intimate relationship(s); recognition that others have concern for one's growth; physical satisfaction with sexual life/needs for touch are being met.

with a collectivist orientation, in which relationship harmony seems to be more closely related to self-esteem in predicting life satisfaction.

Sense of Control. The results of numerous studies indicate that people experience positive outcomes when they perceive themselves as having an impact on what happens to them, and they experience negative outcomes (e.g., depression) when they perceive a lack of personal control. Perceived control is associated with emotional well-being, successful coping with stress, better physical health, and better mental health over the life span. Having an internal locus of control has been associated with lower levels of anxiety and depression and higher levels of self-esteem and life satisfaction. Higher levels of perceived self-control predict healthier behavior, including exercise participation and weight control, and in turn are affected by participation in positive health practices such as exercise.

Realistic Beliefs. Epictetus stated that "people are disturbed not by things, but by the view which they take of them" (Ellis, 1984, p. 200). Ellis noted that people have a tendency to disturb themselves through the perpetuation of their irrational beliefs, the major ones being: (a) I must be loved or approved of by everyone, (b) I must be perfectly competent and productive, (c) it is a catastrophe when things go other than the way I might wish, (d) life must be absolutely fair, and (e) it is better to avoid life's difficulties than to take responsibility for changing them.

Adler referred to internal beliefs as one's private logic, which in turn guides both feelings and behaviors (Sweeney, 1998). The greater the discrepancy between one's private logic and reality, the greater the potential for unhealthy behaviors in response to life events. Healthy people are able to process information accurately and perceive reality as it is rather than as they wish it to be. Thus, people who have realistic beliefs are able to accept themselves as imperfect. In fact, longitudinal studies suggest that accurate appraisals of the self and social environment are essential to positive mental health.

Emotional Awareness and Coping. To experience and positively manage one's emotions is one index of healthy functioning. Many individuals are limited in their ability both to experience and to express joy, anger, affection, and related human emotions. As a consequence, the quality and quantity of relationships within their lives are limited. By contrast, healthy functioning is reflected in rich, varied, and frequent expressions and responses to people and events within one's daily experiences.

Numerous studies report a significant relationship between thoughts, feelings, and illness, with positive emotionality being a major component of mental health and subjective well-being, a negative correlate with depression, and an accurate predictor of physical as well as psychological health. Negative emotions such as anxiety and depression are associated with immune system suppression and a consequent increase in the potential for illness. Hostility, for example, has been shown to be a major contributor to high blood pressure, coronary artery disease, and death, particularly among people with a Type A personality. On the other hand, the appropriate expression of negative emotions combined with the presence of positive emotions seems to strengthen immune function.

Problem Solving and Creativity. Intellectual stimulation, including problem solving and creativity, is necessary for healthy brain functioning and hence quality of life across the life span (i.e., use it or lose it). Thinking involves problem solving, and effective problem solving involves creativity. Effective problem solvers have more positive health expectancies, higher expectancies for control, fewer irrational beliefs, and a lower tendency toward self-criticism than do ineffective problem solvers. Effective problem solving also correlates with reduced anxiety and depression, increased stress hardiness, and overall psychological adjustment.

Creativity has been identified as a universal characteristic of self-actualizing people, all of whom demonstrate originality, expressiveness, imagination, inventiveness, and problem-solving ability. It is a multidimensional phenomenon involving the ability to develop new or different concepts, ideas, structures, or products. Creativity is optimized in individuals with high self-esteem and has a positive effect on life satisfaction, mental health, and overall wellness.

Sense of Humor. Humor, a cognitive and emotional process, includes both recognition and appreciation of humorous stimuli and creation of humorous stimuli. Especially when accompanied by laughter, humor causes the skeletal muscles to relax, boosts the immune system, increases heart rate, stimulates circulation, oxygenates the blood, massages the vital organs, aids digestion, and releases chemicals (endorphins) into the brain that enhance a sense of well-being. Humor has been associated with reduced depression and increased pain relief, higher levels of self-esteem and lower perceived levels of stress, more positive and self-protective cognitive appraisals when dealing with stress, and a greater positive response to both positive and negative life events. Humor facilitates the enjoyment of positive life experiences and has a positive effect on physical health.

Humor also allows cognitive shifts that help individuals gain insights into their personal problems, increase social cohesion, defuse conflicts, and reduce feelings of hostility. However, humor that has a put-down component is related to health problems, whereas a positive sense of humor enhances healthy aging. Humor promotes creativity, improves negotiating and decision-making skills, improves individual and group performance, relieves stress, and bestows a sense of power.

Nutrition. There is a clear relationship between what we eat and our health, moods, performance, and longevity. The eating and drinking habits of Americans have been implicated in 6 of the 10 leading causes of death, including the fact that two in three Americans are considered to be overweight. Dietary quality is influenced by factors such as self-actualization and social support in addition to dietary intake. Factors such as loneliness, poor physical health, and lack of meaningful social contacts result in lowered dietary quality. Successful aging requires a nutritionally complete diet and adequate exercise, suggesting the need for a life span approach to nutritional wellness.

Exercise. Regular physical activity, or exercise, is essential in the prevention of disease and enhancement of health and is important for healthy aging. The benefits of exercise for physical and psychological well-being have been clearly established. Exercise increases strength as well as self-confidence and self-esteem. In addition, there is a significant correlation between physical fitness and improved emotionality as well as cognitive functioning. Exercise training has been shown to significantly decrease state–trait anxiety scores, decrease mild depression, reduce stress, and beneficially affect a variety of chronic illnesses.

Self-Care. Taking responsibility for one's wellness requires personal habits of preventive behavior as well as remedial treatment. Three aspects of self-care constitute this dimension: safety habits that we learn to protect ourselves from injury or death; periodic physical, medical, and dental checkups; and avoiding harmful substances, both those that we might ingest and toxic substances in the environment. Positive self-care improves the quality of life and extends longevity, whereas failure to engage in preventive self-care habits leads to decline in physical functioning and increased mortality.

Stress Management. Stress affects both psychological and physiological functioning and has a specific depressant effect on immune system functioning. People who are stress-resistant experience more positive and beneficial immune system responses, greater resistance to psychosocial stressors, and a more internal locus of control. They also experience more positive mental health and greater physical health. In contrast, the effects of chronic stress are major contributors to escalating health care costs, reaching over $150 billion annually by the turn of the last century.

Stress management is the ability to identify stressors in one's life and to reduce or minimize stress by using strategies of stress reduction. The negative effects of stress can be reduced or eliminated through self-regulatory strategies such as biofeedback and relaxation techniques, social support, and behavioral/environmental methods such as assertiveness and communication skills training, changing mistaken ideas, problem solving, and exercise.

Gender Identity. Gender identity, a basic conviction that one is male or female, refers to subjective feelings of maleness or femaleness and is culturally constructed or defined. Gender role identity, in contrast to gender identity, reflects one's identification with social prescriptions or stereotypes associated with each sex, to which one may or may not conform, rather than the introspective, self-definition of one's gender. Gender role socialization, a process that begins at birth and continues throughout the life span, results in culturally appropriate gender role behaviors being rewarded for both males and females. For example, men are rewarded for engaging in traditionally "masculine" behaviors such as achievement, competition, and independence, whereas women are rewarded for engaging in nurturing, supportive, interdependent, and empathic relationship behaviors. These gender differences have been linked to wellness and illness in adulthood. American women, for example, more readily report illnesses and use the health systems. Women also outlive men by an average of 7 years.

Cultural Identity. Culture is a multidimensional concept that encompasses the collective reality of a group of people. Cultural identity incorporates racial identity, acculturation, and an appreciation for the unique aspects of one's culture and is positively related to well-being. It is a positive personal strength that enhances growth and development across the life span.

Cultural identity affects self-perceived health and wellness because the concepts of health differ according to culture. Psychological stress and behavioral deviance are culturally defined and are often explained in terms of culturally specific religious or spiritual frameworks. In a Western context, for example, happiness is explained as being positively correlated with independence and an internal locus of control. In contrast, the subjective evaluation of happiness in Eastern societies places greater emphasis on relationship harmony and interpersonal contentment.

Life Task #3: Work and Leisure

Work and leisure (defined in the original Wheel model as work, recreation, and leisure) provide opportunities for pleasurable experiences that are intrinsically satisfying and provide a sense of accomplishment. They challenge or engage our senses, skills, and interests, frequently absorbing us in activities in a state of consciousness called *flow* (Csikszentmihalyi, 2000). This is an optimal state in which an individual loses awareness of self and time while being highly engaged in the task at hand. Excitement and joy are enhanced while anxiety and boredom are minimized.

Work. Work serves the major functions of economic support, psychological purposes, and social benefits and was considered by Adler (1927/1954) to be the most important task for maintenance of life. He further defined work as an activity that is useful to the community (others), whether for monetary gain or otherwise. Work satisfaction, comprised of challenge, financial reward, coworker relations, and working conditions, is one of the best predictors of longevity as well as perceived quality of life. People who view their career as a calling tend to experience the highest work satisfaction. Feelings of competence in work tasks also have a positive effect on life satisfaction, and work experiences and work outcomes are consistently and positively related to self-reported emotional well-being. The meaning of work and time commitments related to work must be balanced, in a healthy individual, with time, energy, and satisfaction devoted to family and friends. Factors affecting positive well-being in the work environment also may be obtained through participation in leisure activities.

Leisure. Adler referred to leisure, or play, as a "minor life task." Leisure activities, including physical, social, intellectual, volunteer, and creative, have a positive effect on self-esteem and perceived wellness and increase one's sense of emotional well-being. Life satisfaction is influenced by leisure congruence, defined as the selection of leisure activities consistent with one's personality type. Participation in certain types of leisure activities, notably exercise, is an important means of reducing the effects of stress. Leisure activities also mediate the effects of stress by providing social support and developing psychological hardiness.

Life Task #4: Friendship

The friendship life task incorporates all of one's social relationships that involve a connection with others, either individually or in community, but do not have a marital, sexual, or familial commitment. Adler (1927/1954) considered social interest as innate to human nature, noting that we are all born with the capacity and need to be connected with each other. Empathy, cooperation, and altruism are all manifestations of social interest. Those who regularly devote time to helping others are as likely to experience health benefits as those who exercise or meditate. The desire for interpersonal attachments is a fundamental human motivation, reflected in the need for frequent, positive interactions with the same people, and the search for a long-term, stable, and caring support network.

There is a strong positive connection between friendship quality and sense of well-being, including physical as well as mental health and happiness across the life span. Alternatively, dissatisfaction with close friendships or intimate relationships is predictive of depression. People with satisfying social relationships are more likely to avoid health-damaging behaviors, such as smoking, drinking, and not using seat belts, and are more likely to consume a nutritious and healthy diet.

Social support, the degree to which a person's basic social needs are met through interaction with others, is positively correlated with both physical and emotional health and provides a buffer against stress. Friendships enhance self-esteem, and friendship satisfaction is among the strongest predictors of positive self-esteem. Friendships also prevent feelings of loneliness and are essential for positive growth and development. In contrast, research from a variety of studies shows that people who are socially isolated—those who are unmarried, divorced, widowed, people with few friends, and people who have few social contacts—are much more likely to die from a variety of diseases than those who have happy, fulfilling social lives.

Life Task #5: Love

Relationships that are formed on the basis of a long-term, mutual commitment and involve intimacy compose the life task of love. Characteristics of healthy love relationships include the following: (a) the ability to be intimate, trusting, and self-disclosing with another person; (b) the ability to receive as well as express affection with significant others; (c) the capacity to experience or convey nonpossessive caring that respects the uniqueness of another; (d) the presence of enduring, stable intimate relationships in one's life; (e) concern for the nurturance and growth of others; and (f) satisfaction with one's sexual life or the perception that one's needs for physical touch and closeness are being met. The life task of love necessitates having a family or familylike support system that has the following nine characteristics: (a) shared coping and problem-solving skills; (b) commitment to the family; (c) good communication; (d) encouragement of individuals; (e) expression of appreciation; (f) shared religious/spiritual orientation; (g) social connectedness; (h) clear roles; and (i) shared interests, values, and time.

The feeling of being loved and valued by others, a feeling unrelated to the number or structure of social relationships, has been identified as the core component of social support. For those who answer "no" to the question, "Do you have anyone who really cares for you?" the risk of premature death and disease from all causes is three to five times higher. Thus, it is not surprising that mortality rates are consistently higher for divorced, single, and widowed individuals of both sexes and all races. Interestingly, people who are unhappily married or in negative relationships are less healthy than those who are divorced, whereas divorced people have higher rates of heart disease, cancer, pneumonia, high blood pressure, depression, alcoholism, traffic accidents, homicide, suicide, and accidental death than do people who are married. People who are divorced also have poorer immune system function and are less resistant to disease. These effects are not limited to any one culture. A recent study of Chinese adults, for example, showed that those with the greatest marital maladjustment experienced more psychiatric symptoms, had lower scores on measures of purpose in life, and perceived their health as poor (Shek, 1995).

For men, women, and children, committed relationships provide protection against physical and mental illness, increased longevity, and a greater sense of well-being, and promote better physical and emotional responses to stress. For example, adolescents who live in families that are more cohesive report less depression and fewer stressful life events. Older people who feel that they have at least one person who cares about them and whom they care about in return report both greater life satisfaction and less difficulty adjusting to the challenges of later life.

SUMMARY

The Wheel of Wellness was the first holistic wellness model developed with a foundation in counseling theory. As such, it has been used extensively as a basis for assessment (see chapter 5) and interventions (see chapters 18–20) to enhance the well-being of people across the life span. The depiction of spirituality as the core of the Wheel has intuitive appeal to many people, thus increasing the usefulness of the model as a structure for designing interventions to enhance holistic wellness. Studies using this model, summarized in chapter 4, resulted in a second counseling-based wellness model that differs from the Wheel in being empirically rather than theoretically grounded.

DISCUSSION QUESTIONS

1. What did Adler mean by the terms *socio, teleo,* and *analytic*? How do the socio-teleo-analytic dimensions further understanding of individual wellness?
2. Explain the five main life tasks depicted in the Wheel of Wellness model. How are these tasks interrelated in a healthy person?
3. What are the subtasks of self-direction? How do they function to promote or hinder individual wellness?
4. How is Adler's concept of holism important in understanding wellness?

WEB RESOURCES

- **Adler School of Professional Psychology, http://www.adler.edu/,** is one of several accredited schools of professional psychology specializing in advanced training in Adlerian Individual Psychology.
- **The Alfred Adler Institutes of San Francisco and Northwestern Washington: Distance Training in Classical Adlerian Psychotherapy, http://ourworld.compuserve.com/homepages/hstein/,** provides links to training opportunities in Adlerian Psychology as well as training audio- and videotapes and referrals to practicing clinicians.

4

The Indivisible Self:
An Evidence-Based Model of Wellness

Jane E. Myers and Thomas J. Sweeney

Sexton (2001) presented a case for evidence-based models to inform clinical practice throughout the helping professions. From this perspective, theoretical models require empirical testing and validation. The expectation is that new models will evolve through empirical testing and these in turn must be described and further examined. Following this process, our research in wellness began with extensive literature searches and the development of a heuristic, theoretical model, the Wheel of Wellness (Myers, Sweeney, & Witmer, 2000b; Sweeney & Witmer, 1991; Witmer & Sweeney, 1992). An assessment instrument based on this model, the Wellness Evaluation of Lifestyle (WEL; see chapter 5; Myers, Sweeney, & Witmer, 2000a; Witmer, Sweeney, & Myers, 1993), was used to gather data on the wellness of adults across the life span. Analysis of our database gathered using the WEL over more than a decade led to the development of a new evidence-based model of wellness, which we call the Indivisible Self, or IS-Wel. In this chapter, the statistical foundation for the model is presented and the components of the model are described.

STATISTICAL FOUNDATION OF THE IS-WEL: EXPLORATORY AND CONFIRMATORY FACTOR ANALYSES

Hattie, Myers, and Sweeney (2004) examined the database developed by Myers using the four early versions of the WEL (e.g., Myers, Sweeney, & Witmer, 1996b, 2000a; Myers, Witmer, & Sweeney, 1995; Witmer, Sweeney, & Myers, 1993). Although the psychometric properties of the WEL were supported and evidence of good reliability, construct validity, and both convergent and discriminate validity were provided, in the final analysis the data did not support the hypothesized circumplex model. Both exploratory and confirmatory factor analyses were included in these studies, beginning with a maximum likelihood exploratory factor analysis specifying 17 clear factors, using half of the 3,993-person database. This specification was based on the assumption that the theoretical Wheel of Wellness model indeed included 17 discrete factors of wellness, though related in that all components of human functioning are related.

Importantly, each set of items among the 103 included in the dataset loaded only on their expected factor, and the average factor loadings on the expected factor ($M = .62$) was 29 times greater than on the off-loadings ($M = .02$). Five clear factors emerged from the analysis that were defined as second-order factors. The initial 17 scales of the WEL emerged as independent factors; however, the grouping of the factors was not according to the initial hypothesized Wheel. In reviewing the correlations between the second-order factors, Hattie et al. (2004) found some evidence of the circumplex patterning presented in the original model, as would be expected if the relationships form a "wheel," at the scale level. In the circumplex structure, there are larger correlations near the diagonal and decreasing correlations further away, but the correlations did not increase again as desired in the new, emerging model.

A confirmatory factor analysis was conducted specifying a restricted factor pattern in which each item was allowed to load only on its expected scale. Next, the scales were restricted to load only on the appropriate second-order factors (as identified in the exploratory factor analysis), and these five loaded onto a single third-order factor. Figure 4.1 presents the standardized estimates from a structural equation model (AMOS; SPSS Inc., 2003) at the second and third levels. The goodness-of-fit index, the root-mean-square error of approximation (RMSEA), was .042, $/\chi^2(2533) = 8,261$, which is indicative of acceptable fit of the data to the theoretical model (Browne & Cudeck, 1993). Hattie et al. (2004) noted:

> [E]ach of the standardized factor loadings is statistically significantly different from zero and quite substantial. Wellness, the higher order factor, is best referenced by our Creative and Coping Self, and least by our Physical Self, although all five contribute substantially to overall wellness. (p. 357)

Relationships among the higher order wellness factor, five second-order factors, and 17 subfactors are depicted in the structural model. Extensive analysis of these statistical relationships over a 6-year period, and consideration of both the theoretical and practical significance of each, resulted in the development of the Indivisible Self Model of Wellness (IS-Wel; Myers & Sweeney, 2004b; Sweeney & Myers, 2005).

THE INDIVISIBLE SELF

The IS-Wel model is shown in Figure 4.2, and definitions of the single first- and five second-order factors are provided in Table 4.1. The third-order factors were defined in chapter 3, and because the original 17 factors were confirmed, the definitions are not repeated here. Some of these factors were renamed both to simplify understanding of the relationships among the

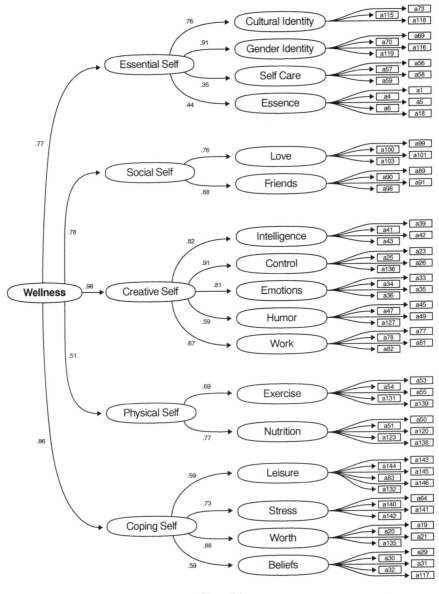

Figure 4.1
Structural Model Created From the
Wellness Evaluation of Lifestyle (WEL) Database

components and to clarify the meaning of the factor (e.g., Emotional Awareness and Coping was renamed Emotions; Problem Solving and Creativity was renamed Thinking; Sense of Humor was renamed Positive Humor). The model also reflects the contextual nature of human functioning, in that we are both affected by and have an effect on our environment.

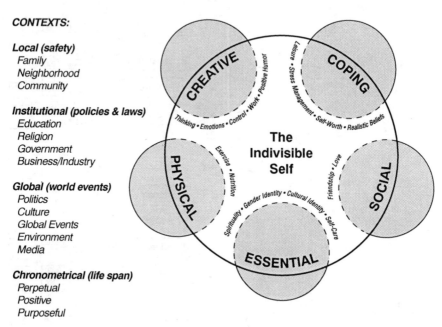

CONTEXTS:

Local (safety)
Family
Neighborhood
Community

Institutional (policies & laws)
Education
Religion
Government
Business/Industry

Global (world events)
Politics
Culture
Global Events
Environment
Media

Chronometrical (life span)
Perpetual
Positive
Purposeful

Figure 4.2
The Indivisible Self: An Evidence-Based Model of Wellness

The Higher Order Wellness Factor

To fully understand the meaning of the factors that emerged from the exploratory and confirmatory analyses and that compose the structural model, it was necessary to examine the individual items in the WEL. We were surprised to find that a study of the items measuring wellness at first made the higher order factor quite difficult to interpret, as all items in the instrument loaded highly on this factor. For example, an item in the Spirituality scale read, "I engage in prayer, meditation, or individual spiritual study is a regular part of my life." An item in the Humor scale read, "I frequently see humor even when engaged in a serious task," and an item in the Self-Care scale read, "I do not use tobacco." How these disparate concepts and items could load so strongly on a single factor at first seemed counterintuitive. It was necessary to reexamine the theory on which the model was based to explain these seemingly unusual results. In chapter 3, Adler's emphasis on holism was discussed. His thesis that we are more than the sum of our parts and cannot be divided provided the essential philosophical foundation for explaining the structural model, and particularly the higher order Wellness factor.

Five Second-Order Factors

Five second-order factors were identified through exploratory and confirmatory factor analyses using the original 17 scales of the WEL. We again looked

Table 4.1

Table 4.1

Definitions of Components of the Indivisible Self

Factor		Definition of Wellness Factor
Single Higher Order Factor		
Wellness		The sum of all items on the Five Factor Wellness Inventory *(5F-Wel); a measure of one's general well-being or total wellness.
2nd-Order Factors	*Corresponding 3rd-Order Factors*	
Creative Self	Thinking Emotions Control Work Positive Humor	The combination of attributes that each of us forms to make a unique place among others in our social interactions and to interpret our world.
Coping Self	Leisure Stress Management Self-Worth Realistic Beliefs	The combination of elements that regulate our responses to life events and provide a means for transcending their negative effects.
Social Self	Friendship Love	Social support through connections with others in our friendships and intimate relationships, including family ties.
Essential Self	Spirituality Gender Identity Cultural Identity Self-Care	Our essential meaning-making processes in relation to life, self, and others.
Physical Self	Nutrition Exercise	The biological and physiological processes that comprise the physical aspects of our development and functioning.
Contexts Local		Those systems in which we live most often—our families, neighborhoods, and communities—and our perceptions of safety in these systems.
Institutional		Social and political systems that affect our daily functioning and serve to empower or limit our development in obvious and subtle ways, including education, religion, government, business and industry, and the media.
Global		Factors such as politics, culture, global events, and the environment that affect us and others around the world.
Chrono-metrical		Movement and change in the time dimension: perpetual, purposeful, and evolving with consequences for later life.

to Adlerian theory as we examined and attempted to make sense of the five factors, which were eventually named the Creative Self, Coping Self, Social Self, Essential Self, and Physical Self. These were seen as the factors composing the *self*, or the *indivisible self*. A brief overview of the meaning of each of the components within the five factors is provided below. The relationship among the factors, as well as contextual variables, is shown in Figure 4.2.

The Creative Self. Adler referred to the Creative Self as the combination of attributes that each individual forms to make a unique place among others in our social interactions (Adler, 1927/1954; Ansbacher & Ansbacher, 1967). Five third-order factors constitute the Creative Self: Thinking, Emotions, Control, Positive Humor, and Work. Both research and clinical experience have revealed that what we think affects our emotions as well as our body. Similarly, emotional experiences influence our cognitive responses to subsequent experiences perceived as similar. Positive expectations result from a perceived sense of control and influence emotions, behavior, and anticipated outcomes. In addition, positive humor has a pervasive influence on physical as well as mental functioning. The ability to think clearly, perceive accurately, and respond appropriately can help decrease stress and enhance the humor response, which in turn affects the immune system positively. Likewise, work is an essential element in human experience that can enhance or exacerbate one's capacity to live life fully.

The Coping Self. The Coping Self includes four components or third-order factors: Realistic Beliefs, Stress Management, Self-Worth, and Leisure. Irrational beliefs are the source of many frustrations and disappointments with life; relinquishing our irrational need to be perfect is one way to help reduce or cope with stress. Likewise, self-worth can be enhanced through effective coping with life's challenges. Finally, leisure is essential to wellness and continual development. Learning to become totally absorbed in an activity in which time stands still helps one both cope with and transcend others of life's requirements. Leisure opens pathways to growth in creative and spiritual dimensions, thus establishing a strong link between the various selves, or second-order factors. The Coping Self, then, is composed of elements that regulate our responses to life events and provides a means for transcending their negative effects.

The Social Self. The Social Self includes the two third-order factors of Friendship and Love, which exist on a continuum and, as a consequence, are not clearly distinguishable in practice. What is clear is that friendships and intimate relationships do enhance the quality and length of one's life. Isolation, alienation, and separation from others generally are associated with a variety of poor health conditions and greater susceptibility to premature death, whereas social support remains in multiple studies as the strongest identified predictor of positive mental health over the life span. The mainstay of this support is family, with healthier families providing the most positive sources of individual wellness. Of course, healthy families can be either biological or families of choice, particularly for adults.

The Essential Self. The Essential Self comprises four third-order factors: Spirituality, Self-Care, Gender Identity, and Cultural Identity. Spirituality has positive benefits for longevity and quality of life, and was viewed by Adler as central to holism and wellness (Mansager, 2000). It incorporates our existential sense of meaning, purpose, and hopefulness toward life. Both gender and cultural identity are filters through which life experiences are seen and affect how others are experienced in response to ourselves. Both affect our essential meaning-making processes in relation to life, self, and others. Self-Care includes proactive efforts to live long and live well, whereas carelessness, avoidance of health-promoting habits, and general disregard of one's well-being are potentially signs of despair, hopelessness, and alienation from life's opportunities, reflected in loss of a sense of meaning and purpose in life.

The Physical Self. The Physical Self factor includes the two third-order factors of Exercise and Nutrition. The physical components of wellness are often overemphasized to the exclusion of other components of holistic well-being. The evidence is compelling with regard to the importance of exercise and nutrition for positive well-being over the life span. Not surprisingly, "survivors," those individuals who live longest, place a priority on both good nutrition and exercise.

Contextual Variables

As humans we do not function in isolation; rather, the importance of context, or systems, for understanding behavior has been well established (e.g., Bronfenbrenner, 1999; Gladding, 2002; Nichols & Schwartz, 2001). Thus, a full understanding of an individual is impossible without or in the absence of knowledge of his or her contextual or environmental situation and influences. As noted earlier, these can operate for better or for worse in relation to individual wellness. The Indivisible Self is both affected by and has an effect on the world around it. In the IS-Wel model, four contexts are defined as important to individual wellness: local, institutional, global, and chronometrical.

Local contexts are similar to Bronfenbrenner's (1999) concept of microsystems. They include interactions with those systems in which we live most often—our families, neighborhoods, and communities. The issue of personal safety within one's local context is paramount, and we often retreat to this context to deal with the challenges and stresses of life.

Institutional contexts—education, religion, government, business and industry, and the media—are similar to Bronfenbrenner's macrosytem and have both direct and indirect effects on our lives. These influences may be quite powerful and, although they can be positive or negative, difficult to assimilate when negative. The influence of *policies and laws* on personal wellness is an important part of this contextual variable.

Global contexts, including politics, culture, global events, and the environment, clearly are made more salient and personal today through the pervasive influence of the media. The effect of CNN news programming during events such as the Iraq War, the Gulf War, the Challenger explosion, and the 9-11 tragedy made these events part of the daily life of all Americans, and indeed people around the world. Anxiety reactions among people widely separated in space and time from these events and the people directly involved in these events have become commonplace. The impact of *world events* on one's wellness is the central concept for this context.

The final context, *chronometrical*, refers to the fact that people change over time in both predictable and unpredictable ways. Wellness involves both acute and chronic effects of lifestyle behaviors and choices throughout an individual's life span (Myers, Sweeney, & Witmer, 2001). We are increasingly finding that the problems of aging are due to lifestyle behaviors and choices and are largely preventable. Thus, wellness choices made earlier in life have a cumulative positive effect as we grow older. Similarly, unhealthy lifestyle choices have a negative effect that intensifies as we age. Consistent with Adlerian theory and research, movement in the time dimension is perpetual and ongoing, positive, and intentional (purposeful) for the achievement of high-level wellness.

Relationship Among Wellness Components

Each of the components of the IS-Wel model interacts with all others to contribute to holistic functioning. Similarly, each contextual factor has an influence or impact on the individual, and the individual affects his or her context. Individually and collectively, these interactions may be for better or for worse. The significance of this model, as was true of the Wheel of Wellness, lies in a positive, holistic orientation, in which strengths in any of the components can be mobilized to enhance functioning in other areas, and to overcome deficits and negative forces that act to depress, demean, or deny the uniqueness and significance of the individual.

SUMMARY

The Indivisible Self, an evidence-based model of wellness, emerged from research with a large database gathered on the earlier theoretical model, the Wheel of Wellness. From a practical standpoint, both models are useful as a foundation for helping people understand holistic wellness and make choices to enhance their wellness across the life span. Both are prisms through which the concept or construct of wellness can be viewed. We continue to gather data relating to both models and recently have begun examination of a new database gathered using the Five Factor Wellness Inventory (Myers & Sweeney, 2004a). A new "prism" for understanding wellness has emerged, including four factors that map onto the well known body–mind–spirit triad (Myers, Luecht, & Sweeney, 2004). While this new model is intriguing, it lacks the richness of earlier models and the variety of components of wellness that can form a focus for strength-based and preventive interventions. However, the four-factor model includes a "common factor" that may provide a means for screening individuals for wellness risk factors through a relatively brief assessment.

We continue to find more questions about the nature of wellness than we are able to answer, and many of these questions lead to the need for reliable and valid assessment as a foundation for empirical studies. Assessment instruments are discussed in chapter 5, following which an entire section of the book is devoted to a review of studies using these and related assessments to explore the meaning of wellness across time and cultures.

DISCUSSION QUESTIONS

1. Explain how the factor analysis of the WEL database led to the new Indivisible Self model of wellness.
2. Using Adlerian theory, explain the meaning of the single higher order wellness factor in the Indivisible Self model.
3. Explain the five second-order factors in the Indivisible Self model.
4. Discuss the contextual variables in the Indivisible Self model.

WEB RESOURCES

- **Understanding Factor Analysis, http: //www.hawaii.edu/powerkills/ UFA.HTM,** provides an overview of factor analysis both conceptually and in terms of the statistical procedures used.
- **The Alfred Adler Institute of San Francisco, http://ourworld. compuserve.com/homepages/hstein/q-a-10.htm,** provides an explanation of Adler's concept of teleological holism.

5

Assessing Wellness:
Formal and Informal Approaches

Jane E. Myers and Thomas J. Sweeney

Although models of wellness are useful for conceptualizing human functioning, what we believe is most important is using these models as a basis for self-understanding and intentional decision making to enhance wellness in a positive direction. To do so most effectively requires some means of assessing how one is doing in each of the areas of well-being. Assessment may be conducted in a variety of ways. In this chapter, informal and formal strategies for assessing personal wellness are discussed. Formal methods include two paper-and-pencil measures: the Wellness Evaluation of Lifestyle (WEL; Myers, Sweeney, & Witmer, 2000a) based on the Wheel of Wellness (Witmer, Sweeney, & Myers, 1998), and the Five Factor Wellness Inventory (5F-Wel; Myers & Sweeney, 2004a) based on the Indivisible Self model of wellness (Myers & Sweeney, 2004b; Sweeney & Myers, 2005).

INFORMAL METHODS OF ASSESSING WELLNESS

Wellness can always be assessed through conversations, or in the case of helping relationships, through clinical interviews. When the model of wellness chosen is parsimonious, having fewer than four or five components, such interviews can occur within a relatively short period of time. However, the content of discussions focused on global aspects of wellness, such as body, mind, or spirit, may be of necessity general, vague, philosophical, or otherwise difficult to quantify. If we assume that some quantification is useful to understanding behavior and to the process of behavior change, as discussed more fully in chapters 16 through 18, then the limitations of clinical interviews as a foundation for creating substantive lifestyle change become readily apparent.

A second and easily accessible means of assessing wellness is through use of simple scaling questions. For example, "On a scale of 1 to 10, with 1 being *low* and 10 being *high*, how would you rate your wellness?" To be more specific and useful, a similar scaling question could be used for each of the components of wellness individually, as well as for overall or holistic wellness. We have also found it useful to ask individuals to make two ratings for each wellness dimension, responding first to "How well do you feel?" and second to "How satisfied are you with your level of wellness in this area?" A sample rating scale for spiritual wellness would look something like this:

Spirituality	Circle the number that best reflects your overall spiritual wellness and your satisfaction with your spiritual wellness.									
Overall wellness	1	2	3	4	5	6	7	8	9	10
Satisfaction	1	2	3	4	5	6	7	8	9	10

The advantage of using scaling questions is that clients can easily self-report their wellness in all of the components and factors in the wellness models, or they can select certain areas of wellness for a focus of discussion and hopefully intervention and positive change. A limitation of this approach is again the global quality of the ratings. Although the definitions of each wellness component may be presented as a stimulus for thinking about self-assessments, it is difficult with a global rating scale to help people think about and focus on specific wellness behaviors and attitudes that might be contributing to their wellness in a particular area. To overcome these limitations, paper-and-pencil assessments with proven psychometric properties can be useful for personal and clinical as well as population descriptions and research purposes.

FORMAL METHODS OF ASSESSING WELLNESS: THE WEL AND 5F-WEL

As mentioned in earlier chapters, our interests in wellness arose from a desire to help all people desire and work toward high-level wellness. As a consequence, we realized a need for formal assessment methods to inform self-understanding and to contribute to an emerging knowledge base of well-functioning. This need was met initially through development and validation of the Wellness Evaluation of Lifestyle (WEL). After 10 years of research involving four separate and increasingly more useful and psychometrically sound versions of the WEL (Myers, Sweeney, & Witmer, 1996b, 2000a; Myers, Witmer, & Sweeney, 1995; Witmer, Sweeney, & Myers, 1993), the 5F-Wel, originally called the WEL-J (Myers & Sweeney, 1996, 2001a), was developed (Myers & Sweeney, 1999a, 2001a, 2004a). Multiple versions of the 5F-Wel, including cross-cultural translations, have made this a useful instrument for clinical as well as research purposes.

The Wellness Evaluation of Lifestyle Inventory (WEL)

The initial version of the WEL (WEL-O; Witmer, Sweeney, & Myers, 1993) included 114 items designed to assess the 17 components in the Wheel of

Wellness. Items were statements (e.g., "I usually achieve the goals I set for myself") that respondents rated using a 5-point Likert-type scale with choices including *strongly agree, agree, neutral or undecided, disagree,* and *strongly disagree.* Over a period of 10 years, the instrument was field tested with a variety of adult populations. Extensive item and scale analyses resulted in several revisions, the most recent being the WEL-S (Myers, Sweeney, & Witmer, 2000a), which includes 131 items.

Test–retest reliability coefficients for the WEL-S scales, established with a sample of 99 undergraduate students (Myers, 1998), ranged from .68 for cultural identity to .88 for nutrition. Internal consistency measures of reliability ranged from a low of .60 for the realistic beliefs scale to a high of .94 for friendship within a larger and more diverse sample of 2,295 adults across the life span. Convergent and divergent validity were investigated by comparing scores on the various WEL scales with similar scales on other instruments. As reported in the WEL manual, Myers (1998) found that scores measuring conceptually similar constructs had high correlations (convergent validity) and scores measuring different constructs had lower correlations (divergent validity).

The WEL is commercially available and remains an important resource for clinical use. Both scale and item scores can be examined and may be helpful in targeting specific areas of wellness for intentional change. The lack of factor-analytic studies limits the usefulness of the WEL for research. Its successor, the 5F-Wel, grew out of factor-analytic studies of the original WEL database.

The Five Factor Wellness Inventory (5F-Wel)

The 5F-Wel measures the factors included in the Indivisible Self model of wellness. It is a paper-and-pencil instrument that includes 73 items measuring the single higher order wellness factor (Total Wellness), the five second-order factors (Creative, Coping, Social, Essential, and Physical Selves), and the original 17 discrete scales measured in the WEL. Most of the scales include 4 to 6 items. An additional 19 items measure the four contexts included in the IS-Wel model (local, institutional, global, and chronometrical). Responses are made using a 4-point Likert-type scale including *strongly agree, agree, disagree,* and *strongly disagree.* The potential for undecided or neutral responses that was included in the original WEL was eliminated in the 5F-Wel. Preliminary studies indicate no reduction in item or scale variance as a result of this change.

The exploratory and confirmatory factor analyses reported in chapter 4 support each of the scales: 17 discrete third-order factors, 5 second-order factors, and a single higher order wellness factor. Alpha coefficients ($N = 2,093$) are uniformly high for the first- and second-order factors: Total Wellness, .94; Creative Self, .92; Coping Self and Social Self, .85; Essential Self and Physical Self, .88. Third-order factor alphas range from .70 to .87 for all but two scales: Self-Care, .66 and Realistic Beliefs, .68. Use of the 5F-Wel in multiple dissertation and other studies provides evidence of both convergent and divergent validity of the scales relative to constructs such as ethnic identity, acculturation, body image, self-esteem, and gender role conflict.

The 5F-Wel is available in three forms for use with different age populations. A ninth-grade reading level version (i.e., all items are ninth-grade reading level or lower) may be used with high school students or adults. Versions created with a maximum sixth-grade reading level and third-grade reading level are useful with middle and elementary school students, respectively. Initial studies with the lower reading level versions to date support the reliability and validity of the scales for use with these populations.

The 5F-Wel has also been translated or culturally adapted (see chapter 12) for use with cultures outside of the United States. The sixth-grade version has been translated into Hebrew (translation by M. Tatar, 1999) and the adult version into Korean (translation by C. Chang, 1998) and Turkish (translation by T. Dogan, 2004). Spanish language translations of the third-grade (translation by J. Villalba) and adult versions (translation by A. Rayle) are in progress.

SUMMARY

Assessment of wellness is required to personalize the meaning of the wellness dimensions presented in the models described in earlier chapters. In addition to informal assessment methods, paper-and-pencil measures with excellent psychometric properties have been developed for clinical and research purposes. These instruments have been central to multiple studies of wellness across ages and populations (examined in more detail in Part II), which have provided a wealth of information to inform theory and practice in wellness counseling.

DISCUSSION QUESTIONS

1. How can wellness be assessed informally? When is informal assessment appropriate?
2. What are the main psychometric differences between the Wellness Evaluation of Lifestyle (WEL) and Five Factor Wellness Inventory (5F-Wel)?
3. What are some important reasons for assessing an individual's wellness?

WEB RESOURCE

- **MindGarden, Inc., http://www.mindgarden.com/,** is a commercial test publisher that publishes both paper and electronic instruments, including the WEL.

PART II

WELLNESS RESEARCH

Theories provide a basis for conceptualizing and understanding phenomena and processes. Swenson (1999; http://www.css.edu/users/dswenson/web/theoryeval.html) suggested the following criteria for evaluating theories: parsimony (explains reality by simplifying), operationality (terms are defined in such a manner that they can be measured), generativity (a good theory generates testable hypotheses), power (the theory is able to account for events accurately), falsifiability (it can be disproven), importance (scope of coverage), internal consistency (concepts are related), organization (explains relationships among concepts), empirical support (evidence supports the theory), and measurement (instruments have adequate reliability and validity to support conclusions). Using these criteria, the Wheel of Wellness and the Indivisible Self models both may be seen as useful and, in fact, good theories to explain the construct of wellness. Numerous studies using these models and associated measures, the Wellness Evaluation of Lifestyle (WEL) and Five Factor Wellness Inventory (5-F Wel), support this conclusion. These studies are summarized in Table II.1.

The wellness models discussed in this book have been used in studies of wellness among various populations, studies examining correlates of wellness, and cross-cultural and cross-national studies. Population studies have included children, adolescents, college students, and young, middle-aged, and older adults. A few of the correlates of wellness that have been examined include short-term state and long-term trait constructs of psychological well-being; components of objectified body consciousness such as body shame and appearance control beliefs; healthy love styles; job satisfaction; mattering; ethnic identity; and acculturation. Cross-cultural and cross-national studies have been conducted with Korean American (Chang, 1998; Chang & Myers, 2003), Native American (Garrett, 1996, 1999), Caribbean American (Mitchell, 2001), and other minority adolescents in the United States (e.g., Rayle, 2002). Adult populations studied have included men, women, African American men, gay men, and lesbians.

The first nine chapters in this part of the book attempt the difficult task of reviewing, summarizing, and integrating the array of wellness research available. Each chapter provides a definition or delimitation of the population or issues to be reviewed, provides a brief discussion of noncounseling wellness models and associated research, and provides an in-depth review of wellness research based in counseling models. An integrative analysis and exploration of the long-range research agenda needed to inform clinical practice is presented in each chapter. In the final chapter of the section, Ginter provides a summary and reflections on the continuing need for wellness research in critical areas across the life span and across populations.

To aid the reader in understanding and evaluating the scope of wellness research, and wellness research needs, a table of doctoral dissertation research and selected additional wellness studies is included here. Table II.1 may be a useful resource for both clinicians and researchers. Additional information and research updates may be found at http://www.uncg.edu/~jemyers/.

Table II.1

Summary of Studies Using the Wellness Evaluation of Lifestyle (WEL) and Five Factor Wellness Inventory (5F-Wel), Including Variables, Methods, Participants, Instruments, and Findings

Author/Citation	Title	Variables	Method and Participants	Instrument	Findings
Amery (2004) and Brown-Baatjies	A study on the wellness of nurses working in oncology in the Nelson Mandela Metropole and City of Cape Town, South Africa	Oncology Nursing Wellness	Descriptive 30 nurses working in oncology wards	5F-Wel	Participants reported high wellness. Essential Self was highest second-order factor. Least well in Realistic Beliefs, followed by Exercise and Nutrition.
Booth (2005)	The relationship among career aspiration, multiple role planning attitudes, and wellness in African American and Caucasian undergraduate women	Multiple role-planning attitudes Holistic wellness Career aspirations	Pearson correlations MANOVAS Multiple regression	5F-Wel Career Aspiration Scale Attitudes About Multiple Role Planning Scale	In progress.
Casey (2005)	Wellness among women hemodialysis patients	Wellness Demographics (age, marital status, income, ethnicity, co-morbidities, length of time on dialysis, history of catheter infections and clotting)	Descriptives Pearson correlations Chi-square 30 adult, English-speaking women hemodialysis patients in California	5F-Wel	In progress examination of wellness among hemodialysis patients and relationship of wellness to dialysis and complications. *(Continued next page)*

Table II.1 (Continued)

Summary of Studies Using the Wellness Evaluation of Lifestyle (WEL) and Five Factor Wellness Inventory (5F-Wel), Including Variables, Methods, Participants, Instruments, and Findings

Author/Citation	Title	Variables	Method and Participants	Instrument	Findings
Chang (1998)	The role of distinctiveness in acculturation, ethnic identity, and wellness in Korean American adolescents and young adults	Differentiation Inclusion Acculturation Assimilation Ethnic identity Wellness Demographics	Pearson correlations MANOVA Multiple regression 208 monolingual and bilingual participants ages 11–25	WEL; 5F-Wel (Korean); cultural adaptation and equivalence of versions comprised initial study	Need for assimilation predicted degree of inclusion; need for differentiation did not. Need for differentiation was negatively related to wellness and acculturation was positively related to wellness.
Connolly (2000)	The relationship among wellness, mattering, and job satisfaction	Holistic wellness Mattering Job satisfaction	Pearson correlations Multiple regression 82 men and women ages 21–62; work settings in Midwest and Southeast U.S.	WEL/5F-Wel General Mattering Scale Job Descriptive Index (revised)	Wellness and mattering predicted job satisfaction, with wellness being the stronger predictor; relationship between job satisfaction and gender found.
Degges-White (2003)	The relationships among transitions, chronological age, subjective age, wellness, and life satisfaction in women at midlife	Transitions experienced and expected; timelines Chronological age Subjective age Overall wellness Life satisfaction	MANOVA Pearson correlations Multiple regression 224 midlife women ages 35–65	5F-Wel Transitions Survey (created for study) Satisfaction With Life Survey Subjective Age Questionnaire	Significant relationship between subjective age and wellness; wellness and household income accounted for a significant amount of variance in life satisfaction. *(Continued next page)*

Table II.1 (Continued)

Summary of Studies Using the Wellness Evaluation of Lifestyle (WEL) and Five Factor Wellness Inventory (5F-Wel), Including Variables, Methods, Participants, Instruments, and Findings

Author/Citation	Title	Variables	Method and Participants	Instrument	Findings
Degges-White, Myers, Adelman, and Pastoor (2003)	Examining counseling needs of headache patients: An exploratory study of wellness and perceived stress	Wellness Perceived stress Mattering	Pearson correlations t tests 60 adult migraine headache patients in private medical clinic	5F-Wel General Mattering Scale Perceived Stress Scale	Lower wellness and higher perceived stress in headache patients than norm group of adults.
Dew (2000)	The relationship among internalized homophobia, self-disclosure, self-disclosure to parents, and wellness in adult gay males	Internalized homophobia Self-disclosure Self-disclosure to parents Wellness	ANOVA t tests 217 volunteers from gay social and professional organizations and university organizations	Nungesser Homosexual Attitudes Inventory General Disclosiveness Scale WEL	No relation between parental disclosure and wellness; self-disclosure and homophobia related to wellness; differences among ages and ethnicities.
Dice (2002)	The relationship among coping resources, wellness, and attachment to companion animals in older persons	Coping resources Wellness Attachment to companion animal	MANOVA Pearson correlations 327 persons 65 years of age and older not residing in long-term care institutions	Coping Resources Inventory WEL Pet Ownership Information Forms	Social, emotional, and total coping resources were higher among current and former pet owners with high levels of attachment than for pet owners with medium and low attachment levels. Significant positive relation between wellness and coping resources for both groups of pet owners. *(Continued next page)*

Table II.1 (Continued)

Summary of Studies Using the Wellness Evaluation of Lifestyle (WEL) and Five Factor Wellness Inventory (5F-Wel), Including Variables, Methods, Participants, Instruments, and Findings

Author/Citation	Title	Variables	Method and Participants	Instrument	Findings
Enochs (2001)	Wellness and adjustment in college freshmen based on type of residence hall and gender	Special freshman residence halls vs. traditional residence halls	t test MANOVA 511 first-year traditional-age freshmen	WEL College Adjustment Scales	Students in freshmen experience halls had higher wellness than students in regular residence halls; significant interactive effect found between wellness and adjustment; gender difference in adjustment (males higher) but not wellness.
Garrett (1996)	Cultural values and wellness of Native American high school students	Cultural value orientation Acculturation Wellness	MANOVAs, ANOVA, Factor Models 155 American; Grades 9–12 20 Native American (NA)	Value Schedule Native American Acculturation Scale WEL	Differences between NAs and non-NAs on acculturation; differences among acculturation levels on wellness; no overall differences between NA and non-NA students on wellness.
Gill (2005)	The relationship among spirituality, religiosity, and wellness for poor rural women	Spirituality Religiosity Wellness	Pearson product moment correlations, ANOVAs, Multiple regression analyses 167 female participants residing in non-metropolitan areas	Spirituality Assessment Scale Brief, multi-dimensional measure of religiousness/spirituality 5F-Wel	In progress.

(Continued next page)

Table II.1 (Continued)

Summary of Studies Using the Wellness Evaluation of Lifestyle (WEL) and Five Factor Wellness Inventory (5F-Wel), Including Variables, Methods, Participants, Instruments, and Findings

Author/Citation	Title	Variables	Method and Participants	Instrument	Findings
Granello (1996)	Wellness as a function of perceived social support network and ability to empathize	Perceived social support Ability to empathize Wellness	Multiple regression Pearson correlations 100 undergraduate students ages 18–47	WEL Norbeck Social Support Questionnaire LaMonica Empathy Profile	No predictive relationship between empathy or social support in relation to wellness.
Hartwig (2003)	The relationship among individual factors of wellness, family environment, and delinquency among adolescent females	Family environment Wellness Delinquency	t tests ANOVA MANOVA 248 undergraduate women ages 18–19	Moos Family Environment Scale 5F-Wel Mak Delinquency Scale	No significant differences between delinquent and nondelinquent females in wellness and family environment.
Hermon (1995)	An examination of the relationship between college students' subjective well-being and adherence to a holistic wellness model	Wellness Perceived psychological well-being	Multivariate regression analysis ANOVA 155 undergraduate students ages 18–51	WEL Memorial University of Newfoundland Scale of Happiness	Ability to self-regulate, identify with work, and friendships contribute most to psychological well-being; significant relationship between wellness and psychological well-being.
Hutchinson (1996)	The relationship of wellness factors to work performance and job satisfaction among managers	Wellness Work performance Job satisfaction	Multiple regression 161 U.S. middle-level managers	WEL Physical Self-Description Questionnaire Job Satisfaction Blank Work Performance Scale	Holistic wellness predicts work performance and job satisfaction better than physical fitness, which currently defines organizational wellness programs.

(Continued next page) |

49

Table II.1 (Continued)

Summary of Studies Using the Wellness Evaluation of Lifestyle (WEL) and Five Factor Wellness Inventory (5F-Wel), Including Variables, Methods, Participants, Instruments, and Findings

Author/Citation	Title	Variables	Method and Participants	Instrument	Findings
Makinson (2001)	The relationship of moral identity, social interest, gender, and wellness among adolescents	Moral identity Social interest Gender Wellness	Pearson correlations SEM 187 adolescents in Grades 9–12; central North Carolina youth organizations	Tennessee Self-Concept Scale Social Interest Assessment Scale (School) 5F-Wel (Teenage)	Social interest, but not wellness, explained variance in wellness; no gender differences in wellness.
Mitchell (2001)	The relationship among acculturation, wellness, and academic self-concept in Caribbean American adolescents	Academic self-concept Acculturation Wellness	Multiple regression Pearson correlations 201 English-speaking Caribbean American adolescents; New York City and Greensboro, NC; public, private, parochial schools	Vancouver Index of Acculturation 5F-Wel (Teenage) Tennessee Self-Concept Scale (Child)	Positive relation between wellness and academic self-concept and acculturation; acculturation and wellness account for variance in self-concept.
Mobley (2004)	The relationship among age, gender role conflict, and wellness in two cohorts of male counselors	Age Gender role conflict Wellness	Correlation ANOVA Multiple regression 287 male professional counselors	5F-Wel Gender Role Conflict (GRC) scales	Gender role conflict was not related to wellness overall; however, some GRC scales, notably restrictive emotionality, were associated with lower wellness. *(Continued next page)*

Table II.1 (Continued)

Summary of Studies Using the Wellness Evaluation of Lifestyle (WEL) and Five Factor Wellness Inventory (5F-Wel),
Including Variables, Methods, Participants, Instruments, and Findings

Author/Citation	Title	Variables	Method and Participants	Instrument	Findings
Myers and Bechtel (2004)	Stress, wellness, and mattering among cadets at West Point: Factors affecting a fit and healthy force	Age Gender Ethnicity Perceived stress Mattering Wellness Pre-post 9-11	Pearson correlations MANOVA *t* tests 179 first-year cadets at West Point	5F-Wel General Mattering Scale Perceived Stress Scale	Significant positive correlations between 17 wellness scales and mattering; negative correlations between perceived stress and some wellness scales; some within-group differences based on gender and age.
Myers, Luecht, and Sweeney (2004)	The factor structure of wellness: Reexamining theoretical and empirical models	Wellness Age Gender Ethnicity	SEM MANOVA Pearson correlations 3,993 adults across the life span	5F-Wel	Identification of new factor structure with four factors: Physical, Mental, Spiritual, and Cognitive-Emotional.
Myers, Madathil, and Tingle (in press)	Marital satisfaction and wellness in India and the U.S.: A preliminary comparison of arranged marriages and marriages of choice	Marital status Marital satisfaction Wellness	Descriptives *t* tests 45 couples in India in arranged marriages	WEL CHARISMA	Differences on 9 scales, some large and medium effects, between sample and WEL norm group; Indian participants scored higher on nutrition, spirituality, and cultural identity. *(Continued next page)*

Table II.1 (Continued)

Summary of Studies Using the Wellness Evaluation of Lifestyle (WEL) and Five Factor Wellness Inventory (5F-Wel), Including Variables, Methods, Participants, Instruments, and Findings

Author/Citation	Title	Variables	Method and Participants	Instrument	Findings
Myers, Mobley, and Booth (2003)	Wellness of counseling students: Practicing what we preach	Wellness variables	*t* tests MANOVA 3-way ANOVA 263 graduate students in counseling; entry-level and doctoral	5F-Wel	Doctoral students report greater wellness; non-Caucasian students report greater cultural identity.
Powers, Myers, Tingle, and Powers (2003)	Wellness, perceived stress, mattering, and marital satisfaction among medical residents and their spouses: Implications for education and counseling	Wellness Perceived stress Mattering Marital satisfaction Medical training	*t* tests 42 couples in medical marriages (i.e., one or both spouses were physicians)	WEL Perceived Stress Scale General Mattering Scale	Resident spouses score higher than norm on wellness, mattering, marital satisfaction; lower on work satisfaction, realistic beliefs. No significant differences between medical and nonmedical spouses.
Rayle (2002)	The relationship among ethnic identity, acculturation, mattering, and wellness in minority and nonminority adolescents	Ethnic identity Acculturation Mattering Wellness	SEM 176 minority and 286 nonminority adolescents	Multigroup Ethnic Identity Measure Stephenson Multigroup Acculturation Scale General Mattering Scale Mattering to Others Questionnaire 5F-Wel (Teenage)	Mattering and acculturation explain adolescent variance in wellness; ethnic identity explains minority variance. No differences between minority and nonminority participants. *(Continued next page)*

Table II.1 (Continued)

Summary of Studies Using the Wellness Evaluation of Lifestyle (WEL) and Five Factor Wellness Inventory (5F-Wel),
Including Variables, Methods, Participants, Instruments, and Findings

Author/Citation	Title	Variables	Method and Participants	Instrument	Findings
Roach (2005)	The influence of counselor education programs on counselor wellness	Total wellness and the 5 second-order factors (Creative, Coping, Social, Essential, Physical) Time in counselor education program (beginning, mid, and end points) Demographics	204 master's-level counseling students age 21–58, enrolled in 3 southeastern universities	Trend analysis in MANOVA ANOVAs	In progress. Preliminary findings indicate that there is no significant trend in levels of wellness among students in counselor education master's programs.
Shurts (2004)	The relationships among marital messages received, marital attitudes, relationship self-efficacy, and wellness among never-married traditional-aged undergraduate students	Relationship self-efficacy Marital messages received (MMR) Marital attitudes (MA) Wellness	Traditional-age, never-married undergraduate students	5F-Wel Relationship Self-Efficacy (RSE) Scale Marital Messages Scale Marital Attitudes Scale Trend analysis, MANOVA, ANOVA 5F-Wel only	MA and family MMR predict Total Wellness (positive scores with higher wellness); MANOVAs: Essential Wellness by MA, Creative Self by RSE, Social Self by RSE, and Total Wellness by RSE (in all cases, more positive MA or RSE groups had higher wellness scores) *(Continued next page)*

Table II.1 (Continued)

Summary of Studies Using the Wellness Evaluation of Lifestyle (WEL) and Five Factor Wellness Inventory (5F-Wel), Including Variables, Methods, Participants, Instruments, and Findings

Author/Citation	Title	Variables	Method and Participants	Instrument	Findings
Shurts and Myers (2005)	The relationships among liking, love, and wellness: Implications for college student romances	Wellness Liking Love	MANOVA 242 undergraduate students, midsize and small colleges in Midwest and Southeast	Rubin Liking Scale Love Attitudes Scale 5F-Wel	Significant differences found for gender, age, and ethnicity. Significant positive relationships were found between liking and all wellness scales. Eros and Storge correlated positively and Mania correlated negatively with total wellness.
Sinclair (2001)	Objectification experiences, sociocultural attitudes toward appearance, objectified body consciousness, and wellness in heterosexual Caucasian women	Objectified body consciousness Objectification experiences Sociocultural attitudes toward appearance Wellness	Multiple regression Pearson correlations 195 female undergraduate students	Objectification Experiences Questionnaire Sociocultural Attitudes Toward Appearance Questionnaire Objectified Body Consciousness Scale 5F-Wel Multigroup Ethnic Identity Measure Stephenson Multigroup Acculturation Scale	Experience and attitudes account for variance in body consciousness. Positive relations between experience, attitudes, and body consciousness; negative relationship between wellness and body shame but not appearance control beliefs.

(Continued next page)

Table II.1 (Continued)

Summary of Studies Using the Wellness Evaluation of Lifestyle (WEL) and Five Factor Wellness Inventory (5F-Wel), Including Variables, Methods, Participants, Instruments, and Findings

Author/Citation	Title	Variables	Method and Participants	Instrument	Findings
Spurgeon (2002)	The relationship among ethnic identity, self-esteem, and wellness in African American males	Ethnic identity Self-esteem Wellness Historically Black college or university and predominantly White institution (HBCU/PWI)	Regression analyses Pearson correlations MANOVAs 245 African American male college students, ages 19–46, juniors and seniors	General Mattering Scale Mattering to Others Questionnaire 5F-Wel (Teenage) 5F-Wel Racial Identity Attitude Scale Rosenberg Self-Esteem Scale	Racial identity and self-esteem did not predict wellness. Significant negative relationship found between preencounter racial identity attitudes and self-esteem. HBCU students scored higher on self-esteem and 6 of 17 third-order wellness factors. PWI students scored higher on Social Self.
Steigerwald (2000)	The relationship of family-of-origin structure and family conflict resolution tactics to holistic wellness in college-age offspring	Wellness Conflict resolution tactics Family-of-origin structure	ANOVA Multiple regression 219 participants, ages 18–25, Midwestern college	WEL Conflict Tactics Scale	Family-of-origin structure was not significantly related to the offspring's holistic wellness.

(Continued next page)

Table II.1 (Continued)

Summary of Studies Using the Wellness Evaluation of Lifestyle (WEL) and Five Factor Wellness Inventory (5F-Wel), Including Variables, Methods, Participants, Instruments, and Findings

Author/Citation	Title	Variables	Method and Participants	Instrument	Findings
Tanigoshi (2004)	The effectiveness of individual counseling on the wellness of police officers	Age Gender Ethnicity Performance evaluation Self-efficacy Stage of change Individual counseling Wellness	60 police officers in New Orleans	5F-Wel	Police officers who received wellness counseling over a 6-week period improved their wellness in almost all dimensions while those in a delayed-treatment control group did not change.
Tatar and Myers (2004)	Wellness of children in Israel and the United States: A preliminary examination of culture and well-being	Wellness Age Gender Country of origin	Factor analysis MANOVA Pearson correlations t tests 240 Israeli middle school students; 377 NC students	5F-Wel (Teenager) Hebrew translation of 5F-Wel (Teenager)	Differences in wellness based on gender, age, country of origin identified.
Vanderbleek (2005)	Couple play as a predictor of couple bonding, physical health, and emotional health	Couple play Couple bonding- satisfaction, conflict resolution, communication, and idealistic distortion Physical health Emotional health	Pearson correlations Regression	5F-Wel	In progress.

(Continued next page)

Table II.1 (Continued)

Summary of Studies Using the Wellness Evaluation of Lifestyle (WEL) and Five Factor Wellness Inventory (5F-Wel), Including Variables, Methods, Participants, Instruments, and Findings

Author	Title/Citation	Variables	Method and Participants	Instrument	Findings
Vecchione (1999)	An examination of the relationship between career development and holistic wellness among college students	Holistic wellness Career development	Multiple regression 160 (109 female, 51 male) undergraduates at a Midwestern university	WEL Career Development Inventory	No relation between career knowledge and wellness; significant negative relationship between career development attitudes and wellness.
Webster (2005)	Toward a lexicon for holistic health: An empirical analysis of theories of health, wellness, and spirituality			5F-Wel	In progress.
Williams (2005)	The relationship among athletic identity, sport commitment, time in sport participation, social support, and wellness in college student athletes	Athletic identity Sport commitment Time in sport participation Social support Wellness	Pearson correlations SEM Mean comparisons MANOVAs Male and female students athletes across multiple sports	WEL Conflict Tactics Scale	In progress.

Note. ANOVA = analysis of variance; CHARISMA = The Characteristics of Marriage Inventory (Rosen-Grandon, 2001); ENRICH = The Enriching and Nurturing Relationship Issues, Communication, and Happiness Inventory (Olson, Fournier, & Druckman, 1983); MANOVA = multivariate analysis of variance; SEM = structural equation modeling.

6

Wellness and Children: Research Implications

Cheryl Holcomb-McCoy

The United Nations Convention on the Rights of the Child (see United Nations International Children's Fund [UNICEF], 1989) specified that all children have "the right to survival; to develop to the fullest, to protection from harmful influences, abuse, and exploitation; and to participate fully in family, cultural, and social life" (UNICEF, 1996, p. 1). This commitment to children has been evidenced by the laws passed to prevent children from being misused in the workplace, to punish adults who physically or psychologically harm children, to provide means for all children to obtain an education regardless of their mental or physical condition, and to support programs for medical care, food, and clothing for children in need (C. L. Thompson & Rudolph, 1999). Yet, the statistics regarding children's health and welfare in the United States are alarming (Federal Interagency Forum on Child and Family Statistics, 2003). For instance, the National School Boards Association (2000) reported that one in five children live in families with incomes below the poverty level, that more than a million children are abused each year, and that 12% of American children suffer from serious emotional disorders but less than a third receive help. The *Healthy Youth 2010* (Towey & Fleming, 2003) initiative states similar statistics today. It is clear that, as a group, children constitute one of the most vulnerable segments of our society.

Children are subject to a wide range of problems and are dependent on families and communities for sustenance and protection. At the same time, childhood offers an important opportunity to set lifelong healthy behavioral patterns. It is during childhood (i.e., the period between infancy and adolescence) when the most rapid growth biologically, cognitively, psychologically, and socially occurs. The role of wellness in the development of children and the effects of childhood wellness on adult development are unknown and should be a focal point of future research. In this chapter, an overview of the scant literature and research that has been conducted on children and wellness is provided. Considering the paucity of research in this area, a large portion of this chapter covers recommendations for future research.

OVERVIEW OF WELLNESS LITERATURE AND RESEARCH

The challenge of research with children is to identify factors or processes that promote and hinder psychological, emotional, and physical wellness (Cicchetti, Rappaport, Sandler, & Weissberg, 2000). Cowen (1991) emphasized the need to build research and prevention programs around multifaceted strategies that have potential for promoting wellness in children. Those strategies include (a) fortifying and building social emotional competence, (b) fostering skills that promote coping and resilience, (c) facilitating proactive social system modification, and (d) promoting opportunities for empowerment. Pedro-Carroll (2001) suggested that resilience, one's achievement of positive developmental outcomes under significantly adverse conditions, is an important component within the context of wellness. She stated that wellness in children can be promoted by "protective factors that are linked to pathways toward resilience, providing supportive scaffolding for children experiencing difficult times" (p. 4). Wyman, Sandler, Wolchik, and Nelson (2000) offered a theoretical framework they termed *cumulative competence promotion* to describe how interventions can be strengthened by using an organizational–developmental model of resilience. Their model involves promoting wellness of children by (a) enhancing protection from the negative impact of adverse experiences and (b) facilitating the child's mastery of healthy developmental milestones. Research on the effectiveness of this model has not been documented.

The research that does exist on wellness and children is scarce. Omizo, Omizo, and D'Andrea (1992), in one of the earliest studies on wellness and children in the counseling field, investigated the effects of wellness promotion guidance activities on elementary school-age children. Participants were fifth graders from two classrooms, divided into an experimental and a control group. The experimental group participated in a 10-week guidance unit covering topics related to wellness (e.g., nutrition, daily exercise, and stress management), then completed measures of anxiety, self-esteem, culture-free self-esteem, and a Wellness Knowledge Test developed by the researchers. Children who participated in the guidance activities had significantly higher levels of self-esteem and knowledge of wellness than did children who did not participate in the guidance activities. The results of the study supported the use of classroom guidance activities in promoting wellness among elementary school-age children. In a noncounseling-related study, Jutras et al. (2003) studied perceptions of wellness among 55 families with diabetic children. On the basis of interviews, Jutras et al. found that perceptions of wellness differ among family members. Children perceived wellness in terms of their school performance and absence of health problems, whereas mothers perceived wellness in terms of their children's socialization patterns. This study showed how definitions and perceptions of wellness are broad and possibly vary according to developmental level and experiences.

Determining the family's influence on children's wellness is another grow-ing area of research. In a longitudinal study, Amato and Booth (1997) exam-ined the effect of changes within the family of origin over time on the psychological and social well-being of children upon entering young adult-hood. Using self-reported, nationally representative data from the Study of Marital Instability Over the Life Course (N = 2,033), the authors examined direct effect, moderated (e.g., gender, age), and mediated models of the as-sociation between changes within the family on adult and child well-being. Amato and Booth suggested that interactions within the family of origin shape a psychosocial milieu for well-being during childhood and later in adulthood, noting that children's wellness is partly a function of events oc-curring within the larger family context. They concluded that family envi-ronment has a direct effect on a child's well-being and later adult life.

In addition to a family's influence on children's wellness, the literature pertaining to children's wellness programs has increased over the past 10 years. For instance, Huettig and O'Connor (1999) described a physical fitness and holistic wellness program for preschool children that stressed the im-portance of play choices, food preferences, spiritual values and ethics, emo-tional health, social development, and intellectual aspects of development. Unfortunately, evaluation of these programs and research on their long-term effects is nonexistent.

RECOMMENDATIONS FOR FUTURE RESEARCH

It is clear that if a paradigm shift to prevention and wellness is to impact chil-dren and the helping professionals who work with them, there is a drastic need for research that explores and examines the construct of children's well-ness. Such research should be based on holistic models such as the Wheel of Wellness (Myers, Sweeney, & Witmer, 2000b) and the Indivisible Self (Myers & Sweeney, 2004b; Sweeney & Myers, 2005) and include consideration of the interaction of the components in these models. Although both models have been studied with adolescent (e.g., Garrett, 1999; Hartwig & Myers, 2003; Mitchell, 2001) and adult populations (e.g., Connolly, 2000; Dew, 2000), no empirical research exists pertaining to the efficacy of these models with children. Examples of needed research based on the tenets of the Wheel of Wellness are provided in this section.

Research Recommendations Based on the Wheel of Wellness

Spirituality. Research on children and spirituality is relatively new and has fo-cused on understanding children's spiritual development (Eaude, 2003), iden-tifying spirituality in young children (Champagne, 2003), and exploring children's dreams and spirituality (K. Adams, 2003). Recent research on the effects of parents' spirituality and religiosity on children's behavior and well-being includes Christian and Barbarin's (2001) findings that African American children of regular church attenders with high levels of religiosity had fewer behavioral problems than those who attended less frequently. Lin (2000) stud-ied 274 families of children with cerebral palsy to determine the relationship of spirituality to coping and adaptation. On the basis of the results, Lin concluded that families coped and adapted better when there was spiritual support. Although spirituality is burgeoning as a new variable in the child development literature, there have been no attempts to look at the significance of spirituality as a component of children's wellness. Studies that examine the effect of spirituality on the overall wellness of children and the salience of the spirituality component when compared with other components would clarify our understanding of spirituality in the lives of children.

Self-Direction. The 12 dimensions of self-direction (e.g., sense of worth, sense of control, realistic beliefs, etc.; see chapter 3) have all been researched independently as variables that affect children's success in school as well as their social and emotional development. In relation to children's overall wellness, the significance of self-direction is not known. Studies that explore the relationships and interactions between the 12 characteristics are greatly needed. Research questions might include, "What is the relationship between children's creativity and sense of worth?" and "How does children's development of cultural identity relate to their overall wellness?"

Work and Leisure. The life task of work and leisure is typically applied to adults or older adolescents. However, work, which for children is school work, and leisure are important aspects of a child's development. There is need for research that explores the salience of children's work and leisure habits to their overall wellness. Longitudinal studies that examine the effect of work behaviors and leisure activities in childhood on wellness in later life would provide invaluable information on the significance of this life task on overall adult wellness. Studies that focus on the relationship between the work and leisure habits of parents to their children's work and leisure habits would contribute much to our understanding of parents' influence on children's wellness. For instance, Freysinger (1994) surveyed 336 married American parents to examine leisure activities parents enjoyed with their children, their reasons for participation, and their level of parental satisfaction. The results indicated that fathers' leisure activities with children and parental satisfaction were positively related. The effect of leisure activities on the participants' children was not investigated in this study. Future research should investigate the relationships between parent–child leisure activities, parental role satisfaction, and children's wellness.

Friendship. Children's social relationships have been a hallmark of child development research for many decades. Similar to research on adults' friendship quality and sense of well-being, research on children has indicated that there is a positive connection between quality of friendships and children's sense of well-being. For instance, Vandell and Hembree (1994) found that children's friendships and peer relationships contributed significantly to their socioemotional adjustment, academic performance, and self-concept. Thus, positive friendships are predictive of better socioemotional and academic adjustment.

Although children's social relationships, particularly friendships, have been extensively researched, there is need for further exploration of the salience of friendship as a component of children's overall wellness. Studies that explore the wellness of children who are socially isolated or experience low-quality friendships are needed. Also, studies that explore the long-term effects of children's friendships on adolescent and adult wellness are warranted. The extent to which this life task accounts for a portion of the variance in wellness is unknown, and if known would provide a better understanding of the impact of friendships on children's overall wellness.

Love. Children's love relationships are typically with significant adults and siblings. Berger (1999) suggested that children need loving bonds with caring adults to develop trusting relationships, solid self-esteem, and a readiness to learn. Although the significance of parents' love and attention in the child's overall development has been well documented (e.g., Erikson, 1997), research that examines the parent–child relationship and the child's overall wellness is needed. Can a child's relationship with a parent predict the child's overall wellness in the present as well as in the future? Studies are needed that focus on children in loving families and their overall wellness. Finally, research that examines the salience of love relationships in children's overall wellness is warranted for us to better understand this life task in relation to the other wellness life tasks.

Additional Recommendations for Research on Children's Wellness

Implementing Diverse Research Methods (e.g., longitudinal studies, qualitative). It is critical that researchers interested in children's wellness conduct longitudinal studies that will assist in our understanding both of the long-term effects of wellness promotion and the intersection of wellness and development. If wellness is viewed not as a static state of being but rather as a state that changes over time as conditions, environments, and life events unfold, then wellness can erode under adverse conditions and can be enhanced by nurturing conditions. This view of wellness can be further understood by examining samples of children over long periods of time.

In addition to longitudinal studies, there is need for studies that utilize a qualitative approach to understanding children's wellness. For example, interviewing and observations of children and their families are needed as a foundation for developing multifaceted approaches to promoting wellness of children. Further, qualitative approaches can help define the meaning of wellness across early life developmental stages.

Developing a Holistic Model for Children's Wellness. The models described in Part I evolved from empirical research conducted primarily with adult populations. Clearly, there may exist a different model structure or structures for children's wellness. Research that examines the relevance of these models with children as well as research that promotes different models of children's wellness is warranted and greatly needed. Large-scale validation studies with samples of diverse children are needed as well as qualitative studies that may determine additional components of wellness for children. Future studies should include validation of the Five Factor Wellness Inventory for diverse groups of children (elementary and middle school versions; Myers & Sweeney, 2005a, 2005b) and perhaps the development of additional valid and reliable instruments to assess children's wellness.

Understanding the Salience of the Wellness Components as They Relate to Children. As noted earlier, the salience of various wellness components (e.g., love, friendship) for children is unknown. Research that explores the influence of the components on children's overall wellness would increase our understanding of what is most important in promoting children's wellness. Studies that incorporate regression analyses (e.g., stepwise regression analyses) and structured models are needed to enable us to predict factors affecting wellness

Understanding the Relationship Between Parental Wellness, Family Developments, and Childhood Wellness. Because parents have a direct influence on children, there is a need for research, both quantitative and qualitative, that examines the relationship between parents' and guardians' wellness and their children's wellness. Do parents who possess high levels of wellness have children with high levels of wellness? And, what processes do parents with higher levels of wellness carry out to promote the wellness of their children? Continuing to increase counselors' knowledge with respect to the connection between parents' wellness and their children's wellness will ultimately assist in intervention planning for both adults and children.

In addition to examining parents' wellness, it is imperative for future studies to examine family development in relation to children's wellness. Given the various types of families (e.g., single-parent families, foster families, blended families), research examining the wellness of children who live in varied settings and wellness promotion strategies that are effective within the context of various family structures is needed.

Understanding Children's Wellness Based on Age Differences. Childhood, the period between infancy and adolescence, is very broad and is the most rapid period of an individual's development. Research that focuses on the wellness of children at different points during childhood would be advantageous. For instance, studies focused on early childhood (from age 2 to 7) wellness and late childhood (from age 8 to 11) would assist in defining developmental components of wellness and in developing appropriate wellness promotion activities for children at specific points in time.

Understanding Children's Wellness Based on Diverse Populations. As counselors' caseloads become more diverse and as the number of immigrants in the United States increases, it becomes imperative that counselors understand the impact of culture on wellness. This is a critical topic because most immigrant populations consist of large percentages of school-age children. Research that examines the "fit" of the models discussed in Part I with diverse populations is needed. Qualitative studies (e.g., interviews of diverse children and their parents) that explore the different factors and components of wellness should be undertaken with diverse samples to further understand how different cultures perceive childhood wellness. Culturally competent researchers who are sensitive to subtle nuances of particular cultures and are sensitive to issues of oppression should be active in this area of research.

Understanding Counseling Interventions That Promote Children's Wellness. For counselors, a clear understanding of how to promote wellness among children is essential. Research that explores the effectiveness of various counseling strategies and techniques that have been proposed for increasing wellness should be implemented. Experimental and quasi-experimental studies on school counseling interventions (e.g., classroom guidance, small groups) should be implemented to determine their effect on wellness. Likewise, programs and special activities that have been developed to promote children's wellness should be evaluated continuously to assess effectiveness and to promote better wellness programs for children.

SUMMARY

Although research, theory, and practice related to wellness have increased over the past 20 years, little attention has been given to researching children's wellness. This is disappointing and surprising, given the importance of early childhood intervention in promoting healthy habits and behaviors in later development. Studies investigating the role of wellness in the development of children and in their later adult development are needed as well as the development of models of wellness specifically for children. Increased attention to child health outcomes and preventative services as identified for *Healthy Youth 2010* (see http://web.health.gov/healthypeople/2010Draft/scripts/text/index) will also assist researchers in identifying areas for further research. Surely, if counselors are to assist clients live better and longer, the promotion of wellness must begin with our youngest clients.

DISCUSSION QUESTIONS

1. Discuss possible research questions and designs related to children and models of wellness (e.g., Wheel of Wellness and Indivisible Self models).
2. Discuss possible research barriers that might occur when implementing research with children.
3. In your opinion, which research questions are most critical to the understanding of children's wellness? Discuss your answers.
4. Discuss differences between children's wellness research and either adolescent or adult wellness research.

WEB RESOURCES

- **The Children's Defense Fund (CDF), www.childrensdefense.org/,** seeks to Leave No Child Behind® by assuring that every child has a Healthy Start, a Head Start, a Fair Start, a Safe Start, and a Moral Start, as well as a supported transition to adulthood. The CDF advocates prevention and works on behalf of poor and minority children and children with disabilities.

- **The Action Alliance for Children (AAC), www.4children.org/,** is an in-depth resource for information about contemporary trends, issues, and policies that concern children and families. The AAC promotes dialogue between policymakers, human service providers, the media, parents, educators, and child-care workers.
- **The American Academy of Pediatrics, www.aap.org/,** is dedicated to achieving the best possible physical, social, and mental health and well-being for all infants, children, adolescents, and young adults. This Web site contains general information for child health, guidelines for specific issues, information for programs and activities, relevant policy statements, publications, and resources.
- **The Child Welfare League of America (CWLA), www.cwla.org/,** aims to get people involved to protect all children, youths, and families from harm and maintain their well-being. The CWLA seeks to have organizations, neighborhoods, families, communities, and government assist youths in becoming healthy and productive members of society.
- **The Child Advocate, www.childadvocate.net/,** aims to build a resource of support for children and their parents; address child mental health, educational, legal, and medical issues; and advocate local, state, and national legislative action for children.
- **The United Nations Children's Fund (UNICEF), www.unicef.org/,** seeks to advance humanity and promote health, education, equality, and protection of children. Programs include HIV/AIDS, child protection, girls' education, immunization, and early childhood.
- **Voices for America's Children, www.childadvocacy.org/,** seeks to be the voice of children in city halls and state houses to make multi-issue, child advocacy organizations that are state and locally based become more powerful and successful.

7

Research on Adolescent Wellness

Andrea Dixon Rayle and Holly J. Hartwig Moorhead

For decades, researchers have investigated various issues concerning individuals in adolescence, the time after childhood in which youths experience significant developmental challenges in preparation for adulthood (Kroger, 1996). Yet today, there remains a lack of consistency concerning when the adolescent period of life begins and ends (Kroger, 1996). The United States government describes younger adolescents as 10 to 17 and older adolescents as 18 to 24 (U.S. Census Bureau, 2000a). In this chapter, the focus is on adolescents between the ages of 10 and 18, a group for whom wellness is imperative if individuals are to live healthy and well across their life spans (Gryzwacz, 1999). Research findings indicate that habits and attitudes developed during adolescence continue in adulthood; thus, wellness is enhanced throughout the life span when healthy behaviors are modeled and taught earlier in life (Omizo, Omizo, & D'Andrea, 1992).

The U.S. government, the American Medical Association (AMA), and the Surgeon General actively support the need for wellness beginning as early as childhood and adolescence by promoting national initiatives such as *Healthy People 2010* and *Healthy Youth 2010*. The *Healthy Youth 2010* publication describes a national initiative to improve adolescent health before the year 2010 and includes 21 central adolescent health/wellness objectives (AMA, 2003). These objectives illustrate goals for reducing possible adolescent unwell and risky behaviors such as substance abuse, violence against others, suicidal ideation, pregnancies among female adolescents, sexually transmitted diseases and HIV, obesity, weapons use, and motor vehicle deaths and injuries. National statistics included in the *Healthy Youth 2010* publication illustrate target percentages for reducing adolescent risky behaviors. For instance, in 1999, 40% of adolescents used tobacco. The goal by 2010 is to reduce this proportion of adolescents who use tobacco to 21%. Similarly, in 1999, weapon use among adolescents was reportedly 6.9%. The target goal for 2010 is to reduce the number to at least 5% (AMA, 2003). These national objectives lend voice to the value of wellness in adolescence, the need to understand current research in the area of adolescent well and unwell behaviors, and the importance of defining future wellness research for this population.

The focus of this chapter is on research involving adolescent wellness. Following an overview of current research, the major findings to date on wellness in adolescence are summarized. We examine studies involving age differences throughout adolescence and other within-group differences and describe the major correlates of wellness in adolescence. Finally, recommendations for future research on wellness in adolescence are provided.

OVERVIEW OF WELLNESS RESEARCH WITH ADOLESCENTS

Historically, studies of wellness in adolescence have focused on the importance of physical health. Multiple studies have examined risk behaviors such as smoking, drug and alcohol use, and early sexual activity, or factors such as exercise, diet, and personal self-care (Jessor, Van Den Bos, Vanderryn, Costa, & Turbin, 1995; Steiner, Pavelski, Pitts, & McQuivey, 1998). For example, Steiner et al. (1998) surveyed 1,769 high school adolescents using the Juvenile Wellness and Health Survey (JWHS-76), which they developed. Following data analyses, five factors were revealed: general risk taking, mental health problems, sex-related risks, eating and dietary problems, and general health problems. Adolescent females experienced more significant difficulties in mental health, sexual risks, general health, and dietary behaviors and lower overall wellness than adolescent males. In addition, in a study with 300 seventh through ninth graders, Jessor et al. (1995) found that positive modeling of healthy behaviors and self-direction, as defined in the Wheel of Wellness to include factors such as nutrition and self-care, may result in fewer self-destructive and problem behaviors and enhanced overall wellness for adolescents.

Over the past 30 years, additional theories of holistic wellness have emerged that expand wellness beyond physical health. Thus, in addition to examining factors related to physical well-being, researchers of adolescent well-being have begun to focus on aspects of what is described as *psychological wellness* or *psychosocial wellness.* Aspects thought to make up or affect psychological and psychosocial wellness in adolescence have been researched broadly and include self-concept, self-worth, self-esteem, academic achievement, spirituality, sense of belonging, mattering, social support from friends and family, and psychological adjustment (Ansuini & Fiddler-Woite, 1996; Marshall, 2001; Rosenberg, 1985; Sussman, Dent, Stacy, Burton, & Flay, 1995; Taylor & Turner, 2001; Walker, 2000).

In a book titled *The Promotion of Wellness in Children and Adolescents* (Cicchetti, Rappaport, Sandler, & Weissberg, 2000), various authors reviewed Emory L. Cowen's research contributions on fostering wellness in children and adolescents, defined as psychological wellness. Cowen's (1994) stance on enhancing psychological wellness for adolescents focused on how influential social environments support the development of wellness. Cicchetti et al. (2000) augmented Cowen's research with additional theoretical ideas by proposing theory, research, and prevention principles that highlight the vast possibilities in fostering positive development and wellness in young people. They identified preventative interventions that have altered psychological wellness in adolescents such as supportive community groups and emphasized the importance of enhancing wellness in a sociocultural context.

Rosenberg and McCullough (1981) and Rosenberg (1985) were among the first to assess adolescent self-concept and self-esteem in relation to psychological well-being in three studies with over 6,000 high school students. Rosenberg (1985) found that self-concept and psychological well-being are more variable and less stable in early adolescence (ages 12–13) and that higher self-esteem leads to greater psychological wellness. He also noted gender differences in wellness, with girls reporting lower self-esteem, self-concept, and total wellness.

Rudolph (2002) studied 460 fifth through eighth graders and found that psychological wellness is affected by stress during adolescence. The results of multiple regression analyses revealed a negative relationship among wellness and both depression and anxiety; moreover, these variables were mediated by stress for both female and male adolescents. In four large-scale studies, involving several thousand high school adolescents in the 1960s and 1970s, Rosenberg and McCullough (1981) noted that adolescents who perceived that they mattered to their parents were less depressed and anxious, and less likely to be involved in risky and unwell behaviors such as smoking, truancy, theft, or vandalism.

Sussman et al. (1995) reported a relationship between behavioral difficulties and deficient psychological and psychosocial wellness among 3,674 seventh- and eighth-grade adolescents. Psychosocial variables related to personality, perceived environment, and behavior systems were studied using a compilation of standardized measures. The results of factor analyses indicated that social support both positively and negatively affected specific aspects of adolescent psychological wellness, such as mental health, and psychosocial wellness including risk taking and general health. Sussman et al. found that although wellness levels among middle school students were negatively affected by participation in poor health practices, social influences and support both positively and negatively affected wellness levels (i.e., unhealthy behaviors encouraged by an adolescent's peer group affect the adolescent's unhealthy actions).

In addition, Walker (2000) investigated spiritual support in relation to community violence exposure, aggressive outcomes, and psychological adjustment among 131 inner-city adolescents using the Spiritual Support Scale. Findings from multivariate analyses indicated that positive spirituality was inversely related to self-esteem and aggressive beliefs. Despite these studies of physical, psychological, and psychosocial wellness, little research has been conducted with adolescents incorporating a holistic approach to wellness.

OVERVIEW OF WHEEL OF WELLNESS RESEARCH AND INDIVISIBLE SELF MODEL WITH ADOLESCENTS

Within holistic wellness models, enhancement of present strengths is emphasized as a way of increasing wellness in specific and overall areas of functioning. Results from several studies indicate that adolescent wellness affects wellness in later adult years, including values, attitudes, beliefs, activities, and experiences (Ansuini & Fiddler-Woite, 1996; Steiner et al., 1998; Werner, 1989). Researchers examining adolescent wellness have begun to view wellness as more than a simple continuum with wellness anchored at one end and sickness anchored at the other end; wellness is neither static nor categorical. Today, concentric holistic models of wellness, specifically the Wheel of Wellness (Myers, Sweeney, & Witmer, 2000b) and the Indivisible Self (Myers & Sweeney, 2004b), guide counseling research conducted with adolescents. Reviewing various studies of adolescent wellness conducted utilizing the Wheel of Wellness model, we found a growing body of empirical research that focuses on this holistic approach to understanding adolescent wellness.

Researchers have used the Wheel of Wellness to assess a variety of psychosocial experiences and factors related to adolescent wellness. These studies incorporated various forms of the Wellness Evaluation of Lifestyle, Teen (Myers & Sweeney, 2001b) and the Five Factor Wellness Inventory, Teen (5F-Wel-T; Myers & Sweeney, 1999b, 2002, 2005b) and have included middle school and high school male and female adolescents of varying racial/ethnic backgrounds. In one study, Makinson (2001) investigated a model for gender, moral identity, and social interest to predict wellness among 187 middle school adolescents using structural equation modeling (SEM). She found that social interest, but not moral identity, explained a portion of the variance in adolescent wellness, but found no gender differences in wellness between males and females.

Garrett (1996) examined cultural value orientation, acculturation, and wellness among 155 Native and non-Native American high school students. Results indicated significant differences between the two groups on wellness, with Native Americans scoring higher on realistic beliefs and cultural identity. Multivariate analyses of variance (MANOVAs) indicated differences between the two groups on acculturation, with higher levels of acculturation to the mainstream culture (i.e., bicultural or assimilated) associated with higher overall wellness for Native Americans.

The relationship between acculturation and wellness was supported in a study by Dixon Rayle (2002), who used SEM to test a model of prediction for wellness in 462 minority and nonminority high school students. She hypothesized that ethnic identity, acculturation, and mattering together would predict wellness but that the model would differ for the two groups. The model tested revealed no significant differences in wellness among minority and nonminority students; however, mattering to others and acculturation explained a portion of the variance in wellness for all adolescents, and ethnic identity level predicted a portion of the variance in wellness for minority students. For the minority students, ethnic identity was the greatest predictor of wellness in five of six areas (spirituality, leisure, love, friendship, and schoolwork).

Chang (1998) found a significant positive relationship between ethnic identity, acculturation, and wellness for a sample of 208 Korean American adolescents. MANOVAs revealed that Korean American adolescents' need to differentiate from the mainstream culture had a negative impact on their wellness. Relatedly, in a study of 201 English-speaking Caribbean American adolescents, Mitchell (2001) found a positive relationship between wellness, academic self-concept, and acculturation. Multiple regression analyses revealed that adolescents' wellness and acculturation experiences accounted for a significant amount of the variance ($R^2 = .083$, $F = 5.90$, $p = .001$) in their overall self-concepts.

Finally, Tatar and Myers (2004) conducted a cross-cultural study of 240 middle school adolescents in the United Stated and in Israel using a Hebrew translation of the 5F-Wel-T. The t test results for comparisons of means between adolescents revealed that those in Israel scored significantly higher on the Coping Self and Social Self factors and those in the United States scored higher on the Essential Self factor. There were no differences on the Creative Self or Total Wellness factors between the Israeli and U.S. adolescents, no gender differences in wellness among the Israeli participants, and only age differences in wellness among the U.S. participants.

CRITIQUES OF CURRENT RESEARCH

Existing research findings have established significant relationships among physical, psychological, and psychosocial wellness and various correlates and moderating factors in adolescent populations. Adolescent wellness has been positively correlated with academic self-concept (Mitchell, 2001), self-esteem (Marshall, 2001), acculturation (Chang, 1998; Dixon Rayle, 2002; Garrett, 1996; Mitchell, 2001), adult wellness (Ansuini & Fiddler-Woite, 1996; Steiner et al., 1998; Werner, 1989), mattering (Dixon Rayle, 2002; Rosenberg & McCullough, 1981), social interest (Makinson, 2001), and social support and modeling (Jessor et al., 1995; Sussman et al., 1995). Empirically supported moderating factors include age (Tatar & Myers, 2004), ethnic identity (Dixon Rayle, 2002; Tatar & Myers, 2004), gender (Garrett, 1996; Rosenberg, 1985; Steiner et al., 1998; Tatar & Myers, 2004), spirituality (Walker, 2000), and stress (Rudolph, 2002). Although these findings are a start to fully understanding wellness among adolescents, current research is limited in scope.

Present studies have not examined either singly or in combination the myriad of possible factors associated with adolescent wellness. For example, numerous wellness constructs have been left unexplored (e.g., safety, life span processes, global events, self-direction), samples exclude segments of the adolescent population, variance within samples largely has been left unexplained, and limited methodologies have been used. Additionally, the Indivisible Self model has not been tested with adolescent populations. Consequently, broad areas of inquiry remain concerning relationships among wellness factors and the appropriateness of existing models for explaining adolescent well-being.

Primarily convenience samples have been recruited to date, excluding marginalized adolescent subpopulations such as at-risk youths and offenders. As a consequence, a complete understanding of wellness within the adolescent population as a whole is not possible at this time. Further, much of the available adolescent research includes data about college students rather than middle and high school age adolescents, failing to describe wellness in the younger spectrum of adolescence accurately. The potential effects of within-group differences, such as age and other demographic factors, on the variance in wellness has gone uninvestigated in existing studies (e.g., current studies do not address how socioeconomic factors or specific ages correspond to differences in wellness within samples).

Finally, wellness research to date is primarily quantitative. Without qualitative data, offering adolescents' personal meaning and interpretation of wellness to accompany quantitative data, the portrait of adolescent wellness is incomplete. Again, within-group variation is an issue in that the wellness of subgroups of the adolescent population remains unknown. Thus, although current research provides an initial framework for understanding adolescent wellness, gaps exist in the areas of wellness that have been studied, which groups have been studied, how wellness has been studied within groups, and the manner in which data have been examined.

FUTURE RESEARCH DIRECTIONS

Simply stated, there is a critical need for research to inform our understanding of adolescent wellness. We need to define and assess adolescents' wellness and provide evidence-based counseling interventions and treatment plans. From reviews of past research, future studies of adolescent wellness should incorporate variations within the foci of studies, larger and more diverse samples, analyses, and methodological strategies.

The foci of future studies should broaden existing knowledge of correlates and predictors of wellness by incorporating a range of psychosocial constructs and adolescent experiences. All components of the Wheel of Wellness and Indivisible Self models, including contextual issues, need to be studied with various adolescent populations. Examples of constructs that need to be studied in relation to adolescent wellness should include relationships, or lack thereof, with parents, siblings, extended family members, friends, teachers, coaches, religious/spiritual figures, and other adult and peer role models. In addition, adolescents' experiences with spiritual or religious teachings and practices, physical wellness behaviors, academic achievement, goal-setting after high school, and leisure activities such as sports, clubs, music, art, and acting should be considered as possible correlates or predictors of wellness. Factors such as psychological and emotional resilience and hardiness should be studied in relation to wellness.

Additionally, the applicability of existing models of wellness should be explored with adolescents. Although researchers have attempted to document the relationship of one aspect of wellness to certain behaviors, outcomes, or characteristics of individuals, few have conducted wellness research based in holistic wellness models. Thus, the need remains for research to examine the interaction of wellness components to illustrate how domains of wellness affect one another. For example, Hartwig and Myers (2003) recommended the use of holistic wellness models for prevention of delinquency, and Makinson and Myers (2003) suggested that holistic wellness models could provide a paradigm shift in conceptualizing violence prevention from a strengths-based perspective. Outcome research to examine the viability of these recommendations is needed.

In future studies, the scope of samples and the location of research should be broadened. For instance, existing studies lack samples with younger adolescents (ages 10–13); diverse race/ethnicity, including immigrant, international, and biracial samples; adolescents from extreme socioeconomic backgrounds (e.g., poverty, privilege); adolescents living in alternative family structures such as those who have been adopted; adolescents who are homeless or runaways; terminally ill adolescents; and gay, lesbian, and bisexual adolescents. In addition, future samples of adolescents might include those living in urban versus rural settings; adolescents of varying religious or spiritual backgrounds; adolescent offenders or gang members; adolescents who have experienced physical or sexual abuse; adolescents who are pregnant, have young babies, or are single parents or head of the household; adolescents who have dropped out of high school; and adolescents recovering from substance abuse. These possible samples are integral for future research to gain a broader understanding of wellness among this age group. Not to be overlooked, however, are those young people who might represent the best models of wellness among their peers. The secrets of those who achieve high levels of wellness might best be discovered through multifaceted research designs.

In conjunction with various foci and samples, future studies should incorporate a variety of methodological approaches and analyses to explore fully wellness within and between groups of adolescents. For instance, there is a dearth of qualitative wellness research with adolescents. Well-designed qualitative studies are needed to help define the meaning of wellness for this population. For instance, do adolescents know the meaning of wellness? How can we discover what wellness means to them within their individual contexts? Interviews and focus-group designs with structured or unstructured interviews, ethnographies, narratives, and case studies would allow for adolescents to openly share their personal definitions, ideas, concerns, and struggles with wellness. This qualitative information would better inform theories of wellness and quantitative research as well as counseling practice. Additionally, using observational approaches along with traditional quantitative (i.e., written and scored assessments) and qualitative (i.e., interviews and focus groups) methods has the potential of contributing greater depth to current wellness research. Creating and implementing standardized methods of observational data collection may provide contextual information about degrees and types of adolescent wellness behaviors that have gone unstudied to date.

Outcome research is needed in varying locations with samples of adolescents. These studies could be conducted in schools, inpatient residential and outpatient agencies, or hospitals exploring the efficacy of wellness-based initiatives based on qualitative and quantitative research. Outcome data can provide important information about the effectiveness of wellness-based interventions. Such interventions may include wellness-based curricula for use with adolescents in schools and empirically supported, wellness-based intervention plans for adolescents and their families seeking assistance through community agencies, hospital settings, and private practice. Studies that examine wellness-based interventions and that provide valuable outcome data have the potential of being beneficial to both clinicians and clients.

Varying methods of data analysis are needed in the future, including regression, factor analyses, correlations, and meta analyses. In addition, few studies of adolescent wellness have included structural equation modeling (SEM), limiting the explanations of relationships among wellness predictors and correlates. In future research, SEM may prove a helpful tool in discovering new aspects of relationships among wellness factors. Also, as previously noted, adolescent wellness research conducted in the future must include samples with greater racial and ethnic diversity; consequently, corresponding analyses should assess potential test bias, especially related to gauging wellness among multicultural populations. Furthermore, beyond examining the variance in wellness among adolescent populations, future data analyses should specifically examine within-group and between-groups differences in relation to racial/ethnic differences, gender, cultural norms, socialization, education, and other relevant characteristics that may prove to be moderators of wellness.

SUMMARY

The purpose of this chapter was to provide an overview of wellness research in professional counseling with adolescents. Adolescence is considered an integral time in individuals' overall growth and development and a time when wellness habits can be learned and enhanced. Existing research is limited in informing researchers and counselors as to what the important correlates and predictors of wellness are with this population, failing to adequately explain areas in which adolescents exhibit low or high levels of wellness, factors that affect adolescent wellness, and how various domains of wellness affect one another among adolescents. Therefore, within the next 20 years, new and varying research studies are needed to discover the changing wellness needs and habits of adolescents. The call for wellness-based counseling services is a reality, and only through a well-established research agenda can mental health providers be prepared to serve their adolescent clients with evidence-based practice.

DISCUSSION QUESTIONS

1. Imagine you are an adolescent of 10–18 years of age; 13–16 years; 17–18 years. Male. Female. From an economically disadvantaged home. From

a middle-class home. From a privileged home. How might you direct future researchers in studying wellness among yourself and your peers?

2. In light of current social, political, national, and international events, what behavioral trends among adolescents could be better helped or explained with additional information about adolescent wellness? What psychological trends within the adolescent population could be better explained with additional information about adolescent wellness?

3. Currently, what are some of the most prominent clinical and research issues within the counseling profession? How do these relate to adolescents? How could more information about aspects of adolescent wellness contribute to prevention, diagnosis, and treatment of these issues?

WEB RESOURCES

- **The Center for Research on Adolescent Health and Development, http://www.crahd.phi.org/,** conducts research, evaluation, and policy studies related to adolescent health and youth development.
- **The National Institutes of Health, U.S. Department of Health and Human Services, http://www.nih.gov/,** conducts research for the purposes of prevention, diagnosis, and treatment of disease.
- **The American Medical Association maintains a page on adolescent health, http://www.ama-assn.org/ama/pub/category/1947.html,** that provides both information and links to resources for consumers and professional service providers.

8

Research on
College Student Wellness

Cynthia J. Osborn

Wellness research with undergraduate college students in the United States now spans 20 to 25 years, and in that time, several models of wellness have been proposed specifically for this population. Although they share a general understanding or definition of wellness (Palombi, 1992), the models vary in terms of their theoretical formulation, dimensions, and how such dimensions or components are emphasized or prioritized. In addition, wellness measures or assessment instruments consistent with these models have been generated, and existing measures have undergone revision and refinement.

In this chapter, wellness research conducted with undergraduate college students is reviewed, and the various models—namely those based in counseling theory—and respective instruments used are briefly described. Overall findings relating to undergraduate sociodemographic characteristics are presented, wellness profiles of undergraduate students are offered, and specific recommendations for further wellness research with this population are discussed.

RATIONALE FOR WELLNESS RESEARCH WITH UNDERGRADUATE COLLEGE STUDENTS

Although college students are regarded as a difficult population to study with respect to alcohol and other substance use (Johnston, O'Malley, & Bachman, 2003), they remain a frequently researched population, particularly in PhD dissertation research (Nelson & Coorough, 1994). Because of their accessibility (e.g., through researcher entry into classrooms and residence halls) and use of health and recreational services on campus, undergraduate college students represent an appropriate population in which to study and promote wellness (Brener & Gowda, 2001; Grace, 1997). Faced with myriad challenges consistent with their chronological and developmental stage (primarily young adulthood), and expected of people who are in various phases of career preparation, college students experience a variety of stressors. Dill and Henley (1998) noted that among nontraditional students (24–54 years old), stressors included balancing school with other obligations, and traditional students (23 years old and younger) reported stressors related to academic performance and peer/social interactions. Wellness efforts with and for this population are therefore indicated.

Approximately 16.5 million undergraduates were enrolled in U.S. postsecondary institutions during the 1999–2000 school year, and the majority were enrolled in either public 2-year institutions (42%) or public 4-year colleges and universities (31%; U.S. Department of Education, 2002). The majority of these students were of traditional age (i.e., 23 years old and younger; 57%), and race/ethnicity was predominantly White (67%), followed by Black (12%), Hispanic (11%), and Asian (5%). Women were a majority of the undergraduate students during this time period (56%), and both full-time and part-time students reported working a considerable number of hours per week (average of 25.5 and 39.5 hours/week, respectively). All in all, the profile of undergraduates suggests that "the postsecondary education system in the United States offers opportunities to a diverse group of individuals" (U.S. Department of Education, 2002, p. 35). Such diversity represents an advantage for wellness research.

NONCOUNSELING WELLNESS MODELS AND RELATED CONSTRUCTS

A number of variables have been studied as correlates of wellness among college students and as precursors to or outcomes of wellness behaviors. For example, studies have examined exercise, nutrition, self-care, eating disorders, and so forth. A few studies have been conducted based on holistic wellness models, such as Hettler's (1984) hexagonal model of wellness, which was developed from a physical health sciences perspective.

Archer, Probert, and Gage (1987) surveyed 3,190 undergraduates from 11 different colleges and universities throughout the United States, using Hettler's (1984) hexagon model to determine (a) the extent to which they believed each dimension affected their health and wellness, (b) which dimensions they believed they needed more information on and assistance with, and (c) their current level of health and wellness in each area. Participants (57% female; 70% 17–20 years old; 85% Caucasian) identified activities that were both beneficial and detrimental to their wellness and indicated factors that were most influential in their decisions to participate in wellness-related behavior. Students believed the physical dimension (nutrition, exercise, sleep) affected their wellness more than any other and that they most needed information and assistance on the occupational dimension. They rated themselves highest in social wellness and lowest in spiritual. Activities perceived as most beneficial to wellness included having a close relationship and exercise; and worrying, poor sleep habits, and procrastination were activities perceived as detrimental to wellness. The top two factors seen as affecting their decision to engage in wellness activities were enjoyment and time. Although it is unclear whether participants were provided an explanation of each wellness dimension (other than its one-word title), Archer et al. (1987) were encouraged that undergraduate students in their study perceived "that the nonphysical dimensions are also as important as the physical dimensions in terms of health and wellness effects . . . [indicating] that students are becoming more aware of the complex interaction between health, behavior, and emotions" (p. 317).

T. B. Adams, Bezner, Drabbs, Zambarano, and Steinhardt (2000) proposed a wellness model also comprising six dimensions (physical, social, emotional, intellectual, spiritual, and psychological) but substituted psychological in place of Hettler's (1984) occupational dimension. Their model is founded on three principles: (a) multidimensionality, (b) balance among dimensions, and (c) salutogenesis (i.e., causing health rather than illness). It is depicted graphically as an upright cone, with the top (more expansive part) of the cone representing wellness, and the bottom (tightly constricted part) of the cone representing illness. The corresponding 36-item Perceived Wellness Survey (PWS) operationally defines wellness as "the sense that one is living in a manner that permits the experience of consistent, balanced growth in the emotional, intellectual, physical, psychological, social, and spiritual dimensions of human existence" (T. B. Adams, Bezner, & Steinhardt, 1997, p. 169).

To test the relationship between spiritual and psychological wellness and the overall model, T. B. Adams et al. (2000) administered the PWS to 112 undergraduate students (81% women; 81% White; average age = 23 years) enrolled in a health education class at a southern state university, along with measures of life purpose (i.e., zest for life, fulfillment, contentment, and satisfaction), dispositional optimism, and sense of coherence (or resilience; Antonovsky, 1987). Higher perceived wellness was significantly related to higher scores on the other measures; optimism and sense of coherence significantly predicted perceived wellness. The results of path analysis suggested that the effect of life purpose on perceived wellness was mediated by optimism and sense of coherence. No implications for college student wellness, however, were provided.

MODELS OF WELLNESS BASED IN COUNSELING

Three models of wellness based in counseling theory (specifically Individual Psychology or Adlerian theory) are presented and described elsewhere in this book: the Wheel of Wellness, the Indivisible Self, and the Four Factor Wellness model (4F-Wel; Myers, Luecht, & Sweeney, 2004). The first two of these models have been used in recent wellness research with undergraduate students, and this section outlines the primary findings from seven of those studies.

Wheel of Wellness Studies Using the Wellness Evaluation of Lifestyle

Hermon and Hazler (1999) surveyed 155 undergraduate students at one midwestern state university to identify relationships between their experience of wellness and their psychological well-being. Wellness was measured using the 114-item Wellness Evaluation of Lifestyle (WEL-O [original version]; Witmer, Sweeney, & Myers, 1993), and a separate measure assessed both state (or affective) and trait aspects of psychological well-being. Students were recruited from communications and organizational behavior courses, and, using multiple regression, results indicated that the two wellness components of (a) work, recreation, and leisure ($\beta = .27$) and (b) self-regulation ($\beta = .28$) were significant contributors to undergraduate students' affective experience of psychological well-being ($R^2 = .35$). Both wellness components ($\beta = .17$ and .27, respectively), along with the wellness component of friendship ($\beta = .26$) contributed to undergraduate students' general life experience ($R^2 = .40$). Hermon and Hazler (1999) concluded that, "The variables of self-regulation and work, recreation, and leisure of the wellness model seem to be the best predictors of a [*sic*] college students' psychological well-being (state and trait)" (p. 341). Although participant characteristics of gender (61% women), age (49% 18–23 years old; 51% 24–51 years old), race/ethnicity (73% Caucasian, 13% African American, 12% Asian/Pacific Islander), and marital status (71% single) were reported, data analyses and interpretation did not take these into consideration.

Enochs (2001) administered the 120-item WEL-S (Myers, Sweeney, & Witmer, 2000a) and a separate measure of adjustment to 511 freshmen (mean age = 18.63 years; 58% female; 80.25% Caucasian, 12.92% African American, and 2.5% Hispanic) enrolled in a southern, state-supported university. Half of the students lived in freshman year experience (FYE) residence halls (i.e., use of tutors- and counselors-in-residence, faculty involvement with students, and community-building activities), and the other half lived in regular halls. Administration occurred at the beginning of spring semester in the residence halls. Using t tests and MANOVAs, Enochs found that students in the FYE halls had significantly higher Total Wellness scores (mean T score = 52.16) and adjustment scale scores than freshmen in regular residence halls (WEL mean T score = 47.79). No significant gender difference in Total Wellness scores was detected. The findings suggest that a programmatic emphasis on campus orientation and resource utilization, academic persistence, and community development for first-year college students in their residence halls may enhance overall wellness. Without baseline measures, however, and not knowing how students are assigned to type of residence hall (i.e., are incoming students able to select the FYE hall?), it is possible that differences in wellness and adjustment may have existed prior to college entry.

In another study of first-year students (Myers & Bechtel, 2004), the revised 103-item WEL (Myers et al., 2000a) was administered outside of introductory psychology class hours to 179 first-year cadets at West Point during two separate, sequential fall semesters. Two other measures assessed perceived stress and mattering (i.e., degree to which individuals perceive themselves to be important to others). The sample was somewhat diverse in terms of race/ethnicity (37% Caucasian, 29% African American, 13% Hispanic, and 8% Asian), but was primarily composed of men (84%) and traditional-age undergraduates (mean age = 19.4 years). Of the six life tasks in the WEL, cadets scored highest on Friendship (mean = 86.84) and lowest on Work (mean = 69.80) and demonstrated significantly higher mean scores on two of the six WEL scales (Friendship and Self-Direction) than an undergraduate norm comparison (Work mean scores were significantly lower). The Total Wellness mean score for cadets was 76.82, comparable with the norm of 76.40. Using MANOVA, significant positive correlations were identified between mattering and Total Wellness, and significant negative correlations were found between perceived stress and wellness in the areas of work, realistic beliefs, and stress management, leading Myers and Bechtel (2004) to conclude that "cadets feel connected with others and experience a greater buffer against stress as a consequence" (p. 480).

The importance of connection with others contributed to a study examining relationships among liking, loving, and holistic wellness (Shurts & Myers, 2005). In this study, 242 undergraduates (75% female; mean age = 25 years; 43% Caucasian, 22% African American, and 28% "other"; 60% single, 33.5% married) at two separate institutions (one small midwestern university and one midsized southeastern university) who were enrolled in "courses in human development and career and life planning" completed a 105-item version of the WEL (Myers et al., 2000a). Two separate instruments were also administered to measure liking (i.e., focus on one's closest friend) and love attitudes.

Shurts and Myers (2005) found that mean scores on the six WEL scales ranged from 74.1 (Work) to 90.8 (Love), with a mean score of 77.4 on Total Wellness, reflecting reasonably high self-assessments of wellness. It is interesting that male undergraduates indicated significantly higher Total Wellness scores than female undergraduates. Positive and statistically significant relationships were identified between liking and each of the six WEL scales, as well as Total Wellness. The strongest correlations between love attitudes and WEL scales were those of Eros love (i.e., romantic love) and the WEL scales of Leisure (.23) and Friendship (.28); Pragma love (i.e., practical/pragmatic love) and Spirituality (.26); and Mania love (i.e., obsessive love) and Self-Direction (–.32). Using MANOVA to identify relationships among subscales on each of the three measures used, Shurts and Myers (2005) concluded that, "Taken together, these findings suggest college students have positive feelings about their close friendships and ability to have success in a nonromantic, intimate relationship," adding that "some love styles are healthier than others."

Indivisible Self Studies Using the Five Factor Wellness Inventory

Spurgeon and Myers (2004) sampled 203 African American male juniors and seniors (mean age = 21.5 years; 91% single; 90% employed at least part time) at a predominantly White institution (PWI; $n = 100$) and a historically Black college or university (HBCU; $n = 103$), both in the Southeast, on their racial identity attitudes, self-esteem, and wellness. Using the 73-item 5F-Wel (Myers & Sweeney, 2004a), Total Wellness mean scores were comparable for participants from HBCUs (73.48) and participants from PWIs (72.77). Examination of other factor scores, however, revealed that participants from PWIs scored signifi- cantly higher on the Social Self wellness factor than participants from HBCUs, which Spurgeon and Myers (2004) noted is inconsistent with prior literature. Overall findings from multiple regression analyses suggested that neither racial identity nor self-esteem significantly predicted the variance in wellness.

Sinclair and Myers (2004) examined the relationship between objectified body consciousness (i.e., viewing self as an object) and wellness in 190 White, heterosexual undergraduate women (67% between ages 19 and 21 years) at a southeastern university. As with Spurgeon and Myers's (2004) study, well- ness was measured by the 73-item 5F-Wel (Myers & Sweeney, 2004a), using the first-order factor of Total Wellness and the five second-order factors in data analyses. A 24-item scale was also administered, designed to measure three aspects or dimensions of objectified body consciousness: surveillance (viewing the body as an outside observer), shame (feeling shame when the body does not conform to accepted societal standards), and appearance con- trol beliefs (amount of perceived control a woman believes she has over her appearance). Participants were recruited from four different classes (coun- seling, human development and family studies, communications, and hu- manities), and class time was used to complete the inventories.

Although wellness scores were not computed for the entire sample, Sinclair and Myers (2004) reported that participants scored highest on the Social Self and lowest on the Physical Self of the 5F-Wel, with Total Wellness approxi- mating a mean score of 80.83. Using MANOVA to determine relationships among the three dimensions of objectified body consciousness and the six factors of the 5F-Wel, Sinclair and Myers (2004) noted that lower surveillance and body shame scores were associated with higher Total Wellness scores. Specifically, the Coping Self (includes stress management and sense of worth) was negatively correlated with both body shame and surveillance, and the Creative Self (includes problem-solving abilities) was negatively correlated with body shame. In addition, the Physical Self was significantly associated with surveillance and appearance control beliefs, indicating that

> a woman who spends time eating a nutritionally balanced diet, main- taining a normal weight, and engaging in sufficient physical activity through exercise . . . is less likely to view her body as an outside observer . . . [that is, she is] more likely concerned with how her body feels than looks. (S. L. Sinclair, personal communication, October 20, 2003)

One unexpected finding was the positive correlation between appearance control beliefs and wellness (on all wellness factors, with the exception of the Essential Self), leading Sinclair and Myers (2004) to speculate "that control- ling one's appearance . . . provides women a sense of competence" (p. 159).

Myers and Mobley (2004) investigated undergraduate performance on the 73-item 5F-Wel (Myers & Sweeney, 2004a), using an existing and unexamined database developed over a 5-year period that included 1,567 undergraduate college students (57% female; 61% Caucasian, 15.5% African American, and

19% other ethnic backgrounds; 86% single, 8.4% married). Of this sample, 83% were traditional college age (i.e., 24 years or younger) and almost 14% were nontraditional, age 25 and over. Comparisons were made between these two student groups, as well as between undergraduate students and nonundergraduate adult participants (*N* = 702) included in the larger database.

Results of Myers and Mobley's (2004) study indicated no difference between the two student groups on Total Wellness (mean score of 76.40), with the Social Self obtaining the highest factor mean score for both groups (87.78) and the Coping Self representing the lowest factor mean score for both groups (69.89). Nontraditional students, however, scored higher on Spirituality (one of four components on the Essential Self factor) and Realistic Beliefs (one of four components on the Coping Self factor) than traditional students, who scored higher on Exercise (one of two components on the Physical Self factor) and Leisure (one of four components on the Coping Self factor). This latter finding is consistent with Dill and Henley's (1998) observation that traditional students reported more vacations, trips, and summer breaks than did nontraditional students. Myers and Mobley's comparisons of undergraduate participants and nonstudent adults indicated that undergraduates scored higher on Exercise and Leisure and scored lower on Self-Care (items that refer to safety behaviors, preventive health behaviors, and avoidance of negative health practices) and Social Self (Friendship and Love) than the nonstudent adults. The authors interpreted these discrepancies to mean that "undergraduate students are challenged relative to the establishment of friendships . . . [and, as a whole] are at risk for lower wellness than nonstudent adults (NSAs), most notably in the area of Realistic Beliefs" (Myers & Mobley, 2004, p. 46).

WELLNESS PROFILES OF UNDERGRADUATE STUDENTS

Results from wellness research with undergraduate students suggest that both physical (e.g., sleep, exercise, leisure activities) and social (e.g., friendships, peer networks) expressions of wellness are descriptive of this particular population. For example, Hermon and Hazler (1999) reported that the wellness component of work, recreation, and leisure contributed significantly to undergraduate students' psychological well-being. Social wellness is also of importance to this population, given its highest rating among theoretical wellness studies (Myers & Mobley, 2004; Sinclair & Myers, 2004; Spurgeon & Myers, 2004). Although traditional undergraduate students (i.e., those 23 years old and younger) regarded their peer and social networks as more important than nontraditional undergraduate students (Dill & Henley, 1998), college students as a whole reported positive feelings about their close friendships and their ability to have success in a nonromantic, intimate relationship (Shurts & Myers, 2005). Nonstudent adults, however, may make better use of and engage in more appropriate or positive friendship and love relationships than undergraduate students (Myers & Mobley, 2004).

Wellness components obtaining lower rankings in undergraduate student samples include spirituality and coping (i.e., realistic beliefs, stress management), although Myers and Mobley (2004) noted that nontraditional students ranked spirituality higher than traditional students. The positive correlation between spirituality and Pragma love reported by Shurts and Myers (2005) suggests that students may be more receptive to a spiritual focus or endeavor when its practical utility for them is clear. Myers and Mobley (2004) observed that undergraduate students struggle with realistic beliefs (a finding consistent with the low Coping scores that Sinclair and Myers [2004] reported among female undergraduates), as well as appropriate self-care. Future research, therefore, must build on the strong physical and social expressions of wellness among undergraduate students, while tapping into and amplifying their spiritual and coping resources.

RECOMMENDATIONS FOR FURTHER WELLNESS RESEARCH

Continued research with undergraduate students must address the unique wellness characteristics of this population, rather than recruiting their participation simply because they are a convenient sample. Five specific recommendations are offered to advance wellness research efforts with college students.

Consistent Use of Wellness Measures

Repeated administrations of wellness measures provide needed psychometric information that allows for instrument refinement. In its relatively brief history, the WEL has undergone a fairly rapid transformation, resulting in the 91-item 5F-Wel and the relatively new 58-item 4F-Wel. These shorter versions may be amenable to undergraduate populations, particularly when used repeatedly at various times over the academic year. It is recommended that researchers and clinicians alike utilize the newer evidence-based wellness instruments along with measures of related constructs such as stamina, sense of coherence, and psychological well-being, as some have already done (e.g., T. B. Adams et al., 2000; Hermon & Hazler, 1999), to continue to sift through and more fully appreciate the multidimensionality of wellness.

Cast a Wider Net

Given that students enrolled in 2-year or community colleges represent the majority of undergraduates today (U.S. Department of Education, 2002), researchers need to study this segment of the undergraduate population. In addition, researchers can target the growing number of older, international, and part-time commuter students now attending college (see Brener & Gowda, 2001), which would also include attention to the type of school or academic setting (e.g., private, urban/commuter, specialized), consistent with previous research (e.g., military academy, historically Black college or university).

Intentionally targeting and recruiting culturally diverse participants makes it possible to conduct analyses based on demographic characteristics. Such efforts would include attention to gender and age comparisons (e.g., Myers & Mobley, 2004; Shurts & Myers, 2005), and investigations of wellness issues that may be more relevant to one gender than the other (e.g., objectified body consciousness; Sinclair & Myers, 2004). Wellness "profiles" based on demographic information could be computed, and wellness strengths and needs of specific ethnic and cultural groups could be identified. This would allow for intragroup comparisons as well (e.g., Spurgeon & Myers, 2004).

Track Wellness Over Time

Longitudinal investigations, as suggested by Myers and Bechtel (2004), are needed to observe college students' participation in wellness programs and the effects of those programs on their overall wellness over the course of their first year or even the entirety of their undergraduate studies. Choate and Smith (2003) infused the Wheel of Wellness model into the first-year college experience of 59 first-semester students at a small, private college in the southeastern United States and administered the WEL during the third class meeting and then again 1 month prior to the end of the semester. Results indicated a significant ($p < .01$) increase in Total Wellness mean scores from pre- (76.1) to post- (81.4) measurement. With the exception of Choate and Smith's work, most of the wellness research conducted thus far has been cross-sectional, providing a very narrow and limited portrayal of undergraduate students' wellness. As a holistic concept, wellness cannot be fully appreciated or understood in a static context. Only over time can the influence of contextual variables (e.g., local, institutional, global, and chronometrical; Myers & Sweeney, 2004b), for example, be appropriately assessed.

Provide Personalized and Normative Wellness Feedback

Personalized feedback has been defined as a summary of self-report information about health-related behaviors (e.g., alcohol consumption, smoking, diet practices, physical activity), often presented with (a) normative, group- or peer-referent comparison data (e.g., how my drinking compares with that of other freshman women at this college) or (b) ipsative or idiographic, self-referent data (e.g., how the amount and frequency of my drinking at the end of the semester compares with what it was at the beginning of the semester), or both (S. E. Collins, Carey, & Sliwinski, 2002; DiClemente, Marinilli, Singh, & Bellino, 2001). Such feedback is intended to promote discrepancy between actual and desired behavior so that the person will be motivated to modify his or her behavior in a positive direction.

The effects of individualized feedback have recently been reported with respect to nutrition (Brug & van Assema, 2000; Oenema, Brug, & Lechner, 2001), cigarette smoking (O'Neill, Gillispie, & Slobin, 2000), and college drinking (S. E. Collins et al., 2002; Walters, 2000; Walters, Bennett, & Miller, 2000). Choate and Smith (2003) referred to the provision of an "individualized wellness profile" to first-year college students, derived from their WEL scores, but did not describe how such feedback was delivered. Feedback has been in the form of print and graphic material, electronic or online information, verbal feedback from a health professional, or a combination of any of these. Providing college students with individualized and normative feedback about their current wellness would be consistent with research in this area. Normative "wellness profiles" offered as a comparison to ipsative or self-referent feedback might be those of their fraternity or sorority, residence hall, or other influential peer group. Repeated administrations and tracking of one's wellness would then gauge how such feedback has affected students' wellness attitudes and participation in wellness activities over the course of a semester (e.g., Choate & Smith) or academic year.

Offer Computerized and Online Completion of Wellness Inventories

Many if not most college students today are computer literate, and colleges and universities routinely offer computer and online accessibility to entice student enrollment and encourage academic persistence. Making available one of the wellness inventories described in this book through an interactive computer program (either in a self-contained package such as a CD-ROM or on a secure Web site) would be consistent with many college students' technological orientation and lifestyle. Personalized wellness feedback could easily be provided, and college students' wellness attitudes and behaviors could be conveniently collected and tracked over time.

Various computer programs are currently available that provide college students with personalized feedback of their health behaviors, specifically alcohol use. One is intended to be completed in the student health center on campus (Multi-Media Assessment of Student Health; Dimeff & McNeely, 2000), with the student using headphones to ensure privacy and minimize disruption. Once the personalized feedback is generated and printed with graphic illustrations, it is reviewed by the student with a health professional. Another similar program has recently been developed (Neighbors, Larimer, & Lewis, 2004) and has not been implemented beyond a research trial. Both programs, however, provide normative feedback about one's alcohol use compared with national norms and norms of the typical student on that college campus. Two programs accessible online are not restricted to students enrolled at a particular institution. One is designed to reduce drinking among college students (www.e-chug.com), and the other, the Drinker's Checkup (www.drinkerscheckup.com; Squires & Hester, 2002), offers assessment of one's alcohol use and is not restricted to college students.

To advance wellness research with undergraduates, it is recommended that the 5F-Wel and 4F-Wel be made available on a secure Web site and that students from various colleges and universities across the United States (and perhaps internationally as well) be recruited to complete one of them anonymously through various incentives (e.g., drawing for gift certificates and other prizes). Such participation could be endorsed by the residence services and student enrollment offices as part of a campuswide wellness campaign and addressing student retention. Students would be provided with an instant personalized "wellness profile" and a comparison profile of their peer group and their wellness tracked over time to ascertain the influence of such self- and norm-referent feedback. The "Wellness Web Site" could also offer students various tips for wellness promotion, as well as links to relevant health-related Web sites. Through such efforts, students, campus communities, and wellness research initiatives would be served.

SUMMARY

College students represent an appropriate population in which to promote and study wellness, and it appears, from research reviewed in this chapter, that interest in and opportunities for such efforts are plentiful. It is recommended, however, that future programmatic and research initiatives emphasize a holistic perspective of wellness rather than a fractured understanding of wellness (e.g., exclusive focus on nutrition, exercise, spirituality, or socialization). As Hermon notes in chapter 24, such an emphasis is rare across college and university campuses today, and yet is essential for addressing such institutional challenges as student retention, academic persistence, and alumni giving.

It is hoped that current and forthcoming findings from wellness research with college students can be used to encourage college administration to invest in campuswide programs (or in residence halls; e.g., Enochs, 2001) for the benefit of students, parents, faculty, and other institutional personnel. In this manner, not only would the topic of investigation be holistic, but the method of implementation and its implications would be comprehensive as well.

DISCUSSION QUESTIONS

1. In light of research findings discussed in this chapter, how would you define wellness for undergraduate college students?
2. What recommendations do you have for disseminating research findings on undergraduate student wellness to (a) college and university administration, (b) college students themselves, and (c) other constituents for the purpose of health promotion? How might such findings be used for the purpose of student recruitment, retention, and academic success?
3. What are innovative methods for conducting research on the topic of undergraduate student wellness? How can such research be conducted in a manner that is enticing and credible for students?

WEB RESOURCES

- **My Student Body,** http://www.MyStudentBody.com/, addresses health-related issues prevalent on college campuses. Links are provided to help students analyze their personal beliefs, behaviors, and consequences, and also to receive the prevention education through interactive tools such as flash animation peer stories and informational segments.

- **The American College Health Association (ACHA), www.acha.org/,** is the chief advocate and leadership organization for college and university health. The ACHA provides education, information, products, communication, and services and encourages research and culturally sensitive practices to help promote the health of students and members of the college community.
- **The Harvard School of Public Health at Harvard University, www.hsph.harvard.edu/,** provides education and information to fortify health capacities and services for communities, inform policy debate, distribute health information, and augment public awareness of health as a public good and essential right.

9

Research on Adult Wellness

Suzanne E. Degges-White and W. Matthew Shurts

During the past three decades, research on wellness and healthy functioning among adults has increased (Pender & Pender, 1987), and conceptual models representing a variety of perspectives and theoretical orientations have been developed to explain the factors and variables that contribute to well-being in this population. Although predominant models share a health-oriented definition of wellness, they differ in both schemas and applications in research and practice. In this chapter, a rationale for conducting wellness research with adults is provided, followed by a summary and critique of studies using various wellness models. Specific attention is given to studies using the Wheel of Wellness (Myers, Sweeney, & Witmer, 2000b) and Indivisible Self models (IS-Wel; Myers & Sweeney, 2004b). An integrative summary of adult wellness research is provided with implications for future research to promote holistic wellness in this population.

RATIONALE FOR WELLNESS RESEARCH WITH ADULTS

The growth and size of the adult population in the United States is unprecedented (U.S. Census Bureau, 2001). This population segment has created a new vision of optimal functioning in contrast to the previously limited view of wellness as simply the absence of illness (Pender & Pender, 1987). Within the auspices of the *Healthy People 2010* initiative (U.S. Department of Health and Human Services, 2000), a set of 10 adult health indicators (e.g., physical activity, obesity, tobacco use, and mental health) was developed representing a combination of behaviors, environmental factors, and health system issues that serve as gauges of health and well-being. Specific adult risk groups, often delimited by education and income, have been identified based on low ratings within these indicator areas. The large number of adults at risk necessitates that further research be devoted to understanding and improving adult wellness. This research need coupled with the dramatic rise of interest in the processes of "successful aging" and "aging well" among the public has resulted in increased research efforts to determine the practices that will facilitate healthy aging (Baltes & Baltes, 1990).

The process of aging well appears to have a measurable relationship with maintaining life satisfaction and overall well-being (Roberts & Chapman, 2000) throughout the adult years. Because choices and behaviors at any life stage can influence future functioning, comprehensive wellness research spanning the periods of young adulthood through older adulthood is warranted. The research presented in this chapter includes studies completed with adults, defined as individuals age 18 and older. Studies with college students and older adults are the subjects of chapters 8 and 10, respectively. Although this still leaves an expansive age range, there is a dearth of research specifically addressing wellness in the general adult population.

WELL-BEING RESEARCH IN THE ADULT POPULATION

Pender and Pender (1987) observed that adults who defined health as the absence of illness were less likely to adopt health-promoting behaviors than those who viewed health as an optimum state of well-being. This finding generated both increased interest in promoting well-being among adults and the development of wellness models and assessment tools. Two similar and related terms, well-being and wellness, have been studied as discrete constructs. Research involving two of the most widely studied constructs of well-being, subjective well-being (SWB) and psychological well-being (PWB), are discussed below, followed by a review of studies using the Wheel of Wellness (Myers, Sweeney, & Witmer, 2000b; Witmer & Sweeney, 1992) and the IS-Wel (Myers & Sweeney, 2004b).

First studied some 50 years ago, SWB comprises life satisfaction, positive mood, and the absence of negative mood (Diener & Lucas, 1999). The measurement of overall happiness, often termed life satisfaction, is useful in assessing temporal feelings about one's present status. In a review of the SWB literature, Diener, Oishi, and Lucas (2003) acknowledged that correlates of happiness across gender, education, profession, or virtually any other demographic variable were difficult to pinpoint.

Moving beyond temporal satisfaction to encompass behaviors, PWB was defined on the basis of engaging in activities in concert with one's true self (Waterman, 1993). Two decades ago, Ryff (1989) developed the first multidimensional model to explain adult well-being based on six needs: autonomy, growth, relationships, purpose in life, environmental mastery, and self-acceptance. Keyes, Shmotkin, and Ryff (2002) investigated the intersection of SWB and PWB in connection with personality factors in a sample of 3,032 adults ages 25 to 74. Results using bivariate correlations and both exploratory and confirmatory factor analyses indicated that SWB and PWB were related, but distinct, constructs. Further, higher scores on both measures were associated with increased education and age.

An earlier study by Ryff and Keyes (1995) focused specifically on PWB within a sample of 1,108 adults (age 25 years and older, mean age = 45.6 years, SD = 14.8). As expected, self-acceptance was found to be positively related to happiness and negatively related to depression. A positive relationship was found between age and well-being, with older participants scoring higher in autonomy and environmental mastery. However, there were declines among older age groups for purpose in life and personal growth, and no incremental changes in self-acceptance. Gender differences were found for positive relations, with women scoring higher than men. Although age and gender do appear related to PWB, a gap still exists between empirical findings and clinical practice. However, associated holistic models of wellness and accompanying assessments incorporate behaviorally focused items that are more immediately useful in determining appropriate wellness-enhancing clinical interventions.

WELLNESS RESEARCH IN THE ADULT POPULATION

Over the past 8 years, numerous empirical studies have been conducted with adults using the Wheel of Wellness and the IS-Wel models. Researchers have explored wellness in concert with career and relationship issues and among populations including medical outpatients and adult women. These studies include clinical implications and, taken together, provide a foundation for exploring wellness research with adults.

Wellness Within Relationships Dyads

The value of social support in relation to wellness is well established (Cohen & Wills, 1985). Myers, Madathil, and Tingle (in press) examined wellness and marital satisfaction of 45 Indian individuals living in India in arranged marriages (50% female; 53% over age 45; 98% with bachelor's degree) as compared with a norm group in the United States in marriages of choice. *T* tests computed to determine differences between the groups revealed that participants from India scored higher on the WEL scales of spirituality, nutrition, and cultural identity, whereas the U.S. sample scored higher on realistic beliefs and work ($p < 1$, large effect), sense of humor ($p < .01$, medium effect), and self-care ($p < .05$, small effect).

Powers, Myers, Tingle, and Powers (2003) examined the relationship among wellness, marital satisfaction, perceived stress, and mattering for medical residents and their spouses ($N = 83$ individuals, 60% residents, 40% spouses; ages 23–38, $M = 30$ years, $SD = 3.03$). Results were compared with existing norm-group scores from members of the general married population ($N = 486$; 40% female; ages 18–101 years, $M = 44$ years, $SD = 19$ years) and counselor education doctoral students. A series of *t* tests was conducted to determine whether differences existed between the groups studied. When compared with the general adult sample, medical residents scored higher on work satisfaction and satisfaction with shared marriage values and lower on realistic beliefs. Residents' spouses scored higher than the general married population on total wellness, mattering, and satisfaction with shared marriage values and lower on work satisfaction and realistic beliefs. These findings suggest that factors more complex than education and marital status determine overall wellness.

Wellness and Career Issues

Hutchinson (1996) examined the relationships among job satisfaction, work performance, and wellness in a sample of 161 American managers (67.7% male; 95.0% Caucasian; 81.7% married/partnered) using the Wheel of Wellness. Multiple regression analyses revealed that several components of wellness (e.g., spirituality, friendship, love, work, leisure, and self-regulation) better predicted job satisfaction and work performance than measures of physical wellness. Hutchinson concluded that offering workplace wellness programs based solely on physical wellness may not be enough to enhance work performance and job satisfaction, two of the primary goals of such programs. A statistically significant proportion of variance in both dependent variables (job satisfaction and work performance) was contributed by occupational or work wellness and intellectual stimulation, problem solving, and creativity, suggesting that a variety of wellness components affect job satisfaction.

Connolly and Myers (2003) completed a similar study of 82 employees (55% female; 82% Caucasian; approximately 60% married/partnered; mean age = 38.2 years, SD = 10.33) in varied positions to determine the variance in job satisfaction that can be accounted for by holistic wellness (using the 5F-Wel) and mattering. Positive, significant relationships were found between job satisfaction and mattering ($r = .22, p < .05$) and job satisfaction and wellness ($r = .29, p < .01$). A significant positive correlation was found between wellness and mattering ($r = .37, p < .01$). The results of regression analyses revealed that both wellness and mattering contributed significantly to the variance in job satisfaction, with wellness the stronger predictor. However, when block variables such as age and job tenure were held constant, the contributions of wellness and mattering to job satisfaction were not significant. Analysis of this study along with Hutchinson's (1996) research presented above suggests that wellness may play an integral role in determining job satisfaction and job performance; however, the exact role has yet to be determined. Various components of wellness were significant for the managers in the former study, yet there may be unique differences among individuals based on position level. The Connolly and Myers study revealed two variables, age and job tenure, that also affect job satisfaction.

Wellness Among Midlife Women

Both wellness and life satisfaction were among the variables explored in a recent study involving 224 women between the ages of 35 and 65 (mean age = 47.33 years, SD = 7.44; 86% Caucasian; Degges-White, 2003). Wellness (assessed with the 5F-Wel) was studied in relation to transitions, life satisfaction, and subjective age, defined as the age that individuals feel and think themselves to be regardless of their chronological age. Participants were divided into three age groups (35–44 years, $n = 87$; 45–54 years, $n = 97$; and 55–65 years, $n = 40$). Total Wellness scores were not significantly different among these groups; however, life satisfaction scores increased in each successive age category. Further, multivariate analysis of variance (MANOVA) calculations showed Total Wellness scores and household income to be significant predictors of life satisfaction. As to the role of social support, sharing a home was significantly related to life satisfaction, $F(1, 222) = 6.358$, $p = .01$, but not to Total Wellness. A one-way analysis of variance revealed that subjective age and chronological age were significantly related to overall wellness, $F(2, 221) = 9.572$, $p < .0001$: Women whose subjective ages were younger than their chronological ages reported higher wellness than women with a reversed age pattern. Degges-White concluded that subjective feelings play an important role in overall wellness.

Wellness Among Medical Patients

The IS-Wel model was the foundation for an exploratory examination of relationships between overall wellness, stress management, and perceived stress in a medical population. Degges-White, Myers, Adelman, and Pastoor (2003) studied 60 patients seeking help from a headache specialty center (mean age = 38.6 years, SD = 13.14; 84% female; 69% Caucasian) using the 5F-Wel and a perceived stress scale. Using t tests, Degges-White et al. compared the sample with an adult norm group and found that the clinical population reported lower Total Wellness, $t(595) = 4.016$, $p < .05$; higher levels of perceived stress, $t(595) = 15.805$, $p < .05$; and similar Stress Management scores. In addition, members of the clinical sample reported significantly lower levels of Nutrition, Exercise, and Sense of Control than the norm group, yet the clinical sample reported a significantly higher score for Spirituality. Although sample size limits the generalizability of the findings, Degges-White et al. concluded that the results supported the need to include spiritually based components in traditional medical treatment. Moreover, the development of specific interventions for headache sufferers based on individual wellness profiles holds promise for mitigating chronic headache problems.

Summary of Adult Wellness Research

From an examination of studies conducted to date, it appears that wellness is more reliably predicted from personality traits and individual dispositions than from demographic variables. However, wellness seems to differ across adult populations and in relation to specific variables examined. For example, the results of Myers et al.'s (in press) study of Indian couples may suggest that wellness as a culturally embedded construct should be explored across cultures and subcultures. Powers et al.'s (2003) study of "medical marriages"—marriages in which one or both partners are physicians and which are often more stressful in the early years than other marriages— revealed higher levels of wellness in medical couples than in a norm group of married adults. Apparently, wellness is associated with relationship satisfaction, education, and occupation. The results of studies incorporating variables such as mattering, job satisfaction, and job performance in relation to wellness (Connolly & Myers, 2003; Hutchinson, 1996) reveal that age and job tenure, often markers of life stage, may mitigate the predictive power of wellness.

Finally, Degges-White's (2003) finding that total wellness was significantly related to life satisfaction for midlife women indicates that the constructs of temporal well-being and optimal functioning are indeed intertwined as are individual attitudes, perceptions, and behaviors, as evidenced by the correlation between subjective age and overall wellness. It is clear that wellness holds an important role in the better understanding of factors such as satisfaction, performance, and functioning in a variety of environments; however, existing studies only begin to address the wide range of issues involving adult wellness.

FUTURE RESEARCH DIRECTIONS

Wellness is a multifaceted construct incorporating multiple behaviors, attitudes, and dispositions, inviting an equally comprehensive and multi-pronged research agenda among adults. Adulthood encompasses many decades of one's life and comprises a variety of transitions experienced in numerous venues, thus a broad-based wellness research agenda is needed to fully capture the complexities and experiences adulthood presents. Four specific areas for future study are suggested below to help move toward this broader research agenda.

Wellness Throughout Adulthood

Many theories of human development and change over the life span have been proposed and validated through theory and research, yet few longitudinal studies of wellness exist. It is has been shown that life satisfaction increases with age (Degges-White, 2003) even while physical health typically declines. In addition, lifestyle choices made by young adults can impact health and wellness throughout the life span. Longitudinal studies are needed to further understanding of the relationship between wellness, adult development, and aging. Investigation of relationships between wellness factors and aging may provide a better understanding of mitigating factors related to coping with change across the adult life span.

Relationships, Family Constellation, and Wellness

The constellation of contemporary families no longer reflects only the once-traditional, now decreasingly visible, nuclear family consisting of mother, father, and children. Age expectations related to partnering and childbearing have relaxed significantly in the past half century, making it increasingly important to understand how wellness is affected at different life stages, not merely chronological ages. Barriers to interracial relationships, gay and lesbian partnerships, single-parent families, single-parent childbearing or adoptions, and a host of other once-indestructible social conventions have diminished. In addition, as individuals live longer, many adults today are becoming caregivers for their aging parents, adding yet another dimension to the family constellation. As a result of these and other changes in contemporary family life, there is a need for better understanding of the role of family constellations, social support, and relationship status in adult wellness. Studies of conventional families as well as members of diverse family constellations are needed to explore factors that contribute to wellness for individuals, couples, and families regardless of gender or family relationship structure across the adult life span.

Career Concerns and Wellness

Contemporary work weeks often stretch beyond the once-traditional 40 hours, second jobs are increasingly essential to balancing family budgets, and leisure time is shrinking rather than increasing. The scope of research devoted to wellness and job performance and satisfaction must be expanded to include a multiplicity of variables (e.g., occupation, career level, hours worked, commute time). As job tenure and job satisfaction were found to be predictors of wellness in two studies (Connolly & Myers, 2003), it seems that longitudinal assessment of wellness and satisfaction among adults will provide important information about these variables throughout the adult career trajectory.

The Mind–Body Connection and Wellness

Perhaps one of the most compelling areas of future research involving adult wellness is the interrelationship between mind and body. The medical community has recognized the strong connection between a positive, wellness-oriented attitude and enhanced physical well-being, but there is still much to learn. To meet this need, attention should be given to a closer evaluation of trends and patterns found in the wellness profiles of individuals who deal most successfully with illness. Resiliency is a valuable tool in responding to unexpected or undesired life events, and it is unknown what specific components of wellness are associated with greater resilience. The role of spirituality in medical care continues to expand as traditional practitioners are exposed to the value of faith and prayer in both coping with illness and recovery. Using wellness assessments that include spirituality and purpose in life may bolster the knowledge base surrounding the mind–body–spirit connection.

Research on wellness of adults, as an overarching construct of combined mental, physical, and spiritual well-being, is relatively recent. As a consequence, there is still a need to explore this triad of components in greater depth across ages, genders, ethnicities, and life stages. To date, research addressing wellness has been conducted with highly specific populations that tend to be nonrepresentative of the overall adult population. By increasing the breadth and depth of wellness research to include the entire spectrum of adults, this very diverse group ultimately will benefit as increased understanding of the strengths and potential challenges to their overall levels of wellness are discovered and utilized to their advantage.

Testing New Models

Both the theoretical Wheel of Wellness and the IS-Wel models have been used in studies with adults. The more recent four-factor model maps more closely on the body–mind–spirit triad (Myers, Luecht, & Sweeney, 2004). These and perhaps new models remain to be tested and verified with a variety of adult populations. Moreover, the contextual variables prominent in the IS-Wel model (see chapter 4) merit study among adults, both in terms of their impact on individuals' wellness and in terms of the potentially selective interaction with the individual factors identified in the model.

SUMMARY

Within the last half-decade, an emphasis on positive well-being and optimizing mental health has taken strong hold across many social science disciplines. However, the empirical study of wellness is still in its infancy. Further studies are needed to provide a strong knowledge base related to wellness of adults so that counselors can develop interventions based on empirical data. Studies that assess changes in wellness and its components over the life span are critical, as adulthood is very much a period of transitions, growth, and continued development.

DISCUSSION QUESTIONS

1. Among adults of various developmental stages, what roles do purpose and meaning in life have in overall wellness? Does this change over the course of the life span?
2. As social mores change and age expectations surrounding significant life events become more fluid, how is adult wellness affected at various stages of development? Does the loosening of social constraints improve or compromise adult wellness?
3. Public health initiatives, such as *Healthy People 2010*, have been gaining influence and recognition throughout the past few years. How do these programs attempt to influence adult wellness at different stages, and what further steps might be taken to assist adults of all ages to strive for optimal well-being?
4. A complaint about the traditional model of mental health and the desire to diagnose individuals with disorders is based on deficits and subnormal functioning. With the new emphasis on mental wellness, how might mental health interventions be implemented so that a similar stigma will be avoided in the case of adults who have scores of below-optimal wellness?
5. There have been many changes in the world over the last 10–20 years. What new trends do you believe most impact adult wellness? How should this affect future wellness research?

WEB RESOURCES

- **AARP Health and Wellness, http://www.aarp.org/health/,** is a sub-page of the American Association of Retired Persons (AARP) main page that provides information on health and wellness for people over age 50. A variety of resources and links are provided.
- **The National Wellness Institute, http://www.nationalwellness.org/,** was founded to integrate the fields of health promotion and wellness. Membership services and annual conference information are provided.
- **Healthy People 2010, http://www.healthypeople.gov,** is the federal site that provides national health promotion and disease prevention objectives for the current decade. Health risk factors as they affect special populations are included.

10

Wellness in Later Life: Research Implications

Jane E. Myers

The number of older persons in the United States approached 36 million in 2002, representing 12.3% of the total population and an 11-fold increase during the 20th century (AARP, 2004). Relatedly, life expectancy increased from 47 years in 1900 to 77.2 years in 2003. Although traditional, stereotypical views of aging present a negative perspective dominated by poor health, disability, functional limitations, and increasing mental illness, recent research on later life reveals that older people typically age well (Johnson, 1995; Myers & Harper, 2004); are resilient in responding to stress, transitions, and change (Carstensen & Freund, 1994); and experience a lower incidence of mental illness than people of younger ages (Gatz & Smyer, 2001). Yet, the tremendous comorbidity of physical and mental health issues results in a lower quality of life for many, and lifestyle choices earlier in life (that could be modified) account for as much as two-thirds of the disease and disability experienced in the later years (G. W. Shannon & Pyle, 1993).

In this chapter, an overview of risk factors provides a foundation for examining research related to successful aging, variously presented in terms such as life satisfaction, quality of life, perceived well-being, subjective well-being, and wellness. Although voluminous literature exists related to aging issues, much of this research examines correlates of later life satisfaction, singly and in combination. Far less research has been conducted using holistic models that emphasize the interaction of key factors that mediate the aging process and promote aging well. Notably, only one empirical study of older persons to date has used the Indivisible Self model (Myers & Sweeney, 2004b; Sweeney & Myers, 2005), and none have been conducted using the Wheel of Wellness (Myers, Sweeney, & Witmer, 2000b; Witmer & Sweeney, 1992).

THE OLDER POPULATION: DEMOGRAPHICS AND RISK FACTORS

The older population, defined in the aggregate as people over age 65, is expected to increase to 20% of the total population by 2030. Although population parameters define some characteristics of this population, these statistics simultaneously obscure significant within-group variation that places many older persons at risk. For example, at present, ethnic minority individuals compose 17.2% of the older population, a figure that will increase by 81% to over 25% of the older population by 2030 (AARP, 2004). Minorities are more likely to live at or near the poverty level. In addition, a gender gap in life expectancy results from women living an average of 19.4 years after age 65 and men living an average of only 16.4 more years. The ratio of older women to older men is 141:100, with four times as many widows as widowers in later life. An additional 8% of older persons are divorced, a significant increase in the last decade (AARP, 2004), and a subgroup especially likely to be among the 10% of older persons who are poor. In fact, the poverty rate for older women continues to be higher than that for older men, with some 20% of older persons being poor or near poor. Double jeopardy, which results when one has at least two risk factors, such as being both a minority and female, results in an even greater likelihood of poverty and associated consequences, including lack of access to health care and a greater incidence of illness.

Recently, just over two-thirds (68.6%) of noninstitutionalized older persons (who make up 95% of the older population) "assessed their heath as excellent or very good (compared with 66.6% for persons ages 18–64)" (see http://www.aoa.gov/prof/Statistics/profile/2003/14.asp). Of course, this means that 31.4%—almost one in three persons—assessed their health as fair or poor. There were few gender differences; however, older African Americans (57.7%) and older Hispanics (60.5%) were less likely to rate their health as excellent or good than were older Whites (75.4%). Despite favorable self-assessments, most older persons have at least one chronic condition and many have multiple conditions that limit their performance of daily living activities. The most common conditions reported include hypertension (49.2%), arthritis (36.1%), heart disease (31.1%), cancer (20.0), sinusitis (15.1%), and diabetes (15.0).

Freedman, Martin, and Schoeni (2002) completed a review of recent research on disability and functional limitations among older adults and concluded that disability in this population has declined significantly in the last decade:

> Yet, 20% of older U.S. adults have chronic disabilities, 7% to 8% have severe cognitive impairments, roughly one-third have mobility limitations, 20% have vision problems, and 33% have hearing impairments. Women, minorities, and persons of low socioeconomic status are especially vulnerable. (p. 3137)

Just under one-fourth (22%) of people 60 and older are obese; only 27% of people age 65–74 and 17% of people 75 and over engage in regular leisure-time physical activity (AARP, 2004). These statistics underscore the need for holistic wellness interventions to help all older people achieve optimum functioning regardless of physical and other limitations.

CORRELATES OF WELL-BEING IN LATER LIFE

A review of the PsycINFO database (American Psychological Association, 2004) resulted in 641 hits for "aging and life satisfaction," 707 hits for "aging and quality of life," 1,335 hits for "aging and well-being," and only 69 hits for "aging and wellness." Space does not permit a full review of this literature; however, a brief review of selected studies reveals a pattern in which correlates of aging and demographic risk factors are highlighted in relation to well-being. It is noteworthy that only 1 of the 69 studies on "aging and wellness" was based in a holistic wellness model; the remaining studies addressed one or more factors associated with well-being and referred to the term *wellness* somewhere in the title or abstract of the article.

Pinquart and Sorensen (2000) conducted a meta-analysis of 286 empirical studies examining the relationship between socioeconomic status, social networks, personal competence, and subjective well-being (SWB) among older persons. They found that all three factors were significantly and positively associated with SWB. Diener and Suh (1998) also conducted a meta-analysis of SWB studies, using large-scale international studies, and found that life satisfaction does not decline with age. However, they also noted that positive affect declines with each successive cohort of older persons. In a subsequent study conducted in Hong Kong, Yeung and Chow (2002) found eight significant predictors of positive SWB: marital status (i.e., married), positive self-esteem, internal locus of control, positive help-seeking attitudes, lower frequencies of financial, emotional, and physical health problems, and lower number of chronic diseases.

A number of variables have been studied in relation to quality of life and life satisfaction for older persons. For example, in a national survey of 999 older Britons, good social relations were mentioned by most (81%) as a primary factor affecting life satisfaction. In addition, social roles, activities, health, psychological outlook, finances, and independence were positive factors, and poor health and low income were negative factors (Bowling et al., 2003). Strawbridge, Wallhagen, and Cohen (2002) also found that absence of chronic conditions and maintaining functioning were positively related to successful aging among 868 respondents age 65–99 years.

Age and sense of control were statistically and substantively related in a study by Wolinsky, Wyrwich, Babu, Kroenke, and Tierney (2003), who also identified the major predictor of sense of control as "mental well-being." Siegenthaler (1996), summarizing a review of literature on leisure participation, noted that "older individuals who participate more frequently and in a greater variety of activities experience greater psychological well being and contentment" (p. 1). Although additional studies could be cited, the point here is that a variety of correlates of successful aging have been identified across studies, and the question of how these correlates interrelate needs to be pursued.

STUDIES OF OLDER PERSONS USING HOLISTIC MODELS OF WELL-BEING AND WELLNESS

Studies of well-being, prominent in the gerontology literature, have emerged largely from the positive psychology movement (Seligman, 1998; Snyder & Lopez, 2001) and thus focus on emotional factors of functioning. For example, Ryff and Keyes (1995), front-runners in the positive psychology movement, noted that deficit models of functioning dominated the psychology literature, in contrast to earlier writings of theorists such as Adler, Jung, Maslow, and Rogers. These authors developed a multidimensional model of well-being comprising six components: self-acceptance, positive relations with others, autonomy, environmental mastery, purpose in life, and personal growth. Through multiple studies of people of varying ages, they determined that older adults view accepting change as an important quality of positive functioning, consider attention to positive relations with others as an index of well-being, and note that sense of humor, enjoyment of life, and accepting change are criteria of successful aging.

T. B. Adams, Bezner, and Steinhardt (1997) developed the Perceived Wellness Model as a means of better understanding subjective perceptions of well-being. They defined perceived wellness as consisting of six dimensions—physical, spiritual, psychological, social, emotional, and intellectual—with wellness consisting of consistent and balanced growth within these dimensions. It is interesting that these dimensions are remarkably similar to Hettler's (1984) hexagon model of wellness (physical, spiritual, occupational, social, emotional, and intellectual). Adams et al. developed the Perceived Wellness Survey (PWS) as a measure of their dimensions and underscored the need to look at wellness as a multidimensional construct. They presented data from multiple studies (including older adult participants) supporting both their model and instrument. However, Harari (2003), analyzing data from 317 participants, found only a single factor underlying the PWS and no support for the six hypothesized scales.

Dice (2002) used the Indivisible Self model and the Five Factor Wellness Inventory to examine the relationship among coping resources, wellness, and attachment to companion animals in a sample of 327 people 65 years of age and older residing in community settings. Using analysis of variance, she found no significant differences in mean wellness scores based on pet ownership status (i.e., current or former pet owner). However, positive relationships were found among wellness and coping resources for both current and former pet owners ($r = .26$ and $r = .63$, respectively) and for those who had never owned pets ($r = .45$). These findings are consistent with earlier studies by Myers (2004) and Hattie, Myers, and Sweeney (2004), who noted strong positive relationships between coping resources and wellness.

DIRECTIONS FOR FUTURE RESEARCH

The scant literature available examining holistic wellness among older adults is surprising. Changing population demographics, significant health and mental health risk factors, and simply the inescapable fact that we all are aging make research in this area a compelling need. Both qualitative studies examining the meaning of wellness to older persons and quantitative studies examining individual components of wellness, the interaction of components of wellness, and wellness within and between subgroups of older persons could provide useful information for professional counselors. Studies of older ethnic minority groups are especially needed, as well as studies incorporating other aspects of diversity (e.g., sexual orientation, disability, spirituality) that could help provide a knowledge base of correlates of wellness as well as differential aspects of wellness among subgroups of the older population.

Studies of wellness factors in relationship to other issues, such as resilience, ego integrity, life satisfaction, and other commonly studied aspects of later life could further understanding of the dynamics of wellness in older adulthood. Cross-sectional studies that reveal correlates of wellness factors are needed. When participants include people of varying ages—for example, the young old, middle old, and old old—results may reveal important differences among age cohorts relative to wellness. Ideally, longitudinal studies will be conducted that will help us better understand whether and how wellness changes across the later life span, and whether there are developmental components embedded in the various wellness factors. Comparisons of older age populations with younger persons, while limited because of cohort effects, could point the way to research questions that can be examined in longitudinal studies.

It is not known whether the factor structure of wellness is stable across age groups or within age groups as diverse as those for adults age 18 to 60 and older persons age 60 and over. Large-scale studies, meta-analyses, and exploratory and confirmatory factor analyses are needed to examine these questions. In addition, the usefulness of various wellness models, particularly the Wheel of Wellness and the Indivisible Self, have not been determined in regard to the older population. The author of this chapter, and both book editors, have assessed wellness for groups of older persons and found that their level of interest in their scores and wellness issues was very high. Many appreciated the Wheel model and felt it accurately reflected their priorities in life. Whether they would respond as positively to an evidence-based model such as the Indivisible Self model has not been determined. If counselors are to develop effective interventions to promote wellness among older persons, the serious gap in knowledge of wellness issues in this population needs to be addressed to provide a firm foundation for evidence-based practice.

SUMMARY

During the last century, increases in the life span were dramatic, and improvements in medical services led to an increasing potential for health in the later years. In the last two decades, common perceptions of aging have shifted, and the span of later life divided into young, middle, and older adulthood. For the first two periods, healthy aging has become a common though by no means universal descriptor; for many older persons, both physical and mental health challenges continue to limit their quality of life. However, what factors contribute most to healthy aging and how wellness affects successful aging have not been determined. Research on wellness in later life is sparse and is needed to inform counselors and other service providers as to how best to promote the well-being of older adults.

DISCUSSION QUESTIONS

1. What characteristics of older persons and subgroups of older persons make them a population at risk in relation to wellness?
2. What kinds of issues would be important to consider when designing studies to examine wellness issues within ethnic minority populations?
3. Review the Wheel of Wellness and Indivisible Self models presented in Part I. How could a study or studies be designed to assess the usefulness of each model as a foundation for counseling older adults?
4. Assume for a moment that there are developmental components in wellness, and that significant changes in wellness occur over the life span. What might those changes be? How could you design a study to test your hypotheses?

WEB RESOURCES

- **AARP**, http://www.aarp.org/, is the Web site for the largest membership organization for older persons in the world. AARP provides information and links to a multitude of sites of interest to older people and that promote wellness in this population, particularly the /health subpage.
- **The Alliance for Aging Research**, http://www.agingresearch.org/, is a nonprofit organization dedicated to supporting and accelerating the pace of medical discoveries to improve the universal human experience of aging and health.
- **The American Society on Aging (ASA)**, http://www.asaging.org/, is a nonprofit organization committed to enhancing the knowledge and skills of those working with older adults and their families. This site contains publications and resources, educational programs and diversity initiatives, and connections to "the largest network of professionals in the field of aging."
- **National Institute on Aging (NIA)—Research Programs**, http://www. nia.nih.gov/Research/Information/, supports extramural research through programs in the Biology of Aging, Behavioral and Social Research, Geriatrics and Clinical Gerontology, and Neuroscience and Neuropsychology of Aging. The NIA Intramural Research Program conducts basic and clinical research in laboratories both in Baltimore and on the National Institutes of Health campus in Bethesda, Maryland.

11

Ethnicity and Wellness

Courtland C. Lee

As the 21st century begins to unfold, demographic realities make it imperative that the concept of wellness be considered within the context of racial and ethnic realities. Population projections for the new century suggest that U.S. citizens from historically minority racial/ethnic groups will supplant citizens of European origin, identified racially as "White," as the majority of the country's population (P. R. Campbell, 1996). In this chapter, a 21st-century paradigm for promoting wellness among people of color is presented, using counseling models such as the Wheel of Wellness and the Indivisible Self (e.g., Myers & Sweeney, 2004b; Myers, Sweeney, & Witmer, 2000b). The chapter begins with an overview of the demographics of these populations, followed by health profiles of African Americans, Asian Pacific Americans, Latino/ Hispanic Americans, and Native Americans. The realities of racism and systemic oppression and their relationship to wellness for people of color are explored, and an ethnic diversity wellness perspective that focuses on cultural dynamics of wellness is discussed. The chapter ends with research implications from an ethnic diversity wellness perspective.

WELLNESS AND ETHNIC DIVERSITY: DEMOGRAPHIC AND HEALTH REALITIES OF THE 21ST CENTURY

To establish a common reference point, it is important to delineate ethnic groups of color. In this chapter, *people of color* refer to people of African American, Asian Pacific American, Hispanic/Latino, and Native American cultural backgrounds. Although it is impossible to detail here the complexity of each ethnic group, the following demographic and health overview should serve as a starting point for wellness-related issues with each group.

African Americans are the currently the largest ethnic group of color in the United States, comprising 13% of the U.S. population (U.S. Census Bureau, 2000b). Within the social sciences literature, the African American experience has traditionally been viewed as a monolithic entity. It is important to understand that there are many aspects and facets to this cultural experience. Among African Americans are distinct ethnic groups such as Jamaican Americans, Caribbean Americans, Nigerian Americans, as well as Black Americans.

Asian Pacific Americans include people whose ethnic heritage originates in East Asia (e.g., Chinese, Japanese, Korean), Southeast Asia (e.g., Vietnamese, Cambodian, Burmese), South Asia (e.g., Indian, Pakistani, Nepali), West Asia (e.g., Iranian, Afghan, Turkish), and the Middle East (e.g., Iraqi, Jordanian, Palestinian). This population has doubled with each passing decade and currently constitutes approximately 4% of the U.S. population (U.S. Census Bureau, 2000b). Chinese comprise the largest ethnic group within Asian Pacific American culture, followed by Filipinos, Japanese, Asian Indians, and Koreans.

Demographers have projected that the Latino/Hispanic community will be the largest ethnic group of color within this century. Currently representing 12% of the U.S. population, the numbers of Latino/Hispanic Americans continue to rise rapidly as a result of continuing immigration and high birthrates (U.S. Census Bureau, 2000c). The largest Latino/Hispanic ethnic groups in the United States are Mexicans, followed by Puerto Ricans and Cubans (U.S. Census Bureau, 2000c).

Contemporary Native Americans are descendants of the original inhabitants of the North American continent. They represent less than 1% of the U.S. population and include more than 500 different cultural communities defined as sovereign entities. The U.S. government recognizes approximately 250 nations, but another 250 Native groups go without formal acknowledgment from the government (U.S. Census Bureau, 2000b).

A life span wellness perspective reveals the following significant points about the health status of people of color in the United States in the early 21st century. In general, African Americans fare worse than any other group, and American Indians and Latino/Hispanics are often disadvantaged in health status compared with White Americans. On average, Asian Americans fare as well as and sometimes better than White Americans on most health indicators (Keppel, Pearcy, & Wagener, 2002). Some examples of differential health status and health risks among minorities serve to underscore the need for wellness research and interventions across populations (see http://www.cdc.gov/omh/AMH/AMH.htm).

- The infant mortality rate is often used as a primary indicator of the overall health status of a group of people. Within the United States, African Americans and Native Americans have higher infant mortality rates than other groups, and although infant mortality rates have been falling for all groups, differences between racial/ethnic groups have persisted (Keppel et al., 2002).
- Immunization is a fundamental component of regular medical care for children, which both measures the extent to which children are protected from childhood diseases and points to whether children have access to medical care. Data suggest that African American and Latino/

Hispanic children who live in socioeconomically disadvantaged circumstances are less likely than nonpoor children to be up to date with recommended vaccinations (Keppel et al., 2002).

- Although deaths among adolescents and young adults are rare compared with deaths among older adults, several causes of death are particularly important for the younger age group, for whom the most common cause of death is not disease but injury. The one fatal disease that significantly affects young people across ethnic groups is HIV. Native Americans are much more likely than members of other groups to die as the result of an unintentional injury or to commit suicide. African Americans are much more likely than members of any other group to be victims of homicide. African Americans and Latino/Hispanic Americans are also more likely to die from HIV-related diseases than members of other groups (Council of Economic Advisors, 1998).

- Chronic diseases such as heart disease and cancer account for the largest fraction of deaths among those age 45 to 64, and smoking is implicated in many of these deaths (Centers for Disease Control and Prevention, 1993). African American men and women have the highest death rates from heart disease and cancer, whereas Latino/Hispanic Americans have lower death rates than White Americans. Asian Pacific Americans generally have the lowest death rates, particularly for heart disease. Native Americans have high rates of heart disease mortality compared with both Latino/Hispanic and Asian Pacific Americans (Geronimus, 1996).

- Coverage by health insurance, either private or public such as Medicaid, is a key indicator of access to medical care. Data suggest that Latino/Hispanic Americans are the most likely to be uninsured. Importantly, for every ethnic group, the rate of uninsured is lower for those with higher incomes (Council of Economic Advisors, 1998); clearly, poverty is linked to poor medical care and a higher incidence of illness and disability.

- There is also evidence that health differences persist into old age. For example, African American and Latino/Hispanic senior citizens are more likely to have disabilities and chronic diseases than their White American counterparts (Schoenbaum & Waidmann, 1997; J. P. Smith & Kington, 1997).

These examples of health disparities and health risk disparities reflect the complex situational and sociohistorical life circumstances of ethnic minorities in the United States.

THE REALITIES OF RACISM AND SYSTEMIC OPPRESSION

Research into the reasons underlying health differences between ethnic groups has focused primarily on differences in socioeconomic status (Williams, 1990). On average, White Americans have better access to resources to ensure a healthy environment and lifestyle. Some research, however, suggests that racism creates stress leading to poorer health among people of color (Williams, Lavizzo-Mourey, & Warren, 1994).

All people of color share the common reality of racism in the United States. While reactions to this oppressive dynamic may differ, its persistence significantly affects the quality of life for ethnic groups of color and should be considered as a significant factor in the etiology of health challenges. The stresses of daily life are compounded for people of color by both overt and covert racism. Racism may operate to limit individuals from a full measure of employment, educational, and social opportunity. Significantly, racism contributes to a phenomenon known as *historical hostility,* which is apparent in the attitudes and behavior of many people of color (Vontress, Johnson, & Epp, 1999).

The essence of historical hostility can be observed anywhere that there has been a long-term pattern of exploitation or oppression between one group of people who is favored on the basis of ethnicity, religion, politics, and so on, and another who is devalued in a common relationship. With respect to the United States, in their collective experience, people of color harbor conscious and unconscious negative emotions produced by traditions of brutality and frustrations that they and their ancestors suffered at the hands of Europeans and their European American descendants (Vontress et al., 1999).

This concept underscores the historical reality of intergroup relations in the United States. Sadly, U.S. history is replete with examples of negative social encounters between European Americans and people from other cultural backgrounds—from the enslavement of Africans to the systematic destruction of Native American culture to the internment of Japanese American citizens during the Second World War. The motivating forces defining these encounters have generally been racism or other forms of social and economic oppression. Over time, the social and political processes associated with racism and oppression in the United States have taken a collective physical, psychological, and spiritual toll on ethnic groups of color. This toll is often seen in intense negative feelings that members of ethnic minority groups possess, either overtly or covertly, toward members of the majority group. Whether these feelings are justified or warranted at any given point in time is generally rendered moot by the nature of the often exploitative and destructive relationship between White Americans and people of color.

The historical persistence of racism and the hostility that accompanies it have significantly affected the health of many individuals from ethnic groups of color. For example, the higher prevalence of hypertension among African Americans compared with White Americans is linked to personal experiences of racism and the implicit hostility, discrimination, and systemic oppression that accompany it (James, 1994). As a consequence of these historical factors combined with the dominant medical model for health care, little or no attention has been paid to issues of prevention, development, wellness, or optimum wellness for people of color.

ETHNIC DIVERSITY:
THE CULTURAL DYNAMICS OF WELLNESS

The challenges to wellness for people of color must be reframed as opportunities to promote optimal health and well-being. Although few studies of wellness among these populations have been conducted, research that has focused on wellness-related issues suggests that several important constructs must be considered in promoting wellness among ethnic groups of color (Chang & Myers, 2003; Dixon Rayle & Myers, 2004; Garrett, 1999; Mitchell & Myers, 2004; Spurgeon & Myers, 2004). The results of this research, though preliminary, point to the possibility of some dynamics that collectively may advance wellness for people of color. These dynamics expand on the major aspects and areas of the Wheel of Wellness (Myers et al., 2000b) and the Indivisible Self (Sweeney & Myers, 2005). Significantly, wellness promotion initiatives for people of color should be predicated on the understanding of these important dynamics, the most important of which appear to be the relationship between ethnic identity and degree of acculturation, kinship, and spirituality. Considered both individually and collectively, these dynamics offer a powerful deterrent to the health challenges exacerbated by racism and systemic oppression in the U.S. social context. While this list is by no means exhaustive, even a cursory review of ethnic groups of color suggests that these are the more salient influences on physical, emotional, and spiritual well-being. Although the influence of these dynamics may vary across individuals, a working knowledge of them and how they may impact health should frame the context of a culturally responsive wellness paradigm.

The Relationship Between Ethnic Identity, Degree of Acculturation, and Wellness

Promoting wellness among people of color may ultimately hinge on an understanding of the concepts of ethnic identity and acculturation and the relationship between them. An appreciation of this relationship, and its influence on physical, mental, and spiritual health and development, is fundamental to understanding wellness.

Ethnic identity refers to an individual's sense of belonging to an ethnic group and the part of one's personality that is attributable to ethnic group membership (Rotheram & Phinney, 1987). Ethnic identity may be considered as the inner vision that a person possesses of himself or herself as a member of an ethnic group. It forms the core of the beliefs, social forms, and personality dimensions that characterize distinct cultural realities and worldview for an individual. Relatedly but in contrast, acculturation, within the context of contemporary American society, refers to the degree to which an individual identifies with or conforms to the attitudes, lifestyles, and values of the European American–based macroculture. For individuals of color, it is generally a process of willing or unwilling attitudinal and behavioral changes brought about by overt and covert pressure from social, educational, or economic institutions within the macroculture (Lee, 1997a).

All aspects of well-being, including physical, mental, and spiritual well-being, are greatly influenced by a sense of ethnic identity and the degree of acculturation among people of color. The relationship between these two concepts shapes attitudes, behaviors, and values. It can be asserted that wellness is enhanced when an individual has a strong sense of ethnic identity and a high degree of acculturation. This is characteristic of those individuals considered to be *bicultural*. In other words, they have a strong sense of belonging to their particular ethnic group while possessing a high degree of identification with or conformity to the macroculture. Bicultural individuals can move comfortably, both physically and psychologically, between their ethnic culture and the macroculture.

Biculturality, therefore, may give people of color a degree of physical, emotional, and spiritual equilibrium that may contribute to health and a sense of well-being. A bicultural individual would be best equipped to handle racism and other systemic stressors that may threaten a sense of wellness. This is a notion that gives credence to the cultural identity subtask of the Wheel of Wellness and the same factor in the Indivisible Self model.

The Kinship Dynamic

Immediate and extended kinship networks must be considered as primary sources for promoting health and normal development among most ethnic groups of color. Such networks may include immediate and extended family, friends, or community cultural resources. Within these networks can be found hierarchical structures and carefully defined age or gender roles that promote a collective unity among people. This collective unity provides the basis for a worldview that emphasizes communalism rather than individualism (Lee, 1997a). This worldview is best captured in the West African cultural ethos that proclaims, "I am because we are and because we are therefore I am." This sense of belonging is an important dynamic seen in the cultural realities of most ethnic groups of color in the United States.

Indigenous kinship support networks are crucial in providing resolution to both situational and developmental life challenges. In many instances, the supportive dynamics of these networks may keep an individual from needing outside decision-making or problem-resolution assistance. Promoting a sense of wellness among people of color must include an understanding of and appreciation for the role of kinship dynamics in health and well-being.

Spirituality

Spirituality, or how one approaches living and dying, is an important foundation of the cultural traditions of all ethnic groups of color. Wellness is often predicated on the influence of spirituality on the lives of people of color. This is because for many people of color, there is often little distinction made between a sense of the spiritual and the secular. The philosophical tenets inherent in spiritual beliefs influence all aspects of human development in the context of culture for ethnic groups of color.

Within the cultural traditions of many ethnic groups of color, institutions or centers that promote spirituality are important sources of physical, psychological, and spiritual support. Likewise, spiritual leaders have been expected to not only provide for spiritual needs but also offer guidance for physical and emotional concerns (Lee & Armstrong, 1995). From the life-affirming traditions inherent in the emotional expressiveness of the Black church (Richardson & June, 1997) to the power found in the traditional healing practices of Native American culture (Garrett & Garrett, 2002), a spiritual legacy of wellness is readily apparent. This spiritual legacy, with its emphasis on inner resolve fostered by an unwavering belief in an omnipotent and all-encompassing higher power, has been a major defense against the onslaughts of racism and systemic oppression for generations. This legacy lends important credence to the notion put forth in the Wheel of Wellness that healthy people have a strong spiritual center (Myers et al., 2000b) and also supports the inseparability of spirituality from other aspects of wellness as part of an indivisible, interacting whole, as presented in the Indivisible Self model.

THE CULTURAL DYNAMICS OF WELLNESS: RESEARCH DIRECTIONS

Any review of the current health status of people of color in the United States makes explicit the need for a research agenda that advances the concept of wellness. Certainly any discussion about the possible existence and relative importance of key cultural dynamics that promote wellness among people of color suggests that there is a need for further research into the viability of these constructs. Recent studies both support the cultural dynamics of wellness previously discussed and suggest the need for further research for promoting this construct among people of color. One aspect that has been investigated is the subtask or factor of cultural identity, especially in relation to ethnic identity and acculturation.

Chang (1998), for example, in a study of the validity of the optimal distinctiveness theory as a predictor of wellness in Korean American adolescents and young adults, found that acculturation had a significant positive relationship ($p < .01$) with total wellness ($r = .15$) and nine subscales of the Wellness Evaluation of Lifestyle, notably problem solving and creativity ($r = .28$), emotional responsiveness ($r = .23$), friendship ($r = .22$), and love ($r = .20$). Need for differentiation from one's ethnic minority culture of origin had a negative correlation with total wellness ($r = -.25$) and 15 of 17 wellness scales. Chang's result underscore the importance of acculturation as a factor affecting wellness for Korean American youths.

Acculturation was also found to be an important wellness variable in an investigation by Garrett (1996), who examined the relationship between cultural values and wellness among 155 ninth- through twelfth-grade students in North Carolina, including 20 Native Americans. He used a version of the Wellness Evaluation of Lifestyle created with a high school reading level (Myers, Sweeney, & Witmer, 1996b) and an acculturation scale adapted to Native

Americans. The results indicated a significant difference between Native American and non-Native American students on acculturation ($F = 11.84$, $p < .001$), with Native American students scoring lower, and no differences between the two groups on any of the wellness scales, with the exceptions of realistic beliefs and cultural identity for which the minority students scored higher. Grade-level and gender differences in wellness were found.

Garrett (1996) also found that mean wellness scores of bicultural and assimilated students tended to be higher than means of students with traditional cultural values. Assimilated students demonstrated higher self-worth, whereas bicultural students had a higher sense of control. He concluded that acculturation is a significant factor mitigating for wellness and is especially a concern for those adolescents who adhere to traditional ethnic group values.

Dixon Rayle (2002) and Dixon Rayle and Myers (2004) studied the relationship among ethnic identity, acculturation, mattering, and wellness in 462 minority ($n = 176$) and nonminority ($n = 286$) adolescents, using a multigroup ethnic identity measure, multigroup acculturation scale, two measures of mattering, and the Five Factor Wellness Inventory, Teenage (5F-Wel-T; Myers & Sweeney, 2002). No significant differences were found when comparing mean scores between the two groups on any measures; however, significant positive relationships were found between the multigroup ethnic identity and self-direction, love, and friendship ($r = .20, .13$, and $.14$, respectively), and significant negative correlations between the multigroup acculturation and spirituality, self-direction, and love ($r = -.12, -.18$, and $-.09$, respectively). For the minority group only, the multigroup ethnic identity correlated positively with spirituality, leisure, love, and friendship ($r = .16$, $.15, .18$, and $.049$, respectively); correlations with the multigroup acculturation were not significant for any wellness scales.

Rayle (2002) also used structural equation modeling to test the hypothesis that the three-factor model of ethnic identity, acculturation, and mattering would predict wellness among adolescents. For all participants, mattering and acculturation significantly predicted wellness but ethnic identity did not. For the minority group, the model provided an acceptable fit to the data: $F(39, N = 176) = 24.61$, $p \le .01$; comparative fit index $= 1.00$; however, path coefficients revealed that only ethnic identity accounted for a portion of variance in five of the six areas of wellness, which is different from both the nonminority model and the model for all participants. The strongest path coefficients were found between ethnic identity and five of the six areas of wellness (spirituality $= .15$, schoolwork $= .51$, leisure $= .85$, love $= .87$, and friendship $= .76$; $p < .05$). On the basis of these findings, Rayle and Myers (2004) emphasized the salience of the minority versus nonminority adolescent ethnic identity development process and possible differences in wellness between the two groups, and suggested that school counselors need to consider these issues when designing interventions, especially for minority adolescents. They also emphasized the need for more research to discover factors affecting the wellness of minority adolescents (see chapter 7).

Spurgeon (2002) and Spurgeon and Myers (2004) examined racial identity, self-esteem, and wellness in 203 African American male college juniors and seniors attending historically Black colleges and universities (HBCUs; $n = 103$) and predominantly White universities (PWUs; $n = 100$) using a racial identity attitude scale, the Self-Esteem Scale, and the Five Factor Wellness Inventory (5F-Wel; Myers & Sweeney, 1999a). They found that racial identity and self-esteem, together, did not predict wellness. However, a negative relationship was found between preencounter racial identity attitudes and self-esteem, a finding consistent with findings by Cross (1971). Multivariate analyses of variance computed between the two groups revealed significant differences between students from HBCUs and PWUs on self-esteem, $F(1, 201) = 16.73$, $p < .05$, with students from HBCUs scoring higher. Students attending PWUs scored higher on the Social Self wellness factor, $F(1, 201) = 9.51$, $p < .05$.

Mitchell (2001) examined the relationship among acculturation, wellness, and academic self-concept for 262 English-speaking Caribbean American adolescents using an acculturation index, the 5F-Wel-T (Myers & Sweeney, 1999b), and a self-concept scale. A regression analysis indicated that acculturation and wellness together predicted a small but significant proportion of the variance in academic self-concept ($R^2 = .083$), $F(3, 196) = 5.90$, $p = .001$; this finding held for both males and females. Mitchell and Myers (2004) also found a significant positive relationship between wellness and academic self-concept ($r = .16$, $p < .05$).

FUTURE RESEARCH DIRECTIONS

This brief review of the scant available literature makes clear that there is a need for future research to continue inquiry on the relationship between ethnic identity, acculturation, and wellness. Significantly, although ethnicity and acculturation have been considered in wellness research, it is apparent that other cultural dynamics have not been given significant attention. Any research agenda regarding the aspects of wellness for people of color must include further consideration of cultural dynamics such as spirituality and kinship.

Hodge and Williams (2002), in their research on African American spirituality, made a strong case for assessment instruments that operationalize spiritual strengths in a clinically useful and culturally sensitive manner. This notion is advanced by the research of Parmer and Rogers (1997) that examined differences in the health concerns, beliefs, practices, and susceptibility to illness relative to gender and religion in African American churches. In a similar vein, much has been written about the role of kinship systems or social networks and support in facilitating the adjustment and assimilation of ethnic groups of color within the majority group in the United States (Kim & McKenry, 1998). In a review of the literature, Wilkinson (1993) contended that the legacy of the extended family system, with strong emotional ties, is an important aspect of family bonding in these groups.

To investigate this contention, Kim and McKenry (1998) conducted a survey of 9,643 respondents that included African Americans, Asian Americans, White Americans, and Hispanic Americans. The survey measured participation in social activities, organization participation, and social support. The findings from this study suggest the importance of social networks and social support in facilitating the social mobility and well-being of African American, Asian American, and Hispanic families. This study lends credence to the importance of further investigating the relationship that the kinship dynamic has for the promotion of wellness among people of color.

SUMMARY

Considering the systemic challenges to the health and well-being of people of color, wellness is a powerful construct. So much of what is known about the status of ethnic groups of color in the United States is framed within a deficit context. Wellness offers a way to reframe that status and consider it from a positive and developmental perspective. To date, few aspects of wellness among people of color have been examined, and wellness has been linked primarily to ethnic identity and acculturation. Further studies are needed across populations and inclusive of variables such as social support, kinship, and spirituality to further understanding of unique aspects of wellness among people of color. It is incumbent on professional counselors to provide leadership in this area and help promote the cultural aspects of wellness for people of color through research and practice.

DISCUSSION QUESTIONS

1. What are some of the major issues related to ethnic identity and acculturation affecting people of color that might be related to their wellness?
2. How might you design a study to determine the effects of biculturalism on wellness?
3. How might researchers ascertain the value of kinship systems and wellness among people of color?
4. Spirituality is a value among many people of color. What are other components of wellness that might be derived from models like the Wheel of Wellness or Indivisible Self for the purpose of empirically testing their meditating influence on quality of life and longevity for people of color?

WEB RESOURCES

- **The Centers for Disease Control and Prevention (CDC), About Minority Health, http://www.cdc.gov/omh/AMH/AMH.htm,** describes the significance of health disparities in the United States and their relationship to racial and ethnic groups. Disease burden and risk factors, plans for elimination of racial and ethnic disparities, environmental justice, farm worker health, and minority health news are discussed.

- The National Institutes of Health (NIH), Minority Populations Gateway, http://hin.nhlbi.nih.gov/minority/minmain.htm, was created by the National Heart, Lung and Blood Institute to improve the health status of minorities worldwide through forums and workshops on minority health. The organization also has community-based initiatives, including education and prevention programs.
- The U.S. Office of Minority Health, http://www.omhrc.gov/omh/sidebar/healthlinks.htm, was created to eliminate minority health disparities through health policies and programs geared toward racial and ethnic minority populations.

12

Cross-Cultural Wellness Research

Catherine Y. Chang, Danica G. Hays, and Moshe I. Tatar

In prior chapters, research on ethnic and diverse groups and wellness was presented; however, the emphasis has been on research within the United States. In light of the growing communication among countries including the United States, the need to study people from varying cultures has increased. In this chapter, issues related to cross-cultural wellness research are discussed, the importance of considering wellness from a global perspective is considered, and challenges associated with cross-cultural wellness research are explored. Issues related to test adaptation in general and test adaptation issues related specifically to wellness are highlighted, and a long-range agenda for cross-cultural wellness research is explored.

WELLNESS: A GLOBAL PERSPECTIVE

Although over 70% of the population of the United States were non-Hispanic Whites in 2000, that number will decrease to 40% by 2100 while Black, Hispanic-origin, and Asian and Pacific Islander populations will increase steadily (U.S. Census Bureau, 2000c; U.S. Department of Commerce, 1996). Lee (chapter 11) noted health risk factors specific to these ethnic populations. Further, the World Health Organization has established the relevance of examining health problems across nations (http://www.who.int/en/). As a consequence of global changes, interest in cross-cultural research has grown (Hambleton & Patsula, 1998). Hambleton and de Jong (2003) noted that "international exchanges of tests have become more common . . . and interest in cross-cultural psychology and international comparative studies of achievement has grown" (pp. 127–128). To date, much of the research in test adaptation has focused on achievement and vocational testing (Chang & Myers, 2003). Austin (1999) suggested that cross-cultural assessment research should be expanded to include a greater focus on personality traits. The assessment of holistic wellness with various ethnic populations represents a unique assessment challenge, in part because definitions of health and mental health vary across cultures (Larson, 1999) and in part because cultural considerations vary across populations. Ultimately, test adaptations are needed to inform our understanding of wellness across cultures.

CHALLENGES TO CROSS-CULTURAL WELLNESS RESEARCH

While it is reasonable to expect cross-cultural similarities in concerns for well-being and survival, it is also reasonable to expect differences. These differences may reflect, or be attributed to, culture-specific contexts. The challenges posed in cross-cultural research on wellness include identification of the values and behaviors that are common in different cultures and those that need to be treated differently. However, before these similarities or differences can be assessed, both culturally sensitive concepts and measures of wellness must be developed. The Wheel of Wellness (theoretical) and Indivisible Self (IS-Wel; empirically based) models and their respective measures, the Wellness Evaluation of Lifestyle (WEL) and Five Factor Wellness Inventory (5F-Wel), are efforts to begin this process. However, there is still need for both tests such as these and models to be adapted for different cultures. Adaptation requires more than mere translation as it requires consideration of cultural differences in addition to language.

Issues in Cross-Cultural Test Adaptation

Brislin, Lonner, and Thorndike (1973) identified test adaptation as the most difficult aspect of cross-cultural research. Since that time, literature related to test adaptation as well as assessment standards that incorporate test adaptation issues has increased substantially (e.g., *Standards for Educational and Psychological Testing*, American Educational Research Association, 1999; *Standards for Multicultural Assessment*, Association for Assessment in Counseling, 2003). Additionally, the International Test Commission (ITC; http://intestcom.org/itc_projects.htm) has developed guidelines for adapting educational and psychological tests and conducted studies to develop strategies for increasing the validity of cross-cultural test adaptations (see Hambleton, 2001; Hambleton & Patsula, 1998).

Hambleton and Bollwark (1991) noted that engaging in cross-cultural research requires one to first assume that the variable of interest exists in both cultures and second that sufficient differences exist for that variable to warrant further investigation. On the basis of these assumptions, they identified four major problems associated with translating tests: (a) identification of "cultural differences between the source and target populations that may affect examinee test performance," (b) identification of "the appropriate language for testing target population examinees," (c) "finding equivalent words or phrases," and (d) "finding competent translators" (Hambleton & Bollwark, 1991, pp. 11–12). Additionally, Van de Vijver and Hambleton (1996) identified three general types of bias in cross-cultural measurement: construct bias (e.g., the variables to be measured only partially overlap across cultures); method bias (e.g., nonequivalent cultural samples, differential response styles, and administration bias); and item bias.

Despite these challenges, test adaptation does have advantages. Adaptation is both less expensive and more expedient than preparing new tests. For example, there is the possibility of utilizing existing norms for a preestablished test. By adapting tests, researchers enhance fairness by enabling people to take tests in their preferred language (Hambleton & Patsula, 1998). Consistent with the ITC guidelines, the adaptation process includes several steps such as literal translations, forward and back translations, consensus to reconcile differences, and field testing (Hambleton, 2001; Van de Vijver & Hambleton, 1996). Forward translations refer to translation from the initial language to the target language, while back translations refer to independent translations from the target language back to the initial language. The back translation is compared with the initial wording to assure consistency and equivalency of concepts. With careful attention to cultural and language differences, technical methods, and interpretation of results (see Hambleton & Patsula, 1998), the test adaptation process can lead to the development of an equivalent inventory developed in one language yet adapted for use in another language.

Test Adaptations of the WEL and 5F-Wel

To date, the WEL and the 5F-Wel have been adapted into Korean (Chang & Myers, 2003), Hebrew (Tatar & Myers, 2004), and Turkish (Dogan, 2004), with a Spanish adaptation in progress (J. E. Myers & A. D. Rayle, personal communication, September 21, 2003). These adaptations used forward and back translations as recommended by the ITC (see Hambleton, 2001; Van de Vijver & Hambleton, 1996) with bilingual individuals fluent in both the target languages and English. A number of interesting challenges arose in the adaptation processes.

Korean WEL. Problems that arose during adaptation of the English WEL into Korean related to differences between the two languages (i.e., language or item bias). The original WEL used a 5-point Likert-type scale with anchors not easily translated into Korean (i.e., *strongly agree, agree, undecided, disagree,* and *strongly disagree*). These response choices were modified to be more clearly understood in Korean, with rough translations back to English meaning *very much like me, like me/that is me, do not know or either way, that is not me/not like me,* and *that is really not like me.* Additionally, several WEL items were modified to reflect differences in meaning between Korean and English. For example, *stress* was the most difficult concept to translate because there is no equivalent term in Korean as it is understood in English. However, the word itself has permeated the Korean language because of Western influences; therefore, *stress* was used, but spelled out phonetically in Korean.

Because Korean Americans may have a different concept about what drugs are illegal and what drugs are legal (e.g., some Korean Americans might consider prescription drugs or drugs sent over from Korea by family members to be illegal), the item "I avoid the use of illegal drugs" was expanded to include examples, such as marijuana, cocaine, and so forth. Some other modifications included the following: The term *gender* was replaced with a phrase indicating qualities of being female and qualities of being male because there is not a Korean word for *gender*. The item "I usually am not in touch with my feelings" was adapted because *in touch* is a colloquial phrase and not translatable to Korean. *In touch* was replaced with a Korean word meaning, "do not think about or do not pay attention to."

Hebrew 5F-Wel. Similarly, several modifications were made during the Hebrew adaptation process to reflect differences between English and Hebrew. The main problems were not with the quality of the translation but were related to the meanings of specific concepts that may be understood differently in the two cultures (i.e., construct bias). For example, a main consideration was definitions of *spirituality*. In Israel, it is difficult for children to differentiate between issues that are related to spiritual concerns and from those issues examining their degree of religiosity. As a consequence, items on the instrument relating to spirituality issues were worded in terms of purpose and meaning in life, consistent with the scale definitions and theoretical base as proposed by Myers, Sweeney, and Witmer (1996a, 2000b).

Further, because of the unique cultural, religious, and national demographic mosaic of Israeli society, within-group differences merit consideration. Aspects of wellness such as cultural identity might be understood differently by different samples within the population. For example, cultural identity may refer to nationality (e.g., Jews vs. Arabs) or religious affiliation (e.g., Orthodox Jews vs. nonobservant Jews) or both. Because the inventory was only administered to non-Orthodox Jewish adolescents, adaptation of the cultural identity section is still in progress.

Turkish 5F-Wel. Adaptation of the Turkish 5F-Wel resulted in item changes in the gender and cultural identity, realistic beliefs, intellectual stimulation, humor, and friendship subscales to help Turkish college students better understand the meaning of the items. Both the work and self-care subscales had very low alphas. In Turkey, college students primarily do not work but only go to school, thus they likely misinterpreted questions concerning "work." Turkey is largely a Muslim country, and alcohol use is forbidden by their religion, Islam. Thus the question on alcohol use could have been misconstrued. As was true for the Korean adaptation, there may be differences in use of drugs and how these are perceived across populations. Finally, few people drive in Turkey. Thus the question of seatbelt use may have been irrelevant.

Findings From the Korean WEL, Hebrew 5F-Wel, and Turkish 5F-Wel Adaptations

Despite challenges associated with adaptations into Korean, Hebrew, and Turkish, all three adaptations resulted in moderate to high alphas for the majority of the subscales and total wellness. As shown in Table 12.1, alphas for the Korean WEL ranged from .66 (love) to .92 (total wellness). The alphas for the remaining four life tasks proposed in the Wheel of Wellness, spirituality, self-direction, work and leisure, and friendship, were .74, .88, .78, and .68, respectively. It is difficult to determine whether the lower alphas for love and friendship are due to translation limitations or to possible differences in the way love and friendship are conceptualized in American and Korean cultures. These differences could be based on the Asian value of

Table 12.1

Alpha Coefficients for Wellness Scales for U.S. Norm Group and Korean, Turkish, and Hebrew Translations/Adaptations of the WEL and/or 5F-Wel

Wellness Scale/Factor	Alpha coefficient				
	U.S. WEL	U.S. 5F-Wel	Korean	Hebrew	Turkish
Creative Self		.90			
Thinking	.79	.84	.69	.62	.55
Emotions	.80	.84	.71	.59	.62
Control	.72	.88	.51	.71	.61
Work	.73	.82	.78[a]	.75	.55
Positive humor	.80	.86	.68	.71	.69
Coping Self		.92			
Leisure	.61	.81	.78[a]	.75	.78
Stress management	.83	.88	.77	.71	.86
Self-worth	.79	.89	.31	.71	.78
Realistic beliefs	.81	.66	.36	.56	.41
Social Self		.94			
Friendship	.87	.89	.68	.76	.69
Love	.89	.91	.66	.86	.64
Essential Self		.91			
Spirituality	.76	.91	.74	.72	.72
Gender identity	.79	.89	.58	.70	.57
Cultural identity	.75	.86	.50	.48	.49
Self-care	.85	.87	.74	.47	.53
Physical Self		.93			
Nutrition	.66	.90	.79	.73	.80
Exercise	.74	.88	.72	.86	.74
Total Wellness	.84	.97	.92	.90	

[a]Work and leisure scales were combined into one scale prior to initial factor analysis of WEL data, at which point they were separated into two distinct scales.

"relationship harmony," commonly noted in studies of collectivist as opposed to individualistic cultures as a factor underlying interpersonal interactions (Chang & Myers, 2003).

Alphas for the Hebrew 5F-Wel ranged from .47 (self-care) to .90 (total wellness). Subscale alphas for the life tasks of spirituality, work, leisure, love, and friendship were .72, .75, .75, .86, and .76, respectively. The lower alphas for self-care (.47) and cultural identity (.48) in the Israeli sample suggest differing views about health promotion and cultural identity in Israel. Cultural identity for this population may refer to nationality and/or religious affiliations.

Alphas for the Turkish 5F-Wel for the life tasks of spirituality, work, leisure, love, and friendship were .72, .55, .78, .64, and .69, respectively. The lowest alphas resulted for the realistic beliefs (.41), cultural identity (.49), and self-care (.53) scales. Lower alphas for these scales within the Turkish population might be due to translation issues or indicative of differing conceptualization of these constructs in the two cultures.

The reliabilities for the Korean, Hebrew, and Turkish scales were fairly moderate to high though not as high as the U.S. alphas. It is interesting that the lowest internal consistency scores resulted for the same three scales for the Turkish and Hebrew translations—realistic beliefs, self-care, and cultural identity—and these were among the lowest for the Korean translation. However, both the self-worth and control scores were also near .50 for the Korean translation. It is difficult to determine if the lower alphas are due to translation limitations or to possible differences in the way these constructs are conceptualized in the three cultures. For example, could it be that traditional Asian values and a collectivist orientation make issues of personal worth and internal control different for Korean youths, necessitating different norms for what might be called "wellness"? Alternatively, is it possible that the lower alphas reflect the pressures experienced by Korean American youths as they try simultaneously to adapt to their culture of origin and American society? Additional studies with larger sample sizes as well as qualitative methodologies might address these and similar questions and help improve the reliabilities of the scales for these adaptations.

A related issue is administration of assessments in English to individuals for whom English is a second language. Myers, Madathil, and Tingle (in press) administered the English 5F-Wel to couples living in India in arranged marriages and compared their scores with those of couples in the United States in marriages of choice. Differences in 9 of 18 wellness scales were found, with Indian individuals scoring lower on sense of control, realistic beliefs, sense of humor, self-care, gender identity, and work and leisure and higher on spirituality, nutrition, and cultural identity. Whether these differences would remain stable if those in India were administered a wellness assessment in their own language is a question that cannot be answered at this time; however, speculation about this question has implications for future test takers who are asked to complete wellness assessments in English rather than in their primary language. Additionally, these differences may be related to construct bias. Individuals in India might not consider these wellness subscales as related to wellness.

In addition, translations for people whose primary language is different from English (e.g., Japanese, Chinese, Spanish, Russian, French, German) are needed to further the knowledge base of wellness across cultures. Numerous adaptation challenges exist in this area, due not only to culture but also to dialects within cultural groups. Recent attempts to develop a Spanish translation of the 5F-Wel, for example, have been hindered by the awareness of more than a dozen possible dialects to serve as the foundation of the translation. With such significant within-group variability to address, the issues of cross-cultural test adaptation become increasingly complex; hence single methodological approaches are inadequate to fully address the issues.

LONG-RANGE AGENDA: FUTURE RESEARCH

The cross-cultural study of wellness remains largely unexplored; consequently, many questions remain concerning the conceptualization of wellness and the applicability of existing wellness measures across cultures. Given the tenets of wellness—prevention and holistic functioning—and the relative infancy of wellness research (Chang & Myers, 2003), the expansion of studies within and between various populations is warranted. Existing studies of cross-cultural wellness (Chang & Myers, 2003; Dogan, 2004; Tatar & Myers, 2004) call for increased assessment and exploration of wellness in diverse populations through increasing sample sizes in currently considered cultures, expanding the number of communities and cultures studied, and exploring the meaning of wellness for each culture. These goals can be accomplished through a variety of methodological perspectives, including qualitative, quantitative, and mixed methodology designs.

Qualitative Perspective

A difficult task associated with measuring wellness involves deciding how different cultures define wellness. Before one can accurately measure wellness cross-culturally with a quantitative tool such as the WEL or 5F-Wel, it is necessary to ensure that a specific culture defines wellness and the components of wellness in like manner. In conceptualizing wellness, it is recommended that one take both universalistic (etic) approaches (i.e., studies that include a limited list of topics and areas of wellness found to be present across various cultures) and relativistic (emic) approaches (i.e., studies that include culture-specific areas of wellness). To access conceptualizations of wellness, interviewing, observation, and ethnographic methods are useful.

Interviews can be categorized into three types: open, semistructured, and structured (Patton, 1990). Using open interviews, researchers may ask participants to define wellness and provide examples of behaviors and attitudes related to those definitions. Alternatively, semistructured or structured interview questions may be developed based on the dimensions of the Wheel of Wellness and 5F-Wel models to facilitate identification of how participants' conceptualizations of wellness are similar to and/or different from these dimensions. Such techniques can help to assess the major life tasks of a particular culture as related to well-being.

Before using interviews as research tools, one important consideration is the influence of investigator and participant bias. One way that a researcher can minimize these types of biases is by having multiple researchers and participants in the study of wellness, a process known as *triangulation* (Lincoln & Guba, 1985). For example, multiple researchers may question Korean Americans about their conceptualization of wellness and then meet to review and reach consensus on chosen terms and descriptors to ensure trustworthiness.

The observation method is another powerful research tool to assess how different cultures conceptualize wellness; it may be used alone or as a triangulation method for other types of qualitative inquiry (Patton, 1990). Researchers may serve as participant observers or outside onlookers for a particular culture. Through observations it may be possible to assess whether behaviors are congruent with the definition of wellness typically found in mainstream America or in the culture being observed. Alternatively, it would be interesting to explore the "fit" of wellness models to particular cultures and determine how each reflects the five second-order factors of the Indivisible Self (i.e., Creative, Coping, Social, Essential, and Physical) and whether or not these tasks are salient for that culture. Information about how the contextual variables interact in various cultures as well as within cultures could be enlightening.

Ethnographic surveys derived from interview or observational data may be helpful to better understand how different cultures conceptualize wellness. A primary benefit of such surveys is that data regarding wellness can be collected from several participants with less time than with other qualitative methods. The data may be compared with cultural conceptualizations of wellness derived from larger samples or methods.

Quantitative Perspective

Because the WEL and the 5F-Wel have been developed and revised over more than 15 years, they are established measures of wellness in the United States and may prove valid assessment tools in other cultures. In cultures in which these instruments have been adapted, there are many opportunities for further research. Existing versions may be reexamined, possibly revising items for subscales with lower alphas and field testing with diverse samples. Thus, there is a need to expand the use of bilingual individuals for test adaptations and field testing for each culture in which the measures are used. Using several translators allows for a more accurate forward-and-back translation process because one can compare translations and ensure that items mean the same things cross-culturally. More bilingual individuals are needed to make confident inferences about the test adaptation process (Chang & Myers, 2003). Once these issues have been addressed, revalidation of existing adaptations may be necessary.

With adaptations of the WEL and 5F-Wel established for specific cultures, wellness between and within groups may be studied. Exploring dimensions of group differences may be useful in understanding the universality and specificity of various components of wellness. Examining group differences may involve comparing 5F-Wel full-factor scale or subscale components of wellness scores of two or more cultural groups within the United States (e.g., Korean Americans and Turkish Americans, Caucasians and Korean Americans), two or more cultural groups internationally (e.g., Korean Americans and Koreans in Korea), as well as subcultures within a larger culture (e.g., Cubans and Peruvians within a Latino community). For group difference studies, wellness could be assessed with both quasi-experimental and experimental research designs. For example, the WEL or 5F-Wel may be given before and after counseling interventions to measure its impact on a group's wellness (see S. L. Smith, Myers, & Hensley, 2002; Tanigoshi, 2004). The 5F-Wel could be administered after a crisis in a particular culture to assess what wellness factors are affected for a particular subgroup such as children.

Longitudinal studies may help to ascertain whether there are wellness changes across the life span and across cultures in predictable ways. Studying age cohorts of a particular culture may provide insight into wellness differences by factors, for example, related to the Coping Self or Essential Self over time. Understanding the development and transitions of wellness across the lifetime in different cultures could present important findings with counseling implications. Similarly, the study of within-group differences in wellness (e.g., adolescents and adults in a Hebrew community, males and females in Korea, individuals with differing occupational identities in Turkey) or the wellness of individuals with different levels of acculturation (e.g., Koreans, first- and second-generation Korean Americans) may require adapting existing versions of wellness instruments. To date, adaptations of age-level versions (third-, sixth-, and ninth-grade 5F-Wel; see chapter 4) remain a fruitful area for cross-cultural wellness research with children.

An interesting area of study is the determination of correlates of wellness across cultures and examination of how these correlates are similar or different in relation to cultural variations. Variables that could be studied include acculturation level, ethnic identity, stress, hardiness, harmony, and mattering, in relation to any or all of the components of existing wellness models. Chang (1998) reported a positive relationship between acculturation and wellness and a negative relationship between need for differentiation and wellness among Korean American adolescents, a component of ethnic identity that includes denial of culture and wellness. The relationship between acculturation, ethnic identity, and wellness warrants additional research within the Korean community as well as with other ethnic and diverse groups (see chapter 11). Concurrent administration of other personality measures along with wellness assessments in various cultures could help determine the convergent and divergent validity of existing wellness scales as well.

An important step toward establishing the validity of models and measurement instruments across cultures is to analyze the factor structure of wellness scores across populations. Whether existing factor structures can be replicated or whether the factor structure of wellness differs across cultures has not been determined. Moreover, with techniques such as structural equation modeling, the significance of factors affecting wellness in different cultures can be more closely examined and compared.

Mixed Methodologies

Perhaps the most central question in cross-cultural wellness research is this: How is wellness similar and different across cultures? This question may be impossible to answer fully because of the difficulty in ascertaining the meaning of cross-cultural wellness from either a quantitative or qualitative perspective alone. Therefore, it may be helpful to integrate these perspectives to allow for more sound conclusions and application of findings. Mixed methodology involves, for example, assessing wellness using case studies or single-case designs to supplement other methods. Because wellness is conducive to optimal mental health (Myers, Sweeney, & Witmer, 2000b), wellness interventions within counseling may be beneficial; individual wellness data may be collected quantitatively (e.g., administration of the WEL or 5F-Wel) and qualitatively (e.g., use of interviews, observations).

SUMMARY

As wellness becomes a global issue, the need for cross-cultural wellness research increases. Important initial strides in cross-cultural wellness research have furthered understanding of wellness from a global perspective; however, a better understanding of the challenges of cross-cultural research, specifically test adaptation issues, is needed. Translations of the WEL and the 5F-Wel illuminated several important issues in test adaptation and cross-cultural wellness research. Additional studies should build on these findings by including more adaptations and studies across cultures using both quantitative and qualitative methodologies. The changing demographics of the United States and indeed the world make understanding and conceptualizing wellness for culturally appropriate counseling a global imperative.

DISCUSSION QUESTIONS

1. What are some arguments for considering wellness from a global perspective?
2. What are some advantages and challenges to cross-cultural wellness research?
3. Describe and provide examples of methodologies for studying cross-cultural wellness.
4. What are some ways to address both within- and between-group issues when developing adaptations of assessment measures for various populations?

WEB RESOURCES

- **The American Educational Research Association (AERA), www.aera. net/,** is a professional association committed to improving the educational process by supporting scholarly investigation related to education and advocating the dissemination and practical application of such research.
- **The Association for Assessment in Counseling and Education (AACE), http://aace.ncat.edu/,** is a professional membership organization of counselors, educators, and professionals that helps the counseling profession progress by supplying leadership, training, and research in the creation, development, production, and utilization of evaluation and diagnostic methods.
- **The International Test Commission (ITC), http://www.intestcom.org/,** assists in the exchange of information among members and promotes their cooperation on the construction, distribution, and utilization of psychological tests and other educational and psychodiagnostic tools. The ITC organizes international meetings and discussions, advocates the publication of relevant information, and promotes international support for research projects relating to the scientific and ethical utilization of tests.

13

Gender, Sexual Orientation, and Wellness: Research Implications

Brian J. Dew and Kathryn S. Newton

Societal attitudes toward gender and sexual orientation have shifted notably in the past 10 years. Gender roles are gradually changing, along with growing acceptance of minority sexual orientations. As a consequence, counselors need to keep abreast of current trends while identifying remaining obstacles to a client's holistic well-being or wellness. Despite our profession's acknowledgment of these shifting social attitudes and perceptions, empirical efforts to examine wellness in diverse genders and sexual orientations remain limited. In this chapter, a rationale for wellness research based on gender and sexual orientation is provided. Existing studies examining the impact of gender and sexual orientation on personal wellness are reviewed, and recommendations for future research are discussed.

RESEARCH ON GENDER

We live in a gendered world: Sex and gender have influenced family, social, cultural, political, and economic structures for as long as humans have inhabited planet Earth. The one absolute biological distinction—reproductive functioning—has been theorized to be a major determinant in how a society distributes work, wealth, and power and assigns value and status to the individual. Western society has historically treated male and female identities as oppositional, mutually exclusive, and bipolar (Bem, 1995) and has pathologized individuals whose gender identity or sexual orientation deviated from established norms (American Psychiatric Association, 2000). However, this polarization of gender is not universal: Other cultures, namely Native American and Asian, have been known to assign a positive social and spiritual status to individuals who occupy a transgendered identity (Bockting & Cesaretti, 2001). In this section, studies that have contributed to better understanding the relationship between gender and wellness are reviewed, and recommendations for future research are presented.

Noncounseling Gender Research With
Wellness-Related Constructs

Two early studies on men correlated gender role conflict and components of well-being. In a study of 190 male undergraduate psychology students at a large midwestern university, Sharpe and Heppner (1991) found self-esteem and intimacy to be significantly negatively correlated with three out of four subscales of the Gender Role Conflict Scales (O'Neil, 1981). These results suggest that male gender role conflict is significantly related to reduced psychological well-being. Given the likelihood of sample bias, the fact that no participant demographic information related to ethnicity, age, or socioeconomic status was provided, nor was a comparative analysis based on these factors presented, no conclusions regarding diverse populations can be drawn from this study.

In a later study, Cournoyer and Mahalik (1995) found that middle-aged men reported lower levels of conflict than younger men related to success, power, and competition, $F(4, 175) = -2.90, p = .002$, but higher levels on conflict between work and family, $F(4, 195) = 2.01, p = .023$. The generalizability of these results is hindered because of sampling limitations, as the entire sample was college educated and ethnic diversity was severely underrepresented. None of the college-age men were married, and only 28% worked at most part time, as opposed to the middle-aged sample in which all were married, had at least one child, and worked full time. It is thus unclear whether the lower level of work and family conflict in college-age men was due to their age or because they simply had no work or family conflicts.

While these studies provided within-group comparisons of male gender and wellness, other researchers have investigated the complex interaction of biological sex, gender role orientation, and wellness. For example, September, McCarrey, Baranowsky, Parent, and Schindler (2001) used the Extended Personal Attributes Questionnaire (EPAQ; Spence, Helmreich, & Holahan, 1979) to divide 379 undergraduate students from a medium-sized Canadian university into four categories: expressive (high feminine, low masculine), instrumental (high masculine, low feminine), androgynous (high feminine and high masculine), and undifferentiated (low feminine and low masculine). Means from these categories were used in comparative analysis with the six subscales of Ryff's Scales of Psychological Well-Being (self-acceptance, positive relations with others, autonomy, environmental mastery, purpose in life, and personal growth; see Ryff & Keyes, 1995). Results of univariate F tests between the four EPAQ categories and all six of the Ryff subscale scores ranged from 21.04 to 34.60 ($p < .001$).

The androgynous group scored highest on all of the well-being subscales, followed by the instrumental, expressive, and undifferentiated groups. This suggests a strong correlation between androgynous gender orientation and overall wellness. As might be expected, women's scores on the expressive subscale were significantly higher than those of men, $F(1, 372) = 31.21$, $p < .001$, and both the expressive and androgynous groups had significantly more women than men (z = 5.49 and 4.69, respectively, p< .01). However, there was no significant difference between men's and women's instrumental scores, $F(1, 372)$ = 1.02, p > .05, where men might have been expected to score higher. Additionally, results from a chi-square analysis revealed significant differences in biological sex among the EPAQ subgroups, $\chi^2(4, N$ = 376) = 21.32, p < .001. Collectively, these results suggest that, although there do seem to be some significant differences between males and females, it cannot be stated that biological sex and gender orientation are synonymous. The generalizability of this study is compromised because of failure to report the ethnic composition of the sample, and, although the age range of the sample was 18 to 50 years, all of the participants were undergraduate students, and the majority were traditional age (M = 22.1 years, SD = 3.20).

Woodhill and Samuels (2003) studied 196 adult men and women using EPAQ scores to place each in one of seven gender categories: positive and negative masculinity, positive and negative femininity, and positive, negative, and undifferentiated androgyny. Multivariate analysis of variance (MANOVA) results indicated that positive androgynous participants scored significantly higher (p < .05) on three of five assessments of psychological well-being (affect, self-esteem, and social behavior) and on the EPAQ identity scale (p < .001). Positive androgynous individuals scored within 1 point of the highest group score on measures of acceptance of others and locus of control. This study confirmed positive and negative androgyny as separate and distinct constructs and established positive androgyny as a predictor of overall wellness. Unfortunately, correlations between biological sex and gender role identity cannot be determined from the results, as the researchers neglected to publish the ratio of men to women within each gender role classification. Additionally, generalizability is limited by both the small sample size and the overrepresentation of women (78.6%) and college-educated participants (68.4%).

Counseling-Based Models and Research

With the emergence of instruments and models specifically for assessing and studying holistic wellness (see Part I; also see Myers & Sweeney, 2004b; Myers, Sweeney, & Witmer, 2000b), there has been an increase in research on wellness in specific populations. Some research has yielded results specific to gender, although no research investigating the relationships between gender, gender identity, gender role orientation, and overall wellness has yet been conducted.

Myers and Mobley (2004) and Myers, Mobley, and Booth (2003) used the Five Factor Wellness Inventory (5F-Wel) database to compare wellness in traditional (n = 1,249; ages < 25 years) and nontraditional (n = 318; ages > 24 years) undergraduate students and counseling graduate students (n = 263). They found no significant gender differences in Total Wellness scores; however, MANOVAs revealed 10 significant gender differences on second- and third-order factor scores. Women scored higher than men on the Essential Self (F = 10.57, df = 22, p < .001) and one third-order factor of the Social Self:

Love ($F = 10.69$, $df = 22$, $p < .001$). Men scored higher on two second-order factors: Physical Self ($F = 36.90$, $df = 22$, $p < .001$), as well as both of its third-order factors (Exercise and Nutrition), and Coping Self ($F = 40.93$, $df = 22$, $p < .001$), as well as three of its four third-order factors (Stress Management, Self-Worth, and Leisure, but not Realistic Beliefs). These results support the results of September et al. (2001) in that men and women demonstrated both similarities (Total Wellness scores) and differences (select second- and third-order scores) in wellness and wellness risk factors. The authors noted the results had limited generalizability given that the samples of both female undergraduates and of nontraditional students were below the national average (12% and 19%, respectively). In their study of primarily first-year counseling graduate students ($N = 263$), Myers et al. (2003) found additional suggestions of gender wellness differences, specifically in gender identity development. Female graduate students (70% of sample) scored statistically higher than male graduate students (27.8% of sample) on Gender Identity ($F = 10.21$, $p = .002$, $d = .26$), although the effect size was small. Entry-level students but not doctoral students scored higher than the norm on Gender Identity, $F(20, 208) = 3.46$, $p = .001$, suggesting that there may be developmental as well as gender differences in gender identity. Again, caution should be used in generalizing the results of this study to other populations owing to differences in academic major, ethnic, educational, gender, age, and socioeconomic factors.

Connolly (2000) used the Wellness Evaluation of Lifestyle (WEL; Myers, Sweeney, & Witmer, 2000a) along with several job satisfaction and mattering instruments to assess 82 individuals working in several work settings. A multiple regression analysis used to determine the relationships among age, gender, wellness, mattering, and job satisfaction revealed that a significant proportion of the job satisfaction variance was predicted by age and gender ($R^2 = .09$), $F(2, 81) = 4.24$, $p = .01$. In the regression analysis, only gender demonstrated a significant contribution to the variance in job satisfaction, $F(4, 81) = -2.06$, $p = .04$. Additionally, although there were no significant differences between Total Wellness scores for men and women, $F(1, 81) = 3.58$, $p = .06$, men scored significantly higher than women on job satisfaction scores, $F(1, 81) = 8.43$, $p = .005$, and on the work subscale of the WEL, $F(1, 81) = 12.31$, $p = .001$. Connolly noted that indications of gender differences in job satisfaction were contrary to previous research, but also cautioned against the possibility of bias in that the sample consisted entirely of volunteers, was 83% Caucasian ($n = 67$), and consisted of participants from a variety of jobs. It is possible that some of the variance found in job satisfaction may be due to a higher ratio of women than men holding jobs that are inherently less satisfying or that offer lower wages or benefits.

Recommendations for Further Research on Gender and Wellness

To date, the nature and extent of relationships among biological sex, gender, gender role orientation, and gender identity remain uncertain. What exactly is a healthy gender identity, and what are the behaviors, traits, and coping skills that support optimal wellness? Suggested areas for further research include replicating existing studies within and between diverse ethnic, age, socioeconomic, educational, and geographic classifications; developing a better understanding of the basis of gender similarities and differences; further exploring gender identity development; and examining gender bias in research and intervention practices.

Replicating Existing Studies. No single study reported here was broad enough to draw any firm general conclusions about gender and wellness in diverse populations. It will be critical to replicate these studies within and between groups of different demographic compositions. Gender, ethnicity, and culture have been shown to interact as contextual factors in many wellness areas, including social support, occupational stress, and perceived coping skills (Abrams, 2003; Luzzo & McWhirter, 2001), yet minimal assessment has been done in this area. Research has tended toward convenience samples of White European Americans and Europeans, predominantly from within higher education or educated professional environments; thus, minority ethnicities and individuals from middle to lower socioeconomic statuses are seriously underrepresented. A review of recently published doctoral dissertations indicates an increase in research studies that explore the interaction of multiple layers of context, culture, and identity, a development that may be an outcome of the increasing emphasis on multiculturalism in counselor training programs.

Developing Better Understanding of Gender Differences and Similarities. There is also a great need for further examination of within-group differences to identify the strengths and risk factors specific to biological sex and to each of the gender role identities (Myers & Mobley, 2004; Myers et al., 2003; Woodhill & Samuels, 2003). Specific recommendations include researching gender-specific predictors of wellness factors as well as developing and testing gender-specific preventative measures and interventions. It is clear that both men and women would benefit from a wellness approach that considers the strengths inherent in both genders and encourages the development of a variety of wellness traits and behaviors, regardless of gender association.

Exploring Gender Identity Development. The results of existing research indicate that individuals who access positive traits and behaviors from across the spectrum have greater levels of wellness (September et al., 2001) and take greater responsibility for personal wellness than those individuals utilizing negative traits or adhering to a rigid gender role identity. What are the personal, environmental, and social factors that influence gender identity development? Changes in gender roles and norms may not be keeping up with the rapid pace of social, cultural, occupational, and other lifestyle transitions. For example, a young boy socialized to his parents' understanding of male gender norms may, as an adult, face significant challenges in relationship, self-care, and the workplace. Longitudinal studies of gender development and wellness may be helpful in exploring and understanding these and related issues.

Examining Gender Bias in Research and Interventions. Critical, and much neglected, areas of research are the effect of gender bias on data collection and interpretation, practitioner case conceptualization, and intervention choices. Woodhill and Samuels's (2003) study excluded 1 transsexual participant who stated biological sex as male and gender as female. September et al. (2001) excluded 5 individuals who did not indicate their sex, equivalent to 1.3% of their sample. In Myers et al.'s (2003) study, 1.9% of the sample did not indicate gender, and Myers and Mobley (2004) noted that 1% of their sample was missing data reporting gender. In much the same way that data collection forms specifying only single or married exclude individuals who are separated, widowed, divorced, or partnered, forms that present the forced choice of male or female exclude an unknown portion of the sample population. Researchers may be consistently excluding a minimum of 1%–2% of their populations because of noninclusive gender options on data collection forms. Future research, particularly on gender role orientation, could include multiple gender categories to capture data from those with nontraditional gender identities. Additionally, use of both qualitative and narrative research approaches may avoid the possible gender bias in existing assessment instruments and allow historically marginalized gendered individuals to more freely and accurately express their experience and identity.

Another important step is to assess gender identity and orientation, as well as gender assumptions in practitioners, counselor educators and supervisors, and students. It would be interesting to know if there is a gender differential in counselors' theory preferences, case conceptualizations, and intervention choices. Do we tend to select therapeutic styles that reinforce or support our personal or cultural construction of gender? If so, to what degree does our personal understanding of gender enhance or interfere with our ability to promote optimal wellness in our clients and students? If future studies can establish a consistent relationship between biological sex, gender role orientation, and overall wellness, an increase in successful preventative measures and interventions that benefit our clients, our communities, our students, and ourselves will be possible.

SEXUAL ORIENTATION AND WELLNESS

Individuals who are sexually and emotionally attracted to persons of the same sex (i.e., lesbians and gay men) or both sexes (i.e., bisexuals) make up between 6% and 10% of the general U.S. population, representing between 14 million and 22 million individuals (Bagley & Tremblay, 1998). Comprising one of the nation's largest nonethnic minorities, lesbians, gay men, and bisexuals are among the most stigmatized minority groups (Luhtanen, 2003). The social, political, and cultural oppression of sexual minorities is maintained by a heterosexist culture and a societal value system that rewards heterosexuality, supposes it is the only appropriate manifestation of sexuality and love, and "devalues homosexuality and all that is not heterosexual" (Herek, 1986, p. 925).

Some of the social challenges and psychological issues experienced by sexual minorities include stigma management, negative public attitudes, employment discrimination, internalized homophobia, and potential family rejection. Specific strategies related to concealing or revealing one's stigmatized sexual orientation are an essential coping mechanism. Although fewer percentages of Americans favor discrimination based on sexual orientation, nearly 50% of Americans still prefer making homosexuality illegal, and 40% of Americans believe that gay men and lesbians should not be allowed to work as members of the clergy, military, or as elementary school teachers (Newport, 2001). So long as there is no federal statutory ban on employment discrimination on the basis of sexual orientation, the legal status of sexual minority employees in the United States remains a complicated matrix of constitutional case law, local and state ordinances and statutes, and contracts and torts case law developments. The acceptance of socially constructed negative attitudes and myths attached to minority sexual orientations remains the leading psychological factor in psychotherapy with lesbians, gay men, and bisexuals (Williamson, 2000). Finally, unlike other minority groups whose family of origin serves as a buffer against discrimination, a person with a same-sex or bisexual sexual orientation is often unable to seek solace from his or her family of origin. As a consequence, members of this population face unique challenges that may hinder their optimal human development or wellness.

Noncounseling Wellness Models and Research Results

A number of studies have examined gender and sexual orientation as correlates of wellness or predictors of health-related behaviors, such as substance abuse (T. L. Hughes & Eliason, 2002), utilization of health care services (Cochran, Sullivan, & Mays, 2003), nutrition (Andersen, 1999), and exercise (Yelland & Tiggemann, 2003). Yet, researchers have rarely selected holistic wellness paradigms when studying gay, lesbian, and bisexual populations. In fact, such empirical investigations with sexual minorities have appeared only in the last 5 years.

In assessing the relationship between sexual identity, life histories, and wellness in lesbian, gay, and heterosexual men and women, Litzenberger (1998) utilized Ryff's (1989) six-dimensional wellness model that included (a) self-acceptance, (b) positive relations with others, (c) autonomy, (d) environmental mastery, (e) purpose in life, and (f) personal growth. Participants included college undergraduates who self-identified as gay men ($n = 60$), lesbians ($n = 53$), heterosexual men ($n = 60$), and heterosexual women ($n = 56$). Gay men reported significantly higher scores on environmental mastery, which indicated high levels of competence in managing their environment and controlling an array of complex external activities. Conversely, gay men scored significantly lower on personal growth, which suggested greater personal stagnation and boredom. Lesbians' scores were significantly lower than all other groups on total autonomy, indicating heightened concern about expectations and evaluations from others and conformity to social pressures. Morris, Waldo, and Rothblum (2001) investigated the relationship between outness in lesbian and bisexual women and psychological well-being among

2,401 respondents (M = 36 years, range = 15–83 years) in a nationwide survey who completed the Lesbian Wellness Survey (LWS; Morris & Rothblum, 1999). The LWS classifies wellness into the following five aspects of lesbian sexuality: (a) sexual orientation (numerical rating of sexual identity), (b) years out (length of time of self-identity), (c) outness/disclosure (amount of disclosure of sexual orientation), (d) sexual experience (proportion of sexual relationships with women), and (e) lesbian activities (involvement with community). A separate measure assessed personal distress and other threats to psychological well-being. Results from structural modeling found that greater comfort with a lesbian or bisexual identity, enhanced community involvement, and longer period of self-identification were related to increased outness, and greater outness was inversely related to psychological distress and decreased suicidality. Path analysis confirmed the model's fit for subsamples of European American and African American women and to a lesser extent for Latina, Asian American, Native American, and Jewish women.

Ketz and Israel (2002) examined the relationship between perceived wellness (PW) and sexual identity among women who have both female and male sexual partners (N = 69; age range = 17–53 years). They found no difference in PW between women who had sex with both females and males and who self-identified as bisexual and women who had sex with both females and males and self-identified as gay, lesbian, or heterosexual, $t(1, 67) = -0.116, p > .05$.

Luhtanen (2003) used multiple regression analysis to investigate and compare predictors of wellness (i.e., self-esteem, life satisfaction, and depression) in 168 lesbian/bisexual women and 152 gay/bisexual men. No significant difference existed between genders; however, possessing a positive sexual minority identity was the leading predictor of psychological well-being in both men and women. Overcoming internalized homophobia, evidenced by the rejection of negative stereotypes, was the leading predictor of sexual minority identity. Generalizability of these results may be limited, as all participants came from the same northeastern city.

Counseling Wellness Models and Results

Although the majority of wellness research with sexual minorities has utilized noncounseling wellness paradigms, two studies have been conducted using the Wheel of Wellness (Myers et al., 2000b) and the Indivisible Self (Myers & Sweeney, 2004b). Dew, Myers, and Wightman (2004) administered the Wellness Evaluation of Lifestyle (WEL; Myers et al., 2000a) to 217 adult gay men to identify the relationships among internalized homophobia, generalized self-disclosure, coming out to parents, and wellness. Gay men were recruited from bars, professional and social organizations, university student groups, and via snowballing and networking methods. Results of multiple regression analysis indicated that, taken together, scores on all five subscales (intent, amount, positiveness, depth, and honesty) of generalized self-disclosiveness and internalized homophobia were significant contributors to gay men's wellness (R^2 = .35). However, results from chi-square analysis failed to indicate a significant relationship between self-disclosure to either mothers or fathers and total wellness, $\chi^2(6, N = 217) = 8.2, p > .05$, although significant relationships ($p < .05$) were found between self-disclosure to mother and both the self-control ($r = .15, N = 217$) and love subscales ($r = .19, N = 217$). The results support previous research establishing internalized homophobia as one of the single greatest impediments to positive mental health in gay men. Furthermore, results were consistent with past research relating generalized self-disclosure to overall wellness, both in gay and nongay populations. However, for gay men, generalized self-disclosure still could exclude disclosure of information related to one's sexual orientation.

Degges-White (2003) measured the relationship between wellness and overall life satisfaction in women of varying sexual orientations ($N = 221$). The 91-item 5F-Wel (Myers & Sweeney, 2001a) was used to obtain total wellness mean scores and a separate measure assessed respondents' overall satisfaction with life. Using analysis of variance, the author found no significant differences for either wellness or life satisfaction among lesbian, bisexual, and heterosexual women. Results from multiple regression analysis indicated that wellness ($\beta = .295$), $F(5, 117) = 3.375, p = .001$, and household income ($\beta = .239$), $t(5, 117) = 2.755, p = .007$, explained a significant percentage of the variance in life satisfaction in heterosexual women, but only wellness ($\beta = .401$), $F(5, 79) = 3.855, p < .0001$, explained a significant proportion of the variance in life satisfaction among lesbians.

SEXUAL MINORITIES AND WELLNESS: A LOOK AHEAD

The results of existing studies suggest that only minimal differences exist in overall wellness among gay, lesbian, and bisexual and heterosexual men and women. Given the myriad social and psychological challenges facing sexual minorities, these findings are surprising. Measurements of life satisfaction, perceived wellness, and sexual identity between gay and nongay participants were largely similar. The most significant differences existed in Litzenberger's (1998) findings of lower scores among gay men in personal growth and lower scores among lesbians in autonomy. However, all research reviewed uniformly acknowledged the importance of developing a healthy minority sexual identity, which incorporates the rejection of negative stereotypes.

Expressions of an integrated sexual identity among sexual minorities include comfort with self-labeling as gay, lesbian, or bisexual; community involvement; and the development of a supportive network of gay and nongay friends. The length of time the individual has identified as gay, lesbian, or bisexual also influences psychological well-being. The positive relationship between generalized self-disclosure and wellness is similar for both heterosexuals and nonheterosexuals. Yet, for sexual minorities, generalized self-disclosure may exclude disclosure of information related to one's sexual orientation. This form of stigma management applies to employers, friends, and family members, especially parents. In each study in which multiple regression analysis was used, development of sexual identity and the influence of internalized homophobia were leading predictors of overall wellness.

By emphasizing wellness among individuals with a same-sex or bisexual sexual orientation, researchers and clinicians transcend traditional measures of pathological assessment and instead focus on a strengths perspective (Myers et al., 2000b). Counselors and other mental health professionals who encourage the maximization of human potential and health promotion may be particularly suited to assist sexual minorities in overcoming traditional stigma and prejudice. Consequently, additional research efforts are needed to assess wellness in this population. In particular, samples including larger ethnic, age, and geographic diversity; assessment of counselors' knowledge of sexual minority development and recognition of internalized homophobia and heterosexism; and further examination of the relationship between self-disclosure of one's sexual orientation and total wellness are needed.

The sample sizes included in the majority of existing wellness research with this population are mostly small, and the percentage of ethnic minorities has often been too minimal to conduct predictive or comparative statistical analysis differentiated by race/ethnicity. In addition, further examination of the relationship between wellness and sexual orientation throughout the life span, including adolescent and older adult lesbians, gay men, and bisexuals is needed. More research is also required that examines the mental health needs of sexual minorities that cannot be identified by their participation in public forums. In particular, inclusion of sexual minorities who do not belong to social, political, or professional groups; visit homosexual-oriented businesses; or participate in gay-related events is desired. Developing methods such as an Internet-based wellness instrument would allow greater access to gay, lesbian, and bisexual individuals whom otherwise would not be included in traditional research methodologies.

Empirical inquiry into a counselor's knowledge and practice with sexual minority clients is necessary. An assessment of potential counselor heterosexism and its impact on the therapeutic relationship is recommended. Evaluation of the clinician's knowledge of minority sexual identity, the impact of internalized homophobia, and consequences associated with self-disclosure of one's same-gender sexual orientation is advised. In addition, an assessment of awareness among mental health practitioners regarding this population's legal and judicial challenges to employment, housing, and parenting is needed. Furthermore, a comparative investigation of the counselor's willingness to discuss all wellness areas, including spiritual topics with heterosexual and nonheterosexual clients, is recommended.

Additional research that examines the relationship between self-disclosure and total wellness is needed. Results from previous research investigating self-disclosure of same-sex sexual orientation and achievement of optimal sexual identity development are equivocal. However, many counselors still consider full self-disclosure as a prerequisite to reaching optimal well-being or wellness. Research that focuses on the relationship of various motives of self-disclosing to family members, especially parents, and total wellness would also be beneficial. In particular, an investigation of such factors as family communication patterns and parenting style might provide insight into the process of self-disclosing to parents and others. Finally, empirical investigation of disclosure patterns within diverse ethnic populations of sexual minorities is especially needed.

SUMMARY

Although the counseling profession has acknowledged changing attitudes toward individuals with varying gender expressions and sexual orientations, there remains scant investigation into obstacles to their holistic wellness. Although limited in number, results from previous noncounseling and counseling-based research have supported greater wellness in individuals who do not conform to strict gender role identities. Rather, research indicates that individuals who integrate positive traits and behaviors from both traditional masculine and feminine gender expressions achieve greater levels of wellness. However, the generalizability of these results remains limited owing to the lack of ethnic, socioeconomic, age, and cultural diversity in study samples.

The majority of wellness research with gay, lesbian, or bisexual individuals has been correlational or predictive of a variety of mental health concerns, such as depression, substance abuse, or suicide. Yet, rarely have wellness paradigms been used to describe this stigmatized population. The results of existing research studies suggest that only minimal differences exist in overall wellness between heterosexual and nonheterosexual orientations. However, the impact of internalized homophobia on one's development of a healthy minority sexual identity was found to be a consistent obstacle to the achievement of higher wellness for gay, lesbian, and bisexual individuals. Furthermore, the integration of effective stigma management strategies, especially the process of self-disclosing one's nonheterosexual orientation, remains an additional challenge to achieving optimal well-being. More investigation into wellness with non-Caucasian, lower socioeconomic, and older sexual minorities is needed.

DISCUSSION QUESTIONS

1. What evidence exists to suggest that an androgynous gender orientation is related to wellness? What implications could this have for further research related to issues of gender, sexual orientation, and wellness?
2. What conclusions can be made from existing gender and wellness research with regard to diverse populations?
3. What comprises a healthy gender expression?
4. How might researchers determine what counseling techniques are best suited to assist clients with overcoming internalized homophobia and promoting overall wellness?
5. What are the strengths and limitations of utilizing the Internet to conduct wellness research with sexual minorities?
6. How might the effect of counselor bias on wellness in sexual minority clients be assessed?

WEB RESOURCES

- **Gender Education and Advocacy, http://www.gender.org/index.html/,** is a national organization that concentrates on the needs and concerns of gender-variant people in society. The organization is dedicated to civil rights, health, and well-being of everyone in a diverse community.
- **International Gender Studies Resources, http://globetrotter.berkeley. edu/GlobalGender/,** is a site that contains research and teaching materials meant to help integrate Women's and Gender Studies into International and Area Studies philosophy and curricula. General and specific bibliographies and filmographies on issues relating to women and gender in Africa, Asia, Latin America, the Middle East and Arab World, and minority cultures in North America and Europe are included.
- **Psychology of Men and Masculinity, http://www.apa.org/journals/ men.html/,** is a journal published twice yearly focused on the dissemination of research, theory, and clinical scholarship that helps to further the field of the psychology of men and masculinity. The discipline concentrates on how gender and the biological and social process of masculinization affect men's psychology.
- **APA Gender Publications, http://www.apa.org/topics/topic_womenmen. html/,** is a Web site dedicated to investigating contemporary psychological issues affecting men and women. It includes links to publications, as well as press releases, journals, and books relating to gender issues.
- **Parents and Friends of Lesbians and Gays, http://www.pflag.org/,** is a national, nonprofit organization committed to celebrating diversity. Its mission involves advocating the health and well-being of gay, lesbian, bisexual, and transgendered persons, their families, and friends through education, support, and initiatives to eliminate discrimination and attain equal civil rights.
- **The Institute for Gay Men's Health, http://www.gmhc.org/programs/ institute.html,** is dedicated to advocating physical, emotional, and spiritual well-being among gay men and their communities. Multiple health and social issues are part of the sexual health agenda for the Institute, particularly those relating to HIV.
- **The National Coalition for Lesbian, Gay, Bisexual, and Transgendered Health, http://www.lgbthealth.net,** is dedicated to improving the health and well-being of lesbian, gay, bisexual, and transgender individuals by way of federal advocacy concentrated on research, policy, education, and training.
- **The Association for Gay, Lesbian, and Bisexual Issues in Counseling, www.aglbic.org,** is a division of the American Counseling Association dedicated to the education of mental health service providers about issues confronting sexual minorities and their loved ones. Resources on such issues as marriage, coming out, spirituality, and substance abuse are provided.

14

Wellness in the Context of Disability

Margaret A. Nosek

The notion that people with disabilities could achieve optimal health, in all of its physical, psychological, and social dimensions, is relatively new in wellness research. This realization gained momentum with the rise of the independent living movement in the mid-1970s, in which people with disabilities demanded acknowledgment of their civil rights and expected to exert control over their lives. Though still far behind the search for cures, the health of people with disabilities is a topic of growing interest and increasingly the focus of federal research funds. As a result, we now have an embryonic body of literature and the beginnings of discussions about how disability puts to the test wellness theory, research, and practice.

Health and wellness in the context of disability have many unique aspects that are not generally known or understood by medical or mental health professionals. These unique aspects interrelate in a complex web of factors that affect the ability of individuals with disabilities to achieve and maintain optimal health and functioning. Consider the case of a 54-year-old woman who had polio as a child and functions with a motorized wheelchair and a variety of adaptive devices. For all of her work life she has never had the opportunity to use the bathroom during the work day. She lives in an apartment complex that has a shared attendant program, but the attendants are not allowed to leave the premises to provide services. Even if she had not been raised with the expectation that she should be totally self-sufficient, or at least give the appearance of such, and even if she could find someone at the hospital where she works to help her at lunchtime, her wheelchair is too large to fit into the stalls of the public restrooms there. As a result, she has had to train her bladder to retain substantial amounts of urine, and she restricts her fluid intake to a minimum. Although this was uncomfortable, it was not a serious problem until recently. She now gets frequent urinary tract infections and is beginning to have some incontinence. Her internist has no idea how she could change her living and working situation to be more conducive to health, so prescribed antibiotics get her through until the next occurrence.

The presentation of this real-life scenario could go on to include the effect of her managed care plan on getting needed prescriptions from her primary care physician, the restrictions it places on seeing specialists, and the limitations it forces on her behaviors and planned activities, as well as the impact this problem has on her self-image, the complicating effect adaptive equipment (wheelchair, seat cushion) or the lack thereof (including an effective female urinal) has on the problem, and the numerous other health problems that stem from frequent urinary tract infections (e.g., yeast infections, antibiotic resistance, skin breakdowns, lowered immunity to other bacterial and viral infections). The solution to this individual's health problems would require massive changes in policies governing the financing and delivery of health care services, rehabilitation services, social support services, and the research and development of adaptive equipment. Her health might also be improved if disability- and gender-sensitive health promotion education and intervention programs were available to her, perhaps something with peer interaction and information about her potential to improve her health. And so the litmus test for wellness theory, research, and practice becomes the question of how effectively it meets the needs of people with disabilities, a population that all of us will one day join.

Despite the effects of the increased risk of developing health conditions that often accompany disability, the stresses that result from living in a society that imposes many limitations and stereotypes on people with disabilities, and the pervasive environmental barriers that restrict socialization and participation in the community, some people with physical disabilities live in a state of vibrant health and, moreover, are able to maintain equilibrium whenever threats to their well-being arise. Our research at the Center for Research on Women with Disabilities focuses on identifying and enhancing the factors that make this possible. This chapter presents an introduction to health disparities in the disabled population with particular attention to the needs of women; some ingredients of wellness in the context of disability; a brief critique of existing wellness models as they apply, or fail to apply, to people with disabilities; and a list of pathways needed for research that will remove some of the health disparities that people with disabilities face.

HEALTH DISPARITIES AMONG PEOPLE WITH DISABILITIES

Healthy People 2010 reports on health status disparities between people with disabilities and people without disabilities (U.S. Department of Health and Human Services, 2000) particularly on measures of physical activity, weight, tobacco use, mental health, and access to health care. Increased functional limitations are strongly associated with aging and with decreased general health status. People with disabilities and chronic illness are less likely than those without disabilities to report regular physical activity (Rimmer, 1999). Regardless of gender, race/ethnicity, or age, people with disabilities have higher rates of obesity than people without disabilities (E. Weil et al., 2002). People with disabilities may be at least three times as likely to experience depression compared with the general population (Turner & Noh, 1988). Disparities in rates of depression have been documented among women with disabilities (R. B. Hughes, Swedlund, Petersen, & Nosek, 2001), especially in the 18–24 age group (National Center for Health Statistics, 2002). Other conditions that are disproportionately high in women with disabilities are chronic pain, fatigue, hypertension, sleep problems, and circulatory problems (Nosek et al., 2004), stress (R. B. Hughes, Taylor, Robinson-Whelen, & Nosek, 2004), and poor nutrition (Stuifbergen & Rogers, 1997). Because of high rates of unemployment combined with low rates of marriage, women with disabilities are disproportionately likely to lack health insurance and tend to delay seeking health care for financial reasons (National Center for Health Statistics, 2002). The combination of all these population characteristics presents an array of risk factors for cardiovascular disease that far exceeds those faced by people without disabilities but has yet to be investigated.

INGREDIENTS OF WELLNESS IN THE CONTEXT OF DISABILITY

Understanding that living with disability carries with it a plethora of risks for additional health problems makes it difficult to imagine how a disabled person could achieve and maintain wellness. To make sense of this, we must hold all preconceptions at bay and examine disability as one component of the context within which we all live. It is largely society and our environment that make disability a disadvantage. Consider the three-legged cat, functional in every way and even content, only in the eyes of some humans an object of pity. Even with progressive disabling conditions, achieving and maintaining wellness is most closely associated with resilience, perseverance, and creative problem solving, among other survival traits. The investigation of wellness in the context of disability, therefore, demands an understanding of the ingredients in this complex recipe.

My colleagues and I at the Center for Research on Women with Disabilities are developing a model to explore the relation of health, wellness, and disability. As rehabilitation researchers and mental health professionals, we talk about health and wellness using a taxonomy of outcomes that includes (a) physical or biological health, including general health status, body mass index, vitality, pain, functional limitations, chronic conditions, and secondary conditions; (b) psychological health, including general mental health, life satisfaction, perceived well-being, and self-esteem; (c) social health, including intimacy, social connectedness, social functioning, and social integration; and (d) spiritual health, including transcendence, meaning or purpose in life, optimism, and self-understanding.

While most of these concepts are commonly understood in health and wellness research, the term *secondary conditions* has only recently come into use. The presence of a physical disability invites the risk of health complications that are greater in number, frequency, and interference than those experienced by people without disabilities (U.S. Department of Health and

Human Services, 2000). As sequelae to primary congenital or acquired impairment, secondary conditions have been defined as the "physical, medical, cognitive, emotional, or psychosocial consequences to which persons with disabilities are more susceptible by virtue of an underlying condition, including adverse outcomes in health, wellness, participation, and quality of life" (Hough, 1999, p. 186). Secondary conditions may be attributed to overuse, underuse, or misuse of an already weakened neuromuscular system; complications due to original injury, disease, or treatment received; coping and lifestyle behaviors; or environmental and attitudinal barriers that limit access to social participation or health-promoting activities (M. L. Campbell, Sheets, & Strong, 1999). Reducing the prevalence and impact of secondary conditions has, therefore, become an important outcome in research on health and disability.

Beneath this taxonomy of health outcomes lies the intricate web of contextual factors, psychosocial factors, and health behaviors that can have a very different configuration for people with disabilities. The contextual factors that are of interest in our research are either internal to the individual or external in the environment and cannot be easily changed, but some of them can be modified through management strategies. These include health history, disability characteristics, demographics, relationships, values and beliefs, life experiences, and environmental resources. The category of environmental resources encompasses many aspects of the micro-, meso-, exo-, and macrosystems in which people with disabilities live, including access to financial resources, education level, the built and natural environment, technology, information from the print and broadcast media and the Internet, instrumental social support and services, and access to health care services. Of the many psychosocial factors identified in the literature on health promotion, our research has shown that self-efficacy (R. B. Hughes, Nosek, Howland, Groff, & Mullen, 2003) and self-esteem (Nosek, Hughes, Swedlund, Taylor, & Swank, 2003) play a major mediating role in accounting for variance in health outcomes among people with disabilities. Some evidence also exists for the inclusion of social connectedness as a mediator (R. B. Hughes, Taylor, Robinson-Whelen, Swedlund, & Nosek, in press).

Health-promoting behaviors in this model related to physical, psychological, social, and spiritual health are similar to those associated with the general population. Also included, however, are those behaviors that relate to disability management, medication management, personal assistance management, prevention of secondary conditions, and maintenance of assistive devices.

This paradigm stresses the powerful influence of the environment on the behaviors and health outcomes of people with disabilities and the strong mediating role of psychosocial factors. Others have approached health and disability using a different configuration of elements. In the Massachusetts Survey of Secondary Conditions (Wilbur et al., 2002), investigators considered access to health care, personal assistance, technology, health behaviors, and employment, socioeconomic status, health insurance, and social support as mediators of the relation between disability and health. In several other investigations, psychosocial variables emerged as predictors of health outcomes. A study of people with mostly physical disabilities found that depression, sense of coherence, and attribution style accounted for 45% of the variance in severity of secondary conditions (Ravesloot, Seekins, & Young, 1998). Depressive symptomatology was also found to be predictive of self-rated health status in a sample of people with multiple sclerosis, along with other demographic and disability characteristics and the number of comorbidities (G. Roberts & Stuifbergen, 1998). The proceedings of a National Institutes of Health conference on the Health of Women with Physical Disabilities (Krotoski et al., 1996) concluded that constructs of health should use a new definition of functioning that addresses the ability to fill social roles and deal with the stress that accompanies living with disability. Whether this variety of models and approaches for investigating health, wellness, and disability reflects creativity or chaos in the field of rehabilitation remains to be determined. While we wait for insight to emerge, a look at how models of health and wellness in the general literature apply, or fail to apply, to those who live with disability will further illuminate issues of interest to researchers.

MODELS OF HEALTH AND WELLNESS AND THEIR APPLICABILITY TO PEOPLE WITH DISABILITIES

Definitions of health, though multidimensional, present a continuum from illness to health. Blair Justice (Justice, 1998) examined health in the context of illness or disability, referring to people with disabilities who live with vitality and participate in society as the "wounded but well" (p. 11). Although the traditional health–illness continuum may have validity for those with acute illnesses, it "clearly excludes individuals with chronic conditions for whom 'cure' or return to pre-diagnosis conditions is not possible, yet who are still able to perform their social roles"(p. 11). It also excludes individuals who have a life-threatening or debilitating illness and cannot perform daily roles but who manifest well-being and wholeness in the presence of their illness or disability. Justice described this phenomenon as one of redefining oneself and conscious shifting in basic self-identity from one of pain and disability to the inner sense of strength and wholeness.

Health promotion models that are in the general literature incorporate many of the same ingredients as in disability research and posit predictive associations. Mediators and moderators of health are variously listed as sense of coherence, competence, resilience, locus of control, or lines of defense and resistance.

An examination of the assumptions underlying one existing model reveals the roots of some of these shortcomings. Pender's Health Promotion Model (see Pender & Pender, 1987) is based on assumptions of the human capacity for reflective self-awareness, including assessment of one's own competencies, and self-regulation, as well as motivation for creating conditions of living through which people can express their unique human health potential, achieve balance between change and stability, and interact with the environment. These capacities and motivations may be severely compromised by the onset of functional limitation and all the psychosocial factors that accompany disability. Pender's model further assumes that health professionals constitute a part of the lifelong interpersonal environment. Certainly, people with disabilities have greater contact with health professionals than do people in general; however, the quality and impact of that contact may have negative as well as positive consequences. Pender's final assumption is that self-initiated reconfiguration of person–environment interactive patterns is essential to behavior change, which again insufficiently acknowledges the powerful external influences accompanying disability that compromise person–environment interactive patterns and serve to weaken individuals' sense of control over their behaviors and the outcome of their behaviors. The reality of living with disability is that it is not that safe to assume engagement in health-promoting behaviors, or receipt of health care services, or strong motivation to bring about change in one's life will be followed directly by improvements in health outcomes.

As with the other models of health or wellness, all of the elements in Myers and Sweeney's model of the Indivisible Self (IS-Wel; Myers & Sweeney, 2004b; Sweeney & Myers, 2005) can be substantially affected by the presence of disability. Volumes have been written about the disability perspective on spirituality, sense of self, self-direction, coping, work, relationships, physical activity, and the environment. The elements of the IS-Wel model (Essential, Creative, Coping, Social, and Physical selves plus contextual elements) are useful in investigating wellness and disability because they are mutually interactive in their contribution to holistic functioning. The authors stated that

> the significance of the wellness perspective lies in a positive, holistic orientation in which strengths in any of the components can be mobilized to enhance functioning in other areas, and to overcome deficits and negative forces which act to depress, demean, or deny the uniqueness and significance of the individual. (Myers & Sweeney, 2004b, p. 241)

Should a deficit occur in physical or mental functioning, this model suggests that the individual's capacity to be creative and cope, to have a social network, and to access environmental resources could be used to compensate for the deficit toward the achievement of wellness and optimal functioning. Although some might disagree that a disability is a deficit or negative force, it would be worth exploring how disability as a context might affect all other elements of this model.

Several brief observations: First, the factor analysis that yielded the five dimensions of self in the IS-Wel model might have had very different results if conducted on data from people with disabilities. In several of our studies, we have observed stratospheric unemployment rates especially among those with more extensive functional limitations. As a consequence, we found an absence of expected associations between work and education level, thinking, perceived control, problem solving, and coping. Second, within the construct of the Essential Self, several of its dimensions would be difficult to measure for some people with disabilities. Ratings on a measure of self-care can go far beyond the norms for the general population. On a continuum from hypochondria to suicidal self-neglect, the choices some individuals make might be interpreted negatively by an observer but might be appropriate reflections of the reality of living with a disability. An example is choosing to spend only a minimum of one's monthly Supplemental Security Income check (generally under $500) on food in order to supplement the state allowance for personal assistance services to cover extra services needed during an illness. How persons with disabilities exhibit self-care requires careful consideration in any effort to measure their wellness within this paradigm. Measurement and scaling issues are substantial in this highly nonnormative and heterogeneous population.

Finally, the Physical Self in this model is described in primarily behavioral terms. Because functional limitations directly affect one's capacity to engage in exercise, the general recommendation of vigorous physical activity for 20 minutes three times a week is simply inappropriate for a substantial segment of the disabled population. Achieving an aerobic effect is generally considered impossible at the highest levels of paralysis or muscle degeneration (although no research has been conducted on the aerobic effects of sexual activity in such individuals). Some types of exercise are contraindicated for people with postpolio syndrome and certain degenerative neuromuscular conditions, just as very low calorie diets are not recommended for people who have weakness from a disabling condition. In view of these limitations, which go far beyond matters of intentional behaviors, the benefits of exercise may not be as great or may be of a different type for people with disabilities, including those benefits mentioned by Myers and Sweeney: increased strength, self-confidence, self-esteem, positive emotionality, cognitive function; reduced anxiety, depression, and stress; improved chronic illnesses; and preserved social identity. Nevertheless, the possible benefits of exercise or related attention to physical wellness and alternative means for achieving wellness need to be studied more extensively for this population.

PATHWAYS FOR RESEARCH THAT WILL MAKE A DIFFERENCE

For each of the constructs and variables mentioned above in the presentation of models of wellness in the context of disability, entire research careers could be built. Before this line of investigation can become integrated into mainstream wellness research, however, some methodological issues must be addressed.

Qualitative Versus Quantitative Methodologies

There are many, many aspects of wellness and disability that have never been investigated scientifically. In the early 1990s, one such example was sexuality and women with physical disabilities. Because we had very limited literature to help us frame the research question, we designed a study that began with qualitative interviews with 31 women. The striking themes that emerged vastly expanded our understanding of the range of factors that affect and are affected by sexuality in women with disabilities. The quantitative study that was based on these findings yielded numerous avenues for further examination that have occupied our team of investigators for the past decade, including funded studies of self-esteem, reproductive health, health promotion, stress, depression, violence, secondary conditions, and aging (see *Sexuality and Disability,* 2001, Vol. 19, Nos. 1 and 3, for articles about the findings of the sexuality study).

Conversely, gaps in quantitative research can be addressed with qualitative studies. A timely example is the problem of obesity. Bodies of literature exist on biomedical and behavioral aspects of weight management, including well-developed guidelines for clinical practice, with almost no attention given to the fact that many women with functional limitations have no way to weigh themselves, nor are they able to engage in activities that will burn off more calories, nor do they always have a say in the food that is put before them or how it is prepared. Qualitative investigation is needed of the weight management frustrations these women experience to develop interventions that will offer them effective medical and behavioral alternatives.

Case Definitions

As mentioned earlier, the heterogeneity and nonnormative nature of the population of persons with disabilities make definitional issues paramount. Simply identifying the point at which someone should be classified as disabled is problematic. Wearing glasses, having one weak leg, or having trouble with math all indicate functional limitations but are not considered disabilities until they interfere with an important life activity. There is quite an ongoing discussion among disability researchers over the benefits and limitations of examining wellness by disability diagnosis versus level of functional limitation. Conducting research by diagnostic category (sampling only individuals with multiple sclerosis, for example) can allow the range of functioning to be so broad as to make the whole notion of central tendency invalid. We encourage researchers to make functioning a higher priority than diagnosis to increase the generalizability of their findings.

Inherent in this same issue is the question of the importance of age at onset of disability. One would expect that having a disabling condition since birth would offer more opportunity to develop coping skills and understand one's limits and potential as opposed to a traumatic onset disability later in life in which the individual is forced to make a rapid adjustment. Our research has shown, however, that age at onset is a variable of weak association with health outcomes. The effect of individual, parental, and societal expectations and attitudes plus personal behaviors and beliefs tends to override the effect of age at onset.

Wellness by Comparison

When researchers find meaning in their data by making comparisons to a norm, people with disabilities are, by traditional definition, at an inherent disadvantage. Take for example a widely used health status measure, the Medical Outcomes Survey Short Form (MOS SF-36 or SF-10; Ware & Sherbourne, 1992), which measures physical and psychosocial functioning. Participants in each of our studies that include this measure generally scored in the lowest percentile on all the physical subscales. This is good, since our intent is to examine health status among women with the most substantial limitations. However, their scores on the psychosocial subscales, though higher, are significantly below the mean for the general population. This raises the question of whether these individuals are indeed functioning poorly on psychosocial dimensions or if the scale itself fails to distinguish psychosocial functioning from physical functioning. New measures are needed for determining health status independent of functional limitations, thus enabling more valid comparisons within and between groups.

Despite these and many other unresolved methodological issues in disability and rehabilitation research, it is necessary to proceed with examinations of certain urgent topics. Discussed earlier were the obesity epidemic and the need for viable and appropriate health promotion interventions for people with disabilities. Aging issues are of increasing urgencies with the retirement of Baby Boomers but are of two distinct types: those related to people who are aging with disabilities (onset early in life) and those related to people who are aging into disability (onset later in life). Attention is finally beginning to turn toward violence against people with disabilities, not only physical and sexual violence but also emotional violence, neglect, and isolation. The lifelong impact on the health of individuals with disabilities who have experienced these forms of violence has yet to be examined.

While these issues focus on improving the health of individuals with disabilities, they also involve health professionals, systems of health care service delivery, and public policy. Although health care systems are becoming more aware of the special needs of active older adults, they are essentially unprepared to handle the special needs of active, younger adults with disabilities. Primary care practitioners do not yet have the training to recognize the possibility that the symptoms of a disabling condition may be masking symptoms of additional conditions, such as osteoporosis and cardiovascular disease, conditions that are usually not expected until much later in life. Educational research is badly needed on effective means for informing medical and mental health professionals about new models of disability, particularly wellness in the context of disability, and enabling them to incorporate this understanding into their clinical practice.

The theme of inadequacy of health care systems has surfaced in almost every study we have conducted, as related to primary care, reproductive health care, physical exams, breast and cervical cancer screening, access to health care, and health care decision making. The effect of the Americans With Disabilities Act of 1990 should have been much greater in creating better access to medical services, but requirements under its provision for equity of service delivery have low compliance levels in medical settings. This lack of physical access and disparity in the quality of health services received by people with disabilities can have a very strong, direct effect on the prevention and treatment of secondary conditions and other health outcomes. Examples used in this chapter have been drawn largely from research with women and some of their unique needs; the issues and challenges associated with the unique needs of men with disabilities also are deserving of attention.

Solutions must come through informed policy decisions at the highest levels. As illustrated by the case study that opened this chapter, policies in many different venues of health care service delivery can have a direct effect on the power of people with disabilities to achieve and maintain wellness. Ultimately, policies reflect funding decisions, and the funding decisions for research, preservice and continuing education, and the implementation of health promotion interventions, must be made by individuals who regard people with disabilities as active members of society and embrace the empowerment model of wellness in diverse contexts. Our job then is to do all within our power and sphere of influence to promote this new and courageous way of thinking.

SUMMARY

Issues of wellness and optimal health in the context of disability have only recently come to the forefront of wellness research. The complexity of factors that intervene in the lives of people with disabilities to foster or prevent wellness provides challenges for research efforts. Existing models of health and wellness have not been fully examined with populations of people with disabilities, and their relevance remains a question. The extent to which physical activity, in particular, can be construed as a hallmark of wellness for people whose physical condition limits such activity has not been studied.

To address what are significant gaps in the literature, both qualitative and quantitative research approaches are needed. The results of this research will guide policy and practice with the very diverse population of people with disabilities. Before appropriate interventions can be developed, an examination of the factor structure and meaning of wellness in comparison with other groups needs to be completed. Such studies will inform the development, refinement, and testing of models to promote the wellness of individuals with disabilities.

DISCUSSION QUESTIONS

1. If the woman in the case study were seeing you for counseling, what counseling techniques might be most effective in helping her make changes toward a healthier lifestyle?

2. Consider the term *physical fitness* in the context of disability. How could the definition and measure of fitness be modified and expanded to be more relevant for people with physical disabilities?
3. How does wellness in the context of disability differ between men and women?
4. In the section "Ingredients of Wellness in the Context of Disability," environment played a major role. Using the case study given, or one known to you, discuss the various aspects of the individual's environment and how it affects his or her ability to achieve and maintain wellness, in its physical, psychological, social, and spiritual dimensions.
5. With the escalating costs of health care and shortening length of hospital stays, there is a simultaneous reduction in funds to provide attendant care services for people with disabilities. How do these funding policies affect the ability of people with disabilities living in the community to recover from illness and regain their independence?

WEB RESOURCES

- **The National Center for the Dissemination of Disability Research,** http://www.ncddr.org/, conducts research and provides technical assistance and demonstration activities that involve the dissemination and utilization of disability research funded by the National Institute of Disability and Rehabilitation Research.
- **The Disability and Health Team, Centers for Disease Control and Prevention (CDC),** http://www.cdc.gov/ncbddd/dh/default.htm, is part of the new National Center on Birth Defects and Developmental Disabilities at the CDC. The team is dedicated to promoting the health of people who are living with disabilities. This Web site describes that work and shares public health information resources.
- **The American Association on Health and Disability (AAHD),** http://www.aahd.us/, seeks to promote health and well-being initiatives for people with disabilities at the federal, state, and local level; decrease the occurrence of secondary conditions in people with disabilities; and bridge the gap of health disparities between people with disabilities and the general public. The AAHD accomplishes its goals through research, education, awareness, and advocacy.
- **The National Center on Physical Activity and Disability (NCPAD),** http://www.ncpad.org/, advocates the health benefits for people with disabilities that can be obtained through participation in regular physical activity. The NCPAD provides contacts, resources, and assistance needed to pursue options for physical activities for people with disabilities.
- **The Center for Research on Women with Disabilities (CROWD), Baylor College of Medicine,** http://www.bcm.edu/crowd/, is a research center that concentrates on issues related to health, aging, civil rights, abuse, and independent living for women with disabilities. CROWD seeks to promote, develop, and disseminate information to increase

the life choices of women with disabilities so that they may fully engage in the community. Researchers build and assess models for interventions to address particular problems affecting women with disabilities.

- **The Research and Training Center on Disability in Rural Communities, University of Montana, http://rtc.ruralinstitute.umt.edu/,** promotes research to solve problems relating to access to transportation and housing, employment and self-employment, independent living services, health and wellness facilities, and inclusion in community activities, that people with disabilities face in rural areas.
- **The Disability Statistics Center, University of California, San Francisco, http://dsc.ucsf.edu/main.php/,** generates and distributes policy-relevant statistical information on the demographics and status of people with disabilities in the United States. The Center concentrates on how that status is changing with respect to employment, access to technology, health care, community-based services, and other facets of independent living.
- **The Rehabilitation Research and Training Center, Health and Wellness Consortium, Oregon Health and Sciences University, http://www.healthwellness.org/,** performs and distributes findings on research studies and training projects on people with long-term disabilities, their families, friends, health care providers, and policymakers.

15

Wellness Research:
An Agenda for the Future

Earl J. Ginter

A number of authors have disputed the value of relying exclusively on illness-based models—exemplified by the *Diagnostic and Statistical Manual of Mental Disorders* (4th ed., Text Revision, *DSM-IV-TR*; American Psychiatric Association, 2000)—to understand human strengths, healing, and wellness (Gazda, Ginter, & Horne, 2001; Ginter & Glauser, 2004; Ivey, Ivey, Myers, & Sweeney, 2005). A series of rectifying articles introduced and outlined the development of a holistic wellness approach that offered a welcomed alternative to the profession of counseling's frequent reliance on information about pathology to extrapolate an understanding of health (Myers, Sweeney, and colleagues; e.g., see Myers, Luecht, & Sweeney, 2004; Myers & Sweeney, 2004b; Myers, Sweeney, & Witmer, 2000b; Sweeney & Witmer, 1991). In fact, the relationship between illness and wellness is complicated and frequently misunderstood. For example, if a client's reason for seeking assistance is not found to match any *DSM-IV-TR* condition, it does not necessarily follow that a status of wellness should be assigned. From a counseling perspective, it is logical and correct to assert that the absence of illness is not to be equated with the presence of wellness. Fathoming the meaning and implications of this assertion is to comprehend one of counseling's qualities that distinguishes it from other mental heath professions.

Concurrent with the efforts of Myers, Sweeney, and colleagues to develop a holistic model of wellness, there were efforts by other researchers interested in studying and sharing their findings on wellness that resulted in an accumulation of evidence to support and clarify aspects of the new model of wellness that was taking form. The sum of all these research endeavors has served to establish a viable framework to stimulate future studies, theory construction, and applications to counseling. The extent of this research becomes even more impressive if, in addition to tallying the number of published articles, other information sources are considered, such as manuscripts with an "in press" status, doctoral dissertations, available but unpublished research manuscripts, and works in progress. At the time this chapter was written, there were over 70 scholarly resources potentially available for the interested researcher to consider in designing a study (J. Myers & T. Sweeney, personal communication, January 19, 2004). Reviewing these sources of information, a researcher will discover a wide variety of variables that have been investigated so far, such as ethnic identity, job satisfaction, acculturation, stress, homophobia, self-disclosure, attachment to animals, delinquency, moral identity, academic self-concept, country of origin, marital satisfaction, love, sociocultural attitudes toward appearance, career development, and conflict resolution. It is also notable that this body of research has attracted the interest of researchers located at six different universities in the United States and four universities outside the country (i.e., Australia's University of Technology, Israel's Hebrew University, South Africa's University of Port Elizabeth, and Turkey's Haceteppe University). Overall, this amassed body of published and ongoing research points to an emerging and empirically supported wellness paradigm based in counseling and depicted through models that promise to provide counselors with a comprehensive understanding of the nature of holistic wellness and how this understanding can be applied in new ways to assist clients to challenge an array of painful realities and achieve hopeful possibilities.

WELLNESS RESEARCH

Chapters 6 through 14 of this section of the book cover some familiar territories (e.g., developmental, ethnicity, cross-cultural, sexual orientation, gender, and disability issues), yet there is much that will be new to the reader, because each territory is traversed following a wellness path that promotes new sights and insights. These chapters review research studies that aim to probe the boundaries of wellness as wellness pertains to specific areas of human existence. While differences in style and other aspects of presentation are found among the chapters, each chapter does provide underlying reasons for why the studies reviewed are important, magnification of pertinent details related to general wellness research and holistic wellness research, discussion of various studies' weaknesses and shortcomings where this was deemed appropriate, and recommendations for future studies that are based on findings in the professional literature. This last provision listed can serve as an excellent source of ready-made research possibilities for future studies. The recommendations are thought provoking and serve to call attention to the type of studies that will make a meaningful addition to the growing body of wellness research.

Before commenting on the findings presented in these chapters, I should note that my intent is not to provide the reader with a sterile, compressed summary of all the material found in chapters 6 through 14 (which are summaries themselves); rather, the aim is to abstract and highlight findings, comments, conclusions, and recommendations I believe to be relevant issues of concern based on my knowledge and experiences. Obviously the delineated approach will be void of the rich detail found in the chapters themselves.

Paraphrasing Hoffer (1951), who was confronted with similar limitations (note that the term *holistic wellness* is inserted into this quote):

> A reader of the remainder of this chapter may quarrel with what is written. The reader may feel that much has been exaggerated and much ignored. But this is not an all-encompassing chapter. What is written represents a chapter of thoughts, and it does not shy away from half-truths so long as they seem to hint at a new approach and help to formulate new questions about [holistic wellness]. "To illustrate a principle," says Bagehot, "you must exaggerate much and you must omit much." (p. 60)

Even though a considerable amount of work is still required by researchers pursuing answers, and despite the restraints imposed by focusing only on portions of each chapter, I believe that much can be accomplished by commenting on the overall importance of holistic wellness to the future of the counseling profession. In a nutshell, holistic wellness as espoused by Myers, Sweeney, and colleagues can infuse and strengthen those characteristic qualities of counseling that define it as a unique profession.

PRÉCIS AND COMMENTARY ON CHAPTERS 6 THROUGH 14

The authors of the nine chapters establish sound reasons for viewing wellness as more than just a topic of study. They provide explanations that illuminate why a consideration of wellness has real potential to serve as a primary contributor to counseling's future.

Wellness' Developmental Links

Chapters 6 to 10 review the connection between wellness and different developmental periods. Many writers since counseling's inception have recognized that developmental issues represent a central point of interest for counseling. In fact, it has been argued that maintaining a developmental perspective is a defining feature of counseling (Ginter & Glauser, 2004). The importance of research that helps counselors better understand what occurs at different stages in life is an irrefutable need, and such an understanding is fostered in five of the nine review chapters in this section. Specifically, the authors of the first five chapters review wellness research for particular periods of the life span and use terms (i.e., children, adolescents, college students, adults, and later life) in their chapter titles that represent a progressive set of age ranges.

While these chapters cover a wealth of information running the length of the entire life span, when compared with one another, there are observable differences in terms of what each offers to enrich counseling research and practice simply because of differences in the amounts of research completed. This seems to be especially true of chapter 6. When this chapter is compared with the other developmental chapters focused on wellness, one finds that children are grossly understudied in terms of wellness, and this has implications for generalizing the findings to children in general. Caution is strongly advised.

When it comes to applying results to a certain age range, there are other reasons for caution. Rather than a paucity of research studies, the way in which developmental terms are defined can be credited with causing a problem for generalizing the results. For example, even though we are far from achieving a complete understanding of "college students," of the developmental periods reviewed in the first five chapters, a large number of researchers have recruited college students as participants. Most researchers are located at universities, and these researchers often obtain research participants who are readily available (i.e., college students). And because college students are not representative of all humans, there is a problem of generalizing the results to other groups. In fact, the existing body of knowledge pertaining to human psychology has periodically been criticized as being, to a noticeable degree, essentially "a psychology of college students." Simply stated, too many researchers have generalized well beyond what was appropriate. Keeping these cautions in mind, it is now time to comment on each chapter.

Children and Wellness. In chapter 6, Holcomb-McCoy reviews wellness research pertaining to childhood and starts by establishing a rationale for why wellness research is needed. Amazingly, this essentially untapped population may be the easiest to reach in terms of its members embracing the importance of wellness and adopting wellness strategies. Both Maria Montessori and Jean Piaget found children to be innately driven to learn; regrettably, this inner urge to learn has yet to be tapped effectively by many present-day educational methods, which closely match those methods used for decades (Bell & McGrane, 1999). Aside from the issue that the period of childhood may provide the best window of opportunity to have individuals identify and incorporate holistic wellness information as "part of the self," we are still left with the issue of too few studies.

While the available research information does not allow for a global conceptualization of what constitutes children's holistic wellness, there are enough research findings available to provide at least a few tentative conclusions. For example, researchers have uncovered an important finding related to holistic wellness for child participants that has possible implications for theory clarification, future research endeavors, and practical applications to counseling children. Specifically, Holcomb-McCoy reports in chapter 6 that Myers, Sweeney, and colleagues' conceptualizations of spirituality as a key wellness dimension finds support among prepubescent participants. It was found that spirituality (exposure to spirituality through parents) was linked to lower levels of reported behavior problems in children. Holcomb-McCoy also points to results that indicate the existence of a positive connection between children's relationships (parental and peer) and self-concept, childhood development, and academic performance. Even with the sparse research efforts found for this age period, and the research weaknesses that Holcomb-McCoy points out, the findings that can be abstracted from the research literature are promising. A tentative, but seemingly justifiable conclusion taken from Holcomb-McCoy's summary is that guidance interventions to help promote children's wellness can be effective.

While much is left to research in this understudied area, I would suggest that researchers in the future also study what hindrances may be present that impede applying what is uncovered about wellness. As a researcher, theorist, and practitioner, I know personally that even "good research findings" are not always embraced (Glauser, Ginter, & Larson, 2004). For example, school systems are frequently reluctant to make any changes even when these systems need to change. Part of this reluctance is probably due to past experiences with one-dimensional, politicized solutions. For example, "Since our children are not performing as well as children in surrounding states, we should extend the amount of time our children are in school." Elementary logic would suggest the flaw to this solution is that increasing exposure to a system that is already failing children is only likely to decrease performance more and increase frustration more. Counselors should not only be researching wellness but also be researching what are the best means to approach school systems so those systems incorporate what we already know (and will learn) about the effect of greater wellness in the lives of children.

Adolescents and Wellness. Compared with what Holcomb-McCoy was able to uncover, Rayle and Moorhead in chapter 7 discovered a greater body of information available for adolescents. For example, these reviewers found wellness linked with academic self-concept, self-esteem, acculturation, social interests, adult wellness, and social support. Significant findings that are intriguing and deserving of greater research scrutiny also were found with minority students, where ethnic identity was reported in one study to predict a portion of the variance comprising aspects of wellness, for example, leisure, love, friendship, spirituality, and schoolwork.

Even though the number of studies that utilize adolescent participants is larger compared with the number of studies devoted to other ages, so far the published studies with adolescents are not free of problems. Rayle and Moorhead note, "much of the available . . . research includes data about college students rather than middle and high school age adolescents, failing to describe wellness in the younger spectrum of adolescence accurately" (chapter 7, p. 72). This pervasive weakness introduces the possibility of distorted conclusions that in truth may or may not apply to adolescents as a whole. As a consequence, we may know less than such studies may imply. The consumer of research should adopt a skeptical attitude whenever a study's participant information is open to misinterpretation because not enough information is presented.

A final issue to consider, one alluded to earlier, is what does a researcher mean exactly when the term *adolescence* in used? This issue was raised by Rayle and Moorhead themselves during their review of this literature. If physiologically adolescence commences with puberty and ends with completion of physiological development, then the period of adolescence ends nearer the point of graduation than matriculation. The reason for accepting this as the endpoint for adolescence is that neurological maturation occurs after the age of 18. Interestingly, even though a case can be made for classifying the traditional college student as falling within the developmental period of adolescence, this still does not offer a final solution because a subtle and more troubling problem still exists. On closer scrutiny of the entire age range (i.e., start of puberty to final neurological maturation), a person may rightly claim, for example, middle school students should be viewed as "categorically different" from juniors in high school because the actual ages that are said to fall within adolescence's boundaries do not blend together in seamless unity. The crucial point is that when the label *adolescent* appears in a publication's title or content, it is critical for the author to provide adequate information to enable readers to ascertain "what segment" of the adolescent group the researcher is addressing. Such information allows readers to better decide the applicability of wellness findings and whether the researcher analyzed the data by "mixing ages" unrecognizable in the actual world of adolescence.

After considering the aforementioned assertions, it seems reasonable that there are times researchers would want to narrow the age band for studying wellness. For a variety of reasons, this narrowing of focus has occurred with the upper end of adolescence when researchers study "college students." The number of studies devoted to college students is great enough to nourish the growth of professional journals such as the *Journal of College Counseling*. It is this developmental group that is reviewed in chapter 8 by Osborn.

College Students and Wellness. Osborn's efforts uncovered a number of theoretical and topic-driven research studies. Within the entire body of research articles devoted to adolescence, Osborn found that a fair number of authors rely on a wellness perspective as a major conduit to investigate the life of college students. Not surprisingly, a number of the wellness research studies reviewed by Osborn represent "noncounseling efforts," and several represent a piecemeal attempt to amass information about a certain health issue common to a college population. Rather than operating from a holistic wellness perspective, these latter studies are focused primarily on topics such as eating disorders, poor eating habits, time mismanagement, poor sleep habits, poor exercise habits, and so forth. These are topics of wide interest to college health educators and researchers operating from medical-based models.

As pointed out by Osborn, even when a more comprehensive stance has been adopted by researchers, such as Hettler's (1984) wellness model (a hexagonal configured model of health with six components labeled physical, emotional, spiritual, occupational, social, and intellectual making up the six portions of the hexagon), these studies frequently lack the extent or intent of a holistic model such as the one advocated by Myers, Sweeney, and colleagues. In relation to this latter model with its subsequent additions, and changes since its initial formulation (i.e., Wheel of Wellness, Indivisible Self, and Four/Five Factor Wellness Model), Osborn was able to isolate and summarize an emerging body of college student research literature that relies on the model's wellness concepts. Of particular interest was Osborn's reference to the use of wellness profiles that have been used in conjunction with Myers, Sweeney, and colleagues' holistic wellness approach; evidence suggests such profiles can serve as meaningful tools to work with college students because they provide personal snapshots of holistic wellness. Such tools can easily stimulate discussion in a counseling session. Also, in relation to this particular model, Osborn reports researchers have found that both physical and social expressions of wellness are descriptive of the college student population. For example, adequate sleep, exercise, and leisure activities along with friendships and peer networks contribute positively to students' sense of psychological well-being. It is clear that wellness is not confined only to the physical area; wellness is multifaceted and its dimensions cannot meaningfully be separated from the interaction of mind and body.

My experience in working with college students—first-year students through those near completion of degree requirements at the University of Georgia—is congruent with the findings uncovered by Osborn in the literature on holistic wellness. A life-skills course offered at the University of Georgia (the curriculum is available for use; i.e., Ginter & Glauser, 2002) covers topics arranged according to an integrative model that depends on four life-skills dimensions that are used to conceptualize the means to maximize personal strengths and obtain wellness. In this course students complete a life-skills assessment (i.e., Life-Skills Development Inventory—College Form; Picklesimer & Gazda, 1996) that provides rich detail of their standing on the four life-skill dimensions. Students transfer information from the assessment to the Life-Skills Wheel, which visually depicts their personal results. Using the Life-Skills Wheel, students determine strengths, how the various strengths are interrelated, and which life-skills area(s) they want to enhance. The end result of this procedure is to call each student's attention to certain aspects of human functioning that are similar to what Osborn uncovered as important components of holistic wellness. For example, students enrolled in the life-skills course frequently report that possessing skills in the following areas are necessary for optimizing their own healthy functioning: effective communication, health and physical fitness, maintaining relationships, stress reduction, critical thinking skills, multicultural skills, problem-solving and decision-making skills, goal setting, and learning more about "who I am." It is encouraging to discover two counseling models developed independently of each other that complement one another and are uncovering compatible results.

Degges-White and Shurts in chapter 9 and Myers in chapter 10 consider research studies that encompass two developmental periods that involve the greatest span of time in one's life. These authors essentially tackle the question, "What does the literature tell us about wellness from a postadolescent perspective?"

Adults and Wellness. In their review of the adult-based wellness literature cited in chapter 9, Degges-White and Shurts found support to conclude that the term *overall happiness* (or life satisfaction) is linked to wellness. It seems noteworthy that it is at this stage in human development when descriptors like *well-being, subjective well-being, overall happiness, life satisfaction,* and *psychological well-being* are found throughout the wellness literature. On first glance these terms may appear to needlessly complicate attempts to glean an understanding of holistic wellness. Each term would seem to complicate this field of study because each requires its own explanation or definition before it is subjected to empirical scrutiny, but seeing these terms from a different perspective reveals something of value to researchers, not as an added burden, but rather as another means to reveal something about the true extension of what wellness means for the adult.

The truest meaning of wellness is in all likelihood both profound and manifold for the adult. The point can be illustrated through use of a commonly heard complaint that poses the following ingredients: An adult reports being physically well, but from a subjective standard feels that there is something lacking that is needed to make life complete. For this person to achieve a state of true holistic wellness might mean the person must first find what is missing. A conclusion that follows from this illustration is that rather than view such terms as obstacles to understanding, it is more likely that they will lead to advances in our knowledge about wellness because a term such as *well-being* may simply represent one of several "hues for wellness," and in that case each term helps to paint a complete picture of holistic wellness. For example, Degges-White and Shurts concluded from their review that overall happiness (or life satisfaction) was found by various researchers to increase with age. This finding is important in several ways because it counters a widely held notion in society that the opposite is true.

Knowledge that corrects mistaken assumptions is invaluable, because the gained knowledge can be applied in ways to increase levels of wellness. For example, based on certain research results reported by Degges-White and Shurts specifically related to job satisfaction and wellness, we may want to reconsider the reasoning behind some programs offered by employers to enhance employee satisfaction and wellness. Programs that are only exercise based, while helpful, may not net the desired results because the literature on adult wellness also points to the importance of opportunities for creativity, problem solving, and intellectual stimulation. Apparently a wide variety of wellness components contribute to job satisfaction; for example, simply allowing office workers access to exercise machines three times a week is inadequate to achieving more beneficial outcomes.

Later Life and Wellness. Chapter 10 covers Myers's review of the wellness literature. Myers has distilled a wealth of information related to adults entering the last stage of their lives and has effectively compressed it into just a few pages. Again, it becomes clear that researchers, theorists, and practitioners interested in learning how wellness interplays with the last portion of one's life will discover (similar to what is uncovered by Degges-White and Shurts in their review) there is a more extensive wellness nomenclature than a novice to the topic might expect. These terms reflect a reality that is too often overshadowed by the commercialization of values that has artificially created the myth that youthful appearance is a critical measure of one's value. In truth, it turns out that being 100, 90, 80, 70, 60, or other ages in between and beyond does not automatically condemn a person to the flat, dull, and rut-filled landscape that is falsely portrayed in the media. Decades ago Erik H. Erikson (1963) wrote about the positive possibilities occurring at the end stage, succinctly capturing these possibilities in his term *ego integrity* (attaining wisdom is one positive outcome).

The contemporary philosopher and social critic Jacques Derrida (see J. Collins & Mayblin, 1996) has cogently argued that all words (including even those printed in research articles) are essentially nothing more than an imperfect means to symbolically categorize and communicate what is experienced. But language itself—despite its inherent shortcomings—can still reveal truths. One such truth is that things exist for a reason, including certain words. The multiplicity of terms found in the literature reflects this truism; these descriptors expose the older adult's experience of perceived wellness much more realistically than the superficial portrayals resulting from a youth-based culture biased toward physical appearance. Myers mentions terms such as *quality of life, perceived well-being, subjective well-being*, and *life satisfaction*. Considering these terms and Myers's summarization of the literature in light of the earlier chapters, it can easily be surmised that the exact personal meaning of the term *wellness* for each older adult is unlikely to be reported as a type of static state that retained the exact same meaning across all the developmental periods experienced. From a developmental perspective, the personal meaning of wellness grows along with the person.

From a holistic wellness standpoint, Myers's review of 69 studies on aging and wellness uncovered that a sense of control is an important indicator of mental well-being in older adults. Also, specifically referring to a study of 999 older adults, Myers reported that 81% of the participants indicated that experiencing "good social relationships" and "independence" were important factors related to the actual felt degree of "life satisfaction." These studies suggest it is important for older adults to see themselves as capable of having meaningful interactions in environments in which they select to actively participate. Furthermore, a tentative and somewhat crude indicator of global wellness for an older adult may be obtainable by initiating a brief discussion with the older adult. Certain types of comments made by the older adult, such as, "I still rely on myself to get around town to visit friends—whenever I want to," can be a quick, qualitative measure that provides a rough estimate of an older adult's perceived sense of wellness. Unlike some cultures that place a value on age-acquired wisdom, an unfathomable number of lost opportunities are probably occurring on a daily basis for some inhabitants of body-conscious cultures, in which individuals fail to see beyond the "wrinkled face and head of sparse white hair." It appears from the literature that life-affirming, proactive adults who in later life see themselves as being in control of their lives have much to teach all those younger about wellness in general, the many faces of wellness through life's journey, and the process of continuous and healthy adaptation.

Wellness' Connection to Ethnicity, Cross-Culturalism, Gender, Sexual Orientation, and Disability

The remaining four chapters in this section review wellness research from different perspectives that add important findings to those already provided by the developmental perspective. Chapters 11 to 14 summarize the research literature from ethnicity, cross-cultural issues, gender and sexual orientation, and disability factors, respectively.

Ethnicity and Wellness. In chapter 11, Lee lays out a case for studying the systemic challenges confronting an individual's health, specifically in terms of the individual's race/ethnicity. Lee highlights both findings that indicate that a number of systemic factors can contribute to ill health of people of color and findings that indicate that a number of systemic factors can serve as buffers for the negative effects fostered by certain "sick" systems. Consistent findings in the literature point to kinship and spirituality (maintaining an active belief and involvement in a church is one example of spirituality) as powerful health-promoting outcomes provided by some racial/ethnic systems. While Lee's chapter requires reading it in its entirety to appreciate the searing logic and carefully thought out consideration of ethnicity and wellness-related issues, a point that deserves emphasizing is Lee's conclusion that it is clearly advantageous for counselors to adopt a wellness perspective in working with clients of color. Infusion of a wellness perspective enables the counselor to move well beyond a deficit approach to helping an ethnic minority client move toward a deeper understanding of how spirituality and kinship can lead to catalytic movement in the client, enabling the client to pull strength from various systems.

Cross-Culturalism and Wellness. In chapter 12, Chang, Hays, and Tatar address wellness from the cross-cultural perspective. This is an area of study that has the potential to establish a true measure of the universal importance of wellness in the world. In addition to informing counselors of the wonderful array of wellness differences throughout the world, an interest in conducting cross-cultural research also will help researchers isolate commonalities of wellness that are not bound to a specific culture but for the time being remain hidden for any number of reasons including language differences. In the area of holistic wellness, Myers, Sweeney, and colleagues have made strides in assessing wellness from a cross-cultural perspective. Such attempts invariably result in unexpected problems. A classic example entails translating an assessment instrument developed in one country for use in another country. A couple of examples will illustrate this type of problem. In Korean, there is no word that corresponds to the word *stress* as used in American culture, and the word *alcohol* has a different connotation in a Muslim culture compared with American culture. Using the word *alcohol* when its use is forbidden by a culture's religion results in the word taking on a new meaning not originally intended.

Reading Chang et al.'s review, it becomes evident that issues surrounding data collection are a major concern for this area of research. I believe the area of cross-cultural research can serve as the equivalent of a much needed "research speed bump"—slowing researchers down long enough to genuinely start considering what might be the best means to collect data. Cross-cultural research provides counselors with an opportunity to get out of the research rut created by continuous use of the same procedures that have dominated the research literature. Additionally, qualitative approaches to data collection, if used correctly, could net important new findings in holistic wellness research. A radical change in research is not what is being advocated. What is being advocated is a counterbalance to current quantitative approaches with alternative methods, such as are found in qualitative methodologies. Using the same old research vehicles to drive counselors to some distant cross-cultural destination is likely to result in the researcher missing a lot of the unique cross-cultural scenery, scenery that would have made the final arrival much more meaningful and important to our understanding of holistic wellness. For example, an advantage of the open-ended interview approach is that the amount of data collected will easily exceed what can be collected through a typical pencil-and-paper assessment with *agree completely* and *disagree completely* closed-ended choices. I firmly believe using data techniques that are more open ended will help prevent us from missing wonderfully revealing information about wellness in all cultures.

Counselors are well aware of the importance of listening in counseling sessions; the same could be said about preparing for cross-cultural research. Keeping an open mind and listening carefully can serve the researcher well in this area of investigation. Adopting this type of attitude will certainly help the researcher decide on the most appropriate means to collect data. Listening carefully usually reveals unique features of a culture that must be considered to conduct a valid research study. I can illustrate this last point by referring to information I located in two different sources, although both sources provided cultural views that converged in their meaning. The first cultural view was found in a book titled *Native American Wisdom*, a work edited by Cleary (1996). I found the following recorded Arapaho proverb: "All plants are our brothers and sisters. *They talk to us if we listen* [italics added], we can hear them" (p. 19). The second source was Davis's (2001) *Light at the Edge of the World,* in which I read the following story related by a phytochemist who was exploring the use of plants growing in remote areas of the Amazon in Brazil:

> The shaman[s] of the Northwest Amazon discovered how to enhance the effects [of a plant] by adding a number of other plants. With the dexterity of a modern chemist, they recognized that different chemical compounds in relatively small concentrations may effectively potentiate one another. In the case of ayahuasca, some twenty-one admixtures have been identified [two of these additions contain tryptamines]. The only way a tryptamine can be taken orally is if it is taken with something that inhibits monoamine oxidase, the enzyme in the stomach. Amazingly enough, the beta-carbolines found in ayahuasca are precisely the kind of inhibitators necessary for the job. . . . Now I ask you how on earth did they [i.e., shamans] figure it out? What are the odds against finding in a

forest of fifty thousand species, two plants, totally different, one a vine, the other a shrub, and then learning to combine them in such a precise way that their unique and highly unusual chemical properties complement each other perfectly to produce this amazing brew that dispatches the shaman to the stars? (pp. 74–75)

The shamans' explanation was that when experiencing a vision state the *"plants speak to them"* [italics added] (Davis, 2001, p. 75). The explanation given by the shamans is elaborated on by the phytochemist's brother, who says "Imagine what it means to really believe that plants sing to you in a different key, to have a taxonomic system that is consistent and true, based on an actual dialogue with plants" (p. 75).

From two different cultures, the people of each culture indicate it is possible to speak to plants. A true tragedy would be to dismiss such cultural-specific claims as unworthy of consideration. If these cultures can learn by "listening to plants," it seems a researcher interested in such cultures could invest time to listen and learn before assuming he or she knows best about how to collect data about holistic wellness.

Gender, Sexual Orientation, and Wellness. Similar to Lee, Dew and Newton in chapter 13 review research in areas that have the potential to generate passionate debate. Much has changed in terms of the general purpose of research devoted to gender and sexual orientation issues in the last 30 years. Of these two areas, relative to most other research areas reviewed thus far, it is the area of sexual orientation that suffers from a surprising dearth of studies in relation to how sexual orientation intersects with wellness. Dew and Newton were much more successful in finding research to summarize in terms of gender and wellness than sexual orientation and wellness. The number of gender-related studies has grown since the 1960s when gender stereotyping became both an issue for societal consideration and research consideration largely due to various feminist movements. By comparison, the study of sexual orientation's connection to wellness lags behind, not only when compared with gender but also when compared with other areas reviewed in the research section.

There are probably many reasons for the relative scarcity of research in the area of sexual orientation and wellness; some of the reasons are probably tied to the changing landscape of the topic area. Over a relatively brief span of time the terms used to denote one's sexual orientation have undergone changes as a result of the proliferation of viewpoints. When I started my undergraduate program in the early 1970s, abnormal psychology textbooks and other sources were still following the earlier *DSM* nomenclature listing "homosexuality" as a form of mental illness (the American Psychiatric Association voted to remove the term from its list of mental disorders on December 15, 1973; see J. C. Coleman, 1976). In roughly three decades, I have seen both changes of magnitude and changes of fine distinctions marking this area of study, and even to this day issues composing this research area are still undergoing rapid changes (e.g., courts are considering the right of gay and lesbian couples to marry and politicians are calling for an amendment to the U.S. Constitution prohibiting such marriages). It is not surprising that any area of study that generates polarizing public debate leaves much to be studied in general, and specifically in terms of wellness' connection. While Dew and Newton's review of the research literature is informative and provides strong support for a concerted research effort being made in the area of sexual orientation, there are particular areas that deserve immediate attention. Individuals who identify with the label *transgender* represent a group that continues to generate profound levels of sexual superstition, a group that has received very limited attention by researchers even though transgendered individuals are the recipients of extreme levels of culturally symptomatic abuse.

Despite the research limitations found in the area of sexual orientation and wellness, Dew and Newton provide a cogent summary of what has been investigated. Even though some of the comments concerning research to date are not especially surprising, Dew and Newton call attention to a finding they did not expect to uncover: that "only minimal differences . . . in overall wellness among gay, lesbian, bisexual, and heterosexual men and women" (chapter 13, p. 135) are found in the literature. This particular finding, along with some others pulled from the literature, is more intriguing than satisfying because these types of results tend to generate many more questions than answers. Of course it should be pointed out that sometimes finding nonsignificant results mirrors reality and such nonsignificant results can open doors to greater understanding. Using the above report of findings to illustrate a point, one might speculate that the results were due to a systemic factor operating in a manner to buffer the negative effects typically found when individuals or a group is confronted with societal obstacles (similar to the type of buffers mentioned in Lee's review). Regrettably, whether this or other possibilities will retain a status of speculation will largely depend on the number of studies that are conducted in the future to decipher the relationship between wellness and sexual orientation.

Disability and Wellness. The review by Nosek offers a concise overview of wellness as it relates to the life experience of individuals with disabilities, and it is in the opening sentence of chapter 14 that Nosek succinctly captures the essence of what makes this particular body of work so timely. Contrary to conventional wisdom, Nosek notes that "people with disabilities could achieve optimal health, in all of its physical, psychological, and social dimensions" (p. 139). My term for what Nosek accomplishes in this sentence is *concept shattering*. The older and erroneous belief, however, still permeates much of U.S. society, including some professions. Nosek is correct to launch the chapter's beginning by noting the shift that has occurred in knowledgeable researchers' thinking about the relationship between wellness and disabilities.

From a research perspective, based on available studies, Nosek argues that expectancies held toward people with a disability have been found to be a powerful factor related to wellness. Individuals with a disability frequently are affected by the positive and negative expectations held by others concerning their potential. Furthermore, if others generally believe a person with a disability cannot achieve a higher level of wellness, then an *artificial disability barrier* has been created.

Nosek indicates that stereotypical thinking about what the word *disability* means has been found to facilitate the occurrence of stress and can lead to intangible but real obstacles to achieving a state of vibrant health. Nosek also reports that contrary to what is sometimes thought, researchers have found that the actual presence of a disability can serve to hone skills of resilience, perseverance, and creative problem solving. Finally, in addition to the findings applicable to expectations and the potential of disabilities to enhance skill development, Nosek calls attention to fours areas of wellness believed to be relevant for working with clients with a disability: physical/biological health, psychological health, social health, and spiritual health. The last area mentioned pertains to optimism, self-understanding, and meaning or purpose in life. All four areas mentioned by Nosek serve to reinforce the importance of using a holistic counseling approach with this population.

Reading chapters 13 and 14 will invariably inject new considerations and subsequent insights for any reader of this material. Both reviews lead a reader to conclude that students of wellness must take into consideration such factors as sexual orientation and disability.

CONCLUSION

Our life journey from a prenatal void of nonexistence to the eventual postmortem experience represents a journey rich in complexity. Arthur Koestler (1978) appreciated this complexity and conceptualized a means to understand the complexity. Koestler coined the term *holon* to refer to the process by which the multivariate nature of our world interacts. A holon is a self-regulating, organized system that is simultaneously a "whole" and an "element"; in other words each holon in the role of an element contributes to the formation of a more complex holon (or whole) that contributes to the next holon seemingly ad infinitum. An example of such a holon hierarchy was provided to by Koestler (1978) and a version of it follows: Subatomic particles coalesce to form an atom, systems of atoms form a molecule, interacting arrangements of molecules lead to an organelle, organelles come together to form a cell type, cells types interact to create a tissue, various tissues in unison form an organ, organs align their operations in ways to form a biological system, and combinations of systems result in a unique organism. It is the world described by Koestler that interests Myers, Sweeney, and colleagues when they theorize about wellness. It is Koestler's level of thinking that differentiates the term *holistic wellness* from related terms. Myers, Sweeney, and colleagues have proposed holistic models that enable counselors to see their clients as the multidimensional beings they are, which facilitates working with clients more effectively. Also, the model shows an appreciation of innate strengths (dimensions of wellness) that reside in all humans and calls attention to how these strengths may differ depending on how far along the person is on his or her life journey.

Reviewing what might be called mental health literature, it becomes obvious to a distiller of such information that it has been strongly influenced by a clinical perspective that relies heavily on pathology and illness. I do not advocate turning away from this information, because, it has real value; rather, what is advocated is the need for a greater balance of different perspectives. It is clear from the various reviews of research studies that the wellness literature can contribute immensely to establishing this balance.

It is interesting to note that the research on holistic wellness parallels in many ways our new understanding of the world's ecology. Through research, we are discovering that holistic wellness is interdependent in nature; its obtainment requires and contributes to wellness realization in others; it requires preservation of diversity; and its maintenance requires the immediate environment lived in by a person (and the larger systems affecting the person) to be healthy, if that person's spiritual growth needs are to be met (see Bender, 2003, pp. 448–449).

While the phrase *paradigm shift* has made a cyclical appearance in the general counseling literature, the phrase has been misused often by some authors who heralded the coming of a significant change in counseling, which in the end almost always proved to be a false prophesy. The theoretical foundation and research findings that pertain to the wellness model advocated by Myers, Sweeney, and colleagues are a better match for what is coming in the future. As we move closer to mid-century, it is predicted that environmental factors will move to center stage, possibly becoming one if not the most important category of factors to affect physiological and psychological wellness (Bender, 2003). The illness perspective promotes waiting until there is an illness reported before an attempt is made to "cure" the problem. This type of approach will ultimately fail because it is a very poor fit for what is predicted for humankind's future. Relying only on an illness perspective is rapidly approaching a state of obsolescence.

Counseling researchers and practitioners now have a sound basis for advancing the profession's knowledge and practice through methods and techniques consistent with its views on life span, optimum development philosophy, and service to its counselees. The next few decades promise even greater strides not only in the United States and its cultures but in other parts of the world as well.

PART III

WELLNESS APPLICATIONS IN COUNSELING: PROFESSIONAL PRACTICE

The American Counseling Association's (1995) Code of Ethics and Standards of Practice for professional counselors begins with a preamble which states that professional counselors "are dedicated to the enhancement of human development throughout the life span . . . and . . . recognize diversity in our society and embrace a cross-cultural approach in support of the worth, dignity, potential, and uniqueness of each individual" (p. 1). The first section of the Code addresses the counseling relationship, and the first statements deal proactively with the need to address client welfare. These statements establish the following: "The primary responsibility of counselors is to respect the dignity and to promote the positive welfare of clients. . . . Counselors encourage client growth and development in ways that foster the clients' interest and welfare" (p. 1). Embedded in these statements is a holistic, wellness-oriented approach to conceptualizing clients and planning effective, growth-oriented, preventive, and remedial interventions.

The need for counselors to have a knowledge base for practice was addressed in prior sections. This knowledge includes theoretical information and models, and research that informs those models. In Part II, in-depth research reviews and analyses were provided, as well as an agenda for research to further the knowledge base of wellness for diverse client populations across the life span. In this section, the application of knowledge in clinical work is emphasized. Specifically, strategies for working with clients to promote positive change are addressed, with examples provided to promote practical applications in varied counseling settings.

Extensive research on human change processes resulted in the development of a model of stages of change that is described in chapter 16. The preponderance of research using this change model has been conducted with addictive behaviors, and applications to wellness are in their infancy. However, in our work we have found that knowledge of the stages and accurate assessment of client stages are important precursors to planning interventions individualized to client needs for a high probability of success. By matching stages of change with specific interventions, we increase the likelihood that clients will change in positive ways and achieve greater wellness. Strategies for helping clients change, based both on their assessed wellness and assessed stage of change, are discussed in chapter 17.

Since the inception of our work in wellness, our major goal has been to help people make choices to become healthier, happier, and more satisfied with their lives. As professionals, our goal is to do the same in the context of our clinical practice. In chapter 18, a model for applying a strength-based wellness approach in counseling is presented. This model is illustrated through a case example of one of our clients. Her life challenges and presenting issues are described from both traditional and wellness perspectives, and the counseling outcomes based on a wellness approach are described. We believe this example will stimulate creative thinking among our readers that will both allow and empower you to apply wellness concepts in your own lives and work settings.

The Wheel of Wellness, and indeed other wellness models, have presented spirituality as the core characteristic of healthy people. As a consequence, chapter 19 is devoted to a close examination of spirituality and wellness and the application of spirituality issues within a wellness-oriented counseling practice. Cashwell provides a brief review of research on the importance of spirituality, then applies spiritual concepts to the counseling relationship. In chapter 20, Young reviews research related to stress management and wellness and provides concrete strategies for reducing stress through a holistic wellness focus. Both of these authors include stimulating questions for self-reflection and personal growth.

The final chapter in this section presents a wellness-oriented, developmental perspective on diagnosis. Ivey and Ivey reflect on the importance of viewing pathology as a normal response to abnormal environmental circumstances. With this philosophy, counselors can implement successful strength-based interventions with even the most difficult clients described by the *DSM-IV-TR* in terms of personality disorders, while simultaneously avoiding the pitfalls of an illness-based model that defines these individuals in terms of pathology rather than potential.

16

Stages of Change and Wellness

Jane E. Myers and Thomas J. Sweeney

No matter how you look at it, change is unavoidable and it is difficult. And, it seems that no matter how desirable it may be, positive
change does not just "happen." If it did, we would not have a world in
which one-fourth of the global population is obese and two-thirds of
the people in the United States are overweight or obese. One-third of
all individuals would not die of diseases related to the health of their
heart and circulatory system. Violence would decrease, and we would
not have to face the startling fact that 51.9% of women and 66.4% of
adult men report having been assaulted as a child by an adult care-
taker (Tjaden & Thoennes, 2000).

How change occurs and what makes change difficult have been studied for
years and are closely examined in Mahoney's (1991) *Human Change Processes.*
Mahoney noted three assumptions

> on which all psychological and educational services rest: (1) that hu-
> mans can, in fact, change; (2) that humans can help other humans change;
> and (3) that some forms of helping are more effective than others in en-
> couraging or facilitating that change. (p. 254)

Prochaska, DiClemente, and Norcross (1992) presented an evidence-based
model for understanding how humans can change. This model evolved from
studies of successful self-changers and the observation that successful change
occurs in stages and follows a "powerful . . . controllable, and predictable
course" (Prochaska, Norcross, & DiClemente, 1995, p. 15). Moreover, they
paired strategies for change with each stage, thus demonstrating specifically
how humans can intervene to help others change (DiClemente, 1993;
DiClemente & Prochaska, 1998).

In this chapter, the Transtheoretical Model developed by Prochaska and his
colleagues is described. This model is consistent with a wellness philosophy of practice in that it focuses on decision making and intentionality as the
foundation of successful change. In addition to describing the stages, strategies for promoting change in each stage are discussed. Research in support
of the Transtheoretical Model is briefly reviewed. Although little published
research using this model to promote positive change as opposed to ceasing

negative behaviors has been conducted, through our teaching and clinical work we have found that the stage model can be applied successfully using a wellness paradigm to create healthy lifestyles. In chapter 17, the applications of the Transtheoretical Model to wellness are addressed.

STAGES OF CHANGE: THE TRANSTHEORETICAL MODEL

Prochaska and his colleagues conducted interviews with over 200 former smokers who quit on their own without outside intervention. They observed a universal, invariant sequence of stages through which all of these individuals progressed to achieve the goal of smoking cessation. Analysis of these stages combined with efforts to promote change through therapeutic counseling and psychology interventions led to the development of "three organizing constructs of the model: the stages of change, the processes of change, and the levels of change" (DiClemente & Prochaska, 1998, p. 3).

Stages of Change

Stages are viewed as dynamic and motivational aspects of the change process that occurs over time. This concept is important in establishing the uniqueness of the Transtheoretical Model, as change is viewed as a process rather than an event. Moreover, this process involves a progression, in a theoretically linear but often cyclical manner, through a series of five stages (or six, if termination is counted as a stage). It is possible at any time during the change process to regress from any stage back to an earlier stage or to the beginning of the change process itself.

Precontemplation. Precontemplation represents the first stage in the process of change. In this stage, individuals either are unaware of a need to change or are unwilling or resistant to change. People who smoke and cite examples of other smokers who lived to a ripe old age, or people who drink excessively and state that they can control their drinking anytime they want, are viewed as being in denial or resistant to change and are in the stage of precontemplation. They are often not aware that they have a problem, may be unaware of the consequences of their behavior or problem, and lack information about their behavior that might raise their awareness of a need to change.

Contemplation. The move to contemplation from precontemplation occurs when an individual becomes aware of the need or desirability for change. Movement to this stage is not equivalent to a commitment to change; rather, during this stage the person thinks about or contemplates change. The hallmark of this stage is an intention to change within 6 months. This is a time for thinking about change and weighing the pros and cons of change. For successful change to occur, the balance has to shift so that the pros for changing are stronger than the cons against changing.

People who try to change and fail, or who think about the pros and cons of change and fail to make a decision to change, may become *chronic contemplators*. These individuals think about change and express a desire to change, but they lack the motivation to implement a successful change process. Often their attempts at change were begun without attention to stages and resources, and fear of failure may become an important feeling that keeps them stuck in the contemplation stage. Chronic contemplation is much more difficult to change than contemplation alone, as it requires a change in belief systems and one's definition of self—often second-order change.

Preparation. The preparation stage may be easily identified when a person indicates an intention to change within the next 30 days, has developed a plan of action, and has made a commitment to a change process. Many people are tempted to jump directly from contemplation, having become aware of a problem, to action, or concrete efforts to change the problem. The preparation stage, however, is essential for researching and choosing change strategies before commiting to a plan.

Action. In the action stage, people are clearly and concretely working to change. Behavior change occurs during this stage. Vigilance is also required, as relapse is an ever-present possibility.

Maintenance. The maintenance stage occurs sometime after action has begun, perhaps 2–3 months later. A minimum of 6 months is required during which the behavior change is maintained before it can be considered a successful change. However, once having maintained a behavior for 6 months, the individual is able to exit the process of change. Relapse prevention is especially important during this stage.

Termination. Termination is the final stage of the change process. At this stage the new behavior is totally integrated into a person's lifestyle and the former behavior is not a consideration. Some would argue that maintenance, or integration of the new behavior into one's lifestyle, is a lifelong effort for a person with an addictive behavior, and that termination in some instances does not occur. Prochaska et al. (1995) acknowledged the difficulty in achieving this stage and suggested a series of standards that separate lifetime behavior maintainers from terminators. These include a new self-image, no temptation in any situation, solid self-efficacy, and a healthier lifestyle.

Processes of Change

The Transtheoretical Model is an integrative model of behavior change that has been "the basis for developing effective interventions to promote health behavior change" (Velicer, Prochaska, Fava, Norman, & Redding, 1998, p. 1). These interventions are based on recognition of the overt and covert strategies and activities that people use for change within each stage. These strategies have been translated into guidelines for intervention to help people change (Prochaska, DiClemente, Velicer, & Rossi, 1993). Five experiential processes have been identified that are primarily used during the early stages of change, and five behavioral processes are defined that are useful in the later stages.

Experiential Processes of Change

Consciousness Raising. Prochaska et al. (1995) described consciousness raising as "the most widely used change process . . . first described by Sigmund Freud, who said that the basic objective of psychoanalysis was 'to make the unconscious conscious'" (p. 27). Becoming aware of a problem or problem behavior automatically raises one's consciousness. Gaining knowledge about the behavior, from any source including family, friends, or coworkers, readings, media, or health care providers, elevates awareness of the behavior and need to change. An individual who is overweight might benefit from a diet analysis and meetings with a dietician to structure an individualized diet that takes into consideration lifestyle factors such as sedentary employment as well as genetic history and risk factors for illness.

Dramatic Relief. Often referred to as emotional arousal, this process helps people become aware of their defenses against change. Significant, sudden, and powerful emotional experiences, or catharsis, may occur when one becomes aware of the significance of a problem behavior. For example, individuals who learn that their heart attack was the consequence of a sedentary lifestyle are likely to express a strong motivation to begin and continue an exercise program. One of the treatments of choice for excessive drinking is a family meeting in which the person with the problem drinking receives feedback from other family members about the impact of the drinking on their relationships and lives; presumably this provides an immediate and powerful awareness of the extent of the drinking problem and creates a motivation to change.

Environmental Reevaluation. Sometimes objects or people in our environment are part of the problem rather than part of the solution. Careful evaluation can help remove barriers to change and optimize assets for change. For example, having large quantities of junk food in the kitchen can be problematic for someone wanting to lose weight; alternatively, an abundance of fruit and bottled water can be useful substitutes when one is hungry or thirsty.

Social Liberation. Social liberation constitutes an external set of circumstances or forces that creates an environment in which change is increasingly possible. Examples are low-fat and low-carb choices on restaurant menus and no-smoking sections in buildings. Advocacy groups for special interests, including sexual minorities and people with disabilities, are part of this important process of change as they enable and empower the individual change process.

Self-Reevaluation. People wanting to change need to reevaluate their strengths, values, and life goals. Consistency is important, and sometimes a realignment of goals and values will help to bring about successful change. A person who claims to be committed to healthful living yet uses humor with a "put down" component that denigrates others may be challenged to redefine the meaning of healthy humor. This same person may need help seeing the negative impact this humor has on his social relationships.

Behavioral Processes of Change

Stimulus Control. Sometimes it is hard to turn down a chocolate sundae when it is offered; better not to be where the offer can be made. Similar to taking action after environmental evaluation, stimulus control requires removing those things that are connected with a problem behavior, in effect removing temptation.

Helping Relationship. Many behaviors are hard to change alone, and other people can be important sources of support. This can be informal, as in support from family and friends. It also can be more formal, through self-help and support groups. Professional counselors and other mental health professionals can be important resources for change, especially with such hard-to-change problems as low self-esteem and feelings of lack of personal control in one's life.

Counter-Conditioning. Counter-conditioning simply refers to substituting healthy behaviors for unhealthy behaviors, and conditioning oneself to enjoy the new choices. For example, many people overeat in restaurants because of the large portions served and their childhood admonitions to "clean your plate." Not going to restaurants, asking for a doggie bag and putting half of the food away before eating, and sharing a meal with a friend are effective ways to change the negative behavior into a more positive one.

Reinforcement Management. Punishment is not an effective way to change a behavior and is rarely used by successful self-changers. Instead, selective reinforcement or rewards for healthy behaviors are needed. Self-praise, gifts to oneself, or asking others to help administer rewards can be useful strategies. Contingency contracts are a useful strategy in this regard. Self-help groups can be useful for meeting this need.

Self-Liberation. Finally, self-liberation requires that one makes a commitment to change, liberating oneself from the control of the negative behavior in one's life.

Levels of Change

DiClemente and Prochaska (1998) noted that the concept of levels has been studied far less than any other part of their model; however, the complexity of human experience requires attention to multiple constellations of factors that can affect successful change. These include situational issues, maladaptive cognitions, interpersonal problems, family and systems problems, and intrapersonal problems.

ASSESSING STAGE OF CHANGE

To successfully implement the stage model and track change over time, some method of assessing stage of change is necessary. The University of Rhode Island Change Assessment (Cancer Prevention Research Center, n.d.) is a paper-and-pencil assessment of readiness to change. Alternatively, change can be assessed informally with a series of six statements:

1. I have not thought about changing this at all. (precontemplation)
2. I have not thought about changing this at all. (contemplation)
3. I am thinking about changing. I have thought about it a lot. (preparation).
4. I am actively trying to change right now. (action).
5. I have changed in this area, deliberately; I need to work on maintaining the changes I have made. (maintenance)

6. I have made all the changes in this area I want to make right now; there is no problem for me in this area. (termination)

RESEARCH ON THE TRANSTHEORETICAL MODEL OF CHANGE

Extensive research has been conducted on the Transtheoretical Model of Change over the past 15 years. Prochaska and his colleagues have received more than $200 million in grant funds to study the application of the model to problems such as smoking cessation (Prochaska, 1994; Prochaska et al., 1994), excessive drinking (Norcross, Prochaska, & Hambrecht, 1991), illegal drug use (Rugel, 1991), exercise adherence (Marcus et al., 1992), obesity (Logue, Sutton, Jarjoura, & Smucker, 2000), and dietary maintenance following cardiac events (C. J. Frame, Green, Herr, Myers, & Taylor, 2001). In virtually all of these studies, identifying the stage of change resulted in significantly more successful outcomes in terms of changing problem behaviors than occurred for nontreatment individuals or individuals in control groups.

Marcus et al. (1992) studied 236 potential exercisers and found that, following a 6-week intervention, most participants increased their stage of exercise adoption. They noted that prior studies have established that helping people progress just one stage can double the chances of successful action in the near future. Logue et al. (2000) found that the Transtheoretical Model allows physicians to recognize when obese patients will be receptive to specific medical treatments. Frame et al. (2001) found that assessing the stage of change and implementing interventions targeted to the stage resulted in significantly greater adherence to cardiac rehabilitation recommendations, potentially reducing the incidence of a second heart attack for the participants.

SUMMARY

The Transtheoretical Model was developed through analysis of successful self-changers. In this model, six universal, theoretically linear stages of change are identified: precontemplation, contemplation, preparation, action, maintenance, and termination. Ten processes of change have also been defined. Through matching the appropriate processes or strategies to the stage of change, the potential for successful change is greatly enhanced. A significant body of research has been developed using the stages of change model. Though most studies have involved addictive and other problem behaviors, several studies have established the usefulness of the model in promoting change in behaviors such as exercise adoption and healthy nutrition. It is clear that this model has great promise for helping people change in positive ways. By combining the stages of change model with models of wellness, we believe people can be helped to choose and maintain any number of healthy behaviors across the life span.

DISCUSSION QUESTIONS

1. List and explain the stages of change. Think about a behavior or habit you have changed successfully. Can you identify progress through these stages as you experienced this change?
2. Review the processes of change presented in this chapter. Identify a behavior that someone could change, then discuss the appropriate strategies for change based on anticipation that the person is progressing through each of the stages of change.
3. Think about a behavior you might change or have thought about changing. Use the stages of change assessment questions to determine your current stage of change. What strategies might help you move to the next stage?

WEB RESOURCES

- **The University of Rhode Island Cancer Prevention Research Center, http://www.uri.edu/research/cprc/,** is an organization formed to help people live longer and healthier lives. The Web site includes links to publications and resources concerning the Transtheoretical Model and behavior change. A detailed overview of the Transtheoretical Model, including a list of published research articles, may be found at http://www.uri.edu/research/cprc/transtheoretical.htm
- **Clinical Applications of the Transtheoretical Model of Readiness for Change, http://www.crhspp.ca/Docs/clapp.htm,** is an online article that summarizes clinical applications of the stages of change model.

17

Moving Toward Wellness: Habit and Behavior Change

Jane E. Myers and Thomas J. Sweeney

Dictionary.com defines a habit as "a recurrent, often unconscious pattern of behavior that is acquired through frequent repetition; An established disposition of the mind or character" (Retrieved May 18, 2004, from http://dictionary.reference.com/search?q=habit). Automatic behaviors and resistance to change are the hallmarks of habits. As noted in the previous chapter, change is difficult. Changing habits is among the most difficult types of change. If habits are to change, intentional and concerted effort is required. Of course, we recommend changing bad habits and changing in the direction of greater wellness.

Strategies for assessing wellness were discussed in chapter 5, and a strategy for assessing stages of change was presented in chapter 16. In this chapter, a series of steps are presented for creating and implementing a successful self-change process that will result in greater wellness. Examples are provided to demonstrate the important linkages between stages of change and intentional decisions to create greater wellness. In contrast to other chapters, this chapter is written from a personal perspective, and the process of moving toward wellness is defined in terms of creating a personal wellness plan for change. If we can create and implement our own plans for successful change, helping others will be easier as a consequence.

CREATING A PERSONAL WELLNESS PLAN FOR CHANGE

Let us start with the assumption that you or a client you are trying to help has decided to change in the direction of being more well. Given the holistic nature of the wellness models described in Part I and the many different components of wellness, the question of where to start immediately becomes important. To attempt to change a lot of things at once surely will result in frustration and failed attempts at change. To help bring focus and direction to the change process, we recommend completing a series of six steps:

Step 1: Assess wellness and select area for change.

Step 2: Assess stage of change for wellness area.

Step 3: Identify baseline information on behaviors/thoughts/feelings related to area selected for change.

Step 4: Conduct additional assessments to learn more about yourself in relation to the change area.

Step 5: Conduct research to learn about the area of change, benefits of change, and strategies for change.

Step 6: Develop, implement, evaluate, and revise as needed a plan for change.

Step 1: Assess Wellness and Select Area for Change

A holistic wellness assessment begins with either a formal (paper-and-pencil or Web administered) measure such as the Five Factor Wellness Inventory or an informal assessment (see chapter 5). Assume an informal assessment at this point, using scaling questions to examine global perceptions of wellness and satisfaction with wellness. On the basis of this assessment, choose one area in which (a) you are less well than you would like to be, (b) you would like to improve from a state of wellness to a state of high-level wellness, or (c) you are basically well but would like to tweak your wellness by adding a new, positive habit. The change you choose could be something quite "simple" (if ever any change is simple!); for example, although your self-care activities are more than adequate, you floss your teeth only sporadically and would like to do so on a regular and consistent basis. Or, perhaps you have gotten feedback from others that you are a very serious person and you would like to learn to laugh more.

Step 2: Assess Stage of Change for Wellness Area

Next, think about your wellness area. Using the assessment questions in chapter 15, assess and note your stage of change. As you complete the stages of change assessment, note the timeline in which you have experienced the change process up to and including the stage you are now in. Make notes of when you first became aware of a need or desire to change, or when you moved from precontemplation to contemplation. How did it happen? Were other people involved? What did they say or do to help arouse your desire to change? What are some things that would tell you if you were truly in contemplation? If you have moved from contemplation to preparation, when and how did that move occur? What are you doing now to prepare for change? If you are in the action stage, when did you move into this stage? What kinds of things are you actively doing to change? How are you monitoring and evaluating your changes?

Step 3: Identify Baseline Information on Behaviors/ Thoughts/Feelings Related to Area Selected for Change

Think carefully about where you are in the change process. We recommend taking at least a week prior to making any changes to establish your stage and your behaviors, thoughts, and feelings in relation to your change. Using a blank piece of paper, create a behavior change worksheet to define the behavior you want to change. On this sheet, answer the following questions (adapted from Myers & Sweeney's *Wellness and Habit Change Workbook*, 2004c):

- As of today's date (note the date), what behavior would you like to change?
- How long have you been aware of/engaged in this behavior?
- When and how did you first become aware of this behavior?
- How do others react to this behavior? What feedback have you gotten?
- Have you tried to change this behavior before? When? How often? What has been the result?
- What barriers do you think will prevent you from changing this behavior successfully?

Next, create a worksheet or use the worksheet in Figure 17.1 to monitor your behavior for at least 7 days. If you truly want your plan to succeed, knowing yourself and your current behaviors and reactions is essential.

Step 4: Conduct Additional Assessments to Learn More About Yourself and Your Change Area

The more you know about yourself, the more you can draw on strengths and resources to help yourself change. Similarly, the more specifically you know about your behaviors, the more easily you can identify your pitfalls for the change process. So, it is important to find out as much as possible about

Figure 17.1
Behavior Monitoring Worksheet

Behavior Monitoring/Recording Worksheet

Define the behavior you want to change:

Date or day/time	What you did (the behavior)	Location	Observers/ others involved	Your thoughts/ feelings
1.				
2.				
3.				
4.				
5.				
6.				
7.				

Note. Copyright © J. E. Myers & T. J. Sweeney, 2004c, reprinted with permission.

yourself in relation to your area selected for change. Useful sources of information include helping relationships, Web-based assessments, and expert consultations. If you are interested in physical fitness, for example, a visit to your physician to assure that you do not have unknown (or known) health issues that might be affected by exercise, or a visit to a personal trainer for an evaluation, could be helpful. If you want to enhance your self-worth, getting help to complete available self-worth assessments could be important for identifying which areas of functioning or what components of self-worth are most important for your initial wellness efforts.

Step 5: Conduct Research to Learn About the Area of Change, Benefits of Change, and Strategies for Change

Sources of information about all aspects of wellness are abundant—libraries, the Internet, family, friends, and helping professionals are some of the more obvious ones. Community education programs where you can take classes in martial arts, yoga, Pilates, the art of making healthy salads, or becoming comfortable with public speaking are examples of other resources that could be useful in the development of your plan. Many agencies and programs, including medical settings, provide useful brochures to help you learn about a particular area of change.

Step 6: Develop, Implement, Evaluate, and Revise as Needed a Plan for Change

Finally, after learning all you can about yourself, your current habits and attitudes, your history, your area of change, and your stage of change, you are ready to begin the process of developing a wellness plan for change. The more concrete and tangible your plan, the greater your potential for success. The less you make assumptions and the more you anticipate and plan, the more easily you will realize your goals. Writing down your plan will help you think about possible strategies and alternatives and will make your plan more concrete. The following items should be included in your plan:

- What are your goals? What is the behavior you want to change and what do you want the results to be?
  - State your long-range goals in terms of your ultimate desired outcome. For example, you might say, "I want exercise to be a regular part of my life that I never have to think about; I just do it every day," "I will enjoy a hearty and healthy laugh at least once each day," "I will have a quiet time for me at least 10 minutes per day, every day, in the morning before I go to work," or "I will floss my teeth daily." When you achieve your long-range goal and reach maintenance or termination, you will miss your target behavior if you do not do it—because it will be your new habit.
  - State your short-range goals in terms of those things you will do on a daily and weekly basis to reach your long-range goal. Again, the more specific and concrete you can be, the greater your chances for

successful change. Note not only the new behaviors but also the time of day you will do them and the amount of time you will devote to this change. An important short-range goal is visual imagery, so plan to spend some time each day thinking about yourself and seeing yourself engaging in your new behavior on a regular basis—and enjoying it!

- What are the methods you will use to reach each goal? Here you need to think about and note the "who, what, when, where, and how" of your behavior change process.
- List and explain the tasks and activities you will use to change your behavior, and include timelines that will result in accomplishment of both your short- and long-range goals.
- Explain the assessment methods (baseline, progress, completion) you will use to monitor your progress and determine the success of your plan. It will be helpful to use a calendar to record and monitor your daily change efforts. Stickers with smiley faces can be positively reinforcing as you look back over your week or month and see all of the days that you successfully engaged in your new behavior.
- List and explain the reinforcers, positive and negative, you will use to promote success. Remember that other people can be very important as reinforcers. One of the most important steps you can take in the change process is to "go public" and let other people know about your desire to change (Prochaska, Norcross, & DiClemente, 1995). Once they know, others can encourage you in your change process and be important sources of support. Be careful not to reward yourself with your problem behavior. For example, if you are trying to lose weight and meet your goals for the week, a banana split may not be the best reward. A new book, movie, dinner with a friend, relaxing bubble bath, or purchase of something you especially like could be a better way to "treat yourself" when you reach a goal.
- List and describe supports and resources you will use to help you change. This could be people, or it could be books, materials, movies, or just about anything that you find meaningful in relation to your area of change. Often information is essential for change; for example, you may need to know more about healthy food choices to create a life-changing diet that you find both satisfying and enjoyable. Sometimes resources are important; for example, we found it easier to implement a daily teeth-flossing plan when Teflon-coated floss became available. You may need help identifying resources, and this could be an important time to seek informal or formal helping relationships to increase the potential for success of your plan for change.
- Develop a timeline for your change, being sure to integrate the stages of change and the time associated with each. For example, if you are planning to move from contemplation to preparation to action, be sure to include 30 days or so for preparation to assure the success of your plan. Following your plan for at least 6 months will be important to

make the behavior change into a new habit or automatic behavior. Including future projections for the change plan over weeks, months, and even years will increase your chances of success.

- Once you have developed your plan, take a moment to reflect on the impact of change on holistic wellness. What other areas of your life will be affected by your change? Noting these areas can be reinforcing and contribute to the overall success of your wellness and habit change plan.
- Building in periodic evaluations of your plan and being willing to modify a plan that is not working well are also important to assure successful change. Rather than ignoring a plan that is not working, reconsider the importance of the change area, and be willing to modify the plan to achieve successful outcomes. When all else fails, be willing to get some outside help to create a new vision of yourself in relation to the change you want to make.

THE IMPORTANCE OF HELPING RELATIONSHIPS

Several times in this chapter we have emphasized the importance of helping relationships in the development and implementation of successful wellness plans. Although we believe that everyone has the potential to be a successful self-changer, we also realize that habits are hard to change, and some are very hard to change. Helping relationships can promote the change process and often help us create change more quickly than we otherwise would do. A full exploration of alternative approaches is not possible here (the interested reader is referred to Milton & Benjamin, 1999, for more extensive coverage of alternative and complimentary therapies).

Changing tangible, easily evaluated, and observed areas of behavior such as levels of activity or food intake may be accomplished with a minimum of outside assistance and a maximum of determination. However, we never underestimate the difficulty of change and encourage others not to underestimate as well. In addition, some areas of change, such as realistic beliefs and self-esteem, are extremely hard to change in the absence of helping relationships, notably professional counseling. Other areas, such as career choice (the Creative Self and especially work wellness) and intimacy (the Social Self, especially love) in relationships may be areas in which professional involvement can help us rewrite our life scripts and move beyond first-order change to a significant second-order change process. How counselors can help others create change from a wellness perspective is discussed in the next chapter.

SUMMARY

The purpose of this chapter was to make change processes tangible through the creation of a personal wellness plan for change. Specific, concrete steps help to ensure success when developing, implementing, and evaluating a personal change plan. Prochaska and his colleagues have recommended strategies for making a change plan successful, such as behavior monitoring, which are linked to the specific stage of change; hence the importance of assessing stage of change in relation to behaviors is emphasized. Moreover, helping relationships are an important resource for promoting strength-based, positive change.

DISCUSSION QUESTIONS

1. Refer to the final discussion question in chapter 16, which asked you to think about a behavior you might want to change. Or, think of another behavior that you would like to change. Complete the worksheets indicated earlier, including the one in Figure 17.1, and reflect on your willingness to develop a plan for change.
2. Develop a wellness plan for change following the steps described in this chapter. How will you evaluate the success of your plan?
3. Discuss the importance of assessing your stage of change and planning strategies appropriate for your stage to assure successful outcomes of your wellness plan.

WEB RESOURCES

- **Behavior Change Links, http://www.social-marketing.com/BCLinks. html,** is a Web site that provides a number of links to sites for information on behavior change strategies and processes.
- **The National Institutes of Health Guide to Behavior Change for Weight Management, http://www.nhlbi.nih.gov/health/public/heart/ obesity/lose_wt/behavior.htm,** is a Web site that provides guidelines for weight management, including the importance people put on weight management, how to set the right goals, and ways to avoid chain reactions while practicing self-monitoring of food intake.
- **The Cognitive Behavior Therapy (CBT) Web site, http://www. cognitivetherapy.com,** provides a description of cognitive behavior therapy and offers resources, training opportunities, contact information for finding a CBT professional, and a description of treatment issues for CBT.

18

Counseling for Wellness

Thomas J. Sweeney and Jane E. Myers

Counseling and counselor education have had their historical roots in a developmental, life span, facilitative philosophy to intervention and human growth since the early part of the 20th century (Hickman & Alexander, 1998; Jones, 1934; Sweeney, 2001). Before "wellness" and holistic approaches to helping were in vogue, counseling literature contained the philosophy and values now embraced by many in the helping professions (Cottingham, 1956; Hill & Luckey, 1969; Hutson, 1968; Miller, 1961; Peters & Farwell, 1967). In keeping with this history, we have used wellness as the underlying philosophical goal for counseling interventions. We have incorporated it into workshops with counselors and other professionals, in classes with undergraduate and graduate students in counseling and other disciplines, and in clinical work with individuals, couples, and groups. We have found it useful in each context. While work is currently under way with elementary through high school students, what follows is drawn principally from work with young to older adults.

Working from a wellness paradigm requires a very different orientation than is customary for most current approaches to helping. While government, business, and insurance leaders are beginning to shift from repair to prevention in their desire to curb escalating costs and to respond to clear evidence that the old systems have failed our society, health care systems, schools, and business environments are still working with old methods, models, and systems of planning and intervention. The tendency may be to follow rather than lead as change agents. Equipped with a different vision and the right methods to improve current systems, counselors have a unique opportunity now to be leaders of change. As a consequence, professional counselors must be informed advocates for the life span, developmental, wellness approach. This approach must involve specific methods and techniques appropriate to outcome measures that will win cooperation if not outright enthusiasm. This chapter is one such effort in that direction by sharing specific steps for using a wellness paradigm in all counseling interventions.

FOUR STEPS TO COUNSELING FOR WELLNESS

Our suggestions for using wellness in counseling incorporate four steps as follows:

1. introduction of one of the wellness models, including a life span focus
2. formal and/or informal assessment based on the model
3. intentional interventions to enhance wellness in selected areas of wellness
4. evaluation, follow-up, and continuation of Steps 2 through 4

Step 1: Introduction of the Wellness Model

The first step in the process of wellness counseling is typically to use relationship structuring time to prepare the counselee for a different vision of what can be accomplished than is customary. Most counselees want and deserve help with their presenting issues. No more time is required to include an expectation that more good can be accomplished than symptom relief or a solution to an immediate issue. After empathizing and showing interest in the presenting issues (this may be near the end of the first session), the first step is to briefly express a desire to encourage wellness as an ultimate goal including a short definition, introducing one of the models (Indivisible Self [IS-Wel] or Wheel of Wellness), and explaining how a focus on healthy living can contribute to overall well-being. A copy of the model is shared with the counselee, and each characteristic in the model is described briefly.

As a scientist-practitioner, the counselor has an opportunity to note that these characteristics are derived from across disciplines through multiple studies over several decades. More than a theory, these are characteristics derived from those who know how to live longer and better. As is often the case, the presenting issues are an expression of lifestyle behaviors, attitudes, and expectations that the counselees are not fully aware contribute to their presenting issues. Our goal includes helping the counselees adopt attitudes and behaviors that address both immediate and longer term improvement in their life circumstances.

The interaction of the indivisible components of the model is an important concept when presenting the wellness model. Change in any one area can contribute to or create changes in other areas, and these changes can be for better or worse. We emphasize the point that wellness is a choice, and that each choice made toward wellness empowers the counselee toward even greater happiness and life satisfaction through enhanced well-being in the areas that contribute to wellness.

When presenting the models, we especially emphasize the three, or even four-dimensional nature of wellness. For example, when using the Wheel of Wellness model, we encourage our counselees to view the model as a round sphere or globe, with spirituality in the center. If one's sense of spirituality is healthy, the middle of the sphere is round and full and provides a firm foundation or core for the rest of the components of wellness. If one's sense of spirituality is somehow flat, the rest of the sphere cannot be firm and round. Similarly, the tasks of self-direction function metaphorically like the spokes in a wheel. So long as they are strong, the wheel can roll along solidly through time and space. If one or more spokes are defective, as in the broken spokes of a bicycle, the wheel is unable to move smoothly through time and space. It is, in effect, similar to a wheel that is out of balance as it travels roughly along the continuums of time and space.

The Wheel represents the components of wellness over the life span, and attention to each component has consequences that multiply over the course of the life span. For those who make wellness choices, the cumulative effect over the life span is one of increasing wellness in all dimensions, thereby contributing to quality of life and longevity. We encourage counselees to take a life span perspective on their total wellness, reviewing the impact of prior choices in each dimension of wellness and projecting the future impact of choices made at this time.

Finally, we ask counselees to review the model and reflect on the personal meaning of wellness. The question may be asked: Would you like to learn how to solve (the presenting issue) alone or would you also like to learn at the same time specific ways to enjoy your life more? Most, if not all, will choose the latter alternative. We then encourage them to define wellness in their own words. They likely will need help reflecting on wellness as a process rather than an outcome. Next, we encourage them to study the components of the model such as the Wheel and reflect on the personal meaning of each concept. Finally, to personalize their view of wellness even further, we encourage informal and sometimes formal assessments of the dimensions of wellness.

Step 2: Formal and Informal Assessment of the Components of the Wellness Models

Assessment of the components of the Wheel of Wellness or IS-Wel requires a procedure for systematically viewing each dimension and measuring one's wellness on a continuum from not well to high-level wellness. We consider health to be a neutral state in which disease is absent. High-level wellness, on the other hand, is a deliberate state in which the process of making choices toward greater wellness becomes self-perpetuating. The purpose of assessment is to provide a basis for developing a personal wellness plan as being a process to assure that change is for the better, and that any changes made will contribute to greater total wellness.

A global self-report assessment of a counselee's functioning in each of the components of the Wheel can be obtained by asking the counselee to rate his or her overall wellness in each dimension on a scale of 1 to 10, with 1 being very low and 10 representing a high level of wellness. With some counselees, it may be helpful to ask for two ratings on a scale of 1 to 10, the first being their perception of their overall wellness in an area, and the second being their level of satisfaction with their wellness in that area. We have found that some counselees report mid to low levels of wellness in an area and also report that they are quite content with their score at a particular point in time and have no desire for change. Of course, such statements are honored in the counseling process. Once counselees have completed their self-ratings, we ask them to reflect on the scores to determine themes and patterns. In addition, we ask them to confirm that these ratings are accurate in terms of how they see their wellness at this point in time.

In addition to or in place of an informal assessment, wellness in each dimension may be assessed using the Wellness Evaluation of Lifestyle or Five Factor Wellness Inventory (5F-Wel; see chapter 5). Counselees are encouraged to reflect on their scores, determine how representative the scores are of their total wellness (i.e., how well the scores reflect their perceptions of their total wellness), then reflect on the pattern of their high and low scores. They are encouraged to select one or more of their low scores as areas for which they would like to develop a personal wellness plan. Alternatively, counselees may choose an area in which they received a high score, yet note this to be an area in which they would like to enhance their personal wellness. In all cases, however, we attempt to build on assets to overcome perceived weaknesses. If positive humor (Creative Self) is an individual's strength, for example, we may help the counselee find humor in the paradox in some of his or her well-intended but self-defeating behaviors, for example, rewarding oneself with a favorite dessert for starting an exercise program when weight control is an ultimate goal (Physical Self). In another case, a counselee high in Social Self could be encouraged to engage friends or family in developing new behaviors associated with leisure (Coping Self).

Step 3: Intentional Interventions to Enhance Wellness: Developing a Personal Wellness Plan

Once wellness in each dimension has been assessed, either informally or formally, we ask our counselees to choose one or more areas of wellness that they would like to change and improve. We do not recommend trying to effect change in all areas simultaneously, for two reasons. First, choosing to change in more than two to three areas will likely represent an overwhelming array of tasks for anyone. Second, because change in one area will cause changes in other areas, awareness of wellness needs combined with change in any one area is likely to increase overall wellness and wellness in specific additional areas of the model.

Once the counselee identifies those dimensions that he or she would like to change in the direction of greater wellness, we work to co-construct a personal wellness plan in each targeted area. The plan begins with a restatement of the definition of wellness for that particular dimension (the definitions found in chapters 3 and 4, Tables 3.1 and 4.1, respectively, may be useful to present to the counselees), followed by a rating scale consisting of the numbers 1 through 10 (Figure 18.1) The counselee is asked to circle, in writing, the number reflecting their wellness in this area. We have developed a set of generic worksheets for use in this step of the process (Myers & Sweeney, 2004c; Myers, Sweeney, & Witmer, 1998). The counselee is asked to write comments on the worksheet concerning his or her satisfaction with

WELLNESS WORKSHEET: POSITIVE HUMOR
Humor, particularly when it is accompanied by laughter, promotes physiological, psychological, and social change. It creates an open flexibility for problem solving, reduces defensiveness, and improves communication while neutralizing stress. Having a positive humor means that you can laugh at your own mistakes and the unexpected things that happen to you. You laugh with others rather than at them, being sensitive to their own self-esteem. You can be playful even when engaging in serious tasks. Humorous situations are sought in media such as cartoons, comedies, and the comics. Playful and humorous exchanges are frequently a part of the interaction with others. Life events from your own experiences and from the daily news can be seen in a humorous light.

Circle the number on the scale below that reflects your perceptions of wellness related to your sense of humor.

1 2 3 4 5 6 7 8 9 10

Very Low Wellness   Very High Wellness

What are your personal strengths and limitations relative to your sense of humor?

Strengths:

Limitations:

Wellness Plan for Positive Humor

Goals:

Methods:

Resources:

Timelines:

Figure 18.1
Sample Wellness Worksheet

___

his or her self-rating. For some counselees with limited sight or other impairments, the counselor records their remarks.

Following a discussion of concerns related to his or her level of satisfaction, the counselee is asked to complete an informal self-assessment of personal strengths and limitations related to the wellness area targeted for change (see questions on worksheet).

The next step is the development of a written behavioral wellness plan. Included are objectives for change, methods to be used to effect change, and resources that will be used as the plan is implemented. If other people are to be involved in the plan in some way, that fact is noted. For example, if a counselee chooses to increase his or her level of exercise but does not enjoy exercising alone, we would discuss ways to select and involve a partner in the exercise plan.

Step 4: Evaluation and Follow-Up

Finally, a discussion of evaluation procedures and timelines is an important part of the behavioral plan. The counselee should be encouraged to commit to an ongoing plan for regular and systematic evaluation, with identified markers that signify progress in making change. For wellness dimensions such as exercise, nutrition, and self-care, it will be easier to list and identify markers of change (e.g., exercised three times this week for 20 minutes each time, ate breakfast daily, lost 2 pounds per week). For other areas it may be more difficult to identify the process and products of the change process. We have found, for example, that feedback from friends and family is a good indicator that efforts to enhance one's sense of humor is having positive results, while feedback from the counselee is necessary to determine when cognitive techniques such as thought-stopping and challenging one's irrational thoughts are having an impact on irrational belief systems.

We encourage counselees to develop both short- and long-range plans to improve their wellness. The counseling process can be a time to introduce them to the model; teach them techniques for self-assessment, planning, evaluation, and follow-up; and encourage them to develop a view of wellness as a lifelong process in which many changes will occur. We have found that many counselees are able to develop and implement their own wellness plans after a short while given only a blank worksheet, whereas others prefer a more focused, step-by-step process involving discussion with a professional. Some areas of wellness are popular in the media today, such as nutrition and exercise, and little outside intervention may be required to help a counselee experience positive change in these dimensions. Other areas, such as emotional awareness and coping and realistic beliefs, may benefit from traditional counseling interventions to facilitate change.

CASE ILLUSTRATION

In most clinical practices, psychological assessment is used to ascertain indices of depression, personality disorder, and related attributes requiring therapeutic intervention. The use of the IS-Wel and 5F-Wel or the Wheel of Wellness Model and WEL by clinicians has been gratifying because of their enthusiasm and that of their counselees in finding a measure that focuses on positive attributes of health suitable for use in treatment planning. The choice of which model to use may be as simple as the one that you find is easiest to explain in plain language. In other cases, you may choose according to counselee preferences for spirituality as central to their lives or according to a desire to simplify the concepts from several to only five with subcomponents as needed.

An example taken from a counselee seen in the practice of one of the authors (Thomas Sweeney) is presented here to exemplify the use in a clinical setting. This case is presented with permission from an article by Myers, Sweeney, and Witmer (2000b). The ethical guidelines of the American Counseling Association (1995) were followed in the development of this case illustration.

Sylvia was a 24-year-old African American female completing a master's degree in health and physical education at a midsize university. Eight months earlier, she had married her childhood sweetheart, who had a bachelor's degree in business and worked as a supervisor for the United Parcel Service. Within the past month, Sylvia had obtained full-time employment as a teacher and coach at a small liberal arts college. Three weeks prior to referral, she had learned that she was pregnant.

Sylvia was asked to see a counselor by her immediate supervisor who had noticed that she seemed distracted and somewhat depressed. When she was asked about these behaviors, she reported feeling overwhelmed, stressed, and unable to concentrate. She was beginning to have arguments with her husband, whom she noted was thrilled about her pregnancy. She herself was "not happy" to be pregnant. While it is beyond the scope of this chapter to provide a complete case and treatment plan, what follows are illustrations of how components of the IS-Wel model were incorporated into such a case from the perspective of an Adlerian counselor (Sweeney, 1998).

Phase 1: Introduction of the IS-Wel Model

Following an intake interview in which she was asked to provide a psychosocial history, Sylvia was asked to reflect on her personal wellness. She noted that wellness to her meant being in good physical condition and not stressed, and that she tried to stay well through exercise. She also noted that she was "very stressed" at that time and that she was not handling her stress well. I provided Sylvia a copy of the IS-Wel, explained the philosophy underlying the model, and briefly reviewed the definitions of the components of the model. Several times during the discussion Sylvia made comments such as these: "Oh, I am not well in that area at all." "I didn't realize that was part of wellness!" "I never thought about that before, but now that you mention it, I am not doing too well." It was noteworthy that she reported eating lots of high-calorie snack foods and at the same time had not yet considered how, or even if, her diet would impact her developing child.

Phase 2: Informal and Formal Assessment

Sylvia was encouraged to assess her wellness informally as we discussed each component of the IS-Wel. She expressed an interest in learning more about specific areas of her wellness by taking the 5F-Wel. By taking the 5F-Wel, she would be able to reflect on the individual items and increase her awareness of her wellness behaviors (or unwellness behaviors). The IS-Wel was scored and a profile developed (see Figure 18.2) that graphically depicted moderately high scores on thinking, positive humor, and work (Creative Self), love and friendship (Social Self), exercise (Physical Self), and cultural and gender identity (Essential Self). She had low scores on spirituality and self-care (Essential Self), control (Creative Self), leisure, sense of worth, realistic beliefs, stress management (Coping Self), and nutrition (Physical Self).

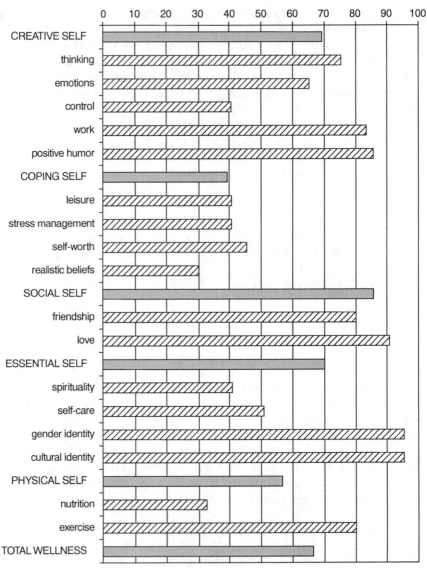

Figure 18.2
Five Factor Wellness Inventory Profile for Sylvia

Phase 3: Development of a Personal Wellness Plan

Sylvia was encouraged to select one or at most two areas of wellness to focus on for improvement. She selected nutrition, in large part because of her pregnancy, and stress management. While working primarily on these goals, I noted that attention to realistic beliefs would be an important strategy for improving her total wellness. Both her sense of worth and control, although not specifically addressed in the wellness plan, would be facilitated as well through achievement of her goals as the plan was implemented. Following our guideline to address no more than two or three dimensions at a time, I was convinced that the total plan would fail if the scope of change attempted was too broad to allow Sylvia to fully experience and appreciate success in the change process. One of our goals is to encourage a counselee and thereby facilitate self-efficacy through successive steps of improvement. This includes taking advantage of Sylvia's "assets" identified in the assessment. These included her sense of humor, her problem-solving attitudes and creativity, her love of physical activity, her network of friends, an intelligent, loving partner and family, and work she feels challenges her capabilities.

An initial step in the development of a personal, behavioral wellness plan includes the establishment of baseline data. In terms of nutrition, Sylvia reported that she snacked constantly on chips and candy and drank at least four to six colas (not diet) daily. Because her husband often worked nights, they did not cook dinner and she would eat snacks for her evening meal. When asked about stress management, she indicated that her typical way of dealing with stress was to let it build up without doing anything about it until she became "like a pressure cooker that just has to let off steam." At that point she would blow up at her husband or another family member, preferring not to show her anger at work in case it affected her performance evaluations. This was especially important during the current probationary period on her job. Since she indicated a desire to work on stress management, we co-constructed a wellness plan in this area. It began in part, however, by uncovering unrealistic beliefs associated with stress.

For Sylvia, there were what Adlerians call *biased apperceptions* about herself, others (especially her partner), life, and how she was to meet her responsibilities that were derived from a brief Adlerian lifestyle assessment. Stress, anxiety, and depression were an outcome of thoughts that included "Winners wear the gold, losers are just losers"; "I don't like unexpected surprises—they mean trouble!"; "Men have it easier than women—and I don't like it!"; and "Weak women are taken advantage of by others; therefore, I must be strong."

Since discovering that she was expecting a baby, Sylvia had "blown up" at her husband at least weekly. Since accepting her new job, she had been too busy to keep up with her friends and she missed them. She had been short tempered with her assistant coaches and found herself crying "for no reason" while driving to and from work. On closer examination, any unhappiness about having a baby was more an expression of stress than her true feelings. Since she was a little girl, she had dreamed of being a mother. Rather than regret or anxiety, she felt the stress in her life was overriding her own excitement.

Stress management for Sylvia included nurturing more positive emotions by confronting her "fictive notions" through thought-stopping and examination of ways to reframe circumstances and expectations. In addition, Sylvia readily acknowledged that she held in her negative emotions until she "exploded." She stated that she never showed her temper with the players she coached, although "she pushed them pretty hard to do their best." After Sylvia had fully shared her account of her predicament, she was asked to describe a "day in the future when she was relaxed, confident, and comfortable." She got teary eyed and said she wasn't sure that she could. We paused for a moment and then I asked if she would like to change the way her life was going. While she readily said "yes," I explained that she may find changing her ways of thinking and responding more challenging than coaching a winning team. In this case, to be strong and not vulnerable meant leaning on those who care about you most and who experience you as a "winner" without competing for it. On the other hand, she had demonstrated a commitment to excellence in other important areas of her life and she had those assets to draw on as her wellness plan was implemented.

Sylvia was helped to construct a stress management plan including objectives, methods, resources, timelines, and evaluation. These included, for example, reestablishing a regular (three times per week minimum) program of exercises appropriate to her condition. She agreed to consult with a staff member in the college to guide her through this process over time. After stress-relaxation response exercises experienced during counseling, she agreed to practice deep-breathing exercises and positive imaging before, during, and after specific times known to be stressful for her (e.g., team practice sessions). She also agreed to keep a log of her responses, others' reactions, and her feelings related to these efforts.

The decision to choose nutrition and stress management for addressing in Sylvia's treatment plan presented an opportunity to consider the implications of working in areas not within a counselor's competence. The wellness models and consequently their corresponding instruments incorporate components drawn from research across disciplines. As a result, many counselors will wish to work collaboratively with professionals in other disciplines (e.g., a nutritionist) and/or continue their education into areas found needed by their counselees.

In the case of Sylvia, the counselor had sufficient knowledge of basic nutritional guidelines to begin the process of examining Sylvia's nutritional habits. However, it also was decided that in order to ensure the best for the unborn child as well as mother, Sylvia needed to consult with her obstetrician as a part of the information and planning process. As a consequence, a dietary plan, regular meals, supplements, and a schedule for visits with weight and other physical indices of positive health were established for tracking throughout the pregnancy and beyond.

Phase 4: Evaluation and Follow-Up

The wellness plans that Sylvia developed included not only baseline data but also strategies, timelines, and techniques for assessing outcomes. The nutrition plan was far easier to develop, implement, and evaluate than was the plan for stress management. In effect, Sylvia agreed to keep a diary of her food intake, read articles, pamphlets, and Web pages on nutrition, with a focus on nutrition during pregnancy, and to take a course in natural-foods cooking. Her husband, mother, and sister agreed to help her plan meals, prepare grocery lists, and prepare nutritious meals. In addition, her physician referred her to a nurse-dietician for consultation.

After 6 weeks, Sylvia had made substantial changes in her daily food and nutrition intake and was determined to make those changes "lifelong." Sylvia's plan for stress management showed that she tended to have a "pressure cooker" explosion on the average of once a week. These were essentially eliminated during the first 6 weeks of implementing her wellness plan, supplemented with weekly counseling sessions. She used a relaxation tape made during one of the counseling sessions to practice between appointments, and she quickly learned the intrinsic satisfaction of control over her emotional outbursts. Her husband joined her for two counseling sessions in which they were both relieved to discover that each could express their fears, hopes, and aspirations for their careers, family, and marriage with mutual support as a foundation.

The case of Sylvia is rich with possibilities for creatively incorporating a new paradigm into the development of a treatment plan. It builds on assets such as her striving for excellence, self-efficacy, and interdependence with others. It challenges both counselor and counselee to think about greater possibilities for living life more fully, free of the "shoulds and oughts" found in her fictive beliefs, and offers renewed hope. More than repairing and supporting, it offers a plan for creating a new outlook on how to make the most of one's attributes, circumstances, and resources.

SUMMARY

The characteristics of healthy people identified through medical and psychosocial research as important components of wellness throughout the life span are the basis of this approach. Optimizing human development is historically at the core of counselor education and counseling practice. Although managed care and insurance company regulations still make it difficult to fully adopt this model in clinical mental health practices at present, it is our belief that this condition will change. This is especially so if entrepreneurial counselors make proposals that incorporate prevention and wellness plans as cost-saving services to employers, insurance companies, and HMOs. Many insurance companies and numerous hospitals are already paying for a wellness emphasis through group psychoeducational interventions with medically related problems. In addition, state and regional wellness council programs in business and industry proliferate as a result of the enormous cost–benefit ratios of such programs. We anticipate that studies currently under way will continue to affirm the cost-effectiveness of prevention as the best health care strategy for future generations.

As an enhancing as well as remedial intervention, counselors can assist counselees in the process of assessing their wellness on components of the wellness models, and in developing wellness plans to facilitate positive growth and change across the life span. The wellness models and methods can be used successfully with couples, families, and groups. In doing so, we apply the same basic principles used in working with individuals. Our goal is to help others to live long and to live well. We believe that this should be the ultimate goal of any effective counseling practice.

19

Spirituality and Wellness

Craig S. Cashwell

> May all beings everywhere, with whom we are inseparably intercon-
> nected, be fulfilled, awakened, and free. May there be peace in this world
> and throughout the entire universe, and may we all together complete
> the spiritual journey.
>
> —*Lama Surya Das*

As you begin to read this chapter, take a few moments to close your
eyes, take a deep cleansing breath, and simply consider the term *spirituality*. What image comes to your mind? Is it the image of a religious
zealot proselytizing for a narrowly defined path? The image of a contemplative living an ascetic life? A focused student of a particular religious tradition? A compassionate servant who takes on a life mission
of serving the poorest of the poor? Whatever your image, this exercise
points out one of the greatest challenges in developing this chapter:
While universal, spirituality also is highly personal and developmental. That
is, each person defines spirituality in her or his personal way, and this
changes over time so that each person defines spirituality differently at
various periods in her or his life.

At the same time, spirituality is universal. Research suggests that 96% of people living in the United States believe in God, over 90% pray, 69% are church
members, and 43% have attended church, synagogue, or temple within the
past 7 days (Princeton Religion Research Center, 2000). Further, this does not
begin to count those people for whom the primary expression of their spirituality occurs outside the context of organized religion. As has been said, we
are not human beings having a spiritual experience but are rather spiritual beings having a human experience. From this perspective, the path toward a
more spiritual life is not one of ascension, but one of descending into the
realm of our Higher or Truer Self. It is this sense that spiritual wellness is at
the core of our existence that has led various scholars to posit that spirituality is the core of wellness and inseparable from all other aspects of wellness
(Chandler, Holden, & Kolander, 1992; Myers, Sweeney, & Witmer, 2000b;
Sweeney & Myers, 2005; Sweeney & Witmer, 1991; Witmer & Sweeney, 1992).
In fact, the words *healing, whole,* and *holy* all derive from the Old English *hal*

and the Greek *holos*, suggesting that what is holy or spiritual is intimately connected to our health and wholeness. This "truth" forms the basis for this chapter. The organization of the chapter includes a working definition of spirituality, a consideration of the translative and transformative purposes of a spiritual life, and implications for counselors and their clients.

DEFINING SPIRITUALITY

Spirituality, because it is both universal and highly personal, is difficult to define (Cashwell & Young, 2005). In fact, Fukuyama and Sevig (1999) asserted that it is not possible to agree on only one definition. When we strive to define spirituality, we discover not its limits, but our own (Kurtz & Ketcham, 1992). As a result, many choose global definitions of spirituality. Unfortunately, such definitions lend themselves to a type of relativism that does not adequately mirror the growing body of literature on spiritual development (Faiver & Ingersoll, 2005).

This being said, the global definition used here is drawn from the work of Chandler et al. (1992), who defined spirituality as "Pertaining to the innate capacity . . . and tendency to . . . transcend one's current locus of centricity, which transcendence involves increased knowledge and love" (p. 169). This definition is offered because it captures the public (exoteric) and private (esoteric) faces of spirituality and the translative and transformative purposes of spirituality (Wilber, 1999).

A common error in the mental health field is to define spirituality based only on its translative (i.e., meaning-making, knowledge-based) purpose; often, this is the only aspect of spirituality given consideration in the scholarly literature. The translative dimension of spirituality understood by many mental health professionals includes how beliefs, creeds, and practices help a person make meaning in a difficult world. As Wilber (1999) asserted, however, spirituality (or religion) serves not only the translative purpose but also a transformative purpose of transcending the ego. In Wilber's nomenclature, while the translative purpose of spiritual beliefs, practices, and experiences serves to fortify the separate self, the transformative purpose serves to shatter the separate self and occasion "a radical transmutation and transformation at the deepest seat of consciousness" (Wilber, 2000). Such transformation often occurs as a result of a peak or mystical experience or a series of such experiences. Wilber (1999) characterized the translative purpose of spirituality as horizontal development (i.e., fortifying the self) and the transformative purpose of spirituality as vertical development. Often, this vertical development is called transpersonal development (literally "beyond the ego").

While the translative and transformative functions of spirituality are presented here as distinct, the interrelationship between the two is vital. With transformative experiences comes the need for integration or translation. Those who are unable to integrate transformative experiences adequately might experience neurosis or even psychosis. This is not a breakthrough, but a breakdown; not transcendence, but a disaster (Wilber, 2000). On the other hand, there exists in the development of many people a point at which translation itself is not adequate. At these points, transformation becomes the spiritual path of growth (Wilber, 2000). Thus, translation and transformation jointly form the spiritual path for the seeker. Important to consider from a wellness paradigm is Maslow's (1970) notion that transcenders might actually be less happy at times than nontranscenders because of their enhanced vision and insight.

In discussing spirituality and wellness, a further distinction needs to be made. When we refer to spirituality, are we referring to spiritual beliefs, practices, or experiences? All three, and the relationship between the three, should be considered. *Beliefs* refer to the purely translative set of ideas and schemas that we hold. Do I hold a set of beliefs closely aligned with a specific world religion? How do I think about concepts such as evil and forgiveness? *Practices* refer to the behaviors that we use to experience and express our beliefs. For example, a person of Jewish faith might read the Torah daily and keep a kosher kitchen. A person who holds Christian beliefs might engage in daily contemplative prayer, whereas a person who holds Buddhist beliefs may engage in vipassana meditation. Finally, *experiences* refer to any occurrences that occasion a deeper and more meaningful connection with the Truer or Higher Self. Such experiences may result directly from the spiritual practices of the person but also may be occasioned by external events, such as the death of a partner.

The most logical interchange between beliefs, practices, and experiences is that they are inextricably connected. For example, a Zen Buddhist might study Zen texts, poems, and sayings to formulate a cognitive schema. Logically, such a person also would integrate a daily practice of meditation and other sitting practices. The spiritual experiences would evolve out of this combination of study and practice. These spiritual experiences (transformations) would then need translation, which might come in the form of further reading or study with a teacher.

For many, though, this connection between beliefs, practices, and experiences is not so clear. Consider, for example, a devout Christian who attends church services regularly but does not seek transformative experiences or, in this case, a closer communion with God but rather attends because, as he says, "I should go." This person enters a worship service with a sense of obligation rather than passion for spiritual growth. Again, the belief system of the person influences both practice and experience, but in a different way. The belief ("God will punish me if I do not attend church regularly") influences the public practice of attending church services. The private practice also is influenced as the individual attends religious services with a sense of obligation and little inherent spiritual experience. As a result, we might expect the person to have limited spiritually transforming experiences.

REVIEW OF EMPIRICAL FINDINGS
ON SPIRITUALITY AND WELLNESS

There is a somewhat limited but growing body of evidence on the impact of a spiritual life on physical and psychological wellness. To date, however, the overwhelming majority of research has been conducted with participants from high-risk groups (e.g., hypertension, depression). As such, most researchers focus on how spiritual practices moderate the impact of life stressors and minimize deleterious benefits of these stressors rather than focusing on the life-enhancing aspects of spiritual practice (J. S. Young, Cashwell, & Shcherbakova, 2000). Reflecting this, the brief review of the literature that follows focuses on aspects of health rather than wellness. Historically, researchers have primarily focused on one aspect of the trinity of beliefs, practices, and experiences, and this review is organized accordingly.

Beliefs

Religious beliefs are defined for measurement purposes by religious involvement. Koenig, McCullough, and Larson (2001) identified 100 empirical studies examining the relationship between religious involvement and well-being (defined as happiness, positive affect, and higher morale). In 79 of the 100 studies, a positive correlation between religious involvement and wellness was found, and only 1 study reported a negative correlation. Further, they found that approximately two-thirds of the studies they reviewed found lower rates of depression among people who were more religious. Also, among people who are depressed, religiosity appears to facilitate more rapid resolution of depression (Koenig, George, & Peterson, 1998).

Conversely, religious struggle may actually increase the risk of mortality, at least among older adults. A 2-year longitudinal study of 595 hospital patients age 55 and older indicated that people who wrestle with religious beliefs during an illness may have an increased risk of dying (Pargament, Koenig, Tarakashwar, & Hahn, 2001). Key risk factors included beliefs that one was being punished by God, feeling abandoned by the faith community, and believing the devil caused the illness. While these studies are of interest, because of the focus on health (rather than wellness) and the aforementioned complex relationship between beliefs, practices, and experiences, these studies provide limited information about the impact of a spiritual life on wellness.

Practices

A full examination of the variety of spiritual practices would fill volumes. Common spiritual practices include prayer, meditation, yoga, chanting, reiki, tai chi, Qigong, shamanism, guided imagery, bioenergetics, psychosynthesis, breathwork, and creative visualization, among others. For the purposes of this review, only two of the more common spiritual practices, prayer and meditation, are discussed.

Prayer. Prayer is a basic element of all theistic religions in the world, though observances and types of prayer vary among religions such as Judaism, Christianity, and Hinduism. While research concerning the impact of prayer on well-being is in the early stages, the results are substantial. Byrd (1988) found that coronary care patients ($N = 393$) who received prayer from a healing circle had lower need of diuretics, lower incidence of pneumonia, lower incidence of cardiopulmonary arrest, and a higher chance of having a good recovery process than among those in the control group. Byrd's study was a true experiment using random assignment to groups and a double-blind methodology. The results were at a magnitude considered sensational in the medical field (Fontana, 2003). Similarly, Koenig, George, Hays, et al.'s (1998) findings suggested that people who engage in religious activities on at least a weekly basis are 40% less likely to have high diastolic pressure or diastolic hypertension.

Meditation. Various forms of meditation, such as mindfulness meditation (vipassana) and transcendental meditation, have been credited with reducing blood pressure, anxiety, addiction, stress, muscle tension, and pain; increasing perceptual/cognitive abilities and motor skills; and increasing self-actualization (Andresen, 2000). Yet, it remains apparent that these are difficult practices to quantify with respect to outcomes and wellness.

Experiences

Spiritual experiences, often referred to as *transpersonal* or *trans-egoic*, afford one a sense of self expanded beyond the ego. Such experiences may occur spontaneously or be occasioned by disciplined spiritual practice such as prayer, meditation, or shamanic journeying. Such experiences are generally only considered useful if they make a difference in the daily life of the individual. A comprehensive review of spiritual experiences is beyond the scope of this chapter. For illustrative purposes, however, near-death experiences (NDEs) are discussed as one type of spiritual experience.

Researchers have found that as many as 40% of people at or near clinical death report NDEs prior to resuscitation (Fenwick & Fenwick, 1995). More important than the occurrence of the NDE is the life-changing impact occasioned by NDEs. Common outcomes include a loss of fear about death, less worry about past grievances and future problems, increased feelings of self-worth and acceptance and concern for others, changed life goals with less emphasis on material values and more emphasis on spiritual values, more emphasis on love and compassion, and a tendency to seek a deeper understanding of life, particularly at a spiritual level (Ring, 1984).

SPIRITUALITY AND WELLNESS: THE MODERATING ROLE OF INTEGRATION

Having highlighted the centrality of spiritual and religious beliefs, practices, and experiences within the overall framework of wellness, a caveat is necessary. Distinguishing between a healthy use of spirituality that fosters positive development and wellness and the unhealthy use of spiritual beliefs, practices, and experiences that enable a person to avoid dealing with unfinished psychological business is essential. Referred to as *spiritual bypass*, individuals may misguidedly use practices that include compulsive goodness, repression of undesirable or painful emotions, spiritual narcissism, spiritual obsession or addiction, blind faith in charismatic leaders, abdication of personal responsibility, and social isolation (Cashwell & Rayle, in press).

Perhaps spiritual bypass is best explained by use of a case example. John, a 37-year-old man who is a self-proclaimed "spiritualist" presented in counseling. He was referred by another counselor who had been unsuccessful in his work with John. Because of his extensive experiences with meditation, yoga, and other spiritual practices, John did not understand why he felt such intense anger toward his ex-wife and toward other women, particularly those in authority positions. In an effort to work within a spiritual framework, the former counselor, well-intentioned but misguided, integrated bibliotherapy readings on forgiveness, temperance, and compassion as adjuncts to the therapeutic process in John's counseling. Failing to fully assess for a core issue, however, the previous counselor did not gather the information that John was a victim of severe physical and psychological abuse from his mother. The divorce became a linked trauma to this early abuse. John had, in fact, used his spiritual practice to avoid the painful "working through" of his anger about the early trauma. In so doing, he had relegated his anger to the realm of the shadow (Jung, 1963). These unresolved conflicts continued to seek expression and often created tremendous intrapsychic conflict. From a wellness perspective, addressing emotional wellness was essential.

The Wheel of Wellness (Myers et al., 2000b; Witmer & Sweeney, 1992) includes spirituality as the core aspect of wellness, characterized as the "hub" of the wheel from which other aspects of wellness emerge as spokes. The Indivisible Self Model of Wellness (IS-Wel; Myers & Sweeney, 2004b; Sweeney & Myers, 2005) suggests that spirituality is an aspect of the Essential Self and, as such, is connected to all other aspects of wellness. Both models suggest that spiritual wellness is vital to holistic wellness. The central issue, however, is how people integrate spirituality into their lives. Some fail to develop their spiritual lives at all; others, however, such as those people in spiritual bypass, overdevelop their spiritual lives without developing in other areas and without an integrated or grounded spirituality. A closer examination is warranted that captures more fully the relationship between spiritual wellness and other aspects of wellness, as people who live longer and better have mastered some skills and habits in all components of wellness (Sweeney & Myers, 2005). While it is possible to consider the impact of various types of religiosity and spirituality on all other aspects of wellness, for parsimony the focus here will be on a few aspects of wellness (emotions, sense of control, problem solving and creativity, self-care, realistic beliefs, and social support) included in the IS-Wel model. Two of the aspects (sense of control and problem solving) are considered together.

Emotions

The previously discussed case of John is a good example of how a poorly integrated spirituality negatively affects emotional wellness. While temperance is an essential aspect of many world religious belief systems, in John's case an overemphasis on forgiveness led him to bypass his unresolved anger from childhood abuse. A second example occurs when people are encouraged to be "strong" and not express their emotions during periods of grief and loss. Messages that the loved one is in a better place or that sufficient faith would preclude sadness often lead to complicated grief reactions.

Sense of Control and Problem Solving

Out of religious and spiritual beliefs and practices emerge very different patterns of exerting personal control, particularly during times of crisis or challenge. Pargament et al. (1988) distinguished between three patterns of coping: (a) *self-directing approach* in which people use the talents afforded them by their Higher Power to handle a situation, (b) *deferring approach* in which people abdicate their personal responsibility and instead defer to a Higher Power, and (c) *collaborative approach* in which people work together with their Higher Power to deal with crisis or difficulty. For those individuals with a theistic belief system, the collaborative approach is captured in the words of the serenity prayer, "God grant me the serenity to accept the things I cannot change, the courage to change the things I can, and the wisdom to know the difference." As an example of various coping strategies, consider a person diagnosed with a life-threatening illness. One might cope by collecting information, consulting with physicians, and advocating for a particular medical treatment without considering the meaning attached to end-of-life issues (self-directing). Another might refuse medical treatment, relying on healing from a Higher Power (deferring). Yet another might both seek medical assistance and rely on spiritual beliefs and practices to cope (collaborative). While more conservative religious groups might argue that the deferring strategy is the "true" faith, Pargament et al. (1988) found that people with a deferring coping strategy had a lower sense of control and poorer problem-solving skills. Only those who used their faith in a way that they claimed some personal responsibility for their well-being (either collaborative or self-directed) had a stronger sense of control and higher problem-solving skills.

Self-Care

Sweeney and Myers (2005) characterized self-care as including care of the physical body but also as a fundamental expression of a desire for living. Conversely, then, lack of self-care is an expression of discouragement with life. Many religions espouse particular guidelines for self-care, including mental and physical exercises and guidelines for nutrition. There are many examples, however, of religious beliefs and practices that might result in a decrease in self-care. Religious addiction and refusal to allow necessary medical treatment are two examples.

Realistic Beliefs

The realistic beliefs construct refers to the ability of individuals to process information accurately and perceive reality as it is rather than as they wish it to be (Sweeney & Myers, 2005). This is consistent with the beliefs of many spiritual teachings in which the goal is the shattering of the illusions created by the mind through disciplined spiritual practice. On the other hand, more dogmatic and rigid belief systems are fraught with "always, never, should, and must" in relation to self and others.

Social Support

According to the IS-Wel model, the indivisible self exists within a social context, including family and community. For many, the community of the church, temple, synagogue, or mosque is a vital and healthy part of the individual's social support system. One need only consider cults led by Jim Jones and David Koresh, however, to see how social support can go awry in the name of religion.

RECOMMENDATIONS FOR SPIRITUAL PRACTICE

The following general recommendations are offered toward self or counselees developing/beginning a spiritual practice:

1. Determine personal goals for beginning a spiritual practice.
2. Learn about a variety of spiritual practices before choosing one. Attending workshops and reading spirituality literature will help in the selection of a practice. (*The Complete Body, Mind, and Spirit* by Nancy Allison, 2001, is a good reference for this purpose.)
3. Choose a practice that is consistent with one's spiritual belief system and likely to facilitate movement toward your goals.
4. Once a practice is selected, make the practice a disciplined one. Build time into each day to practice.
5. Consider beginning your practice within a community, which may help sustain the practice. Further, many forms of spiritual practice, particularly contemplative practices, tend to uncover defense mechanisms and occasion strong emotional reactions, including the expression of anger, anxiety, sadness, or fear. In such cases, a supportive community and the experience of others may help integrate diverse experiences.

SUMMARY

In sum, then, a healthy spiritual life is one that is integrated with other aspects of wellness. A system of healthy spiritual beliefs, practices, and experiences will provide a sense of social support, improve realistic beliefs, support healthy emotions, and facilitate a balanced sense of control over external events. A healthy spirituality also will provide a natural form of stress management as the individual finds meaning in the struggles of everyday life and finds comfort in a disciplined spiritual practice.

DISCUSSION QUESTIONS

In closing, here are some questions to facilitate further exploration and growth. The following questions may be useful for personal reflection, for small group discussion, or with clients.

1. What was the role of religion in your childhood and how do you feel about that now?
2. Do your religious/spiritual beliefs support you toward positive development? How? If not, why? What changes would you like to make?
3. Are you a member of a spiritually oriented or religious community? If so, how is the community supportive of your spiritual development?
4. How do your spiritual practice and experiences influence your daily life?

WEB RESOURCES

- **The Association for Spiritual, Ethical, and Religious Values in Counseling, www.aservic.org/,** is an organization of counselors and human development professionals who are dedicated to creating an environment of spiritual, ethical, and religious exploration and empowerment in the counseling process.
- **The Council on Spiritual Practices, www.csp.org/,** is composed of spiritual guides, experts in the behavioral and biomedical sciences, and scholars of religion who seek to allow the experience of the sacred to become more accessible to people safely and effectively in their daily living.
- **Ontario Consultants on Religious Tolerance, www.religioustolerance. org/,** is a Web site that supports religious freedom, tolerance, and diversity, all considered to be positive values. Over 2,600 related links are provided.

20

A Wellness Perspective on the Management of Stress

J. Scott Young

Andrew Weil, the noted holistic physician and author, tells the story of an American medical student who was excited about the opportunity to practice medicine in Africa (A. Weil, 1999), in a Third World setting where she would have the opportunity to treat a variety of exotic diseases that would challenge her medical knowledge and skill. Weil described her surprise and disappointment when she discovered that the vast majority of her patients presented with complaints identical to those that physicians practicing in the United States and other Western countries encounter regularly. Symptoms such as headaches, upset stomachs, heartburn, and sleep disruption were widespread among the African patients. According to Weil, all of these diseases are considered to have a significant stress-related component. The young physician realized that stress, far from being a problem unique to the modern Western lifestyle, is a reality that all people experience regularly. Weil concluded that the management of stress, conceptualized in its broadest sense, is a crucial life task for people throughout the world.

Given that stress appears to be an actuality for people from every walk of life, including those from both the developed and underdeveloped countries, it is important to understand what stress entails. Stress is a systemic reaction that human beings, as well as other living things, experience when they perceive danger to their physical, emotional, or mental safety (Charlesworth & Nathan, 1984). Because of its multilevel impact on the individual, the effects of stress are felt on the physical, the mental/emotional, and the spiritual level, and therefore techniques for managing stress must necessarily address those same areas. As Myers, Sweeney, and Witmer (2000b) indicated, stress management involves recognizing stressors and utilizing strategies to minimize the impact of stress. Before discussing techniques for treating stress, however, it is helpful to consider the question, "What is the nature of stress?"

A stressor is any event, positive or negative, that causes physiological arousal, emotional discomfort, and disruption or change to a person's life. Distress includes those events we typically think of as stressful, such as sitting in traffic, unreasonable demands from the boss, or the illness of one's child. However, stress also may be of a positive nature. Positive stress is referred to as *eustress*. Examples of eustress include developmental milestones such as marriage, parenthood, and the drive individuals experience to accomplish their goals, to engage in a new activity, or to strive to perform at a high level. Therefore, it is clear that stress is a complex phenomenon that involves external events, one's internal reactions to those events, and the meaning attributed to such events. Not surprisingly, there are models that conceptualize stress from each of these three perspectives (i.e., physiological reactions to stress, life events that increase stress, and environmental/individual influences of stress). Following an overview of these models, the relationship between stress and wellness is examined, techniques for managing stress are explored, and the role of spirituality in stress management is discussed.

MODELS OF STRESS

Physiological Reactions to External Events

Hans Selye (1976) was the first researcher to talk about the impact of threatening stimuli on the physical body. The common experiences of stress such as a racing heart, a churning stomach, and tension in the muscles of the neck and shoulders are recognized as symptoms of stress by most people. All of these reactions are the body's reaction to stress. Stress causes a set of very specific physical changes in the body when one becomes alarmed because of a sense of imminent danger (Simon, 2003). A biochemical reaction prepares the individual to either remove oneself from a threatening situation or to defend oneself against the danger (i.e., the fight-or-flight response). A rush of hormones triggers a biological alarm system that causes rapid breathing, increased heart rate and blood pressure, sweaty or dry palms, agitation, digestive problems, dry throat, and hyperalertness. After a prolonged period, this state of biochemical arousal can become habitual and chronic. Interestingly, one can adjust to feeling stressed to the point that one no longer recognizes the strain stress is causing to the body and mind. This situation is particularly dangerous as a chronic state of tension will eventually lead to physical breakdown and disease. Not surprisingly, as much as 80% of all physical illness is stress related (Simon, 2003).

Life Events and Stress

The second model for explaining the causes and impact of stress focuses on life events and how various situations that people encounter as part of being human contribute to the individual's adjustment. The pioneering research of Holmes and Rahe (1967) examined the impact of life events on the health and adjustment of individuals and demonstrated clearly that both positive events such as marriage, the birth of a child, or the purchase of a new home as well as negative events such as divorce, loss of a job, or the death of a loved one cause stress that may result in an increased likelihood of disease or injury for the individual. An important finding of their research was that stress is cumulative in nature. One life-changing event alone may not prove difficult for the individual to manage; however, the accumulation of multiple stressful events can overwhelm the individual's coping skills. Thus stress can cause physiological breakdown (injury or disease) as well as emotional suffering (anxiety and depression), resulting in a decreased capacity to meet the demands of life. In fact, researchers utilizing the life-change index developed by Holmes and Rahe were able to predict successfully which Navy and Marine personnel would need the most visits to sick bay within the coming 6-month to 1-year period. Similarly, football players who have experienced many life changes consistently experience more injuries during sports participation (Greenstone & Leviton, 2002).

Environment and Stress

According to the third model of stress, which is based on an environmental–interactional approach (Lazarus & Folkman, 1984), the degree to which an event is stressful depends on how stressful events are perceived by the person experiencing them. In other words, individuals make internal assessments of how threatening various events are to them. The degree of perceived threat along with one's ability to cope work together to determine how stressful a particular event is for a given individual at a particular point in time. An individual will be able to cope effectively with a specific event on the basis of

> a number of factors such as their sense of competence to handle the stressor, previous success in dealing with similar situations, the degree to which they feel in control of events, their perceptions of being overloaded or having conflicting needs, and expectations that are either self-imposed or imposed by others. (Lewis, Lewis, Daniels, & D'Andrea, 2003, p. 62)

STRESS AND WELLNESS

The Wheel of Wellness, originally described by Sweeney and Witmer (1991) and Witmer and Sweeney (1992) and updated to represent the results of ongoing research on the nature of wellness (Myers, Sweeney, & Witmer, 2000b), and the Indivisible Self model (IS-Wel) pictorially represent the interconnectedness of the life tasks or factors of wellness (see chapters 3 and 4). These factors interact to produce an individual's overall state of wellness, and when regulated effectively, they increase the individual's capacity for meeting the demands of life. From a wellness perspective, stress may be viewed as an interruption of the state of positive balance that exists when the body–mind–spirit triad is functioning optimally. Stress, due to underdevelopment or interruption in one of the life tasks, manifests as an experience of being physically, mentally, or spirituality out of balance. When one or multiple life tasks are negatively affected, the individual's resilience is compromised. This is the typical scenario when a client presents for counseling. The *Diagnostic and Statistical Manual of Mental Disorders*, currently in its fourth text revision (American Psychiatric Association, 2000), presents a five-axis heuristic for the biological bases of mental disease. The fifth axis is specifically designed to quantify a person's level of stress and is represented as a number between 0 and 100 on the Global Assessment of Functioning scale (GAF). Lower GAF scores indicate a greater amount of overwhelmingly destabilizing stressors and a resulting breakdown in coping.

According to Myers et al. (2000b, p. 255), stress management entails the "ability to identify stressors in one's life and to reduce or minimize stress by using strategies of stress reduction." For a counselor to assist a client in managing stress effectively, the counselor must be able to demonstrate how the client's stress is affecting him or her. Myers et al. (2000b) and Sweeney and Myers (2005) provided examples of how the wellness models can be used to assist clients in assessing their overall states of wellness by rating on a scale from 1 to 10 their functioning in each domain. Stress could be assessed along these same dimensions. If a client can identify that he or she is at a "3" on the work/leisure life task because the client does not enjoy his or her work nor have meaningful leisure activities, the client's potential for mental and physical stress related to this reality is increased. Subsequently, such a client could be encouraged to utilize various stress management techniques (e.g., imagery, exercise, and a spiritual practice) as interventions to reduce the negative impact of nonfulfilling work while they take steps to either find different work, increase engagement in out-of-work interests, or both.

TECHNIQUES FOR MANAGING STRESS

Although research-based guidelines and techniques for management of stress have been readily available for at least the last 30 years, it is evident by the rates of mental and physical disease that the majority of people do not implement these strategies effectively. Subsequently, counselors face the challenge of motivating their clients to adopt a wellness perspective on their lives, thereby utilizing stress management techniques for preventative as well as remedial purposes. For a client to adopt a wellness perspective, proper education, motivation, and support are all crucial. Therefore, it is incumbent on the counselor to understand fully the approaches that exist for assisting a client in managing his or her stress. These techniques fall into three broad categories of approaches: those addressing the physical body, those addressing the mind and mental functioning, and those addressing the spirit. Interestingly, these categories align with three factors of wellness representing the body–mind–spirit triad identified in the most recently developed Four Factor Wellness Model (Myers, Luecht, & Sweeney, 2004).

Body-Focused Approaches to Managing Stress

Techniques for managing stress that seek to alter the individual's physiological responses to distressing stimuli have been well documented and include progressive relaxation and imagery training (Charlesworth & Nathan,

1984). These approaches work by engaging the body's natural relaxation response and are based on the idea that is not possible to be physically relaxed and stressed simultaneously. The relaxation response, like the stress response, is an organic phenomenon that occurs when the body is sufficiently triggered through neuromuscular release to produce calming endorphins that sooth the muscles, lower heart rate and blood pressure, and inhibit the release of noradrenalin, a neurotransmitter that is the precursor to adrenaline release.

Progressive Relaxation. Progressive relaxation, a technique developed in the 1920s by physician Edumund Jacobson, has been systematically studied for years and has been found to be helpful with such issues as anxiety, insomnia, headaches, backaches, and hypertension. Progressive relaxation involves the intentional tensing of major muscle groups for a short period of time (5 to 10 seconds) followed by complete relaxation of the muscles along with focused breathing and mental reminders to release stress and relax (Charlesworth & Nathan, 1984). The technique is designed to release muscular tension that is held in the body, tension that is often out of the individual's awareness. When a state of overall muscular relaxation is achieved, one experiences a state of calmness and peacefulness. Like all stress management techniques, the success of this technique is improved with regular practice even in times of low stress so that when stress is greater, the individual is confident in his or her ability to utilize the technique effectively.

Imagery Training. According to Charlesworth and Nathan (1984), imagery training, also called visualization, involves using pleasant visual images to control upsetting thoughts and obtain a state of deep physical relaxation. However, for the approach to work, the individual must be able to generate appropriate mental images that are then practiced sufficiently so that the images can be sustained as long as needed. Suggested images include a tropical island, a cloud, a valley, a willow tree, a beach, a field of flowers, a forest, a stream, and so on. One learns that although unwanted thoughts may come, one has the power to return the mind to the desired calming image. This technique is enhanced when all five senses are engaged to bring the image into clear focus. For example, if a client were working to develop a pleasant scene that involves the safety and comfort of a mountain meadow, he should be encouraged to smell the flowers growing along the edge of the meadow, to feel his head laying against the soft grass, to listen to the sound of a stream that runs nearby, and to taste the breeze on his lips. Once such an image becomes tangible to the person and is paired with relaxation, the person, when under times of stress, can much more easily draw on the calming scenes to induce a state of mental relaxation.

Exercise and Nutrition. Another approach to managing stress through the body (i.e., physical wellness) is with the use of proper exercise and nutrition. The U.S. public, through both print and television media, is constantly barraged with information on weight loss, diet, and physical fitness. Yet, health promoters tell us that over the last 30 years only about 25% of the population has engaged in a regular fitness program (B. Hunt, personal communication, December 15, 2003). Furthermore, this percentage has not varied greatly even with the tremendous increase in focus on physical fitness and diet within the culture. Therefore, it appears that the greater availability of information about physical fitness and nutrition does not necessarily lead to greater behavior change. Nevertheless, it is well established that physical health, including good cardiovascular fitness, more muscle mass, and healthy diet (i.e., lower fat and higher protein), supports a greater capacity for the body to manage stress and avoid disease. For counselors this translates into the need to provide clients with good information related to the effects of exercise and diet on depression, anxiety, and other mental disorders, and physical diseases that are aggravated by stress. Additionally, counselors can assist clients in understanding the role that caffeine, sugar, and processed foods have on anxiety and nervousness as well as sleep and other lifestyle issues, thereby assisting clients in developing a wellness perspective on their lives.

MENTAL APPROACHES TO MANAGING STRESS

Cognitive Restructuring

Cognitive restructuring is a well-established approach that is designed to help reduce self-induced stress. By relying on faulty or negatively oriented patterns of thinking, the person generates stress by taking as fact distorted beliefs about themselves, their abilities, attributes, or a particular situation in which they find themselves. Cognitive restructuring was designed to assist clients in bringing about changes to any number of problematic thought processes, thereby altering behaviors and feelings. In terms of stress management, counselors assist clients' use of cognitive restructuring through a five-step process (Lewis et al., 2003) as follows:

1. The client recognizes that his or her cognitions act as a go-between for the physiological arousal that emotions stimulate rather than what clients often believe, which is that their feelings "come out of nowhere and make me feel bad."
2. The client systematically considers the irrational nature of his or her thoughts and identifies dysfunctional thinking patterns.
3. The client learns how dysfunctional (i.e., unrealistic) thoughts impact stressful emotions and create a physiological stress reaction.
4. The client, with the assistance of the counselor, determines ways to modify irrational thinking by intentionally replacing negative thoughts with more adaptive ones.
5. The counselor supports the client as he or she works to formulate new patterns of thinking by helping the client evaluate his or her success in change, thus enhancing wellness in both the Creative Self and Coping Self as depicted in the IS-Wel model.

Assertiveness Training

Like cognitive restructuring, assertiveness training relies on first helping a client to recognize thinking patterns that govern their interactions with other people. However, unlike cognitive restructuring, assertiveness training also involves bringing about direct change in patterns of social behavior by carefully training the client in new ways of communicating, negotiating, and overcoming fear, while at the same time working to change faulty beliefs about oneself in relationship to others.

Because many people who have difficulty managing stress effectively typically have trouble with their beliefs about themselves, they will also have faulty beliefs about how they are perceived by others (Patterson, 2000). These beliefs and behavior patterns often lead to chronic ways of interacting with others that cause the person to behave in an overly passive or overly aggressive manner. Either of these patterns are a formula for increased stress and the negative emotional states that accompany it. Through assertiveness training, clients can learn their typical patterns of behavior in relationship to others and make necessary adjustments. Learning to communicate directly, giving and receiving positive and negative feedback, learning to say "no," making requests of others without attempting to control them, and handling confrontations are all important assertiveness skills that relate to one's perceived level of stress (Patterson, 2000).

From the perspective of wellness, a client's cognitive and mental self may be conceptualized as "in shape" or "out of shape" in much the same way as the physical self might be. Subsequently, nearly any client can benefit from carefully considering the beliefs and thoughts that underlie common moods and feeling states. Even a client who is not in a state of severe psychological decline can benefit from better cognitive conditioning. Given that stress is a reality of modern life, counselors can utilize cognitive restructuring and assertiveness training to assist many clients in optimizing their mental health, reducing negative stress responses, and enhancing wellness. This focus on empowering the Creative Self and Coping Self will affect all other aspects of wellness in a positive manner (Myers & Sweeney, 2004b).

SPIRITUAL APPROACHES TO MANAGING STRESS

In the previous chapter, Cashwell provides a thorough overview of both the nature of spirituality and means by which one may expand one's spiritual connections (i.e., prayer and meditation). What is interesting and relevant to the current discussion is the role that such spiritual activities can play in the management of stress. For example, research into the effects of prayer on the person praying suggests that people who pray believe that prayer offers both physical and psychological benefits. These people may be correct as prayer is correlated with life satisfaction and well-being and appears to act as a buffer to stress (M. W. Frame, 2003). Although it is not yet known how prayer creates these positive benefits, there is some preliminary evidence that even anonymous intercessory prayer can benefit the person who is prayed for; however, this remains a controversial and inconclusive area of research (Richards & Bergin, 1997).

Nevertheless, given their potential for bringing physical and mental calm, as well as a sense of life satisfaction, spiritual approaches to managing stress are important. Such approaches are unique in that spiritual beliefs work by positively shaping the adherent's perspective on life events. In other words, a spiritual understanding of self engages the belief that one's life can be understood in a broader context in which there is a meaning and purpose inherent in all experiences and/or that there is a supportive divine being overseeing one's unfolding. Therefore, spiritually oriented techniques for managing stress cannot be applied in the same way as those discussed earlier in this chapter. This is due to the fact that prayer is only prayer if one is sincerely seeking a connection to the divine. Therefore, it cannot be faked. By contrast, exercise is beneficial whether one enjoys the process or not!

More than the other techniques of stress management, spiritual activities involve specific attitudes about one's life and the convictions that flow from these attitudes. Nevertheless, it can be argued that spirituality is the most important and far-reaching stress management "technique" available, if spirituality is theoretically the central attribute of healthy individuals (Myers, Sweeney, & Witmer, 2000b). This means that if one believes one's life has inherent value that is divinely ordained, it follows that all life experiences are of consequence—both the good and the bad. Further, a spiritual perspective aids in the process of making meaning out of negative life events and in accepting things that cannot be changed. For example, some researchers suggest that spirituality plays an important role in a number of life issues such as aging, death anxiety, alcoholism, and attitudes toward work (Kelly, 1995).

There is a growing body of research findings that religious faith and spiritual commitment serve to mediate a broad range of stress responses such as marital stability, longevity, recovery from surgery, addiction, and overall satisfaction with one's life (Kelly, 1995). Similarly, a study by J. S. Young, Cashwell, and Shcherbakova (2000) found that spirituality served to mediate the negative effects (i.e., anxiety and depression) of stressful life events. Prayer and meditation can be conceptualized as means for maximizing a client's spiritual potential. In addition, they can be used as interventions to prevent stress-related difficulties or to facilitate a client's return to a state of wellness.

SUMMARY

From a wellness perspective, stress occurs when environmental, psychological, or physical demands outdistance the individual's current capacity to meet them. A deficit in any of the primary life tasks of wellness provides an opening for stress to become unmanageable. Therefore, the counselor can, together with a client, assess for stress issues by looking at a client's functioning along the life task dimensions. If it is determined that stress management is needed, a variety of techniques for managing stress are available. These can be used to remediate or prevent stress in relation to its impact on the physical, mental/emotional, or spiritual functioning of the person. Given the position of spirituality at the center of the Wheel of Wellness model, the approach to stress management that may be the least expendable for overall wellness is a fulfilling connection to the divine through a significant spiritual or religious connection. Counselors wishing to assist clients with stress management should become adept at utilizing the techniques described and, along with clients, form a plan for managing stress as a lifelong skill to be mastered.

DISCUSSION QUESTIONS

1. How is stress best understood in terms of its relationship to general wellness?
2. Develop an explanation of stress and wellness that you could use with various types of clients (children, adolescents, adults, older adults) to explain the role of stress in their life.
3. Which of the stress management techniques discussed in this chapter are most applicable to the client populations with which you work or intend to work as a counselor? Why?
4. Practice several of the techniques discussed in this chapter with a friend or colleague. Determine what additional training you need to execute these approaches effectively with clients.

WEB RESOURCES

- **Andrew Weil's Self Healing Strategies Web site, www.drweilselfhealing. com/,** offers articles and suggestions based on integrative medicine, which combines the most optimal ideas and practices of alternative and traditional medicine to enhance the body's healing processes.
- **The Holmes-Rahe Scale, found at www.geocities.com/beyond_ stretched/holmes.htm,** offers a personal stress test commonly used to evaluate the significance and impact of major life events.
- **Stress Management and Emotional Wellness Links, www.imt.net/ ~randolfi/StressLinks.html,** offers links to manage stress and rejuvenate emotional wellness through strategies such as restructuring thinking, relaxing one's body, and seeking help from professional organizations.

21

Wellness and the *DSM-IV-TR*: A Developmental Approach for Clients in Severe Distress

Allen E. Ivey and Mary Bradford Ivey

Severe client distress as manifested in *Diagnostic and Statistical Manual of Mental Disorders* (4th ed., Text Revision, *DSM-IV-TR*; American Psychiatric Association, 2000) diagnoses such as depression, the personality "disorders," and even schizophrenia can be reframed, reconceptualized, and treated with a wellness approach (Ivey & Ivey, 1998, 1999). In this chapter, the focus is on clinical and theoretical perspectives learned from a journey that began in microcounseling (Ivey & Ivey, 2003), the well-known original skills training program used widely in counselor education and translated into 17 languages. The journey reached full development with the publication of *Developmental Counseling and Therapy: Promoting Wellness Over the Lifespan* (Ivey, Ivey, Myers, & Sweeney, 2005). A brief overview of the developmental model with a practice focus is provided in this chapter. A systematic approach that shows how to use developmental counseling in the interview is described, and special attention is given to issues of wellness from a developmental framework.

DEVELOPMENTAL COUNSELING AND THERAPY: INTEGRATING WELLNESS IN THE SESSION

Developmental Counseling and Therapy (DCT; Ivey, 1986/2000; Ivey et al., 2005) originated in the early 1980s with the discovery that Piagetian cognitive-emotional developmental concepts have value and use in the counseling and therapy process. Both Piagetian and DCT concepts are based on an educational, wellness perspective. They are developmental in that they optimistically anticipate that people can expand their cognitive, emotional, and behavioral repertoire.

Much like growth in other areas of human development, one's full potential can be stunted or blocked because of a variety of environmental, physical, or emotional conditions. As with counseling philosophy and practice from its inception (Sweeney, 2001), through DCT we seek to optimize each client's capacity to experience and respond effectively to life's tasks and challenges through positive interventions designed to maximize the client's capabilities. As a consequence, we believe that everyone, regardless of stage of life or prior circumstances, can be helped to experience life more fully and positively through DCT assessment and interventions.

DCT is also rooted in Platonic philosophy, which has useful parallels to Piagetian thought (see Table 21.1). Plato's Allegory of the Cave in the *Republic* (Cornford, 1941/1982) focused on the evolution of consciousness from embedded sensory experience to sophisticated multiperspective dialectic thinking. A distinction should be made between the concepts of stage, as used by Piaget, and of cognitive-emotional style as presented in this chapter. Piaget's stage concepts are related to age and cognitive competence. For example, a child must develop sufficient horizontal development (competence) in concrete cognitive tasks if he or she is to move to the next stage. Stages are considered to be sequential, whereas in the DCT model, styles are seen as both sequential and holistic. Thus, DCT uses Piagetian concepts of sensorimotor, concrete, and formal operations metaphorically; clients at all ages can move freely from one style or orientation to another.

Developmental Assessment

The DCT model includes specific assessment procedures so that counselors can determine the cognitive-emotional style presented by the client. The task of the counselor in the early stages is to match his or her language and cognitive-emotional style to that of the client—while later mismatching may be useful to help clients move to new styles of experiencing the world. Each client tends to have a preferred cognitive-emotional style, and we as counselors are most likely to help clients if we work with them within their style

Table 21.1

Platonic, Piagetian, and Developmental Counseling and Therapy (DCT) Views of Cognitive-Emotional Development

Worldview	Plato	Piaget	DCT
The concrete world of appearances	Imagining (*eikasia*)	Sensorimotor Preoperational	Sensorimotor/ Elemental
	Belief (*pistis*)	Concrete operations	Concrete/ situational
The abstract world of ideas and thinking	Thinking (*dianoia*)	Formal operations	Formal/reflective
	Knowledge (*episteme*) Intelligence (*noesis*)	Postformal operations	Dialectic/systemic

Note. From *The Thought and Language of the Child*, by J. Piaget, 1955, New York: New American Library (Original work published 1923).

orientation. By matching their style, we communicate our understanding of clients' meaning-making processes (i.e., accurate empathy). During the DCT assessment questioning sequence, for example, the counselor may explore issues with the sensorimotor style, in which here-and-now experiencing is stressed ("What are you feeling, hearing, seeing, right now?"). To do this we start by asking the client to respond to an open-ended question such as "Tell me what happens for you when you think of your family?" Some clients have difficulty with this line of questioning if they do not experience life events in a sensorimotor way. It is really important, however, that the counselor is patient and uses microcounseling skills to anchor the sensory aspect of the experience to a location in the body (e.g., I feel it in my heart, my head, the back of my neck, etc.).

After carefully summarizing content and feelings and mirroring the body movements and posture of the client as well, the counselor asks, "Have you ever had this feeling as located in your body before?" We then ask that they describe the second experience with a focus on concreteness and linearity ("Could you give me a specific example? What happened before it happened? What occurred after?"). Some clients can be so concrete and provide so many specific details of their experiences that others may tire of listening to them. Other clients will not be linear, and even the counselor may have difficulty reflecting what has been shared. Either way, the counselor has valuable information about blocks in the client's developmental thinking and experiencing process and where further work is needed. More often, the second incident is described successfully and the assessment process continues.

Movement across the Platonic line to formal operational abstractness occurs when we ask clients to reflect on their experience. This involves asking, "You have described two events (summarize contents and feelings, location in the body); what do these two events have in common? What meaning do you make of them? or What sense do you make of that?" "As you reflect and look back on what you said, what occurs for you?" This line of questioning gives the counselor an assessment of the client's "if this, then that" capabilities in coping with life events and their consequences. If the assessment has progressed as it should, clients are often able to see connection among the events rather easily. If not, they may be experiencing a formal operational block. This is another valuable bit of information for the counselor in intervention planning.

Dialectic/systemic assessment examines systems of knowledge. Cultural and life history come in here as well as multiple perspective thought. Often clients have internalized "rules" about themselves, life, and other people that were adaptive at earlier stages of their development but are inappropriate to present circumstances. The counselor will use the theme or rule derived by the client from what the two events had in common; for example, "When something goes wrong in relationships, it is my fault and I must do something to make things right." The questions to the client follow with, "Where do you think that rule came from? Is that always a good rule to follow? Could there be a better rule for different situations?" This begins what we consider to be the *deconstruction* of faulty self-evaluations developed as a child as well as beliefs instilled by oppressive environments in the home, school, community, and larger society. Likewise, we cooperate and act as a friend in walking with the client metaphorically in the co-construction of new more adaptable thoughts, beliefs, and behaviors.

Developmental Interventions

In the intervention stage, as might be anticipated, the DCT counselor knows that different client styles are best served using varying approaches. Table 21.2 presents examples of intervention strategies associated with each cognitive-emotional style. While one style may be most prominent in a particular intervention, many are multidimensional and may affect more than one cognitive-emotional style. In addition, a sensorimotor strategy such as imagery is often followed in counseling by concrete discussion of the story associated with the image, then formal reflection of the image and the story. In some cases, counselors will also encourage clients to examine the systems and contextual issues related to the image.

Mary Ivey was the first to apply the four-style model to children, both for diagnosis and for assessment, and she presented a model for using DCT in cases of childhood neglect or abuse. Elementary-level children in particular often appear with the sensorimotor style (e.g., tears, overwhelmed by anger, random verbalizations), although most are concrete operational. Nonetheless, the four-style intervention proves effective. With careful listening and repetition of stories, many children can achieve understanding of patterns often associated with formal operational thought. Systemic issues of family, community, and complex treatment systems are, of course, resources the counselor needs to use to ensure change. This brief summary of DCT provides a foundation for examining wellness-based interventions with severe clinical issues.

A WELLNESS APPROACH TO *DSM-IV-TR*

The first fully integrated presentation of DCT as an overall framework for assessing and treating *DSM-IV* issues appeared in 1998 (see Ivey & Ivey, 1998). The foundational belief of a wellness approach to severe distress is that these issues are a logical response to biological and psychological trauma. The DCT counselor will see even the most distressing behavior as learned protective mechanisms used by the client. Troubling syndromes are viewed as the patient or client's best effort to adapt to severe stressors often beyond his or her control. This wellness approach used a five-step conceptual model of severe stress, an expansion of the basic borderline triad described by Masterson (1981):

1. Environmental or biological insult (may lead to)
2. Stress and physical/emotional pain, which is a threat to attachment and safety (this in turn may lead to)
3. Sadness/depression (may lead to)

Table 21.2

Illustrative Strategies Corresponding to Each Developmental Counseling and Therapy (DCT) Style

Predominantly Sensorimotor/ Elemental Strategies	Predominantly Concrete/ Situational Strategies
Bodywork—acupuncture, massage, yoga	Assertiveness training
Catharsis	Behavioral counts and charts
Exercise—walking, jogging, swimming	Brief therapy
Focusing on emotions in the here and now	Cognitive automatic thoughts chart
Gestalt here-and-now activities	Crisis intervention
Guided imagery	Decision and problem-solving counseling
Medication	Desensitization and establishment of anxiety
Meditation	hierarchies
Psychodynamic free association	Narratives and story telling
Relaxation training	Psychoeducational skills training
	Reality therapy
	Rational emotive behavioral therapy
	"ABCDEF" analysis
	Thought stopping

Predominantly Formal/ Reflective Strategies	Predominantly Dialectic/ Systemic Strategies
Adlerian therapy—early recollections	Advocacy for social justice
Bibliotherapy	Community or neighborhood action
Cognitive therapy	Community genogram
Dream analysis	Family dream analysis
Logotherapy	Family genogram or chart
Narratives, reflecting on stories	Multicultural counseling and therapy
Person-centered therapy	
Psychodynamic therapies	
Rational emotive behavior therapy	
Reflection on narratives	

Theories and Strategies Applied Across All Four Styles

Consciousness-raising groups
Developmental counseling and therapy
Feminist therapy
Multicultural counseling and therapy
Self-help groups (e.g., Alcoholics Anonymous, Adult Children of Alcoholics, eating disorders)
Trauma therapy *if* it also takes a look at systemic effects on the person.

4. Defense against the pain and, in severe cases, Axis II developmental personality styles (these in turn may lead to)
5. Axis I defensive structures (termed "disorders" by *DSM-IV-TR*)

Each of these steps leads to varying intervention suggestions. At the first
level, we see the need for a preventative approach, part of the general wellness orientation. We can help clients most effectively by providing sane environments for living and healthy growth. But, as natural stress occurs, stress

management interventions can be used. If these fail, expect the client to experience some depression, although it may be masked as anxiety or other presenting issues. Depression itself can be managed very well through standard treatments such as those listed in Table 21.2. The importance of a multilevel treatment plan is emphasized in the DCT model.

The wellness models described in Part I are foundational to a holistic approach to helping. Each of the dimensions of the Indivisible Self (IS-Wel) model (Myers & Sweeney, 2004b; Sweeney & Myers, 2005) speaks to health and well-being. For example, facilitating your clients' awareness of themselves as a cultural being can be critical as cultural identity is a key aspect of wellness. The IS-Wel model contains multiple areas amenable to treatment, not only as preventive strategies but also as treatment strategies for severe disorder, including depression and Axes I and II diagnostic issues.

When under stress, one of the first components of wellness to suffer is one's sense of humor. Positive humor is an antidote to the toxicity of stress. Both physiological and emotional benefits accrue through a good belly laugh. In fact, one of the surest signs of client progress in counseling is demonstrated when clients can laugh at aspects of their predicament or self. Likewise, through the DCT assessment and intervention process, client emotional responsiveness is broadened; that is, positive emotions are felt more fully as natural and desirable. When depression is turned to righteous indignation about unjust circumstances, greater sense of worth, control, and realistic beliefs provide energy for more appropriate responses to otherwise deadening experiences. The Coping Self is empowered to effect positive change.

Within the Wheel of Wellness and IS-Wel models are components now widely recognized for ameliorating depression, anger, and anxiety with such different qualities as exercise, nutrition, and spiritual practice. Both microcounseling and DCT methods are well suited to helping clients address their most basic daily needs for good health while reaching dialectically for meaning, purpose, and contentment within life as they have yet to live it. Even the most challenging "disorders" are opportunities to promote greater wellness as counselors help their clients co-construct new rules for life events and circumstances.

Axis II personality disorders are termed *developmental personality styles* by DCT. These styles are believed to be used to mask underlying depression. For example, when one works effectively with the antisocial or borderline style, underlying depression often appears. While people do indeed likely have natural biological predispositions, years of experience in family, schools, and culture tend to produce certain ways of relating to others. Each developmental personality style has a positive aspect, which itself can help lead counselors and therapists to more effective treatment decisions. Just one example of this would be the obsessive-compulsive personality style. This style's positive aspect is the recognition that maintaining order and a system is necessary for most job success. We can expect this client to manifest perfectionistic and inflexible behavior in the session, often with little access to emotion. The developmental family history is often one of overattachment with a focus on achievement and perfection. There is considerable concreteness in the obsessive-compulsive style. The positive treatment approach suggested by DCT includes reflecting and provoking feeling to help the client experience the sensorimotor style, helping the client discover her or his personal needs, and formal operational work toward developing a more fully aware self-concept. These goals may be achieved by a variety of strategies drawn from many differing theories of counseling and therapy as shown in Table 21.2.

Axis I issues are viewed in the DCT model as the failure of Axis II developmental personality style defensive structures. While severe difficulties that result in a diagnosis such as schizophrenia or clinical depression may at least be partially related to biological conditions, the multilevel treatment suggested in DCT remains relevant. In DCT, we acknowledge that medication is a valid treatment, and we can anticipate that over the years many psychologists and, we suspect counselors as well, will have prescription privileges, but we also seek to remove medication as soon as client crisis is managed.

Whereas *DSM-IV-TR* and the medical/illness model view "disorder" as existing in the patient, the DCT counselor will view the same behavior as severe distress located both in the person and the environment. These counselors are also culture focused, realizing that many client issues are the result of racism, anti-Semitism, sexism, heterosexism, or other culturally sanctioned oppression. Rather than just treating the individual, counselors are encouraged to work to treat the environment and also encourage clients to work to eliminate oppressions that might have caused their distress (e.g., through rape prevention groups, workers' rights movements, community anti-Semitism programs).

IMPLICATIONS FOR THEORY, RESEARCH, AND PRACTICE

Perhaps the central implication of the DCT approach to severe client distress is the emphasis on person–environment contingencies. Whereas the traditional counseling and therapy approach is to place the problem ("disorder") in the client, the DCT counselor stresses the importance of examining racial, ethnic, gender, sexual orientation, and other types of oppression. It does little good in the long run to treat a person of color or a woman for depression if the real problem is an oppressive and insensitive environment.

Yet, most of psychology and psychiatry still treat clients and patients from a White European, Western view in which distress is located in the person. The professional helping field learned about posttraumatic stress disorder (PTSD) from Vietnam veterans who challenged the medical establishment. These veterans helped us see that external stressors bring about severe internal distress. But, the medical and psychological establishment still defines PTSD as something "in the individual" and gives minimal attention to environmental concerns and developmental history.

SUMMARY

In this chapter, we suggested that present conceptions of severe emotional distress as presented in *DSM-IV-TR* are oppressive and designed to facilitate provider comfort and financial gain. As a consequence, social action may be as important as individual treatment in facilitating client developmental growth. The origins and progress of the microcounseling and DCT models reflect a 35-year effort to reframe the meaning and treatment of severe distress. The specifics of microcounseling are straightforward and backed by over 450 databased studies (Daniels, 2003), whereas the more recent DCT model may be described as a conceptual system to organize well-known and useful treatment systems into a coherent whole. In addition, the DCT approach offers its own treatment alternatives. Prevention, a developmental approach, and social justice action provide the foundation of a wellness orientation to severe emotional distress.

DISCUSSION QUESTIONS

1. Developmental Counseling and Therapy (DCT) stresses the importance of defining client cognitive-emotional style and then matching counseling interventions to that style. What is your own preferred cognitive-emotional style? What therapeutic strategies are likely to be effective with that style?
2. What are your reactions and thoughts about DCT's central statement on *DSM-IV-TR*: "so-called disorder is a logical response to overwhelming and/or insane social/environmental conditions?" Do you view client difficulties as "in the client," "in the system," or in some balance of the two?
3. How can aspects of wellness models such as the Indivisible Self be applied in working with clients with severe distress? What are the benefits of taking such an approach?
4. Social action has been presented as central to a wellness approach to counseling and therapy. How can social action be implemented in working with specific types of clients?

WEB RESOURCES

- **Microtraining Associates, http://www.emicrotraining.com/,** provides a list of videos and books for microcounseling, Developmental Counseling and Therapy, and multicultural issues. This is an educational commercial site with numerous resources helpful for counselor training.
- **The Multicultural Counseling Competencies, http://www.counseling. org/resources,** presents the competencies endorsed by the American Counseling Association competencies as essential for all professional counselors as they provide specifics for a culturally competent practice.
- **Multicultural Counseling Competencies Individual and Organizational Development 0803971311.html/,** is a site that extends the multicultural counseling competencies to organizational development.
- **The online article, http://www.findarticles.com/cf_dls/m0KOC/3_5/ 83037909/p1/article.jhtml,** is a useful explanation of how to apply Developmental Counseling and Therapy in work with children.

PART IV

WELLNESS APPLICATIONS IN COUNSELING SETTINGS AND COUNSELOR EDUCATION

The major proposition of the preceding chapters is that wellness is a desirable goal for all counseling interventions; this proposition is not only relevant but essential to a saner, healthful, and vibrant society. School and workplace violence, mental health drug treatment for children and adults, and spiraling costs for health conditions associated with obesity, smoking, and related high-risk lifestyle behaviors head the list of ills that afflict the United States, the wealthiest, most powerful nation in the world. These are all the symptoms of a bankruptcy that points to serious structural problems that transcend simple solutions. As a consequence, we do not propose that through counseling alone these issues can be resolved. We do believe, however, that with a clear vision of what constitutes a vibrant, healthful school, work, or community setting, over time, even our greatest challenges can be met and a new, better environment for living long and well can be created.

We see professional counselors as empowered agents of change because of their historical roots in an optimum, developmental philosophy of helping all persons over the life span and the growing evidence of the efficacy of such a position. The preceding chapters on research are only the beginning of what is to come in evidence-based practices. As a result, the following chapters provide a foundation and blueprint for helping to create change through schools, community mental health agencies, colleges and universities, business and industry, and counselor education.

School personnel and children are under unprecedented pressure to "produce" and not be "left behind." In chapter 22, Villalba and Borders offer an alternative to the assessment-driven school curriculum. Parents will no doubt welcome an alternative that balances academic achievement and joy in the lives of their children. Indeed, learning has its own intrinsic satisfactions when nurturing learners is the goal. Using a developmental plan of integrating wellness activities through the existing curriculum from elementary through middle and high school, all the components of wellness can be addressed. There is no better place to start with a wellness initiative than in the schools. As these authors note, however, wellness in the schools is for everyone—staff, administrators, and all who will assist them. Some schools have already begun to adopt a wellness approach, and we expect more to follow.

Carney and Hazler invite the reader in chapter 23 to imagine "what if" community mental health agencies exemplified wellness instead of solution-focused interventions. Obviously there is nothing wrong with helping clients solve problems. Like the words to the song, however, "Is that all there is?" Using the Indivisible Self model as a foundation, they propose that the crises in funding for mental health agencies could well be moderated, if not overcome, with a paradigm shift in what the public expects and gets from such agencies. Self-help and alternative care is big business today because more people want to have a part in their own well-being. Community agencies have an opportunity to reinvent what it is they do and for whom.

While traditional college-age students have been among the most abundant subjects for wellness research, Hermon notes that higher education institutions in general have yet to embrace a holistic student development approach to their education. There are exceptions, fortunately, and more could be evolving with proper leadership from counseling and student development personnel. Many of the larger institutions are building aesthetically pleasing recreation facilities where exercise is considered to be the primary, if not only, component of wellness. Smaller, liberal arts colleges, however, have a mission to educate the "whole" person and find a holistic approach compatible with this mission. Hermon provides examples in chapter 24 of various methods for helping integrate wellness into the campus community for staff as well as students.

The traditional Employee Assistance Program came about as a result of burgeoning costs through lost employee productivity and health care programs. Impetus for change will not be philosophical in this sector, as benefit-to-cost ratios drive business decisions. That is good for a wellness program if it is holistically designed and accountable in its outcomes. Both are possible but it is not the norm through most efforts to date. In chapter 25, Connolly provides an inside look at the business community and its unique opportunities for professional counselors with a holistic wellness agenda and a knowledge of those whose needs they can serve.

Witmer and Granello complete the circle of participants in our vision of wellness within the various settings by applying it to counselor education. In chapter 26, they challenge us to be what it is we want others to become: deliberate, positive, and developmentally appropriate in choosing wellness as a way of life, not just more methods and techniques to use with others. National counselor education standards require that faculty define their vision and mission for their program and assess it accordingly. Witmer and Granello provide a template for how any counselor education program can integrate, adopt, or incorporate wellness into its programs. The only question remaining based on the evidence already available: Why wouldn't they do so?

22

Wellness Applications in Schools

José A. Villalba and L. DiAnne Borders

There perhaps has never been a more critical time to talk about wellness in the public schools. The current emphasis on student academic achievement and school accountability, one facet of the No Child Left Behind Act, has created unfortunate, deleterious (and perhaps unintended) effects (Amrein & Berliner, 2003). As a result of the current focus on achievement, schools are neglecting nonacademic, negative effects such as stress, peer pressure, and poor self-esteem, which may have a detrimental impact on the social–emotional development of children and adolescents (Ainslie, Shafer, & Reynolds, 1996; Alves-Martins, Peixoto, Gouveia-Pereira, Amaral, & Pedro, 2002; Kiselica, Baker, Thomas, & Reedy, 1994; Santor, Messervey, & Kusumakar, 2000). Teachers, school counselors, and other school personnel are feeling overwhelmed and even unappreciated as a result of the disproportionate importance placed on academic achievement as opposed to academic development and general well-being of their students (Hayes, Nelson, Tabin, Pearson, & Worthy, 2002; Martinez & Martinez, 2002; Myrick, 2003).

Researchers have added their perspective on high-stakes testing and academic-achievement-oriented schools, reporting the failure of high-stakes tests to produce motivated and higher achieving students (Amrein & Berliner, 2003) and questioning the statistical validity and reliability of large-scale state assessments (Yen & Henderson, 2002). Even popular media have sounded the alarm. Writing in *Newsweek*, Tyre (2003) reported that nearly 20% of elementary schools in the United States had eliminated recess to allow additional instructional time. Counselors would easily predict the negative consequences from such a move, both from developmental, learning perspectives—children need activity and, without it, are less focused and more fidgety in the classroom—and from a wellness perspective—inactivity contributes to poor physical health and obesity. Some parents and educators have fought back, lobbying for mandated daily recess (Tyre, 2003); organizing citywide family nights with no homework, team practices, or club meetings (Steptoe, 2003); or establishing schoolwide or systemwide wellness-based programs for students and staff (Gallagher & Satter, 1998; Steptoe, 2003;

www.ridgewood.k12.nj.us). Clearly, there is both a strong need and a public outcry to promote wellness in public schools.

In this chapter, we propose that intentional application of a wellness perspective can enhance not only the school counseling program but also the entire school climate. First, we identify how components of wellness models are—or could be—reflected in a school's curriculum, counseling program, and other school activities. Then we provide specific examples of wellness-based school counseling activities that are appropriate at various developmental levels. Lastly, we suggest ways that wellness concepts can be applied to staff development.

WELLNESS MODELS AND THE SCHOOL CLIMATE

An emphasis on wellness is a natural fit for school counselors (Myers, Sweeney, & Witmer, 2001; Omizo, Omizo, & D'Andrea, 1992). In fact, it could be said that school counselors have always promoted wellness, even when the term was not in vogue. Like wellness, school counseling programs are rooted in proactive, prevention models and developmental theories, and they are comprehensive and holistic in nature (Borders & Drury, 1992; Myrick, 2003; Omizo et al., 1992; Paisley, 2001; Sweeney, 2001). Nevertheless, school counselors' work could be enhanced by an explicit application of a wellness perspective. Wellness models (e.g., Myers & Sweeney, 2004b) provide a broad framework for assessing, planning, and evaluating not only a school counseling program but all aspects of a school. Determining effective and ineffective factors in school counseling programs as well as throughout the school environment currently is considered one of the many responsibilities of school counselors (Dahir & Stone, 2003; Lapan, 2001).

In fact, these wellness models clearly set forth that schools are a key source of influence on a child's wellness; this is particularly true for elementary and middle school students, as school is a focal point of their lives, given their developmental tasks (Cowen, 1991). For example, in the Wheel of Wellness model (Myers et al., 2001), education is one of seven "life forces" that interact dynamically with a person's life tasks. In the Indivisible Self wellness model (IS-Wel; Myers & Sweeney, 2004b), education is one of several "institutional contexts" that "affect our lives in both direct and indirect ways." Importantly, the influence of education is often "powerful, difficult to assimilate, and again may be positive or negative." Indeed, environmental contexts such as schools may enhance or erode wellness (Cowen, 1991). Thus, assessment of the wellness climate of a school would provide information critical to the health of all members of a school community. In a consultant role, school counselors then can use such an assessment to help school staff revise policies and practices as needed, design needed programs, and identify appropriate outcome variables.

Using a wellness model as a gauge of a school's health, school counselors are likely to find both positive and negative components at work in their school, including those within and external to the school counselor's purview (see Gallagher & Satter, 1998). For example, physical education classes and sports programs clearly contribute to the Wheel of Wellness's (see chapter 3) Exercise factor; health and sex education classes support Nutrition, Gender Identity, and Self-Care; Safety Patrol, "bully proofing," conflict resolution, and drug prevention programs likely contribute to Sense of Control, Stress Management, and Problem Solving; cultural celebrations during Black History Month and Hispanic Awareness Month support Cultural Identity; senior service projects enhance Sense of Worth; safety issues related to a specific community can be addressed and resolved through Problem Solving and Creativity; and a school counselor's classroom guidance units, small-group activities, and individual counseling sessions most often address issues related to Emotional Awareness and Coping, Realistic Beliefs, Sense of Control, Sense of Worth, and Self-Care. Of course, the existence of these courses, programs, and activities is no guarantee that they are positive influences, so that some assessment of effectiveness also is required.

However, positive wellness components in a school sometimes are contradicted by other (well-meaning) activities. For example, the Parent Teacher Association (PTA) at one school in our area designated funds for Project Fit America equipment and for pizza and ice cream rewards for guidance classroom of the month (Nutrition and Exercise factors)! In some areas, school accountability measures, as well as budget cuts, have led to cutbacks or elimination of physical education offerings and sports programs (Exercise factor), music and drama programs (Creativity and Cultural Identity factors), and in-school suspension programs (Sense of Control factor). Stressed school administrators and teachers may act in ways that negatively affect students' (and their own) Sense of Worth.

Wellness, then, need not be just an appropriate and positive, abstract philosophy in a school. Through application of wellness models such as those described in Part I, concrete assessment, enhancement, and evaluation of a school's wellness climate can be achieved.

IMPLICATIONS FOR PRACTICE: WELLNESS FOR CHILDREN AND ADOLESCENTS IN SCHOOLS

Children and adolescents enrolled in schools find themselves in ever-changing environments as schools evolve in size, student body demographics shift, and the academic achievement focus increases. The changes experienced within the school environment by students are amplified, often times at stress-inducing levels, by biological and psychological development. Wellness models, such as the Wheel of Wellness and the IS-Wel, may be used to enhance the academic environment of these children and adolescents while relieving some of the psychosocial pressures experienced in schools, as highlighted by Holcomb-McCoy in chapter 6. School counselors can and should play a key role in promoting a philosophy of wellness in their schools.

In a review of the 17 factors in the Wheel of Wellness, and the third-order factors in the IS-Wel model, it is apparent that some of the tasks require a person to be more mature, more emotional, and more intellectually developed than others. Therefore, school counselors in specific educational settings (elementary, middle, or high school) may elect to focus on a certain task or factor when designing and implementing developmentally appropriate wellness activities for students in their schools. For example, elementary school counselors may elect to deal with more concrete concepts, such as taking care of one's body and the importance of eating healthy foods. Middle school counselors can direct their wellness exercises toward more abstract concepts related to a student's self-control and effectively managing stressful situations. Finally, high school counselors can address more ambiguous concepts, such as self-worth and planning a desirable, realistic future.

School counselors may use individual, small-group, and classroom guidance counseling modalities to deliver wellness information to students. Because the possible combination of counseling modalities, wellness factors, and educational settings yields a large number of options and possibilities for applying wellness models in the schools, we have elected to provide examples of general strategies for each educational level. In addition, an example of how to deliver wellness information using a selected counseling modality is presented for each of the three educational settings. Consistent with the wellness models and philosophy espoused in this book, changes in any one area of wellness will contribute to changes in all areas; hence we recommend starting with specific programs within a general goal of infusing wellness throughout the school environment.

Elementary Schools

An effective strategy for dealing with wellness in the elementary school setting is to help children understand the importance of basic wellness activities. Potential wellness factors to be addressed throughout this initial educational level may include Self-Care, Exercise, Nutrition, and Sense of Humor. School counselors and other educators can help children realize the importance of establishing positive personal habits with regard to basic hygiene, physical activity, eating a well-balanced diet, and, in essence, enjoying the positives in their lives.

According to Holcomb-McCoy, in chapter 6, large-group guidance lessons on wellness increased participants' wellness knowledge when compared with children not receiving large-group guidance wellness instruction. Elementary school counselors interested in highlighting the importance of wellness to young children may use a classroom guidance unit centered on self-care, composed of, for example, five different lessons. Potential lessons can include medical and dental hygiene, not talking or interacting with strangers, behaving in a safe manner so as to reduce harm to self and others, getting sufficient rest, and saying no to drugs and alcohol. School counselors also may design self-care lessons in collaboration with classroom teachers in an effort to infuse wellness topics throughout the curriculum. Finally, school counselors may enhance their self-care unit, thereby increasing the impact and applicability of the lessons, by using art, books, videos, music, and dance activities (Myrick, 2003).

Middle Schools

The factors Problem Solving and Creativity, Stress Management, Sense of Control, and Emotional Awareness and Coping are developmentally appropriate wellness areas of focus for middle school counselors. Middle school students' ability to observe concepts and ideas from less concrete and more abstract perspectives should enable them to better grasp notions of imagination, coping with stressors, locus of control, and understanding and controlling one's feelings. Middle school students familiar with wellness concepts, perhaps from experiences in the elementary settings, may be encouraged to draw on their wellness knowledge to facilitate their grasp of developmentally appropriate factors.

Middle school children, particularly adolescent girls, may experience poor self-image because of peer and societal pressures (Akos & Levitt, 2003). Akos and Levitt proposed group counseling as one way in which school counselors can help middle school students with poor self-esteem and a negative self-image. A wellness-centered small-group activity, composed of six to eight sessions, can help middle school children with an unhealthy body image to be more emotionally aware. More importantly, a counselor-led small-group counseling intervention can help children cope with negative feelings and beliefs. Furthermore, Akos and Levitt indicated the importance of including parents of children with poor self-image and coping skills in the process of enriching their psychosocial well-being.

High School

The four self-direction factors—Gender Identity, Cultural Identity, Sense of Worth, and Realistic Beliefs—may be addressed by high school counselors. Although gender and cultural identity development, for example, begin to occur as early as age 3 or 4, it is not until children are in high school that they begin to think of themselves as members of a particular gender or ethnic background and the implications of their membership in these groups (Helms, 2003). High school counselors can serve as a conduit for wellness education to high school students, particularly with such abstract and mature factors.

Although it may be extremely difficult for high school counselors to see many students on an individual counseling basis, in light of their multitude of responsibilities and large caseloads, they may use individual counseling in working with cultural identity development issues. High school students, as they learn more about their racial/ethnic group through academic endeavors and social interactions, may begin to experience guilt, anger, or resentment toward their race/ethnicity or those who are racially/ethnically different (H. L. K. Coleman, Casali, & Wampold, 2001). Individual counseling with a school counselor who is knowledgeable about multicultural counseling theories and techniques can provide a student who experiences feeling cultural identity confusion or discomfort with the wellness skills to cope with his or her situation. Through counseling interventions, students are provided with a safe and private forum to discuss their own beliefs and opinions about belonging to a particular cultural group, in addition to their thoughts about members of other cultural groups (Villalba, 2003). The long-term benefits of sharing and facilitating cultural identity development and wellness in high school students include better understanding of oneself, others, family, and society. It also may improve race relations in a high school, as well as reduce conflict and violence, another desired outcome from a wellness perspective.

IMPLICATIONS FOR PRACTICE: WELLNESS FOR SCHOOL STAFF

School counselors also may apply wellness concepts to staff development across all educational settings. Teachers, teaching assistants, administrators, office staff, and other school support staff would benefit from school counselor workshops and activities related to the philosophy of wellness, such as the Wheel of Wellness and the IS-Wel. Although staff development through wellness may seem like a cumbersome and overwhelming responsibility for school counselors, the promotion of schoolwide well-being will enrich the academic experience of students and families. In addition, school staff that are aware and knowledgeable of wellness concepts may be more likely to apply healthy strategies in the curriculum and throughout the school.

A staff development workshop is one method a school counselor could use to address wellness concepts with school staff. Similar to classroom guidance interventions, it is possible for school counselors to organize and implement a workshop whereby all school staff partake in wellness self-assessment and exercises. School counselors could lead staff in discussions around the current academic achievement focus in schools and how that focus affects the school environment. During the workshop, school counselors can facilitate a forum in which school staff learn how focusing on the IS-Wel or Wheel of Wellness may lead to healthier physiological and psychological well-being, both in school and away from school. School counselors also can help staff realize the benefits of modeling wellness concepts and behaviors to students. Finally, once the wellness staff development workshop is over, school counselors can continue to promote wellness throughout the school year by planning year-round activities focused on wellness, such as guest speakers, newsletters, and after-school gatherings. In essence, school counselors should strive to make the educational setting a bastion of wellness for school staff and students alike.

In terms of measuring wellness throughout the school environment, school counselors can administer and instruct school staff on using the Wellness Evaluation of Lifestyle (WEL) assessment tool, perhaps during the staff development workshop (Myers et al., 2001). The WEL can be used by all school staff to help them determine their own individual wellness. School staff members' WEL results may contribute to their understanding of how they manage their professional and personal responsibilities. Consequently, school counselors may use the staff's WEL results to gauge the school wellness climate, thereby facilitating their role in fostering a positive learning and teaching atmosphere (Lapan, 2001). Also, school counselors may establish advisory groups comprising school staff, which may determine the effectiveness and ineffectiveness of school policies, physical plant, and curriculum practices, using data generated by the WEL.

A system that incorporates several of the above recommendations is being implemented in a local school by Myers and Sweeney (see chapter 5). School faculty and staff were trained in the concepts and philosophy of wellness. In addition, the Five Factor Wellness Inventory was being used to assess the wellness of third-, sixth-, and ninth-grade students at the school. The entire process was undertaken by a schoolwide wellness committee, charged with promoting collaboration and commitment to wellness. Potentially, the ideas, services, and programs organized and implemented by the schoolwide wellness committee could extend to parents and other community members connected to the school.

SUMMARY

The discerning reader may have noticed that we have directly discussed all aspects of the Wheel of Wellness and IS-Wel (Myers et al., 2001; Myers & Sweeney, 2004b; Sweeney & Myers, 2005) except for one, spirituality. Some might argue that spirituality is an inappropriate topic for the school setting. Yet, Myers et al.'s definition of spirituality suggests other more basic and critical considerations. In particular, the emphasis on "a deep sense of wholeness or connectedness" seems a powerful goal for a school community. Others (e.g., August & Hakuta, 1997; Purkey & Schmidt, 1996) have discussed the importance of "inviting" schools, in which students feel safe and connected to their teachers, and have identified the contributions these factors make to students' academic success and psychosocial well-being. Putting these factors within the realm of spirituality, however, emphasizes their centralness to a student's being, well-being, and development, and thus the relevance of a spiritual dimension to a school counselor's work.

We have argued that wellness is—and should be—a central concept underlying a school counselor's work, particularly in light of current pressures on schools, school staff, and school students. Wellness models make clear the importance of education to one's development and well-being and emphasize education's connection with many other aspects of one's well-being. That larger perspective is greatly needed and, we hope, will become a guiding principle for school counselors' work.

DISCUSSION QUESTIONS

1. What are some ways that your school promotes wellness? What are some ways that your school seems to detract from the wellness of students and staff?

2. Is it possible for schools to balance the emphasis on accountability measures and academic achievement with monitoring the psychosocial development and well-being of students and staff? Why or why not? How?
3. Discuss the appropriateness of using spirituality as a guiding concept in the schools.
4. How might you introduce your school's staff to a workshop addressing the importance of school wellness? How could you help them to be receptive to measuring the school's wellness climate using the Wellness Evaluation of Lifestyle?
5. How could children and adolescents in your school be introduced to wellness concepts? How could they practice wellness in the school environment and in the home?

WEB RESOURCES

- **Healthier Schools, www.healthierschools.org/,** provides an in-depth description of Healthier Schools New Mexico and A Model of Coordinated School Health, which includes nutrition, health education and life skills, physical education and activity, staff wellness, family and community partnership, health and safe environment, social and emotional well-being, and health services.
- **The National Education Association (NEA) Mental Health Page, www. neahin.org/programs/mentalhealth/,** provides NEA members with information, education, and training about contemporary mental health topics.
- **The Web site, http://www.mnschoolhealth.com/index2.html/,** is a cooperative effort between Minnesota's Departments of Health and Education. It has numerous tips on wellness and how healthy living can lead to better academic experiences. The "starter kit/start here" button on the left side of the menu bar provides an overview, and summaries are provided for useful Web links.

23

Wellness Counseling in Community Mental Health Agencies

JoLynn V. Carney and Richard J. Hazler

A married couple asked if they could discuss their experiences at a local mental health clinic. They were not displeased with the counselors or the agency and were learning a lot, but they had a nagging feeling that something was missing.

The wife described her therapeutic work as dealing with depression with aspects of posttraumatic stress disorder (PTSD) from an early childhood experience. The husband was trying to deal with an adult form of attention deficit hyperactivity disorder (ADHD) and what some people thought was his overpowering personality. Their preteen daughter was having discipline problems and experimenting with cutting herself. They each talked of coming to understand their problems and working directly on them as individuals and as a family. Their language included terms like *solution-focused, cognitive-behavioral,* and *homework exercises.* The drugs they were taking could be cited and their use explained. The couple saw themselves as making progress, sort of, but it seemed something was missing.

Neither this couple's problems nor process is unique. Their counselors were providing quality professional service. Yet, this brief interaction exemplifies what is generally not being offered in mental health agencies today—a focus on wellness and the whole person, including how the non-cognitive-behavioral aspects of their life provide choices, opportunities, and strength. To strengthen this wellness focus, community mental health agencies (CMHAs) need to look beyond specific client problems to a more systemic view of the needs, desires, and conditions experienced by individuals and communities so that a therapeutic foundation based on the widest variety of available strengths and prevention opportunities can be built.

WELLNESS POTENTIAL IN A MANAGED CARE ENVIRONMENT

CMHAs were forced to become more business oriented when federal funding began a downward spiral starting in the 1970s. Physical management required close attention to finding financing for all clients in ways that were balanced with agency expenses. The rapid growth of managed care added more burdens by promoting shorter counseling interventions based on official diagnostic criteria, medication management, emergency services, and increased paperwork to verify diagnosis, treatment planning, and outcomes (Cypres, Landsberg, & Spellmann, 1997). These shrinking resources and expanded service demands have put the viability of CMHAs' health focus into question for the future unless they can find new ways to support the full range of treatment and prevention they were initially designed to provide.

The time is critical for CMHAs to find prevention and treatment options that make them truly community mental health service agencies rather than problem treatment facilities. The way to do so is through a wellness model, a holistic/wellness/prevention-based approach with a long history of advocacy by the counseling profession (Sweeney, 1995a, 2001). Unfortunately, researchers, theorists, practitioners, and CMHAs continue to build their efforts around a deficit diagnosis and treatment model. Holistic, wellness, and prevention issues are increasingly being sought by the public, and the sooner CMHAs recognize and act on this financial and service potential, the more they will ensure an influential future role in society.

Validation for wellness efforts by agencies and counselors is provided in this chapter along with specific benefits of a wellness model to CMHAs, including examples of proven direct and indirect wellness therapeutic approaches. The future is envisioned though the Wellness Mall model for practical application with individuals, communities, organizations, businesses, and even financial investors and as a challenge to create outside our normal day-to-day boxes.

A MODEL FOR IDENTIFYING WELLNESS OPPORTUNITIES

Broader and more effective integration of wellness into CMHA practices requires a model on which to identify appropriate opportunities for inclusion. Two directly related models that have received significant attention for their philosophical foundations in counseling, cross-disciplinary emphasis, and supportive research are the Wheel of Wellness (see Myers, Sweeney, & Witmer, 2000b) and the Indivisible Self model of wellness (IS-Wel; Myers & Sweeney, 2004b). The five factors of the IS-Wel provide opportunities to identify resources and practices that can be matched with specific wellness needs of clients and the community. Recognizing and taking actions to include them in the efforts of CMHA is one way to begin designing a community wellness approach to mental health.

The Physical Self (see chapter 2), which emphasizes exercise and nutrition, is perhaps the most commonly recognized wellness focus. The Creative Self combines thinking, emotions, control, positive humor, and work in ways that can enhance or exacerbate one's capacity to live life fully. The Social Self relates to friendship and love, including issues such as family, friends, isolation, and intimacy. The Coping Self relates to the ways in which people manage their lives such as leisure activities, stress management techniques, sense of self-worth, and the degree to which people hold realistic beliefs. The Essential Self relates to existential aspects of oneself, including spirituality, self-care, gender identity, and cultural identify. Together they provide an effective way to conceptualize holistic wellness for individuals and communities.

These categories have research support for inclusion as mental health issues and also provide vehicles for identifying actions that support them. CMHAs have the potential to expand their practice by identifying additional preventive measures that will attract clients and by implementing wellness techniques directed at these categories within currently used therapeutic models. Financial and practice success comes to those who act not only on what is being done but also on what creatively can be done better. The rewards will go to those who take a viable wellness model and begin finding ways to integrate it into a full range of applications.

AGENCIES NEED A WELLNESS MODEL TO SURVIVE AND EXPAND

CMHAs can either act on wellness or miss their greatest opportunity in decades. The longer a nearly total emphasis remains on getting every dollar out of managed care companies and the government for diagnosis and treatment of mental illness, the more opportunities to be mental health leaders rather than followers will be missed. The wellness market in the private sector is growing rapidly, and the time to get in the business is now.

"If I have to" is the way people think about copayments under managed care plans, but they are quite willing to purchase nonreimbursed self-care alternatives. A 1998 study by Landmark Healthcare and Interactive Solutions confirmed what professionals are seeing. Alternative forms of health care were used by 42% of respondents in the previous year, 45% said they would pay out of pocket to get the care they felt they needed, and 71% believed there would be increasing public demand for alternative health care opportunities.

Americans today are more knowledgeable and assertive about things that affect their health than even two decades ago. They view TV news shows, documentary specials, and talk shows about the variety of ways to understand and care for their mental, emotional, physical, and spiritual health. Magazines, newspapers, and even drug companies run regular ads, columns, and multipage special sections on health and wellness topics. CMHA's will miss the boat if they do not get on board this movement soon.

Sociological issues are also providing pressure to expand treatment and prevention models. No longer are White European models for medicine and mental health accepted as right for everyone. Attention to diversity, including racial, ethnic, religious, and gender issues, among others, are pressuring physical and mental health establishments to be more responsive to differences in the ways people define, establish, and maintain an effective and well-rounded life.

WELLNESS MODEL BENEFITS TO AGENCIES

People are ready and willing to pay for their health. Fitness centers, natural food stores, sleep centers, homeopathic services, massage establishments, church-related support centers, and a host of other human service opportunities have become commonplace without the support of managed care companies. All get their support from people wanting something more than basic mental or physical health care and are willing to pay directly with less paperwork and no middleman for the service providers.

If the prospect of additional paying customers is not enough encouragement for CMHAs to expand into a wellness model, then how about a healthier, more effective staff as another outcome? Wellness models for Employee Assistance Programs have demonstrated savings for businesses on insurance costs, fewer workdays missed, and better productivity of staff (Emener, Hutchison, & Richard, 2003). Integrating wellness opportunities into CMHAs would create opportunities to offer services to staff and therefore provide a healthier environment in which they would live and work. Such an environment would reduce the common problems of burnout and turnover in agencies.

Bringing alternative forms of prevention and support services together in a more holistic model will also facilitate community wellness. People are pressing communities to be more responsive to wellness choices, as exemplified by the overwhelming reduction in places where people can smoke and the increase in recreation opportunities. Businesses are recognizing the economic value in society's desire for greater wellness, and CMHAs have the historical and service orientation to become major players in this trend.

COMPLEMENTARY PATHS TO WELLNESS

Opportunities for CMHAs to expand from the illness model into more wellness-oriented models are multiplying. They include activities that can take place in counseling sessions, indirect additions to the agency's environment, development of new services, and formal collaborations with local wellness service providers.

Wellness Approaches to Therapy: Direct Wellness Strategies

Direct treatment strategies that incorporate a wellness perspective can be infused throughout the entire counseling process. A wellness approach to therapy can begin at intake with a thorough assessment of clients' nutritional and exercise routines (i.e., Physical Self). Self-care issues can be intentionally incorporated into every session, and important gender, cultural, and spiritual issues also help to focus counseling interactions (i.e., Essential Self).

Viable approaches available to clients include but are not limited to acupuncture, therapeutic touch, imagery, and the creative arts, including dance/movement therapy. Additional innovative approaches that have been tested in practice are eye movement desensitization and reprocessing

(EMDR), thought field therapy, spiritual therapy, and body-centered therapies (Corsini, 2001; S. Shannon, 2002). EMDR, developed by Francis Shapiro, is a technique for cognitive restructuring of traumatic events by desensitizing clients to those events and reducing traumatic symptomatology. Clients image the traumatic events, allowing themselves to reexperience all of the associated emotions and physical sensations while attending to an external left-right stimulus that may be eye movement, audio tones, or hand taps (Shapiro, 2002). Thought field therapy (TFT) is an integrated, meridian-based, mind–body–energy psychotherapy that is incorporated into treatment while clients are focused on their problems. TFT helps lessen clients' negative emotions, activating a number of designated acupuncture points by tapping those areas, which is said to then neutralize or eliminate the energetic cause of the client's problem (Diepold, 2002). A full exploration of alternative approaches is not possible here, but two creative strategies should stimulate thoughts of others.

Aromatherapy and Flowers. Aromatherapy and flowers provide a complementary avenue to increase a wellness focus, because smell is one of the strongest senses that can increase clients' overall sense of well-being. The benefits associated with using aromas in healing (e.g., Cooksley, 2002) have made it a staple in other professions (e.g., nursing). Clients can explore applications of basic scents in their lives, such as lavender as a calming agent, citrus as an uplifting agent, and rosemary and clary sage as mental clarity agents. Staff can also benefit by using vaporizers or spritzers to infuse scents into the environment. One caveat is to assure that people with allergies or scent sensitivities are not negatively affected by these approaches.

Floral work provides an additional alternative vehicle for creative expression, exploration of wellness, strengths, and deficits. The intent is to tap client senses, emotions, and cognitions by simultaneous stimulation of smell, sight, and touch. The olfactory, optical, and tactile senses can elicit repressed feelings, memories, and thoughts, making the use of flowers in counseling another creative art like music, dance, drama, imagery, drawing, literature, humor, and play that promote attention to all five wellness factors. No floral design skills or knowledge is necessary to promote expression of feelings and thoughts from children, adults, individual, or group clinical issues such as grief and loss, depression, self-esteem, trust, or to build group cohesion.

Introducing flowers and plants into clients' environments can connect them in a significant way to the lifecycle of the Earth and its healing forces. The seasons are mirrored in the musty leaves and mum plants of fall; the sight of poinsettias in winter; the pungent odors of hyacinths and lilies in the spring; the feel of warm earth under our feet and blossoms everywhere we look in the summer. The Eden Alternative (http://www.edenalt.com/) is just one example in which plants, music, pets, and other "normal" aspects of living are introduced into long-term care settings for older people, resulting in increases in health and quality of life (Barba, Tesh, & Courts, 2002).

Music in Therapy. Tapping into music inspires delight and relaxation with important therapeutic benefits that can heal the body, strengthen the mind, and unlock the creative spirit (e.g., D. G. Campbell, 1997). A range of sounds from nature to classical symphonic works can be integrated with counseling for issues such as stress reduction, chronic pain, anxiety, depression, and ADHD. Music therapy for homework assignments can foster creativity, imagery, and visualization much more effectively than behavioral logs have accomplished. Tapping the Creative Self and Coping Self, music therapy can help balance mood and therapeutic effect when clients choose music and sounds that match their personal preferences (Sultanoff, 2002). Counselors can encourage clients to trust their own sensitivities to music they love and experiment with their musical tastes to find what works best for them therapeutically.

Indirect Wellness Strategies for Therapy

Indirect treatment strategies may encourage client relaxation and involvement in waiting-room activities. One simple approach is to include music in the waiting-room atmosphere where its healing properties can begin producing positive effects before a counselor is ever seen. A second strategy, already found in many agencies, is the incorporation of living plants into the waiting room. The interconnection between people and plants is an excellent vehicle for increasing client and staff overall wellness in CMHAs. Plants not only have a calming effect on people, but they also moderate the humidity and pollutants in a room.

Why not make the waiting room a healing room? For example, through our work with flowers, clients have shown us that they choose a particular flower that often holds an unconscious meaning to them. Imagine the positive energy in a waiting room where clients are relaxed and involved as opposed to sitting in isolation, staring at the walls, avoiding eye contact, and mindlessly flipping through a magazine. Music, plants, flowers, and sand trays in the waiting room can help tap client Coping and Creative Selves even before counseling begins.

Collaborative Wellness Services

Expanding an agency's wellness agenda in financially viable ways benefits from introducing alternative services available in the community, but not necessarily in the agency itself. Collaborative arrangements are not new to problem treatment where, for example, schools, CMHAs, rehabilitation services, and children's services often work together with an individual or family. It is not common, however, when it comes to connecting service providers for wellness efforts. The potential for new and collaborative wellness efforts is continually expanding as the examples that follow may suggest.

Physical Modality Collaborations. A focus on wellness is incomplete when the Physical Self is not addressed. It appears clear that a common role for diet is played in the etiology of mood disorders and the risk of cardiac mortality from research results across 60 countries (Settle, 2002). Nutrition, diet, and exercise have been linked to migraines, depression, postpartum mood disorders, cognitive development, ADHD, and schizophrenia. Collaborative relationships developed between CMHAs and nutritionists, herbologists, and physical trainers could make significant differences for clients.

Mind–Body Collaborations. Overwhelming evidence supports the mind–body interface. Biofeedback, which primarily allows clients to observe, become more aware of, and learn to control their bodily processes, is highly empowering as it enables clients to bring mind–body processes under conscious control. Meditation, progressive muscle relaxation, hypnosis, self-hypnosis, and breath work all focus on the same underlying theme of client empowerment. These self-regulating experiences become powerful preludes to control in other aspects of client lives and mental health issues such as anxiety, depression, attention deficit, and addictions (Moss, 2002).

Mind–Body–Spirit Collaboration. Counseling for spiritual wellness is a paramount way to use the spirituality that is a natural part of being human to improve client quality of life (see chapters 18 and 19). The holistic interface of our body, mind, and spirit improves mental and physical health by training and focusing our mental activity. "The spirit–emotion aspects interface and guide healing and health by structuring the broadest beliefs, attitudes, and perspectives with which we create our existential viewpoint" (Wyker, 2002, p. 288). Simultaneously assisting clients' personal and spiritual development will have each contributing to the other in an overlapping and interactive manner, clearly benefiting client growth as reflected in the Indivisible Self model (see chapter 3). Collaborations with systems that support client spiritual development, such as spiritual centers encompassing ecumenical approaches to spirituality, retreat centers, or courses such as the popular "Course in Miracles" (Foundation for Inner Peace, n.d.), might all hold unique value for CMHAs and their customers.

RESEARCH FOR ETHICAL PRACTICE, MARKETING, AND WELLNESS PROMOTION

Combining research with the practice of wellness interventions must be planned before action is taken. Doubters will have appropriate concerns that the viability of wellness actions and collaborations mentioned here are not sufficiently supported by research, which can in turn open individuals and agencies to ethical examination and potentially expensive lawsuits. What the concern does not take into account is the nature of mental health counseling and how all prevention and intervention techniques only become viable as we use and refine them through application and research. We would not, for example, be using person-centered, cognitive-behavioral, or brief therapy models today if they had not been utilized before adequate research was available. The initial application process allows necessary research to be accomplished.

Once research is identified as a critical need in the integration of wellness approaches for CMHAs, the next question becomes how is it to be supported with limited resources? Several primary sources are available, including federal and state health and mental health agencies, hospitals, medical care providers (even HMOs and drug companies), higher education, local governments, service organizations, churches, and investors. Federal agencies such as the National Institutes of Health (NIH), the National Institute of Mental Health (NIMH), and the Substance Abuse and Mental Health Services Administration (SAMHSA) fund health-related projects and are potential sources of money for larger projects, but they cannot be relied on to support the many needed smaller and ongoing projects. Higher education is increasingly expecting research by faculty, which in our field is primarily the applied research that CMHAs need, thereby creating a common mission for their collaboration.

THE WELLNESS MALL

Doubters will say, "This all sounds great, but who will pay for the facilities and personnel needed for implementation and research since, even if they wanted to, NIH, NIMH, SAMHSA, and other large-scale government sources cannot support more than a fraction of local initiation efforts?" The truth is that many individuals and groups could provide the needed support based on their current activities and motivation. Local governments are increasingly funding projects for the health and well-being of constituents. Ball fields, recreation buildings, arts centers, and community gathering places are just a few of the expanding efforts to meet community wellness needs. Service organizations are continually looking for ways to provide human and financial support to projects aimed at bettering the lives of people in their communities. Religious organizations are another big contributor to projects that promote human learning, health, and wellness, and recent government rulings have opened additional doors to making them full-fledged community collaborators. By consolidating the many public service wellness activities, a critical step toward maximizing the use of community resources will be achieved.

Private investment is another major underutilized resource that could provide support for funding, implementation, and evaluation of wellness programs. Investors are generally not seen as a critical part of community projects, but that is only because nonprofits like CMHAs rarely invite their involvement with an incentive for profit. Nonprofit organizations and profit-making ones can collaborate in fully developed wellness programs that would include profitable products and services. Imagine a Wellness Mall complex where health food stores, massage businesses, exercise studios, a gardening center, arts studio, book store, education center, counseling services, spiritual center, computer training, biofeedback labs, climbing walls, a children's exercise playground, a senior center, community government, and more bring people together in search of health and a sense of community. Many of these would be for-profit establishments, including family stores and retail chains. The incentive for private investment in wellness is present if we can look beyond a limited traditional vision of what mental health services entail to have CMHAs lead in collaboratively building a wellness culture throughout our communities.

SUMMARY

The circumstances that have pressured CMHAs to take a more business-oriented approach to mental health care have created pressures to look toward a wellness approach to provide better services in a more competitive atmosphere. Such an approach can viably provide wellness benefits to individuals, families, and communities to the business benefit of CMHAs. Examples of wellness-oriented therapeutic techniques that would fit such a model were provided along with the rationale and collaborative design for needed research to expand the model in the future. Finally, a vision of a collaborative Wellness Mall was offered as the concrete conceptualization of how this wellness model could be used to promote the collaborative efforts of CMHAs, service organizations, community governments, and large and small businesses to produce places of both socially and economically responsible wellness for whole communities. Economics and human health will continue to be tied even more closely together in the future, and a holistic wellness model can provide the vehicle to support both sides of that equation.

DISCUSSION QUESTIONS

1. How can a community needs assessment be used to establish a holistic wellness program that fits the mission of your mental health agency?
2. What incentives and barriers are faced by your agency staff (e.g., counselors, psychiatrists, psychologists, social workers) in adopting a holistic wellness model to service?
3. Who should you enlist in promoting interest among businesses, service organizations, local governments, and schools in developing a communitywide wellness program?
4. What could you do to build consensus among all stakeholders for a wellness model?
5. How could a wellness plan and applied research strengthen the agency's future viability?
6. What specific topics would you include on your agency's client evaluation form to serve as feedback on the effectiveness and benefits of a holistic wellness program?

WEB RESOURCES

- **The National Institutes of Health (NIH), www.nih.gov/,** is a chief distributor of medical and behavioral research for the United States. The NIH aims to nurture creative discoveries, develop and renew prevention resources, increase the knowledge base in the medical and associated sciences, and promote the highest level of integrity, accountability, and responsibility for scientific conduct.
- **The National Institute of Mental Health, www.nimh.nih.gov/,** seeks to improve mental health through support of research on the mind,

brain, and behavior. The Web site provides links to news and research related to mental health as well as funding information.

- **The National Center for Complementary and Alternative Medicine, nccam.nih.gov/,** is part of NIH that explores complementary and alternative healing processes in the frame of rigorous science, training of researchers, and dissemination of information to the public and professionals.
- **The Substance Abuse and Mental Health Services Administration, www.samhsa.gov/,** was created to help people who are at risk for substance abuse or mental illness develop resilience and receive assistance with recovery. Among the extensive topics on the Web site are homelessness, HIV / AIDS and hepatitis, criminal and juvenile justice, older adults and children and families.

24

Wellness Counseling in Colleges and Universities

David A. Hermon

A vice president of student affairs experiences a sense of frustration and futility after reviewing narrative data from a recent student focus group. While the students reported that they were pleased with the quality of their academic training, the new recreational center on campus, and student services in general, they felt a lack of connection with the campus community and a lack of opportunities for deciding on, setting, and meeting personal and lifestyle goals.

Several students commented that they considered making an appointment at the college counseling center, but they decided that their interest in exploring how they were doing in various psychosocial and nonacademic areas of their lives and making plans for the future did not represent enough of a "problem" to schedule a counseling appointment at the center. Other students reported a desire to explore the fit between their chosen academic major and their values to solidify career goals. On further inquiry, it was clear these students knew that the university career services center provided a great deal of information on how to choose a major and job placement opportunities; however, the students did not know if exploring such a fit would be something the career staff would help them work on and they did not follow up.

These students were making good progress academically and did not have problems that would require remediation or signal staff to intervene. The vice president was frustrated knowing that the university spends considerable time and resources to hire professionals who could assist students in grappling with these more proactive and preventative issues; however, their priority is to handle campus emergencies and attend to more remedial forms of student assistance. Clearly, hiring and staffing is not the problem, but embracing and communicating a holistic developmental vision throughout campus to students, faculty, and staff is required.

The American higher education system is eclectic and complex. The Boyer Commission (1998) found the majority of U.S. universities to be decentralized and heavily focused on graduate study, grants, and research. The commission encouraged a broader definition of scholarship, an emphasis on undergraduate education, and a need for community building. Wellness programs in higher education are one strategy for developing community on campus and for addressing the dynamic and complex interactions characteristic of holistic development for college students (Evans, Forney, & Guido-DiBrito, 1998). Holistic wellness models based in counseling theory, notably the Wheel of Wellness, and the evidence-based Indivisible Self model (both presented in Part I) are consistent with college student development models and with the American College Personnel Association's (1998) philosophy that student development is an essential purpose of higher education and the responsibility of the student affairs division. In this chapter, examples of wellness programs in higher education for students, faculty, and staff are presented, along with implementation strategies and networking ideas for wellness counseling. Inclusion of wellness in the curriculum and implications for theory, research, and practice provide an agenda for colleges to advocate for and embrace the holistic development of college students.

WELLNESS PROGRAMS IN UNIVERSITY SETTINGS

While the number of campus-identified "wellness" programs is increasing, existing programs tend toward an exclusive focus on physical and health promotion aspects of wellness. Universities, particularly land grant research universities, have received tremendous financial support to build wellness and recreation centers that include trendy amenities (e.g., rock-climbing walls, water slides, food courts) in addition to traditional amenities formerly housed in recreation intramural buildings (Reisberg, 2001). In comparison, holistic wellness programs are rare and likely to be found in liberal arts colleges congruent with the mission of developing the whole student.

Institutional Factors

Green Mountain College's Bozen Wellness Center demonstrates how a wellness program can match a unique institutional mission (www.greenmtn. edu/living/counseling_ctr.asp). This center provides environmentally friendly opportunities to enhance student and community development consistent with the college's mission. Counselors are part of a multidisciplinary team that includes career specialists, acupuncturists, massage therapists, campus nurses and doctors, and the campus chaplain. The center's goals are to help students grow in the areas of emotional, spiritual, physical, and career wellness, and to build students' efficacy to influence all of life.

Counselors working at smaller liberal arts campuses, with a more centralized student affairs structure, are typically required to wear more "hats" in their professional life. They have a unique opportunity to integrate holistic wellness directly in their work with students but have the disadvantage of fewer student affairs units with whom to network and refer students. These counselors must use the expertise of community resources (e.g., hospitals, community wellness centers) for wellness programming on campus, in the same way small liberal arts colleges incorporate community groups in their crisis and emergency response teams.

Major research universities with decentralized organizational structures create both unique barriers and benefits for counselors. Large university counselors typically have a more limited scope of work and greater demand for services. This requires counselors to be knowledgeable of available campus resources to best address various wellness issues. For example, a counselor may do a wellness assessment and develop an individual wellness plan that requires directing a student to another student affairs unit to assist in implementing the student's plan. This requires the counselor's awareness of campus resources and a campuswide holistic wellness philosophy of student development. The first can be learned; the second is a greater challenge. It requires enthusiasm for change in organizational philosophy embraced at the top levels of administration, establishment of a shared vision communicated throughout student affairs units, and substantial commitment of other student development professionals.

Helping Students Create Wellness Plans

Characterizing the roles of counselors in liberal arts colleges and research universities is difficult because local demographics will dictate how best to meet the wellness needs of both traditional and nontraditional students in building community at a wide variety of campuses (Hermon & Davis, 2004; Terenzini et al., 1994). Given the challenge of defining the scope of college counseling across settings, the five factors of the Indivisible Self (Myers & Sweeney, 2004b; see Part I) provide one example of how wellness domains can provide a foundation and organizational structure for college counselors to help students create wellness plans.

Essential Self. The Essential Self includes having a sense of purpose, being hopeful, being responsible for health promotion, and having a well-formed sense of gender and cultural identity. Several student affairs units may be helpful to counselors to promote the Essential Self, including community service and service learning programs; health services; international student services; leadership programs; lesbian, gay, bisexual, and transgender (LGBT) student services; multicultural student services; religious programs and services; and a women's center. These units can provide expertise and be valuable resources for individual wellness plans.

Social Self. Developing quality relationships and having support in times of isolation and alienation are crucial during the college years (Chickering & Reisser, 1993). In addition to helping students grapple with these Social Self issues, the following student affairs offices may be helpful for implementing individual wellness plans: student activities, commuter services and off-campus housing, orientation and new student programs, residence life and housing, and Greek affairs.

Creative Self. Key variables to address in the Creative Self factor include helping students develop clear thinking, control and manage their emotions, use humor positively, and develop a plan for vocation and use of their leisure. Career planning and placement, and programs offered through liberal arts academic units (e.g., literature, fine arts, drama, music), may assist the counselors' plan for students in developing the Creative Self dimension.

Coping Self. Managing stress, setting realistic expectations, finding *flow* (Csikszentmihalyi, 2000) experiences, and coping with life's challenges are important aspects of the Coping Self factor and increase self-efficacy (Myers & Sweeney, 2004b). In addition to these fairly common issues worked on in counseling sessions, some students may be assisted in meeting their Coping Self needs through programs offered in connection with disability support services, financial aid offices, and topical programs offered through residence life.

Physical Self. The college years are a critical period in developing lifelong healthy lifestyles; thus the Physical Self, including exercise, diet, and nutrition, is the most widely programmed and researched wellness dimension (Bates, Cooper, & Wachs, 2001). However, counseling in the Physical Self domain remains limited. When counseling does include the Physical Self, it tends to focus on the dysfunctional aspects of self (i.e., students with eating disorders). Hence, to be proactive, counselors are encouraged to network and use, for example, nutritionists from dining and food services and recreation and fitness program staff in assisting students to develop wellness plans to address the Physical Self factor.

WELLNESS FOR STAFF AND FACULTY

Although the discussion thus far has focused on college students, primarily undergraduates, campus faculty and staff also have a strong desire to be part of a community that is renewing and healthy (affording opportunities for recreation and preventative health care), offers cultural events, and enjoys collaborative norms (Woodard & Komives, 2003). Therefore, a comprehensive wellness program on campus should include all members of the campus community.

Successful corporate wellness programs found in Employee Assistance Programs (EAPs) can provide models for campus wellness programs. Such programs can increase faculty and staff interaction and improve morale. The development of healthier lifestyles, reduced absenteeism, and decreased health care costs are potential benefits of incorporating wellness programs for faculty and staff (Vickio, Mangili, Keller, & Colvin, 1994). The wellness program Vickio et al. described included day-long programs on a variety of topics (e.g., relaxation, gardening, cooking, karate, line dancing, step aerobics, goal setting, stress management, healthy food alternatives, etc.).

Depending on size and institutional mission, some college and university wellness programs primarily serve students, whereas others are open to all members of the campus and surrounding community. An inclusive program requires efforts to communicate that staff and faculty are welcome participants. Reger, Williams, Kolar, Smith, and Douglas (2002) illustrated how a participatory planning approach, commonly used in complex organizations, can be used to implement a wellness program at a large land-grant research university (West Virginia University). This approach included weekly sessions aimed at identifying and addressing key needs of the campus and promoting participation and ownership of the wellness program. The authors demonstrated how the model can be used to break through institutional barriers often found at bureaucratic institutions, increase community involvement, and help in the identification and use of key campus resources to create an effective university wellness program.

WELLNESS IN THE CURRICULUM

In addition to co-curricular wellness programs, wellness may be addressed in curricular units or entire classes. For example, I teach a health, wellness, and stress management class in the counseling department. Other classes offered on campuses such as psychoneuroimmunology, nutrition, and exercise science may enhance a holistic view of development by including the perspective of other academic disciplines. Through general education courses, counselors and student development specialists can help students develop a sense of direction and purpose in life grounded in a wellness philosophy. These classes may address critical campus issues (e.g., retention), student development, tenets of holistic wellness, and colleges' goal of a well-rounded education by integrating academic and co-curricular experiences to foster growth in areas such as integrity, citizenship, leadership, and psychological development. Some examples may illustrate how wellness can be infused in the curriculum to complement the mission of the college as a learning community and demonstrate commitment to the growth and development of the whole student.

Marshall University in Huntington, West Virginia, created a 1-credit-hour course, UNI 101, that helps students transition to the university and addresses five aspects of wellness: physical, personal, academic, social, and career. The class is team taught by a professor and student development professional, with guest lecturers speaking to salient campus topics (e.g., relationships, diversity, meditation, importance of healthy lifestyle choices at this stage in students' lives). The desired outcomes include greater self-knowledge, increased awareness of campus resources, acclimation to the university environment, and academic retention.

The WEL (Myers, Sweeney, & Witmer, 2000a) is administered in a 1-credit-hour course on wellness and risk reduction at The College of St. Benedict/St. John's University in Minnesota. Students develop individual wellness plans based on the Wheel of Wellness and their WEL results. In addition to increasing students' wellness, a research team, composed of interdisciplinary faculty and staff (nutritionist, nurse, student health office professionals), is collecting data to examine the relationship between wellness and learning outcomes.

In addition to creating new courses to address shared goals of student development and wellness, wellness can be incorporated into existing courses. S. L. Smith, Myers, and Hensley (2002) integrated holistic wellness concepts in a career and life planning course in Louisiana. The class used a wellness assessment (the WEL) to provide students with data that offered a new perspective on lifestyle, vocational, and avocational choices. This larger contextual perspective complemented traditional career theory and decision-making models, allowing students to develop life plans and implement choices consistent with their preferences and wellness goals. A posttest after the course revealed higher levels of wellness among students in the class.

IMPLICATIONS FOR PRACTICE

Colleges and universities today compete with a greater number of groups for fewer state funds. The result is that colleges are forced to do more with less and document specific outcomes. Wellness programs, along with all student development programs and services in higher education, face stringent tests to document their worth to students and the campus community. Programming on campus is based on context and need, is grounded in theoretical assumptions, and is designed to promote student learning. The development of community by involving various units on campus, however, is a factor too frequently missed in program design. The collaboration, often seen in responses to campus crises, is the same as that required in proactive student development and wellness programs. Why would campus decision makers not prefer a wellness initiative over a crisis response?

To be proactive, counselors, student development practitioners, student affairs deans, and vice presidents must first assess current wellness programs (if they exist), identify units that could be team members for such programs, and develop initiatives to address holistic development consistent with the university's mission. In this chapter, holistic wellness as a unifying theme for student affairs units has been encouraged. Addressing salient campus issues, demonstrating the fit of the wellness program to the educational mission of the university, and adhering to the development of the whole student are crucial to documenting the value of these programs to the larger campus community. Involvement will be greater if there is a shared sense of expectation, organization, creation, planning, and implementation of such programs.

The first step in developing an applied, action-oriented plan is to identify the issues facing higher education. Brainstorming the various levels of issues is important: ongoing issues, issues unique to your campus (e.g., attrition rate), and national trends that may affect your campus now or in the future (e.g., population aging). Next, identify how holistic wellness programs can address current issues (both remedial and developmental) and possible future issues (proactive). Based on the former, plan wellness intervention programs, identify variables that can be measured, and form a team to collect and analyze data. Keep in mind that the mechanism for data collection should aid in immediate modification of the newly created programs and help document the longer term benefits.

Collecting longitudinal data on the impact and benefits of campus wellness programs is crucial to documenting the value-added nature of these initiatives. Items that assess benefits of wellness programs may be included in university graduation follow-up surveys. These can be a part of a feedback loop that begins the process of modifying, adding to, and maintaining campus wellness programs. Additional follow-up with alumni at multiyear intervals can document the value of the wellness program at a critical developmental period in students' lives, thus providing data supporting the value of the program to the campus community.

SUMMARY

Optimal student development and learning take place when curricular and co-curricular experiences challenge students to make connections between ideas, events, and skills consistent with universities' and colleges' purposes and priorities. As illustrated earlier, wellness programs as holistic student development models can serve as unifying themes for institutions that desire to develop the whole person. Additionally, holistic wellness serves as an agent to address the Boyer Commission's (1998) call for increasing a sense of community in higher education, a community that promotes purpose, health, citizenship, responsibility, altruism, and understanding of the need for interdependence.

Examples of wellness programs in higher education curricula and co-curricula support the benefits of wellness programs in the campus community. Given the wide variety of higher education institutions with diverse missions and the changing demographics of today's college students, administrators, professors, staff, and students need to reexamine their current institutional mission. Having done so, they then need to consider how to define, plan, and develop full ownership of holistic wellness programs in their campus community.

Increasing competition for money for higher education makes action research necessary to document wellness program outcomes and desired educational outcomes. Furthermore, action research provides an opportunity for data-driven reflection and modification to improve programs. By using questions such as those provided below, counselors can help campuses structure further discussions and plan effective wellness programs.

DISCUSSION QUESTIONS

1. List all of your college's desired outcomes for a graduate. How do these outcomes match the mission of the college?
2. List the current ongoing issues on your campus and issues unique to your campus (e.g., retention) and national issues and trends. How could a campus wellness plan and action research strategy address these issues and prove to be of value to the institution?
3. How would a holistic wellness program fit (if a wellness plan currently exists, how well does it fit) the mission of the college?
4. To what extent would campus professionals support (if a wellness plan exists, how well do they support) a holistic wellness model? If not, how can you structure a meeting to discuss and form a consensus (recognizing that not everyone will agree, at least initially)?

5. List the student affairs units at your college that you would want to assist with planning (and ultimately owning) an overall wellness model for your campus community. What would be the barriers and hurdles of networking with these various units?
6. What specific items would you include on your college's graduation questionnaire that would serve as feedback on the effectiveness and benefits of a holistic wellness program?

WEB RESOURCES

- **Boise State University's (BSU) Web site, www.boisestate.edu/healthservices/wellness/index.asp,** describes the holistic approach, which focuses on prevention and health support, adopted by Wellness Services at Boise State University. The provision of educational opportunities, leadership programs, and collaboration with the community are chief components on the agenda.
- **Bradley University's Web site, www.bradley.edu/eddev/cwc/wellness.html/,** describes campuswide programs and activities within eight dimensions of wellness: physical, intellectual, emotional, social, occupational, spiritual, environmental, and safety. The Wellness Program assists students in making healthy, responsible decisions.
- **Green Mountain College's Bozen Wellness Center, www.greenmtn.edu/living/counseling_ctr.asp,** provides professional and considerate support to help students and the Green Mountain College community grow in the areas of physical, emotional, spiritual, and career wellness, and to assist them appreciate the ability they have to influence life.
- **Rice University's Wellness Center, www.ruf.rice.edu/~wellness/,** strives to build programs that promote and strengthen behaviors in students that encourage a higher quality of life and well-being. The center offers leadership, services, and expertise to help students manage their academic lives and better their knowledge of health, attitudes, and behavior.
- **Wheeling Jesuit University's Wellness Program, www.wju.edu/academics/wellness.asp,** describes a graduation requirement that educates students by methodically supplying them with opportunities for growth. It encourages students to take responsibility for their personal growth through a variety of structured co-curricular activities outside of class.

25

Wellness Counseling in Business and Industry

Those who have been studying wellness should feel gratified at the attention it receives in organizational literature, yet discouraged at the same time by the lack of comprehensiveness found in the programming the literature informs. The Indivisible Self Model of Wellness (IS-Wel; Myers & Sweeney, 2004b; Sweeney & Myers, 2005) provides a framework from which to understand the dynamics of health and the continuum of healthfulness or wellness. When used in business and industry settings with its companion assessment tool, the Five Factor Wellness Inventory (5F-Wel; Myers & Sweeney, 2004a), and subsequently as a guide to program design, employers and employees alike can begin to conceive of wellness in a more inclusive manner.

In this chapter, the emergence of wellness and health promotion programs in business and industry is explored, and the failure of traditional worksite wellness programs to meet the holistic needs of employees is considered. The need to assess wellness in business and industry is emphasized as a foundation for establishing interventions, such as support groups and training modules, which counselors operating from a strength-based wellness paradigm can implement.

EMPLOYEE HEALTH PROGRAMS: TRADITIONAL PERSPECTIVES

Employee health is often addressed with regard to work stress, emphasizing physical responses to stress on the job. During the 1980s and 1990s, disease and illness related to stress cost U.S. industries billions of dollars per year in absenteeism, compensation claims, and health care costs. Wellness programming emerged as employers began to realize the inevitable link between employee health, job satisfaction, and job performance. The purpose of traditional wellness programs was to reduce health care costs and motivate employees to adopt better health habits (Paxton, Meeting, & Falconer, 1993). These grew out of models based primarily in physical health professions, and typically employees' mental health was overlooked in the workplace (Csiernik, 1995). Currently, some organizations promote psychological wellness for employees through stress reduction (Anonymous, 1999); however, the preponderance of programming remains focused on physical health. Despite the relationship between physical and psychological health, or the mind–body connection, physical health screenings (e.g., cholesterol, diabetes) and fitness memberships dominate corporate wellness programs, commonly called health promotion programs. While these components are necessary to minimize physical health symptoms in the workplace, they fail to meet the needs of the total employee (Goetzel, Ozminkowski, Sederer, & Mark, 2002).

Employee Assistance Programs (EAPs), designed to meet the mental health needs of employees, have enjoyed success when rolled into benefit and flexible account packages. The National Worksite Program (NWP) was formed by the Washington Business Group and the National Institute of Mental Health to respond to employers' lack of awareness of mental health problems, specifically depression, in the workplace. Glover-Burgess (1999) reported that of the 17 million adults with depression, 70% are in the labor force, costing nearly $24 billion to employers. In spite of these costs, businesses continue to struggle with how to cope with the recognition and treatment as well as the stigma of mental health problems. The NWP provides employers needed tools to reduce the costs associated with mental health problems, including training and educational materials that cover a spectrum of issues from recognizing depression to reintegrating employees with depression into the workplace.

There is little doubt that programs offered by the NWP and EAPs have helped destigmatize mental health in the workplace and have lowered health care and productivity costs, yet the objective of these programs is deficit based and reactive rather than preventative and proactive. Issues that are related to mental health in the workplace, for example, stress management, role ambiguity, job satisfaction, and discrimination, yet are not mental problems per se are often left unaddressed by these programs (Kahnweiler & Riordan, 1998). Mental health is of concern in the workplace when it is thought of as illness related or with negative connotations and, frankly, when it negatively impacts the bottom line. Yet mental health exists on a continuum, and it is time to address not only the pathological end of that continuum but the normal, developmental end as well. In doing so, there is opportunity to leverage employees' mentally healthy selves.

The work of organizations like the NWP should be applauded, as they have supported employers and employees alike in regard to managing psychopathology in the labor force. It is the lack of proactive and preventative worksite wellness programming in support of a range of physically and mentally healthy behaviors that drives the remainder of the discussion in this chapter. Continuing to ignore the spectrum of employee health will do little to help employers create a workforce that can respond to growing demands. By implementing the IS-Wel (see Part I) as a training and development mechanism, professional counselors in business and industry can broaden how wellness is defined and measured in those settings.

PROFESSIONAL COUNSELORS BRINGING WELLNESS TO BUSINESS AND INDUSTRY

Professional counselors, grounded in strength-based developmental wellness theory, research, and career development, are well positioned to reconstruct the role of wellness in business and industry to include proactive interventions supporting mentally healthy employees. Allan Wright, managing partner of Wright and Partners in the United Kingdom, noted that professional counseling is one of the best ways of improving performance at work (Wright, 1998). The unique preparation, philosophy, and skills that differentiate professional counseling from lay activities such as coaching or mentoring are essential assets in favor of professional counselors. We cannot emphasize enough the importance of employee development grounded in sound theory, research, and practice.

The uniqueness of the three wellness models presented in Part I lies in their genesis in counseling theory. Of particular interest to business and industry is the notion of Adler's indivisible self, which informs the evidence-based model named for that concept. The belief that the self cannot be compartmentalized runs contrary to a common workplace maxim often invoked when personal issues arise on the job, "It's just business, it's not personal." Yet business and work are personal; in fact, Adler posited that work is the most basic of life tasks, as it determines individuals' ability to provide for and contribute to self, others, and society at large (Adler, 1927/1954; Herr & Cramer, 1996). Work provides individuals with the ability to attain economic, social, and psychological benefits (Herr & Cramer, 1996). Successful accomplishment of the work task is essential for individuals to obtain a sense of worthiness, competency, belonging, and meaning in life (Herr & Cramer, 1996; Sweeney, 1995b, 1998).

Meaningful work, however, has become elusive in a contemporary workplace affected by downsizing, reengineering, flatter organizational structures, technological advances, and outsourcing (Moomal, 1999). Despite more than $300 million spent per year on employee training and development, workers remain challenged by the need to successfully balance task and interpersonal factors in the workplace, factors often reflected in emotional health (Berry, 2000; Mitner & Thomas, 2000). Dewe and O'Driscoll (2002) studied managers' views on stress and who should be responsible for addressing job-related stress. Despite training, many managers were ambivalent about their roles and their organizations' responsibility to address stress-related problems in the workplace. Though companies are aware of the impact of stress-related depression and physical problems, few have offered stress management programs. Equally important, employees in the greatest need of help often do not seek it (Cryer, McCraty, & Childre, 2003). If managers are uncertain of whether they should attend to stress or depression in the workplace and employees do not seek attention, then training around stress management and awareness of depression may be for naught.

Not many would argue that the training employees receive on work-oriented tasks is more highly valued than "soft skill" training (stress management, interpersonal relations, conflict, etc.) because they are more readily linked to organizational goals and the bottom line. These training goals are by definition objective; they can be seen, measured, and quantified. There is a parallel between this line of thinking and how wellness is traditionally defined and measured in organizations. Blood pressure, cholesterol, and weight, for example, can all be measured, and the money organizations spend on treating health-related problems can be quantified by the extent to which health improves. However, health care costs are still high and 147% higher for those who consider themselves stressed or depressed (Cryer et al., 2003). The question must be asked: What can be accomplished via training and development around stress or other emotional issues from a wellness perspective?

By no means is it suggested that successful training and development programs pointed at task and business practices lack value. Rather, organizations are challenged to enhance the way they conceive of employee wellness by offering more comprehensive programming guided by models such as the IS-Wel model, which encourage both assessment and training components. When used by counseling professionals in the workplace, these models provide a means to balance work-related factors and interpersonal factors across a wellness continuum.

Assessing Wellness

At the front-end of any effective employee development intervention is meaningful assessment. With the glut of online surveys and psychometrics, organizations find themselves well equipped to measure employees' personality type, intelligence, leadership skills, and even psychopathology. Typical wellness assessments, reflective of the programming they shape, tend to measure physical aspects of health (e.g., hypertension, obesity) as opposed to holistic health (e.g., sense of humor, self-worth). The 5F-Wel (Myers & Sweeney, 1999a, 2004a), which measures the components of the IS-Wel model, allows industry counselors to build employee wellness interventions focused on overall wellness (higher order wellness factor) and the five second-order factors of the 5F-Wel (i.e., Creative Self, Coping Self, Social Self, Essential Self, Physical Self; see Part I).

The IS-Wel model and 5F-Wel provide a wealth of organizational assessment opportunities, not only measuring the components of Self but total wellness. At the most basic level, the 5F-Wel can be used to conduct culture audits, broad-based assessments of organizational culture from an employee wellness perspective. Because of the models' exclusivity, results will provide a range of data across all levels of the organization.

Wellness and Job Satisfaction

The world of work and work satisfaction are clearly wellness-related issues (Adler, 1927/1954; Connolly, 2000). Wellness as defined by the Wheel of Wellness model (see Part I) was found to predict employee job satisfaction among 82 employees in varied positions (Connolly & Myers, 2003). In this study, regression analysis was used to determine the extent to which the variance in job satisfaction could be attributed to holistic wellness and mattering. While both were found to be significant predictors, holistic wellness was a stronger predictor of job satisfaction.

When correlated with a widely used measure of job satisfaction, the Job in General Scale (Balzer et al., 1997), Connolly (2000) found that the Work scale on the Wellness Evaluation of Lifestyle (WEL; Myers, Sweeney, & Witmer, 2000a) provided an adequate measure of employee job satisfaction. As the Work scale on the WEL is a component of the Creative Self, this scale can approximate employees' level of contentment with work in addition to their capacity to successfully reap the benefits of work as posited by Adler. The Creative Self is a window to employees' perceptions of their own uniqueness and sense of importance in their social settings including the workplace. Taking into account the importance of all components of Self, results of the inventory can be used to emphasize employees' strengths and to design developmental interventions to serve both employee and organizational needs.

Support Groups and Training Modules

Employee support groups are an example of wellness-based interventions that can lend balance to each factor. Kahnweiler and Riordan (1998) examined the use of support groups at Kodak, AT&T, and Motorola. These organizations recognized that employees have affiliations beyond the workplace. The support group concept helped leverage employees' common interests and challenges by helping them cope with special issues unique to those affiliations (e.g., working parents, women executives, white men, gays and lesbians, and Latinos).

Support groups for managers-in-training were also helpful. As increasing span of control combined with diminished loyalty and commitment among employees leaves new managers pressured to produce more with less, such pressure translates into stress that resides within the manager and often projects toward subordinates (Kahnweiler & Riordan, 1998). Because professional counselors are able to facilitate group dynamics, they can guide support groups to include stress management, career development, communication skills, conflict resolution, diversity, and myriad wellness-related issues within the topics of discussion.

The support group model is among the most effective means of delivering wellness programming in terms of both cost and time. On- and off-site training workshops and seminars also provide effective ways of conducting such training. They allow issues to be discussed proactively with professional counselors rather than reactively after worksite problems occur. Counselors can invite employees who participate in wellness programs to consider, for example, the IS-Wel model to assist them in recognizing and defining personal and work-related problems that need attention.

When personnel problems occur in the workplace, business effectiveness suffers. Berry (2000) encouraged businesses to employ full-time resident counselors to treat high levels of tension, compulsive behavior, no-show workers, communication breakdowns, and other behavioral symptoms in the workplace. Problems like these can be expected, yet when left unattended, pose a threat to the Self (or Selves) and overall wellness according to research reflected in the IS-Wel model. For example, discrimination and sexual harassment threaten the Essential Self; the Creative Self is harmed by negative thoughts and unrealistic expectations for self and others. Professional counselors' expertise with diversity training can help deconstruct cultural biases and discrimination on the job. Counselors also are well positioned to train employees to use cognitive-behavioral techniques to cope with stress, conflict, and negative thinking that can preclude mentally healthy behaviors in the workplace. Management trainees can use knowledge of their Essential Self and Creative Self to grow in self-awareness and awareness of others as they learn to lead and motivate subordinates.

Despite the myriad problems that can occur, there are also virtues in the workplace. The Social Self is shaped by interpersonal relationships that are typically available in the workplace. Wellness programming should include ways in which employees can find expression for social needs and connections at work. Because the preponderance of worksite wellness programs emphasize the Physical Self, counselors can work within these programs to bring balance to wellness initiatives by providing referrals to other disciplines in health care. In fact, Dixon, Mauzey, and Hall (2003) suggested that professional counselors gain knowledge and expertise in exercise physiology given the relationship between physical activity and mental health.

IMPLICATIONS FOR RESEARCH AND PRACTICE

Professional counselors will do well to learn three of the most important words in business and industry: *return on investment* (ROI). Outcomes of wellness programming using the IS-Wel model should be measured quantitatively and qualitatively such that ROI can be realized. Pre- and postprogram measures and satisfaction surveys should be introduced as stages in the program design subsequently validating the methods and interventions used.

Organizational researchers and practitioners have long welcomed professional counselors into business and industry upon recognizing the potential for positive effects on employee development, performance, satisfaction, and health (Berry, 2000; McBryde, 1988; D. Roberts, 1983; Mitner & Thomas, 2000). However, there is a paucity of research explicating the presence of professional counselors in these settings. This discussion is beyond the scope of this chapter, yet it should be noted that in addition to outcome research designed to measure ROI and the success, for example, of an IS-Wel program, validating the efficacy of counseling professionals in business and industry settings is essential. It behooves professional counseling associations and counselors themselves to educate human resources and organizational development experts about how counselors can add value and how they are trained and credentialed to do so. Marketing efforts should include professional counselors' knowledge of assessment, consultation, wellness, human development, psychology, career management, adult education and learning style, group/team dynamics and development, program design, and change, as these typically reflect organizational needs.

SUMMARY

Wellness programming can focus on the strengths inherent in the workplace as well as on preventing and solving problems that can create distress. Support groups and psychoeducational modules that emphasize the dynamic interaction of the Self (or Selves) in the context of the workplace will advance a proactive approach to employees' striving for a well-balanced lifestyle. For businesses, our goal is helping them achieve a better bottom line with less employee costs and greater productivity.

DISCUSSION QUESTIONS

1. What steps would you take to counsel a manager who wanted to improve wellness on his or her team?
2. What would you include in a proposal to an organization that has invited you to bid on designing a wellness program using the IS-Wel?
3. How would you measure the outcome of an IS-Wel program?

WEB RESOURCES

- **Acumeans, Inc., www.acumeans.com/,** is Dr. Kathleen M. Connolly's private counseling and consulting practice Web site that provides information on organizational consulting, counseling and psychotherapy, clinical hypnosis, and career development. Acumeans, Inc. delivers an array of mental health, organizational, and career services.
- **Formerly the Washington Business Group, The National Business Group on Health, www.wbgh.com/,** is a non-for-profit organization that represents employers, health care companies, and benefit consultants. The Group is committed to finding cutting-edge solutions to the nation's most important health care and benefit issues.
- **The National Business Coalition on Health (NBCH), www.nbch.org/,** is a national, nonprofit membership organization of employer-based health coalitions. NBCH and its members are committed to value-based purchasing of health care services through the cooperative effort of public and private purchasers in order to have the country advance toward safe, efficient, and high-quality health care.
- **The Organizational Development Institute, www.odinstitute.org/,** is a nonprofit educational association created to encourage an understanding of the field of organization development (OD). Every year the Institute publishes *The International Registry of OD Professionals and OD Handbook* and meets twice a year to keep the members and the public informed on current developments in the field.

- **The Society for Human Resource Management, www.shrm.org/,** is the world's largest association committed to human resources management. The Society serves the need of human resource professionals by providing resources to and a means for the advancement of the human resource profession.

26

Wellness in Counselor Education and Supervision

J. Melvin Witmer and Paul F. Granello

> In order to grow we must let go of what we are at the moment so that we can become that of which we are capable.
> —*J. M. Witmer* (1985)

For the first time in human history, we know the characteristics of a well person and the qualities of a healthy lifestyle. A defining characteristic of the profession of counseling is its roots in a philosophy that seeks to maximize each person's development over the life span. Wellness is the hallmark characteristic of those whose lives achieve the balance between self, life, and others.

Counselor education has made great strides as a discipline in the last few decades. However, a paucity of research exists concerning knowledge of our pedagogy for training and instruction. What are the best methods for training counselors? What teaching styles should be used? Are there different teaching techniques that should be used at varying stages of the student's cognitive development? We believe that one reason for this lack of investigation into the pedagogy of counselor education has been the absence of a unifying philosophy of instruction for programs. Without clearly articulated, unifying values about the goals of counseling, methods and techniques are a proverbial "bag of tricks." We beg the question as educators when "effective techniques" do not specify the desired ultimate outcomes of our counseling interventions.

We believe that a wellness philosophy of instruction can provide both an orienting guide in deciding what methods and curricula lead to producing effective counselors and a clearer connection between our past and our future as a profession. It also can serve as a guide in the development of a cohesive counselor education program. Such a philosophy includes the achievement of learning objectives that promote the balanced health and optimal well-being of the students and faculty within a counselor education program. As a consequence, the work of faculty and students will consider all dimensions of human functioning, both intrapsychic and interpersonal, from the perspective of the well-being of the total person.

Given our historical roots as a profession and the social and behavioral health realities of the future, a wellness philosophy is a highly appropriate direction for the development of our profession (Myers, 1992; Myers, Sweeney, & Witmer, 2000b; Watts, 2004). To help articulate such a position, in this chapter we identify key participants in the process (i.e., faculty, students, and ancillary faculty and staff), guidelines for applying a wellness philosophy to training, curricular models to create experiences related to wellness, and a wellness orientation for site supervisors who help to shape the persona of the professionals under their supervision. Addressing each of these topics will enhance the process of creating a developmental, strength-based approach to counselor education.

PREPARING FOR A WELLNESS EMPHASIS: IDENTIFYING PARTICIPANTS

The first steps to implementing a wellness philosophy in counselor education programs require consideration of (a) faculty leadership, (b) student experiences, and (c) interdepartmental and interdisciplinary affiliations.

Faculty Leadership

Faculty leadership is a prerequisite for creating a wellness community in a counselor education program. Furthermore, it is highly desirable if not essential that faculty members demonstrate a healthy lifestyle and provide opportunities for students to develop their wellness potential. The example set by the faculty and advanced students is integral to building a community that cares and encourages its members to strive for wellness (Witmer & Young, 1996). A dysfunctional faculty, like a dysfunctional family, creates conditions and experiences that result in unhealthy student behavior. When a new faculty member is recruited, one criterion should be the expectation to commit to a wellness philosophy through personal and curricular participation. Although one faculty member may take the responsibility for developing expertise in wellness, it is only with the commitment, support, and involvement of all faculty that guidelines for such a program can be implemented.

In-service activities should include training and dialog to promote understanding of the wellness philosophy and the model to be used for faculty, student, and both curricular and co-curricular activities. On completion of a wellness assessment (see chapters 5 and 18), each faculty member may develop an Individual Wellness Plan (IWP; see chapter 18) in which they would establish goals and priorities for their own wellness lifestyle. Periodic reporting, sharing, and revising of this plan is part of ongoing involvement of faculty in a wellness community.

Student Experience

Counselor education program literature should clearly reflect a wellness philosophy and the expectations for each student to participate in personal self-disclosure and self-growth as part of the wellness goals of the training

(Council for Accreditation of Counseling and Related Educational Programs [CACREP], Standards Section II.E., 2001). Before admission, potential students need an orientation to the wellness expectations of the program. A wellness philosophy would include a statement that students are expected to make a commitment to personal growth and professional competence through opportunities that enhance functioning in all areas of wellness. Students should be exposed to wellness both within the classroom and outside of the classroom in the form of extracurricular activities such as social advocacy projects, guest speakers on health topics, or perhaps a yearly programwide Wellness Fair in which student, faculty, and staff present on topics related to wellness (see examples at http://www.csi-net.org/advocacy). The purpose is to provide students with experiences in which they receive consistent and supportive messages about the importance of developing their own well-being as counselors in training.

Interdepartmental and Interdisciplinary Affiliations

Adopting a wellness philosophy for a counselor education program and the type of program culture/community that would result also entails forming interdisciplinary relationships with faculty and programs outside of counselor education. Academics are urged to move beyond their specific disciplines and find means for interdisciplinary research and instruction. Entirely new research agendas and methods of preventative counseling can develop from cross-discipline collaborations. Wellness as a philosophy is sufficiently broad to allow for inclusion of professionals from disparate fields. For example, colleagues from nutrition, exercise, health and medical sciences, psychology, or physiology may have a great deal to offer our students concerning health and well-being.

APPLYING A WELLNESS PHILOSOPHY TO COUNSELOR EDUCATION

Wellness-oriented counselor education programs are structured to create curricular and co-curricular learning experiences for achieving wellness goals. Both faculty and students are given an opportunity to explore, develop, and attain a more balanced state of optimal health. These programs might follow some basic guidelines or goals such as the following:

1. Counselor education programs will promote the individual and collective well-being of faculty, students, supervisors, and clients.
2. Faculty will be encouraged to optimize a personal healthy approach to their teaching, research, and service.
3. Students will be encouraged to optimize their personal adjustment in the process of becoming a professional counselor.
4. Students' ability to assess, identify, and engage in healthy lifestyle habits will be supported by the faculty.

5. Field supervisors will be supported by the faculty in developing enhanced wellness and professional competence.
6. Field supervisors will nurture and assist in the development of their supervisees' strengths and positive psychological attributes.
7. Client strengths and positive attributes will be assessed, recognized, and viewed as essential elements in treatment planning by students, field supervisors, and faculty.

MODELS FOR IMPLEMENTING A WELLNESS PHILOSOPHY INTO THE CURRICULUM

There are numerous ways to implement a wellness philosophy into the curriculum of a counselor education program. When one considers the immediate and long-range benefits of a wellness community and curriculum in the preparation of counselors, the impact could be comparable with other major developments in counselor education during the half century of its identity as a separate profession (Myers, Mobley, & Booth, 2003). Three differing models for such integration are presented: a Course-Specific Model, an Infusion Model, and a Holistic Wellness Model. Each of these models has strengths and limitations, and each represents a different level of "buy in" to a wellness philosophy as a guiding force for educating counselors.

Course-Specific Model

The Course-Specific Model of applying a wellness philosophy involves the creation of a single, stand-alone course on wellness. There are many examples of wellness courses across the United States in counselor education programs. Mel Witmer developed a course in the early 1980s at Ohio University, originally called "Biofeedback, Stress Management, and Self-Control" and later changed to "Wellness and Stress Management Over the Life Span." Paul Granello at Ohio State University currently teaches a course titled "Advanced Interventions: Prevention and Wellness." At the University of North Carolina at Greensboro, Jane Myers teaches "Counseling for Wellness and Habit Change," and Tom Sweeney teaches a similar course at Ohio University. Mark Young at the University of Central Florida offers "Counseling for Wellness." No matter what the title, all of these courses are based on teaching a philosophy of counseling that does not focus on the traditional pathological models of psychology but takes a more positive and developmental approach to understanding and enhancing human growth and experience. These courses focus on lifestyle and instructing students on how to help themselves and their clients make positive and lasting attitudinal, cognitive, and behavioral lifestyle decisions.

The advantages of the Course-Specific Model are that little overall change need occur to a counselor education program. Either the new course is added as an elective or it is substituted for an old requirement. The limitations or weaknesses of this model are also apparent in that whenever any topic in counseling is limited to one course (e.g., multiculturalism), the risk is that students will not generalize what is learned in the course, resulting in the material being isolated from other counseling courses and topics. Likewise, when the faculty member's teaching responsibilities or availability changes because of administrative or career choices, such an experience for students can literally disappear from the curriculum. Finally, a major disadvantage of this model, when implemented in isolation from discussion by the whole faculty, is the tendency to see the wellness emphasis as the unique specialty of one faculty member rather than being the underlying philosophy embraced by the faculty as a whole.

Infusion Model

An Infusion Model seeks to alter the curriculum by not adding new courses or radically changing the structure of an existing curriculum but rather by inserting wellness objectives and assignments into existing course work. Infusion Models have been promoted by our national Standards (CACREP, 2001) since the inception of CACREP for topics associated with multiculturalism, spirituality, and outcome research in counselor education programs (Granello & Granello, 1998).

Infusing a wellness philosophy into a counselor education program would entail examining the syllabi for each of the program courses and determining whether wellness-related objectives or assignments could be added to the CACREP core experiences. Using the CACREP nomenclature, some examples of how wellness objectives or assignments might be related or infused into existing counselor education program curricula core areas may be helpful here.

Foundations of Counseling/Professional Identity. As part of professional orientation, the unique history of counseling as evolving from a developmental, life span, strength-based approach can be emphasized. Wellness as a topic is related in that individuals must strive for well-being not only across the developmental stages of their life span but also between professional demands and private life. A foundation of counseling course is an excellent place to discuss the need for students to balance their own self-care with the current demands of graduate school and plan for the inherent challenges in our profession where burnout rates are high. Because this is usually the first course a student takes, it is an excellent place to introduce a wellness model. The Wellness Evaluation of Lifestyle Inventory (WEL) or Five Factor Wellness Inventory (5F-Wel) can be administered and an IWP created by each student to be followed and reviewed periodically during their time in the program.

Social and Cultural Diversity. Social and cultural values are central to one's personal philosophy and approach to life. Readiness for change is embedded in family, community, and related values learned while growing up, and sensitivity to their impact on well-being is a critical dialectic competency for all counselors. Everything from one's likes and dislikes of food, exercise, spiritual practices, and approaches to friendship are affected by social and cultural experiences. Examination of how these factors help to influence choices for positive well-being or not is important to both counseling students and those they will serve. Students can discuss the understanding of what is "well" in the context of different cultural understandings of the construct. What factors in the culture contribute to wellness and what factors contribute to illness? What forces in the larger (majority) culture influence wellness?

Human Growth and Development. The meaning of wellness may change given the developmental stage of the client. How do the characteristics of a well person emerge, and how can they be nurtured in each developmental stage? Students can discuss how they would modify taking a wellness approach by adapting it to a major life transition facing an individual at a particular life stage. The Wheel of Wellness (Myers, Sweeney, & Witmer, 2000b; Witmer & Sweeney, 1992) and the Indivisible Self (IS-Wel; Myers & Sweeney, 2004b; Sweeney & Myers, 2005) models call attention to issues related not only to physical but also to emotional development. As a result of research with colleagues in Israel, safety was added as a contextual issue in the IS-Wel model before 9/11. Now safety issues are rampant in communities both within the United States and throughout the world. Safety issues for both genders and people of different ages are relevant in terms of how they affect development. How to cope with, ameliorate, and transcend such concerns is both an opportunity and challenge.

Career Counseling. Some of the most compelling findings associated with living long and living well are associated with one's work or lack thereof. The role of career satisfaction can be discussed as important to the overall well-being of individuals. How does career satisfaction contribute to wellness over the life span? How can leisure help to compensate for a lack of control at work, dissatisfaction with working conditions, or inadequate use of one's talents and gifts in the workplace?

Helping Relationships. Theories of helping that relate to human development and positive cognitive-behavioral attributes can be stressed as a comparison with theories that have a more pathological focus. The theories of Adler (1927/1954), Maslow (1962), and Rogers (1961) posit positive motivations behind human behavior and place an emphasis on human development. They can be compared and contrasted with theories focused on remediation and treatment. The aforementioned theories are consistent with a wellness philosophy that promotes the individual's dynamic striving toward ever-increasing holistic health. Discussion of transtheoretical models of human behavior change is useful in avoiding the more traditional classical models taught in such courses. For example, the instructor may wish to introduce one or more alternatives such as REPLAN (M. E. Young, 2004) or the Transtheoretical Change Model of Prochaska, DiClementi, and Norcross (1992; see also chapter 16).

Group Counseling. Group experiences provide an opportunity to discuss the nature of social support in helping individuals make positive lifestyle changes. Groups can be used to review and revise IWPs, provide support, and provide a safe setting for practicing new behaviors. Additionally, the psychoeducational group can be presented as an excellent model for wellness-based interventions. Conyne, Wilson, and Ward's (1997) work provides a good discussion of teaching the various models of group work (task, counseling, psychoeducational, and psychotherapy).

Assessment. Students can learn to assess positive health dimensions and individual psychological and social qualities as well as use instruments that focus on psychopathology, such as the Minnesota Multiphasic Personality Inventory. For example, measures of social psychological attitudes provide students with assessment scales and rich data for conducting a variety of psychosocial assessments. Students can perform a wellness self-assessment with one or two volunteers using an instrument such as the 5F-Wel or WEL Inventory (see chapter 5). The results of these assessments can be used to develop an IWP.

Research. Students can be encouraged to review relevant outcome research with regard to prevention and etiology of mental and emotional disorders. They can learn about the societal impact of mental illness in terms of human cost, demands on the medical system, and economic impact. Exploration of cost-effective and prevention-oriented methods can be emphasized for educational, business, and community settings.

Legal and Ethical Issues. One possible discussion that might be useful for students while taking an ethics course is to study the counselor's scope of practice with regard to wellness. For example, are counselors within their scope of practice to recommend exercise to clients with depression? Another useful discussion is the ethics regarding "do no harm," sometimes interpreted to mean the least restrictive means possible to treat clients. Given that many clients' problems are due to lifestyle factors that could be improved by taking a wellness approach, would it be less ethical to conduct a diagnosis and treatment plan from a pathological philosophy as opposed to a strength-based wellness perspective? Could the use of such a less restrictive method constitute harm to the client?

Diagnosis or Clinical Pathology. The discussion of wellness is an important concept for understanding mental illness (see chapter 21). Discussions concerning how society defines mental health and mental illness go hand in hand. It is important to discuss with students the overpathologizing of American society and the economic motives behind this trend. For example, with millions of prescriptions for antidepressants being distributed annually, a discussion can be held around society's values with regard to the use of medications to control mood. A wellness philosophy that places an emphasis on nonchemical controls of mood is a significant contrast.

Practicum/Internship. An assignment of working with a client to help the client make a positive habit or lifestyle change can be useful for students. Skills learned in assessing individual well-being in the assessment course can be applied to develop an individual wellness plan for a client. Students can be assigned a project that targets an at-risk population with a psychoeducational prevention activity.

Consultation. Students can learn to identify and better understand how the political, economic, and social forces in the community affect health resources. With this knowledge, strategies for interacting with and influencing these organizations can be developed. A possible assignment is a community or organizational wellness project in which students team up and conduct a needs assessment, analyze the data, design a wellness program, implement the program, and assess outcomes.

School Guidance and Counseling. School counselors can be taught to develop guidance plans that are holistic in nature. An assignment can be made to develop a comprehensive guidance plan that stresses a schoolwide wellness philosophy. Such a plan would focus on the health and wellness of the students from a multidisciplinary approach and support both the academic achievement of the student and character education.

College Student Development. The holistic movement from the in loco parentis model of students services to the contemporary idea of developing the whole student is a core premise for college student development classes. However, wellness differences in traditional and nontraditional students (Hermon & Davis, 2004; Myers & Mobley, 2004) and the definition of the well person must be addressed. An assignment to develop a campus-based wellness program to meet individual needs may be worthwhile. As noted in chapter 4, some universities are using the wellness models described in Part I for programming and administering wellness instruments to all entering freshmen and tracking their progress over time.

The Infusion Model has some advantages over the Course-Specific Model. The major advantage is that by infusion, wellness is not isolated in one course. Therefore, students are more likely to see the relationship of the topic to all aspects of the curriculum and their interdependence. There are also limitations with regard to the use of an Infusion Model for the curriculum. First, even though wellness is infused across course work, it is unlikely to provide a program with an overall philosophical orientation to wellness. Second, there is no planned carryover of the topic into noncurricular activities and the general culture of the program.

Holistic Wellness Model

A model of counselor education that is fully based on a wellness philosophy incorporates wellness into both the course work and the noncurricular and lifestyle experiences of the faculty and students. Under this model, a wellness philosophy would be incorporated into every facet of the program from faculty participation, student admissions, and course work to co-curricular activities and field-work experiences. This saturation approach is intended to help faculty and students develop a wellness community within the program that will become part of a lifestyle in their career and personal life.

Communication of the wellness philosophy would be inherent in all program recruitment materials, on Web pages, and on official admissions forms. Students could be asked to submit a personal wellness statement as a part of their admissions packet for the program. Once admitted, each student would complete a wellness assessment and develop an IWP that includes goals and priorities until completion of their degree. Periodic review and reporting of progress along with any revision of the IWP would need to be made. The counselor education program review and retention policy would include statements on personal adjustment and wellness along with the academic standards required.

Course work in such a program would include a training focus on primary and secondary prevention. Students would learn to assess client strengths as well as pathology, and how to work with clients on setting positive lifestyle goals and achieving them. Students and faculty would be challenged to set their own wellness goals and work toward achieving them. Regardless of the model used, the following options can be incorporated into the degree program: self-directed readings of wellness concepts and practices via online instruction, individual counseling, and personal growth through group process.

WELLNESS-ORIENTED SUPERVISION

Thus far in this chapter, we have discussed the application of a wellness philosophy for counselor education to both students and faculty. Field supervisors are a critical component of the student's graduate training experience. Supervisors are in a unique position to set healthy examples for students, or they can convince students that burnout and stress are "just part of the job." The need for a healthy relationship between field supervisors and supervisees is apparent, but very little has actually been written on how to plan and create the conditions for such a relationship to occur. Applying a wellness philosophy to intentionally create a health- and growth-focused relationship between supervisors and supervisees seems highly applicable. Perhaps if supervisors demonstrated through their own behavior an emphasis on the importance of well behaviors for their supervisees, our profession would suffer less from the effects of stresses, burnout, and impaired counselors (Granello, 2000).

Examples of the application of a wellness philosophy to the supervisory relationship include the following:

- In-service training and opportunities for supervisors to have their own wellness assessments and create their own wellness plans.
- Supervisors can be taught how to monitor students' wellness not only in relation to client management and therapy but also as healthy caregivers.
- Internship requirements might include the completion of a given number of wellness assessments, wellness plans, and counseling. To the extent possible, the wellness plan could be implemented under the direction of the supervisor. A possible version of this assignment might be to conduct a dual assessment of a client using the standard illness model and a wellness assessment using a wellness model for a total-person perspective in the context of the life situation. Students would do treatment planning with both and implement whatever is practical given the educational or clinical setting.

SUMMARY

In this chapter, alternatives suitable for incorporating a wellness philosophy and its methods into counselor education were described. Philosophy is not as commonly discussed as it once was in counselor education (Sweeney, 2001); as a consequence, the importance of philosophy for prompting questions of "why" about the purpose and outcomes desired in counseling may have been lost. We have proposed that our answer to the question of "why" is to provide professional counselors with more than knowledge or skills but also with a reason for what they do with clients. Equally important, professional counselors should experience all aspects of wellness, for example, the sense of worth, control, emotional responsiveness, and humor, that come from making positive choices about living their own lives. Proposing to reduce the stress response in clients is not enough if their helpers are on the road to burnout themselves.

Counselor education can be at the forefront of preparing professional counselors who model, teach, and apply wellness principles in all settings and with all clients. Optimum wellness and enhancement of human potential are a part of our history. Counselor educators can now make it the defining philosophy of our future.

DISCUSSION QUESTIONS

1. How does a wellness philosophy approach to counselor education differ from a generalist approach in which various theories, methods, and techniques are presented and students are expected to choose what they prefer from among them?
2. What obstacles are likely to deter faculty from adopting a wellness philosophy and curriculum? Are the reasons valid compared with the outcomes possible through a systemic wellness approach to preparation?
3. What resistance might you expect from students when introduced to habit change that would improve their overall wellness and lifestyle? How might these be approached through a coordinated curriculum?
4. What assets (programs, people, resources) are likely to exist within a university community that would support and enhance a wellness approach to counselor education? Where might alliances be made to sustain a program or individual faculty member in taking a wellness approach to preparation of counselors?
5. What kinds of baseline data could be collected to help measure change over time related to philosophy, values, attitudes, methods, and outcomes as a result of a wellness approach?
6. To what extent might faculty, programs, and facilities outside counselor education be a part of the total wellness requirements or opportunities for students? For example, is there a "wellness center" that includes exercise and nutritional programs? How can students learn to create or utilize community resources to improve their wellness and that of their clients?

WEB RESOURCES

- **The Association for Counselor Education and Supervision (ACES), http://www.acesonline.net/home.htm,** seeks to improve the education, credentialing, and supervision of counselors through accreditation processes and professional development programs. The ACES purpose is in accordance with the American Counseling Association and involves advancing counselor education and supervision to better the guidance, counseling, and student development services rendered in all settings.
- **Chi Sigma Iota, International (CSI), http:/www.csi-net.org/,** is the international honor society in counseling for students, professional counselors, and counselor educators. CSI's mission is to promote scholarship, research, professionalism, leadership, and excellence in counseling, and to recognize high attainment in the pursuit of academic and clinical excellence in the profession of counseling.
- **The Council for Accreditation of Counseling and Related Educational Programs, http://www.counseling.org/cacrep/,** is an independent agency recognized by the Council for Higher Education Accreditation to accredit master's degrees in the profession of counseling. This Web site serves students, educators, and practitioners.
- **The Council on Rehabilitation Education, http://www.core-rehab. org/,** promotes the successful delivery of rehabilitation services to individuals with disabilities, continuing review and improvement of master's degree–level rehabilitation counselor education programs, and program self-improvement rather than outside censure.
- **National Wellness Institute, http://www.nationalwellness.org/,** was founded to bring together the health promotion and wellness fields to promote a holistic outlook toward well-being. The Institute seeks to enhance the professional and personal growth of wellness professionals in all disciplines.

Epilogue:
Future Directions in
Wellness Counseling

Thomas J. Sweeny and Jane E. Myers

You must be the change you wish to see in the world.

—*Gandhi*

This is the first effort to bring together 15 years of work on the topic of wellness and its implications for counseling theory, research, and practice. We, the editors, have been engaged with this topic for so long that it was refreshing to study thoughts, experiences, and hopes for wellness through the works of other authors and their chapters. While it is gratifying to see what is being done not only in the United States but in other countries as well, one has the distinct feeling that the real work has only begun.

Myers, Sweeney, and Clarke (2004) conducted an e-mail survey of 250 counselor education programs through the Chi Sigma Iota electronic mailing list of Chapter Faculty Advisors followed by qualitative interviews of respondents. Of 32 programs responding, 27 reported specific wellness efforts including research, courses, and infusion methods. We think it was notable that two-thirds ($n = 21$) of the programs were accredited by the Council for Accreditation of Counseling and Related Educational Programs (CACREP). While the core CACREP Standards do not address wellness per se, more accredited program faculty may be attuned to the unique history and values of the counseling profession regarding optimizing human development. With several limitations in such a study as this one, little more can be offered at this time except to note that 10% of those programs surveyed ($N = 250$) do have wellness activities in some measure and that this modest number represents a baseline from which to grow in the future. We believe that a survey of this nature would have had few if any respondents if conducted 10 years ago. We expect even more wellness activities will be reported in the future.

We now have measurable concepts and the tools to test hypotheses. Our instruments are evolving as they always will be, but they are already proving useful. The level of readiness for changes in education, business, and government policies and practices is more evident than ever before. As a result, the time seems right for imaging a new future for the health and well-being of the United States.

In the early stages of planning this book, we wanted the U.S. Secretary of Health and Human Services, the Honorable Tommy Thompson (2003), to contribute in some way. His staff reported, however, that because of department policy he could not do so. Nevertheless, we believe that his leadership and vision are indicative of what the future holds for health care in this country. Like him, we believe that promoting a wellness lifestyle is the only viable alternative to the ever-growing morass of problems that plaque our country at the present time. Fortunately, he has used his position to advance a wellness perspective for the health of this country, and we are at liberty to quote him from his many public appearances available on the Internet. From the remarks of the Honorable Tommy Thompson:

> Americans spend $1.4 trillion on health care each year. Seventy-five percent of those dollars are spent treating chronic diseases. If they had practiced healthier habits, Americans could have saved a great deal of money—and they could have spent that money, time, and effort on other priorities. . . .
>
> So major questions facing every American are: *How will I lead my life? What habits will I develop?*
>
> We cannot be neutral. If we have not made an effort to develop the right habits, chances are good that we are practicing the wrong habits. We all have loved ones who suffer from diseases that are largely preventable. My own father had diabetes. He died from a heart attack associated with diabetes. Many of my friends have had heart attacks. Many more suffer from asthma.
>
> Once I saw firsthand and understood the pattern that caused all this destruction, I wanted to stop it whenever I saw it. And I still do.
>
> I released a report in September 2003 [U.S. Department of Health and Human Services, 2003] that showed that health promotion is part of a wise business strategy.
>
> The costs to U.S. businesses of obesity-related health problems in 1994 added up to almost $13 billion, with approximately $8 billion of this going towards health insurance expenditures, $2.4 billion for sick leave, $1.8 billion for life insurance, and close to $1 billion for disability insurance.
>
> On an individual level, it costs an average of $2650 to insure an American without diabetes for a year. It costs $13,243 to insure an American who does have diabetes. That is why employer spending on prevention is a wise investment that pays off. It pays off in lower health care expenses. It pays off in lower absenteeism and higher productivity.
>
> The recently passed Medicare law moves our health care system from a focus on treating disease to a focus on preventing disease. Our doctors will not be satisfied just to keep people alive; they will also keep them well. *From now on, we will measure success not by the absence of illness, but in the quality of life.*
>
> Personally, I have lost more than 15 pounds. As a result I have much more energy and stamina now that I am not lugging around the equivalent of a bowling ball. How tired would you be if you had to carry a bowling ball around with you all day every day? And how good would it feel at the end of the day when you got to put it down? That is how I feel since I lost weight.
>
> This brings us back to the key questions: *How will I lead my life? What habits will I develop?*

The purpose of this book is to provide the knowledge and means for professional counselors to help individuals and institutions across the life span to answer these questions with specific, positive, life-enhancing declarations. It is clear that children need to learn as early as possible how to make healthy choices and develop lifelong habits in all aspects of their lives. No less important are older persons and the opportunities that they have to change old habits and improve the quality of their lives. In short, wellness can be a priority for everyone.

While the physical aspects of wellness and health are often addressed, this work emphasized all aspects of wellness over the life span. Drawing on the research and methods across disciplines to create a holistic approach to health and wellness clearly serves the purposes of all citizens. Those of us in the counseling profession can welcome and encourage best practices among other professions that help us achieve our mutual goals. Together, let us hope to see the evidence of our efforts in more citizens who live long and live well.

References

AARP. (2004). *Profile of older Americans*. Washington, DC: Author.

Abrams, L. S. (2003). Contextual variations in young women's gender identity negotiations. *Psychology of Women Quarterly, 27*, 64–74.

Adams, K. (2003). Children's dreams: An exploration of Jung's concept of big dreams. *International Journal of Children's Spirituality, 8*, 105–115.

Adams, T. B., Bezner, J. R., Drabbs, M. E., Zambarano, R. J., & Steinhardt, M. A. (2000). Conceptualization and measurement of the spiritual and psychological dimensions of wellness in a college population. *Journal of American College Health, 48*, 165–173.

Adams, T. B., Bezner, J., & Steinhardt, M. (1997). The conceptualization and measurement of perceived wellness: Integrating balance across and within dimensions. *American Journal of Health Promotion, 11*, 208–218.

Adler, A. (1954). *Understanding human nature* (W. B. Wolf, Trans.). New York: Fawcett Premier. (Original work published 1927)

Ainslie, R. C., Shafer, A., & Reynolds, J. (1996). Mediators of adolescents' stress in a college preparatory environment. *Adolescence, 31*, 913–924.

Akos, P., & Levitt, D. H. (2003). Promoting healthy body image in middle school. *Professional School Counseling, 6*, 138–144.

Allison, N. (2001). *The complete body, mind, and spirit*. Columbus, OH: McGraw-Hill.

Alves-Martins, M., Peixoto, F., Gouveia-Pereira, M., Amaral, V., & Pedro, I. (2002). Self-esteem and academic achievement among adolescents. *Educational Psychology, 22*, 51–61.

Amato, P. R., & Booth, A. (1997). *A generation at risk: Growing up in an era of family upheaval*. Cambridge, MA: Harvard University Press.

American College Personnel Association. (1998). *ACPA's statement of ethical principles and standards*. Washington, DC: Author.

American Counseling Association. (1995). *Code of ethics and standards of practice*. Alexandria, VA: Author.

American Educational Research Association. (1999). *Standards for educational and psychological testing*. Washington, DC: Author.

American Heritage Dictionary of the English Language. (2000). Boston: Houghton Mifflin.

American Medical Association. (2003). *Healthy Youth 2010*. Retrieved January 16, 2004, from http://www.ama-assn.org/ama1/pub/upload/mm/39/hy2010revised.pdf

American Psychiatric Association. (2000). *Diagnostic and statistical manual of mental disorders* (4th ed., Text Revision). Washington, DC: Author.

American Psychological Association. (2004). *PsycINFO*. Washington, DC: Author.

Americans With Disabilities Act of 1990, 42 U.S.C.A. 12101 *et seq.* (West 1993).

Amrein, A. T., & Berliner, D. C. (2003). The effects of high-stakes testing on student motivation and learning. *Educational Leadership, 60,* 32–38.

Andersen, A. E. (1999). Medical information for nonmedical clinicians and educators treating patients with eating disorders: Psychotherapists, educators, nutritionists, experiential therapists, and coaches. In P. S. Mehler & A. E. Andersen's (Eds.), *Eating disorders: A guide to medical care and complications* (pp. 202–213). Baltimore: Johns Hopkins University Press.

Andresen, J. (2000). Meditation meets behavioral medicine: The story of experimental research on meditation. *Journal of Consciousness Studies, 7,* 17–73.

Anonymous. (1999). Mental illness in the workplace. *Management Review, 88,* 9.

Ansbacher, H. L. (Ed.). (1969). *The science of living: Alfred Adler.* Garden City, NY: Doubleday.

Ansbacher, H. L., & Ansbacher, R. R. (Eds.). (1967). *The individual psychology of Alfred Adler.* New York: Harper & Row.

Ansuini, C. G., & Fiddler-Woite, J. (1996). The source, accuracy, and impact of initial sexuality information on lifetime wellness. *Adolescence, 31,* 283–290.

Antonovsky, A. (1987). *Unraveling the mystery of health.* San Francisco: Jossey-Bass.

Archer, J., Probert, B. S., & Gage, L. (1987). College students' attitudes toward wellness. *Journal of College Student Personnel, 2,* 311–317.

Ardell, D. (1977). *High level wellness: An alternative to doctors, drugs, and disease.* Emmaus, PA: Rodale Press.

Association for Assessment in Counseling. (2003). *Standards for multicultural assessment.* Alexandria, VA: Author.

August, D., & Hakuta, K. (Eds.). (1997). *Improving schooling for language-minority children: A research agenda.* Washington, DC: National Academy Press.

Austin, J. T. (1999). *Culturally sensitive career assessment: A quandary.* (ERIC Document Reproduction Service No. EDCE99211)

Bagley, C., & Tremblay, P. (1998). On the prevalence of homosexuality and bisexuality in a random community survey of 750 men aged 18 to 27. *Journal of Homosexuality, 36,* 1–18.

Baltes, P. B., & Baltes, M. M. (1990). Psychological perspectives on successful aging: The model of selective optimization with compensation. In P. B. Baltes & M. M. Baltes (Eds.), *Successful aging: Perspectives from the behavioral sciences* (pp. 1–34). New York: Cambridge University Press.

Balzer, W. K., Kihm, J. A., Smith, P. C., Irwin, J. L., Bachiochi, P. D., Robie, C., et al. (1997). *Users' manual for the Job Descriptive Index and the Job in General scales.* Bowling Green, OH: Bowling Green State University.

Barba, B. E., Tesh, A. S., & Courts, N. F. (2002). Promoting thriving in nursing homes: The Eden Alternative. *Journal of Gerontological Nursing, 28,* 7–13.

Bates, J. M., Cooper, D. L., & Wachs, P. M. (2001). Assessing wellness in college students: A validation of the Salubrious Lifestyle Scale of the Student Development Task and Lifestyle Assessment. *Journal of College Student Development, 42,* 193–203.

Bell, I., & McGrane, B. (1999). *This book is not required* (Rev. ed.). Thousand Oaks, CA: Pine Forge.

Bem, S. (1995). Dismantling gender polarization and compulsory heterosexuality: Should we turn the volume down or up? *Journal of Sex Research, 32,* 329–333.

Bender, F. L. (2003). *The culture of extinction: Toward a philosophy of deep ecology.* Amherst, MA: Humanity Books.

Berger, E. (1999). *Raising children with character: Parents, trust, and the development of personal integrity.* Fort Lee, NJ: Jason Aronson.

Berry, J. (2000). Consulting to management. *Journal of Management Consulting, 11,* 29–31.

Bockting, W. O., & Cesaretti, C. (2001). Spirituality, transgender identity, and coming out. *Journal of Sex Education & Therapy, 26,* 291–300.

Booth, C. (2005). *The relationship among career aspiration, multiple role planning attitudes, and wellness in African American and Caucasian undergraduate women.* Unpublished doctoral dissertation, University of North Carolina at Greensboro.

Borders, L. D., & Drury, S. M. (1992). Comprehensive school counseling programs: A review for policymakers and practitioners. *Journal of Counseling & Development, 70,* 487–498.

Bowling, A., Flessig, A., Gabriel, Z., Banister, D., Dykes, J., Dowding, L. M., et al. (2003). Let's ask them: A national survey of definitions of quality of life and its enhancement among people aged 65 and over. *International Journal of Aging and Human Development, 56,* 269–306.

Boyer Commission on Educating Undergraduates in the Research University. (1998). *Reinventing undergraduate education: A blueprint for America's research universities.* New York: Carnegie Foundation for the Advancement of Teaching.

Brener, N. D., & Gowda, V. R. (2001). U.S. college students' reports of receiving health information on college campuses. *Journal of American College Health, 49,* 223–228.

Brislin, R. W., Lonner, W. J., & Thorndike, R. M. (1973). *Cross-cultural research methods.* New York: Wiley.

Bronfenbrenner, U. (1999). Environments in developmental perspective: Theoretical and operational models. In S. L. Friedman & T. D. Wachs (Eds.), *Measuring environment across the life span: Emerging methods and concepts* (pp. 3–28). Washington, DC: American Psychological Association.

Brown-Baatjies, O., & Amery, S. (2004). *A study on the wellness of nurses working in oncology in the Nelson Mandela Metropole and City of Cape Town, South Africa.* Unpublished doctoral dissertation, Nelson Mandela Metropolitan University, South Africa.

Browne, M. W., & Cudeck, R. (1993). Alternative ways of assessing model fit. In K. A. Bollem & J. S. Long (Eds.), *Testing structural equation models* (pp. 136–162). Newbury Park, CA: Sage.

Brug, J., & van Assema, P. (2000). Differences in use and impact of computer-tailored dietary fat-feedback according to stage of change and education. *Appetite, 34,* 285–293.

Byrd, R. C. (1988). Positive therapeutic effects of intercessory prayer in a coronary care unit population. *Southern Medical Journal, 81,* 826–829.

Campbell, D. G. (1997). *The Mozart effect: Tapping the power of music to heal the body, strengthen the mind, and unlock the creative spirit.* New York: Avon Books.

Campbell, M. L., Sheets, D., & Strong, P. S. (1999). Secondary health conditions among middle aged individuals with chronic physical disabilities: Implications for unmet needs and services. *Assistive Technology, 11,* 105–122.

Campbell, P. R. (1996). *Population projections for states by age, sex, race, and Hispanic origin: 1995–2025* (PPL-47, U.S. Bureau of the Census, Population Division). Washington, DC: Government Printing Office.

Cancer Prevention Research Center. (n.d.). *University of Rhode Island change assessment.* Kingston, RI: Author.

Carstensen, L. L., & Freund, A. M. (1994). The resilience of the aging self. *Developmental Review, 14,* 81–92.

Casey, K. (2005). *Wellness among women hemodialysis patients.* Unpublished doctoral dissertation, San Jose State University.

Cashwell, C. S., & Rayle, A. D. (in press). Spiritual bypass. In D. S. Sandhu (Ed.), *Spirituality as the fifth force in counseling and psychology: Implications for research, training, and practice.* Alexandria, VA: American Counseling Association.

Cashwell, C. S., & Young, J. S. (2005). *Integrating spirituality in counseling: A guide to competent practice.* Alexandria, VA: American Counseling Association.

Centers for Disease Control and Prevention. (1993). Cigarette smoking-attributable mortality and years of potential life lost—United States, 1990. *Morbidity and Mortality Weekly Report, 42,* 645–648.

Centers for Disease Control and Prevention. (2002). State-specific prevalence of obesity among adults with disabilities: Eight states and the District of Columbia, 1989–1999. *MMWR Weekly, 51,* 805–808.

Champagne, E. (2003). Being a child, a spiritual child. *International Journal of Children's Spirituality, 8,* 43–52.

Chandler, C. K., Holden, J., & Kolander, C. (1992). Counseling for spiritual wellness: Theory and practice. *Journal of Counseling & Development, 71,* 168–175.

Chang, C. (1998). *The role of distinctiveness in acculturation, ethnic identity, and wellness in Korean-American adolescents and young adults.* Unpublished doctoral dissertation, University of North Carolina at Greensboro.

Chang, C. Y., & Myers, J. E. (2003). Cultural adaptation of the Wellness Evaluation of Lifestyle (WEL): An assessment challenge. *Measurement and Evaluation in Counseling and Development, 35,* 239–250.

Charlesworth, E. A., & Nathan, R. G. (1984). *Stress management: A comprehensive guide to wellness.* New York: Ballantine Books.

Chickering, A. W., & Reisser, L. (1993). *Education and identity* (2nd ed.). San Francisco: Jossey-Bass.

Choate, L. H., & Smith, S. L. (2003). Enhancing development in 1st-year college student success courses: A holistic approach. *Journal of Humanistic Counseling, Education and Development, 42,* 178–193.

Christian, M. D., & Barbarin, O. A. (2001). Cultural resources and psychological adjustment of African American children: Effects of spirituality and racial attitudes. *Journal of Black Psychology, 27,* 43–63.

Cicchetti, D., Rappaport, J., Sandler, I., & Weissberg, R. (2000). *The promotion of wellness in children and adolescents.* Washington DC: Child Welfare League of America Press.

Cleary, K. M. (Ed.). (1996). *Native American wisdom.* New York: Barnes & Noble.

Cochran, S. D., Sullivan, J. G., & Mays, V. M. (2003). Prevalence of mental disorders, psychological distress, and mental services use among lesbian, gay, and bisexual adults in the United States. *Journal of Consulting and Clinical Psychology, 7,* 53–61.

Cohen, S., & Wills, T. A. (1985). Stress, social support, and the buffering hypothesis. *Psychological Bulletin, 98,* 310–357.

Coleman, H. L. K., Casali, S. B., & Wampold, B. E. (2001). Adolescent strategies for coping with cultural diversity. *Journal of Counseling & Development, 79,* 356–364.

Coleman, J. C. (1976). *Abnormal psychology and modern life* (5th ed.). Glenview, IL: Scott, Foresman.

Collins, J., & Mayblin, B. (1996). *Introducing Derrida.* Victoria, Australia: McPherson's Printing Group.

Collins, S. E., Carey, K. B., & Sliwinski, M. J. (2002). Mailed personalized normative feedback as a brief intervention for at-risk college drinkers. *Journal of Studies on Alcohol, 63,* 559–567.

Connolly, K. (2000). *The relationship among wellness, mattering, and job satisfaction.* Unpublished doctoral dissertation, University of North Carolina at Greensboro.

Connolly, K. M., & Myers, J. E. (2003). Wellness and mattering: The role of holistic factors in job satisfaction. *Journal of Employment Counseling, 40,* 152–160.

Conyne, R. K., Wilson, F. R., & Ward, D. E. (1997). *Comprehensive group work: What it means and how to teach it.* Alexandria, VA: American Counseling Association.

Cooksley, V. G. (2002). *Aromatherapy: Soothing remedies to restore, rejuvenate and heal.* Paramus, NJ: Prentice Hall.

Cooper, S. (1967). *The antecedents of self-esteem.* San Francisco: Freeman.

Cooper, S. E. (1990). Investigation of the Lifestyle Assessment Questionnaire. *Measurement and Evaluation in Counseling and Development, 23,* 83–87.

Cornford, F. (Trans.). (1982). *The Republic of Plato.* London: Oxford University Press. (Original work published 1941)

Corsini, R. J. (2001). *Handbook of innovative therapy* (2nd ed.). New York: Wiley.

Cottingham, H. F. (1956). *Guidance in elementary schools: Principles and practices.* Oxford, England: McKnight & McKnight.

Council for Accreditation of Counseling and Related Educational Programs. (2001). *CACREP accreditation standards and procedures manual.* Alexandria, VA: Author.

Council of Economic Advisors. (1998). *Changing America: Indicators of social and economic well-being by race and Hispanic origin.* Washington, DC: Author.

Cournoyer, R. J., & Mahalik, J. R. (1995). Cross-sectional study of gender role conflict examining college-aged and middle-aged men. *Journal of Counseling Psychology, 42,* 11–19.

Cowen, E. L. (1991). In pursuit of wellness. *American Psychologist, 46,* 404–408.

Cowen, E. L. (1994). The enhancement of psychological wellness: Challenges and opportunities. *American Journal of Community Psychology, 22,* 149–179.

Cross, W. E. (1971). The Negro-to-Black conversion experience: Toward a psychology of Black liberation. *Black World, 20,* 13–27.

Cryer, B., McCraty, R., & Childre, D. (2003). Pull the plug on stress. *Harvard Business Review, 81,* 102–107.

Csiernik, R. (1995). Wellness, work and employee assistance programming. *Employee Assistance Quarterly, 11,* 1–13.

Csikszentmihalyi, M. (2000). *Beyond boredom and anxiety: Experiencing flow in work and play.* San Francisco: Fetzer.

Cypres, A., Landsberg, G., & Spellmann, M. (1997). The impact of managed care on community mental health outpatient services in New York State. *Administration and Policy in Mental Health, 24,* 509–521.

Dahir, C. A., & Stone, C. B. (2003). Accountability: A M.E.A.S.U.R.E. of the impact school counselors have on achievement. *Professional School Counseling, 6,* 214–221.

Daniels, L. R. (2003). Assessment of social support among veterans with military-related post-traumatic stress disorder: A study of the Social Support Questionnaire. *Dissertation Abstracts International: Section A, Humanities and Social Sciences, 63*(11-A), 4092.

Davis, W. (2001). *Light at the edge of the world.* Washington, DC: National Geographic Society.

Degges-White, S. (2003). *The relationships among transitions, chronological age, subjective age, wellness, and life satisfaction in women at midlife.* Unpublished doctoral dissertation, University of North Carolina at Greensboro.

Degges-White, S., Myers, J. E., Adelman, J. U., & Pastoor, D. D. (2003). Examining counseling needs of headache patients: An exploratory study of wellness and perceived stress. *Journal of Mental Health Counseling, 25,* 271–290.

Dew, B. (2000). *The relationship among internalized homophobia, self-disclosure, self-disclosure to parents, and wellness in adult gay males.* Unpublished doctoral dissertation, University of North Carolina at Greensboro.

Dew, B. J., Myers, J. E., & Wightman, L. F. (2004). *Wellness in adult gay males: Examining the impact of internalized homophobia, self-disclosure, and self-disclosure to parents.* Manuscript submitted for publication.

Dewe, P., & O'Driscoll, M. (2002). Stress management interventions: What do managers actually do? *Personnel Review, 31*(1/2), 143–165.

Dice, C. (2002). *The relationship among coping resources, wellness, and attachment to companion animals in older persons.* Unpublished doctoral dissertation, University of North Carolina at Greensboro.

DiClemente, C. C. (1993). Changing addictive behaviors: A process perspective. *Current Directions in Psychological Science, 2,* 101–106.

DiClemente, C. C., Marinilli, A. S., Singh, M., & Bellino, L. E. (2001). The role of feedback in the process of health behavior change. *American Journal of Health Behavior, 25,* 217–227.

DiClemente, C. C., & Prochaska, J. O. (1998). Toward a comprehensive, transtheoretical model of change: Stages of change and addictive behaviors. In W. R. Miller & N. Heather (Eds.), *Treating addictive behaviors* (pp. 3–24). New York: Plenum Press.

Diener, E., & Lucas, R. E. (1999). Personality and subjective well-being. In D. Kahneman, E. Diener, & N. Schwarz (Eds.), *Well-being: The foundations of hedonic psychology* (pp. 213–229). New York: Russell Sage Foundation.

Diener, E., Oishi, S., & Lucas, R. E. (2003). Personality, culture, and subjective well-being: Emotional and cognitive evaluations of life. *Annual Review of Psychology, 54,* 403–425.

Diener, E., & Suh, M. E. (1998). Subjective well-being and age: An international analysis. *Annual Review of Gerontology and Geriatrics, 17,* 304–324.

Diepold, J. (2002). Thought field therapy: Advancements in theory and practice. In F. P. Gallo (Ed.), *Energy psychology in psychotherapy: A comprehensive sourcebook* (pp. 3–34). New York: Norton.

Dill, P. L., & Henley, T. B. (1998). Stressors of college: A comparison of traditional and nontraditional students. *The Journal of Psychology, 132,* 25–32.

Dimeff, L. A., & McNeely, M. (2000). Computer-enhanced primary care practitioner advice for high-risk college drinkers in a student primary healthcare setting. *Cognitive and Behavioral Practice, 7,* 82–100.

Dixon Rayle, A. (2002). *The relationship among ethnic identity, acculturation, mattering, and wellness in minority and nonminority adolescents.* Unpublished doctoral dissertation, University of North Carolina at Greensboro.

Dixon Rayle, A. & Myers, J. E. (2004). Wellness in adolescence: The roles of ethnic identity, acculturation, and mattering. *Professional School Counseling, 8,* 81–90.

Dixon, W. A., Mauzey, E. D., & Hall, C. R. (2003). Physical activity and exercise: Implications for counselors. *Journal of Counseling & Development, 81,* 502–505.

Dogan, T. (2004). *Wellness of college students in Turkey.* Unpublished doctoral dissertation, Hacetteppe University, Ankara, Turkey.

Dreikurs, R. (1967). *Psychodynamics, psychotherapy, and counseling.* Chicago: Alfred Adler Institute.

Dreikurs, R. (1971). *Social equality: The challenge of today.* Chicago: Regnery.

Dunn, H. L. (1961). *High-level wellness.* Arlington, VA: R. W. Beatty.

Dunn, H. L. (1977). What high level wellness means. *Health Values: Achieving High Level Wellness, 1,* 9–16.

Eaude, T. (2003). Shining lights in unexpected corners: New angles on young children's spiritual development. *International Journal of Children's Spirituality, 8,* 151–163.

Ellis, A. (1984). Rational-emotive therapy. In R. J. Corsini (Ed.), *Current psychotherapies* (3rd ed., pp. 196–238). Itasca, IL: Peacock.

Emener, W. G., Hutchison, W. S., & Richard, M. A. (2003). *Employee Assistance Programs: Wellness/enhancement programming*. Springfield, IL: Charles C Thomas.

Enochs, W. K. (2001). *Wellness and adjustment in college freshmen based on type of residence hall and gender*. Unpublished doctoral dissertation, University of Arkansas.

Erikson, E. H. (1963). *Childhood and society* (2nd ed.). New York: Norton.

Erikson, E. (1997). *The life cycle completed: An extended version with new chapters on the ninth stage of development*. New York: Norton.

Evans, N. J., Forney, D. S., & Guido-DiBrito, F. (1998). *Student development in college: Theory, research, and practice*. San Francisco: Jossey-Bass.

Faiver, C., & Ingersoll, R. E. (2005). Knowing one's limits. In C. S. Cashwell & J. S. Young (Eds.), *Integrating spirituality into counseling: A guide to competent practice* (pp. 169–184). Alexandria, VA: American Counseling Association.

Federal Interagency Forum on Child and Family Statistics. (2003). *America's children: Key national indicators of well-being*. Washington, DC: Government Printing Office.

Fenwick, P., & Fenwick, E. (1995). *The truth in the light: An investigation of over 300 near death experiences*. London: Headline.

Fontana, D. (2003). *Psychology, religion, and spirituality*. Malden, MA: BPS Blackwell.

Foundation for Inner Peace (n.d.). *A course in miracles*. Tiburon, CA: Author.

Frame, C. J., Green, C. G., Herr, D. G., Myers, J. E., & Taylor, M. L. (2001). The stages of change and dietary fat and fruit and vegetable intake of patients at the outset of a cardiac rehabilitation program. *American Journal of Health Promotion, 15*, 405–413.

Frame, M. W. (2003). *Integrating religion and spirituality into counseling: A comprehensive approach*. Pacific Grove, CA: Brooks/Cole-Thompson Learning.

Freedman, V. A., Martin, L. G., & Schoeni, R. F. (2002). Recent trends in disability and functioning among older adults in the United States. *Journal of the American Medical Association, 288*, 3137–3146.

Freysinger, V. J. (1994). Leisure with children and parental satisfaction: Further evidence of a sex difference in the experience of adult roles and leisure. *Journal of Leisure Research, 26*, 212–226.

Fukuyama, M. A., & Sevig, T. D. (1999). *Integrating spirituality into multicultural counseling*. Thousand Oaks, CA: Sage.

Gallagher, P. A., & Satter, L. S. (1998). Promoting a safe school environment through a schoolwide wellness program. *Focus on Exceptional Children, 3*, 1–12.

Garrett, M. (1996). *Cultural values and wellness of Native American high school students*. Unpublished doctoral dissertation, University of North Carolina at Greensboro.

Garrett, M. T. (1999). Soaring on the wings of the eagle: Wellness of Native American high school students. *Professional School Counseling, 3*, 57–64.

Garrett, M. T., & Garrett, J. T. (2002). "Ayeli": Centering technique based on Cherokee spiritual traditions. *Counseling and Values, 46*, 149–158.

Gatz, M., & Smyer, M. (2001). Mental health and aging at the outset of the twenty-first century. In J. Birren & K. W. Schaie (Eds.), *Handbook of the psychology of aging* (5th ed., pp. 523–544). San Diego, CA: Academic Press.

Gazda, G. M., Ginter, E. J., & Horne, A. M. (2001). *Group counseling and group psychotherapy: Theory and application.* Boston: Allyn & Bacon.

Geronimus, A. (1996). Excess mortality among Blacks and Whites in the United States. *New England Journal of Medicine, 335,* 1552–1558.

Gill, C. (2005). *The relationship among spirituality, religiosity, and wellness factors for poor rural women.* Unpublished doctoral dissertation, University of North Carolina at Greensboro.

Ginter, E. J., & Glauser, A. S. (2002). *Life-skills for college: A curriculum for life.* Dubuque, IA: Kendall/Hunt.

Ginter, E. J., & Glauser, A. S. (2004). Assessment and diagnosis: The developmental perspective and its implications. In R. R. Erk (Ed.), *Counseling treatment for children and adolescents with DSM-IV-TR disorders* (pp. 2–36). Upper Saddle River, NJ: Pearson.

Gladding, S. (2002). *Family therapy: History, theory, and practice* (3rd ed.). Upper Saddle River, NJ: Merrill-Prentice Hall.

Glauser, A., Ginter, E. J., & Larson, K. (2004, April). *Appreciating the difficult other: Advocating for the disruptive student.* Paper presented at the American Counseling Association's Annual Convention, Kansas City, MO.

Glover-Burgess, A. (1999). Managing workplace depression. *Behavioral Health Management, 5,* 37–38.

Goetzel, R. Z., Ozminkowski, R. J., Sederer, L. I., & Mark, T. L. (2002). The business case for quality mental health services: Why employers should care about the mental health and well-being of their employees. *Journal of Occupational and Environmental Medicine, 44,* 320–331.

Grace, T. W. (1997). Health problems of college students. *Journal of American College Health, 45,* 243–250.

Granello, P. F. (1996). Wellness as a function of perceived social support network and ability to empathize. *Dissertation Abstracts International: Section B. The Sciences and Engineering, 57*(2-B), 0985.

Granello, P. F. (2000). Integrating wellness practice into private practice. *Journal of Psychotherapy in Independent Practice, 1,* 3–16.

Granello, P. F., & Granello, D. H. (1998). Teaching students to utilize outcomes research. *Counselor Education and Supervision, 37,* 224–237.

Greenstone, J. L., & Leviton, S. C. (2002). *Elements of crisis intervention: Crises and how to respond to them* (2nd ed.). Pacific Grove, CA: Brooks/Cole.

Gryzwacz, J. G. (1999). Growing up healthy: The ecology of child well-being. *Family Relations, 48,* 433–435.

Hambleton, R. K. (2001). The next generation of the ITC test translation and adaptation guidelines. *European Journal of Psychological Assessment, 17,* 164–172.

Hambleton, R. K., & Bollwark, J. (1991). Adapting test for use in different cultures: Technical issues and methods. *Bulletin of the International Test Commission, 18,* 3–32.

Hambleton, R. K., & de Jong, J. H. A. L. (2003). Advances in translating and adapting educational and psychological tests. *Language Testing, 20,* 127–134.

Hambleton, R. K., & Patsula, L. (1998). Adapting tests for use in multiple languages and cultures. *Social Indicators Research, 45,* 153–171.

Harari, M. J. (2003). A psychometric investigation of a model-based measure of perceived wellness. *Dissertation Abstracts International: Section B. The Sciences and Engineering, 63*(7-B), 3474.

Hartwig, H. (2003). *The relationship among individual factors of wellness, family environment, and delinquency among adolescent females.* Unpublished doctoral dissertation, University of North Carolina at Greensboro.

Hartwig, H., & Myers, J. E. (2003). A different approach: Applying a wellness paradigm to adolescent female delinquents and offenders. *Journal of Mental Health and Counseling, 25,* 57–75.

Hattie, J. A., Myers, J. E., & Sweeney, T. J. (2004). A factor structure of wellness: Theory, assessment, analysis, practice. *Journal of Counseling & Development, 82,* 354–364.

Hayes, R. L., Nelson, J., Tabin, M., Pearson, G., & Worthy, C. (2002). Using school-wide data to advocate for student success. *Professional School Counseling, 6,* 86–94.

Helms, J. E. (2003). Racial identity in the social environment. In P. B. Pedersen & J. C. Carey (Eds.), *Multicultural counseling in the schools: A practical handbook* (2nd ed., pp. 44–58). Boston: Allyn & Bacon.

Herek, G. M. (1986). The social psychology of homophobia: Toward a practical theory. *Review of Law and Social Change, 14,* 923–934.

Hermon, D. (1995). *An examination of the relationship between college students' subjective well-being and adherence to a holistic wellness model.* Unpublished doctoral dissertation, Ohio University.

Hermon, D. A., & Davis, G. A. (2004). College student wellness: A comparison between traditional- and nontraditional-age students. *Journal of College Counseling, 7,* 32–39.

Hermon, D. A., & Hazler, R. J. (1999). Adherence to a wellness model and perceptions of psychological well-being. *Journal of Counseling & Development, 77,* 339–343.

Herr, E. L., & Cramer, S. H. (1996). *Career guidance and counseling through the lifespan: Systematic approaches* (5th ed.). New York: Harper Collins.

Hettler, W. (1984). Wellness: Encouraging a lifetime pursuit of excellence. *Health Values: Achieving High Level Wellness, 8,* 13–17.

Hickman, L. A., & Alexander, T. M. (1998). *The essential Dewey: Vol. 1. Pragmatism, education, and democracy.* Bloomington: Indiana University Press.

Hill, G. E., & Luckey, E. B. (1969). *Guidance for children in elementary schools.* New York: Appleton-Century-Crofts.

Hodge, D. R., & Williams, T. R. (2002). Assessing African American spirituality with spiritual ecomaps. *Families in Society, 83,* 585–601.

Hoffer, E. (1951). *The true believer: Thoughts on the nature of mass movements.* New York: Harper & Row.

Holmes, T. H., & Rahe, R. H. (1967). The social adjustment rating scale. *Journal of Psychometric Research, 11,* 213–218.

Hough, J. (1999). Disability and health: A national public health agenda. In R. J. Simeonson & L. N. McDevitt (Eds.), *Issues in disability and health: The role of secondary conditions and quality of life* (pp. 161–203). Chapel Hill: University of North Carolina, FPG-Child Development Center.

Huettig, C., & O'Connor, J. (1999). Wellness programming for preschoolers with disabilities. *Teaching Exceptional Children, 31,* 12–17.

Hughes, R. B., Nosek, M. A., Howland, C. A., Groff, J. Y., & Mullen, P. D. (2003). Health promotion for women with disabilities: A pilot study. *Rehabilitation Psychology, 48,* 182–188.

Hughes, R. B., Swedlund, N. Petersen, N., & Nosek, M. A. (2001). Depression and women with spinal cord injury. *Topics in Spinal Cord Rehabilitation, 7,* 7–24.

Hughes, R. B., Taylor, H. B., Robinson-Whelen, S., & Nosek, M. A. (2004). *Stress and women with physical disabilities: Identifying the correlates.* Manuscript submitted for publication.

Hughes, R. B., Taylor, H. B., Robinson-Whelen, S., Swedlund, N., & Nosek, M. A. (in press). Enhancing self-esteem in women with physical disabilities. *Rehabilitation Psychology.*

Hughes, T. L., & Eliason, M. (2002). Substance use and abuse in lesbian, gay, bisexual and transgender populations. *Journal of Primary Prevention, 22,* 263–298.

Hutchinson, G. (1996). *The relationship of wellness factors to work performance and job satisfaction among managers.* Unpublished doctoral dissertation, University of North Carolina at Greensboro.

Hutson, P. W. (1968). *The guidance function in education* (2nd ed.). New York: Appleton-Century-Crofts.

Ingersoll, R. E. (1998). Refining dimensions of spiritual wellness: A cross-traditional approach. *Counseling and Values, 42,* 156–165.

Ivey, A. (2000/1986). *Developmental therapy.* North Amherst, MA: Microtraining.

Ivey, A., & Ivey, M. (1998). Reframing *DSM-IV-TR*: Positive strategies from developmental counseling and therapy. *Journal of Counseling & Development, 76,* 334–350.

Ivey, A., & Ivey, M. (1999). Toward a developmental *Diagnostic and Statistical Manual*: The vitality of a contextual framework. *Journal of Counseling & Development, 77,* 484–490.

Ivey, A., & Ivey, M. (2003). *Intentional interviewing and counseling: Facilitating client development in a multicultural world* (5th ed.). Pacific Grove, CA: Brooks/Cole.

Ivey, A., Ivey, M., Myers, J., & Sweeney, T. (2005). *Developmental counseling and therapy: Promoting wellness over the lifespan.* Boston: Lashaska Houghton Mifflin.

James, S. A. (1994). John Henryism and the health of African American Americans. *Culture, Medicine and Psychiatry, 18,* 163–182.

Jessor, R., Van Den Bos, J., Vanderryn, J., Costa, F. M., & Turbin, M. S. (1995). Protective factors in adolescent problem behavior: Moderator effects and developmental change. *Developmental Psychology, 31,* 923–933.

Johnson, T. F. (1995). Aging well in contemporary society. *American Behavioral Scientist, 39,* 120–130.

Johnston, L. D., O'Malley, P. M., & Bachman, J. G. (2003). *Monitoring the Future national survey results on drug use: 1975–2002. Vol. II: College students and adults ages 19–40* (NIH Publication No. 03-5376). Bethesda, MD: National Institute on Drug Abuse.

Jones, A. J. (1934). *Principles of guidance* (2nd ed.). New York: McGraw-Hill.

Jung, C. G. J. (1963). *Memories, dreams, reflections.* New York: Pantheon.

Justice, B. (1998). *A different kind of health: Finding well being in spite of illness.* Houston, TX: Peak Press.

Jutras, S., Morin, P., Proulx, R., Vinay, M., Roy, E., & Routhier, L. (2003). Conception of wellness in families with a diabetic child. *Journal of Health Psychology, 8,* 573–587.

Kahnweiler, W. M., & Riordan, R. J. (1998). Job and employee support groups: Past and prologue. *Career Development Quarterly, 47,* 173–188.

Kelly, E. W. (1995). *Spirituality and religion in counseling and psychotherapy: Diversity in theory and practice.* Alexandria, VA: American Counseling Association.

Keppel, K. G., Pearcy, J. N., & Wagener, D. K. (2002). *Trends in racial and ethnic-specific rates for the health status indicators: United States, 1990–98.* Hyattsville, MD: National Center for Health Statistics.

Ketz, K., & Israel, T. (2002). The relationship between women's sexual identity and perceived wellness. *Journal of Bisexuality, 2,* 227–242.

Keyes, C. L., Shmotkin, D., & Ryff, C. D. (2002). Optimizing well-being: The empirical encounter of two traditions. *Journal of Personality and Social Psychology, 82,* 1007–1022.

Kim, H. K., & McKenry, P. C. (1998). Social networks and support: A comparison of African Americans, Asian Americans, Caucasians, and Hispanics. *Journal of Comparative Family Studies, 29,* 313–334.

Kiselica, M. S., Baker, S. B., Thomas, R. N., & Reedy, S. (1994). Effects of stress inoculation training on anxiety, stress and academic performance among adolescents. *Journal of Counseling Psychology, 41,* 335–342.

Koenig, H. G., George, L. K., Hays, J. C., Larson, D. B., Cohen, H. J., & Blazer, D. G. (1998). The relationship between religious activities and blood pressure in older adults. *International Journal of Psychiatry in Medicine, 28,* 189–213.

Koenig, H. G., George, L. K., & Peterson, B. L. (1998). Religiosity and remission of depression in medically ill older patients. *American Journal of Psychiatry, 155,* 536–542.

Koenig, H. G., McCullough, M. E., & Larson, D. B. (2001). *Handbook of religion and health.* London: Oxford University Press.

Koestler, A. (1978). *Janus: A summing up.* New York: Random House.

Kroger, J. (1996). *Identity in adolescence: The balance between self and other* (2nd ed.). London: Routledge.

Krotoski, D. M., Nosek, M. A., & Turk, M. A. (Eds.). (1996). *Women with physical disabilities: Achieving and maintaining health and well being.* Baltimore: Paul H. Brookes.

Kurtz, E., & Ketcham, K. (1992). *The spirituality of imperfection: Storytelling and the journey to wholeness.* New York: Bantam.

Landmark Healthcare and Interactive Solutions. (1998). *The Landmark Report on public perceptions of alternative care*. Sacramento, CA: Landmark.

Lapan, R. T. (2001). Results-based comprehensive guidance and counseling programs: A framework for planning and evaluation. *Professional School Counseling, 4*, 289–299.

Larson, D. D. (1999). The conceptualization of health. *Medical Care Research and Review, 56*, 123–136.

Lazarus, R. S. (2003). Does the positive psychology movement have legs? *Psychological Inquiry, 14*, 93–109.

Lazarus, R., & Folkman, S. (1984). *Stress, appraisal and coping*. New York: Springer.

Lee, C. C. (1997a). Cultural dynamics: Their importance in culturally responsive counseling. In C. C. Lee (Ed.), *Multicultural issues in counseling: New approaches to diversity* (2nd ed., pp. 15–30). Alexandria, VA: American Counseling Association.

Lee, C. C. (1997b). *Multicultural issues in counseling: New approaches to diversity* (2nd ed.). Alexandria, VA: American Counseling Association.

Lee, C. C., & Armstrong, K. L. (1995). Indigenous models of mental health intervention: Lessons from traditional healers. In J. G. Ponterotto, J. M. Casas, L. A. Suzuki, & C. M. Alexander (Eds.), *Handbook of multicultural counseling* (pp. 441–456). Thousand Oaks, CA: Sage.

Lewis, J. A., Lewis, M. D., Daniels, J. A., & D'Andrea, M. J. (2003). *Community counseling: Empowerment strategies for a diverse society* (3rd ed.). Pacific Grove, CA: Brooks/Cole-Thompson Learning.

Lin, S. (2000). Coping and adaptation in families of children with cerebral palsy. *Exceptional Children, 66*, 201–218.

Lincoln, Y. S., & Guba, E. G. (1985). *Naturalistic inquiry*. Newbury Park, CA: Sage.

Litzenberger, B. W. (1998). The development of sexual orientation: Identity, emotional well-being, and life histories of lesbian, gay, and heterosexual men and women. *Dissertation Abstracts International: Section B. The Sciences and Engineering, 58*(10-B), 5649.

Logue, E., Sutton, K., Jarjoura, D., & Smucker, W. (2000). Obesity management in primary care: Assessment of readiness to change among 284 family practice patients. *Journal of the American Board of Family Practice, 13*, 164–171.

Luhtanen, R. K. (2003). Identity, stigma management, and well-being: A comparison of lesbians/bisexual women and gay/bisexual men. *Journal of Lesbian Studies, 7*, 85–100.

Luzzo, D. A., & McWhirter, E. H. (2001). Sex and ethnic differences in the perception of educational and career-related barriers and levels of coping efficacy. *Journal of Counseling & Development, 79*, 61–67.

Mahoney, M. (1991). *Human change processes*. New York: Basic Books.

Makinson, L. (2001). *The relationship of moral identity, social interest, gender, and wellness among adolescents*. Unpublished doctoral dissertation, University of North Carolina at Greensboro.

Makinson, L., & Myers, J. E. (2003). Wellness: An alternative paradigm for violence prevention. *Journal of Humanistic Counseling, Education and Development, 42*, 165–177.

Mansager, E. (2000). Individual psychology and the study of spirituality. *Journal of Individual Psychology, 56,* 371–388.

Marcus, B. H., Banspach, S. W., Lefebvre, R. C., Rossi, J. S., Carleton, R. A., & Abrams, D. B. (1992). Using the stages of change model to increase the adoption of physical activity among community participants. *Health Promotion, 6,* 424–429.

Marshall, S. K. (2001). Do I matter? Construct validation of adolescents' perceived mattering to parents and friends. *Journal of Adolescence, 24,* 473–490.

Martinez, T. P., & Martinez, A. P. (2002). Texas tragedy: No Hispanic child left behind? *Hispanic Outlook on Higher Education, 12,* 11–14.

Maslow, A. H. (1962). *Toward a psychology of being.* New York: van Nostrand.

Maslow, A. H. (1970). *Motivation and personality* (2nd ed.). New York: Harper & Row.

Maslow, A. H. (1971). *The farther reaches of human nature.* New York: Harper & Row.

Masterson, J. (1981). *The narcissistic and borderline disorders.* New York: Brunner/Mazel.

McBryde, R. (1988). The counselor, the agency, and organization development. *Canadian Journal of Counseling, 22,* 44–52.

Miller, C. H. (1961). *Foundations of guidance.* New York: Harper & Brothers.

Milton, D., & Benjamin, S. (1999). *Complementary alternative therapies: An implementation guide to integrative care.* Chicago: American Hospital Association Press.

Mitchell, N. (2001). *The relationship among acculturation, wellness, and academic self-concept in Caribbean American adolescents.* Unpublished doctoral dissertation, University of North Carolina at Greensboro.

Mitchell, N., & Myers, J. E. (2004). *Promoting school success for Caribbean-American adolescents: The role of acculturation, wellness, and academic self-concept.* Manuscript submitted for publication.

Mitner, R. L., & Thomas, E. G. (2000). Employee development through coaching, mentoring and counseling: A multidimensional approach. *Review of Business, 21*(1/2), 43–48.

Mobley, K. (2004). *The relationship among age, gender role conflict, and wellness in two cohorts of male counselors.* Unpublished doctoral dissertation, University of North Carolina at Greensboro.

Mokdad, A. H., Marks, J. S., Stroup, D. F., & Gerberding, J. L. (2004). Actual causes of death in the United States 2000. *Journal of the American Medical Association, 291,* 1238–1245.

Moomal, Z. (1999). The relationship between meaning in life and mental well-being. *South African Journal of Psychology, 29,* 36–41.

Morris, J. F., & Rothblum, E. D. (1999). Who fills out a "lesbian" questionnaire? The interrelationship of sexual orientation, years "out", disclosure of sexual orientation, sexual experience with women, and participation in the lesbian community. *Psychology of Women Quarterly, 23,* 537–557.

Morris, J. F., Waldo, C. R., & Rothblum, E. D. (2001). A model of predictors and outcomes of outness among lesbian and bisexual women. *American Journal of Orthopsychiatry, 71*, 61–71.

Mosak, H. H., & Dreikurs, R. (1967). The life task: III. The fifth life task. *Journal of Individual Psychology, 5*, 16, 22.

Mosak, H. H., & Dreikurs, R. (1973). Adlerian psychotherapy. In R. Corsini (Ed.), *Current psychotherapies*. Itasca, IL: Peacock.

Moss, D. (2002). Biofeedback. In S. Shannon (Ed.), *Complementary and alternative therapies in mental health* (pp. 136–158). New York: Academic Press.

Myers, J. E. (1992). Wellness, prevention, development: The cornerstone of the profession. *Journal of Counseling & Development, 71*, 136–139.

Myers, J. E. (1998). *Manual for the Wellness Evaluation of Lifestyle*. Palo Alto, CA: MindGarden.

Myers, J. E. (2004). *Manual for the Five Factor Wellness Inventory*. Greensboro, NC: Author.

Myers, J. E., & Bechtel, A. (2004). Stress, wellness, and mattering among cadets at West Point: Factors affecting a fit and healthy force. *Military Medicine, 169*, 475–483.

Myers, J. E., & Harper, M. (2004). Evidence-based effective practices with older adults: A review of the literature for counselors. *Journal of Counseling & Development, 82*, 207–218.

Myers, J. E., Luecht, R., & Sweeney, T. J. (2004). The factor structure of wellness: Reexamining theoretical and empirical models. *Measurement and Evaluation in Counseling and Development, 36*, 194–208.

Myers, J. E., Madathil, J., & Tingle, L. R. (in press). Marriage satisfaction and wellness in India and the U.S.: A preliminary comparison of arranged marriages and marriages of choice. *Journal of Counseling & Development*.

Myers, J. E., & Mobley, K. A. (2004). Foundations of wellness promotion for undergraduate students: Lessons from between and within groups comparisons. *Journal of College Counseling, 7*, 40–49.

Myers, J. E., Mobley, K., & Booth, C. S. (2003). Wellness of counseling students: Practicing what we preach. *Counselor Education & Supervision, 42*, 264–274.

Myers, J. E., & Sweeney, T. J. (1996). *The Wellness Evaluation of Lifestyle, Form J* (5th ed.). Greensboro, NC: Authors.

Myers, J. E., & Sweeney, T. J. (1999a). *The Five Factor Wellness Inventory* (1st ed.). Greensboro, NC: Authors.

Myers, J. E., & Sweeney, T. J. (1999b). *The Five Factor Wellness Inventory, Teen (Middle School), Hebrew*. Greensboro, NC: Authors. (Translated by Moshe Tatar, Hebrew University, Jerusalem, Israel)

Myers, J. E., & Sweeney, T. J. (2001a). *The Five Factor Wellness Inventory* (2nd ed.). Greensboro, NC: Authors.

Myers, J. E., & Sweeney, T. J. (2001b). *The Five Factor Wellness Inventory, Teen* (2nd ed.). Greensboro, NC: Authors.

Myers, J. E., & Sweeney, T. J. (2002). *The Five Factor Wellness Inventory, Teen (Middle School)* (3rd ed.). Greensboro, NC: Authors.

Myers, J. E., & Sweeney, T. J. (2004a). *The Five Factor Wellness Inventory* (3rd ed.). Greensboro, NC: Authors.

Myers, J. E., & Sweeney, T. J. (2004b). The Indivisible Self: An evidence-based model of wellness. *Journal of Individual Psychology, 60,* 234–244.

Myers, J. E., & Sweeney, T. J. (2004c). *The wellness and habit change workbook.* Greensboro, NC: Authors.

Myers, J. E., & Sweeney, T. J. (2005a). *The Five Factor Wellness Inventory, E (Elementary School).* Greensboro, NC: Authors.

Myers, J. E., & Sweeney, T. J. (2005b). *The Five Factor Wellness Inventory, Teen (Middle School)* (3rd ed.). Greensboro, NC: Authors.

Myers, J. E., Sweeney, T. J., & Clarke, P. (2004). *Wellness in counselor education: A preliminary study.* Unpublished manuscript.

Myers, J. E., Sweeney, T. J., & Witmer, J. M. (1996a). *Manual for the Wellness Evaluation of Lifestyle.* Palo Alto, CA: Mindgarden.

Myers, J. E., Sweeney, T. J., & Witmer, J. M. (1996b). *The Wellness Evaluation of Lifestyle, Form G* (3rd ed.). Palo Alto, CA: Mindgarden.

Myers, J. E., Sweeney, T. J., & Witmer, J. M. (1998). *Workbook for the Wellness Evaluation of Lifestyle.* Greensboro, NC: Authors.

Myers, J. E., Sweeney, T. J., & Witmer, J. M. (2000a). *The Wellness Evaluation of Lifestyle, Form S* (4th ed.). Palo Alto, CA: Mindgarden.

Myers, J. E., Sweeney, T. J., & Witmer, J. M. (2000b) The Wheel of Wellness counseling for wellness: A holistic model for treatment planning. *Journal of Counseling & Development, 78,* 251–266.

Myers, J. E., Sweeney, T. J., & Witmer, J. M. (2001). Optimization of behavior: Promotion of wellness. In D. C. Locke, J. E. Myers, & E. L. Herr (Eds.), *The handbook of counseling* (pp. 641–652). Thousand Oaks, CA: Sage.

Myers, J. E., & Williard, K. (2003). Integrating spirituality into counseling and counselor training: A developmental, wellness approach. *Counseling & Values, 47,* 142–155.

Myers, J. E., Witmer, J. M., & Sweeney, T. J. (1995). *The Wellness Evaluation of Lifestyle, Form R (Revised)* (2nd ed.). Greensboro, NC: Authors.

Myrick, R. (2003). *Developmental guidance and counseling: A practical approach.* Minneapolis, MN: Educational Media Corporation.

National Association of Social Workers. (1995). *Encyclopedia of social work* (19th ed.). Washington, DC: Author.

National Center for Health Statistics. (2002). *Healthy women with disabilities: Analysis of the 1994–1995 National Health Interview Survey* (Series 10 Report). Washington, DC: Author.

National School Boards Association. (2000). Educational vital signs. *American School Board Journal.* Retrieved from http://www.asbj.com/evs/00/children.html

National Wellness Institute. (1983). *Testwell.* Stevens Point, WI: Author.

Neighbors, C., Larimer, M. E., & Lewis, M. A. (2004). Targeting misperceptions of descriptive drinking norms: Efficacy of a computer delivered personalized normative feedback intervention. *Journal of Consulting and Clinical Psychology, 72,* 434–447.

Nelson, J. K., & Coorough, C. (1994). Content analysis of the PhD versus EdD dissertation. *Journal of Experimental Education, 62,* 158–168.

Newport, F. (2001, June 4). *American attitudes toward homosexuality continue to become more tolerant: New Gallup poll shows continuation of slow, but steady, liberalization of attitudes.* Retrieved October 19, 2003, from http://sodomylaws.org/usa/usnews32.htm

Nichols, M. P., & Schwartz, R. C. (2001). *Family therapy: Concepts and methods* (5th ed.). Boston: Allyn & Bacon.

Norcross, J. C., Prochaska, J. O., & Hambrecht, M. (1991). Treating ourselves vs. treating our clients: A replication with alcohol abuse. *Journal of Substance Abuse, 3,* 123–129.

Nosek, M. A., Hughes, R. B., Swedlund, N., Taylor, H. B., & Swank, P. (2003). Self-esteem and women with disabilities. *Social Science and Medicine, 56,* 1737–1747.

Nosek, M. A., Robinson-Whelen, S., Morgan, R., Petersen, N., Taylor, H. B., & Byrne, M. (2004). *Secondary conditions in women with physical disabilities: Measurement issues, prevalence, and predictors.* Unpublished manuscript.

Oenema, A., Brug, J., & Lechner, L. (2001). Web-based tailored nutrition education: Results of a randomized controlled trial. *Health Education Research, 16,* 647–660.

Olson, D. H., Fournier, D. G., & Druckman, J. M. (1983). The Enriching and Nurturing Relationship Issues, Communication, and Happiness Inventory. In O. C. S. Tzeng (Ed.), *Measurement of love and intimate relations: Theories, scales, and applications for love development, maintenance, and dissolution* (pp. 137–143). Westport, CT: Praeger.

O'Neil, J. M. (1981). Patterns of gender role conflict and strain: Sexism and fear of femininity in men's lives. *Personnel and Guidance Journal, 60,* 203–210.

O'Neill, H. K., Gillispie, M. A., & Slobin, K. (2000). Stages of change and smoking cessation: A computer-administered intervention program for young adults. *American Journal of Health Promotion, 15,* 93–96.

Omizo, M. M., Omizo, S. A., & D'Andrea, M. J. (1992). Promoting wellness among elementary school children. *Journal of Counseling & Development, 71,* 194–198.

Paisley, P. O. (2001). Maintaining and enhancing the developmental focus in school counseling programs. *Professional School Counseling, 4,* 271–277.

Palombi, B. J. (1992). Psychometric properties of wellness instruments. *Journal of Counseling & Development, 71,* 221–225.

Pargament, K. I., Kennell, J., Hathaway, W., Grevengoed, N., Newman, J., & Jones, W. (1988). Religion and the problem-solving process: Three styles of coping. *Journal for the Scientific Study of Religion, 27,* 90–104.

Pargament, K. I., Koenig, H. G., Tarakeshwar, N., & Hahn, J. (2001). Religious struggle as a predictor of mortality among medically ill elderly patients: A 2-year longitudinal study. *Archives of Internal Medicine, 161,* 1881–1885.

Parmer, T., & Rogers, T. (1997). Religion and health: Holistic wellness from the perspective of two African American church denominations. *Counseling & Values, 42,* 55–67.

Patterson, R. J. (2000). *The assertiveness workbook*. Oakland, CA: New Harbinger.

Patton, M. Q. (1990). *Qualitative evaluation and research methods* (2nd ed.). Newbury Park, CA: Sage.

Paxton, W. E., Meeting, D. T., & Falconer, R. C. (1993). Controlling health care costs with wellness programs. *The CPA Journal, 63*, 32–36.

Pedro-Carroll, J. (2001). The promotion of wellness in children and families: Challenges and opportunities. *American Psychologist, 56*, 993–1004.

Pender, N. J., & Pender, A. R. (1987). *Health promotion in nursing practice* (2nd ed.). Norwalk, CT: Appleton & Lange.

Peters, H. J., & Farwell, G. F. (1967). *Guidance: A developmental approach.* Chicago: Rand McNally.

Peterson, C., & Seligman, M. (Eds.). (2004). *Character strengths and virtues: A handbook and classification.* Washington, DC: American Counseling Association.

Piaget, J. (1955). *The thought and language of the child.* New York: New American Library. (Original work published 1923)

Picklesimer, B. K., & Gazda, G. M. (1996). *Life-Skills Development Inventory— College Form.* Athens, GA: Authors.

Pinquart, M., & Sorensen, S. (2000). Influences of socioeconomic status, social network, and competence on subjective well being in later life: A meta-analysis. *Psychology and Aging, 15*, 187–224.

Powers, A. S., Myers, J. E., Tingle, L. R., & Powers, J. C. (2003). Wellness, perceived stress, mattering, and marital satisfaction among medical residents and their spouses: Implications for education and counseling. *The Family Journal, 11*, 1–11.

Princeton Religion Research Center. (2000). Americans remain very religious, but not necessarily in conventional ways. *Emerging Trends, 22*(1), 2–3.

Prochaska, J. O. (1994). Strong and weak principles for progressing from precontemplation to action on the basis of twelve problem behaviors. *Health Psychology, 13*, 47–51.

Prochaska, J. O., DiClemente, C. C., & Norcross, J. C. (1992). In search of how people change: Applications to addictive behaviors. *American Psychologist, 47*, 1102–1114.

Prochaska, J. O., DiClemente, C. C., Velicer, W. F., & Rossi, J. S. (1993). Standardized, individualized, interactive, and personalized self-help programs for smoking cessation. *Health Psychology, 12*, 399–405.

Prochaska, J. O., Norcross, J. C., & DiClemente, C. C. (1995). *Changing for good.* New York: Avon.

Prochaska, J. O., Velicer, W. F., Rossi, J. S., Goldstein, M. G., Marcus, B. H., Rakowski, W., et al. (1994). Stages of change and decisional balance for 12 problem behaviors. *Health Psychology, 13*, 39–46.

Purkey, W. W., & Schmidt, J. J. (1996). *Invitational counseling: A self-concept approach to professional practice.* Monterey, CA: Brooks/Cole.

Ravesloot, C., Seekins, T., & Young, O. R. (1998). Health promotion for people with chronic illness and physical disabilities: The connection between health psychology and disability prevention. *Clinical Psychology and Psychotherapy, 5*, 76–85.

Reger, B., Williams, K., Kolar, M., Smith, H., & Douglas, J. W. (2002). Implementing university-based wellness: A participatory planning approach. *Health Promotion Practice, 3,* 507–514.

Reisberg, L. (2001, February 9). Colleges replace drab gyms with sleek, playful facilities. *Chronicle of Higher Education, 47,* A38–A39.

Richards, P. S., & Bergin, A. E. (1997). *A spiritual strategy for counseling and psychotherapy.* Washington, DC: American Psychological Association.

Richardson, B. L., & June, L. (1997). Utilizing the resources of the African American church: Strategies for counseling. In C. C. Lee (Ed.), *Multicultural issues in counseling: New approaches to diversity* (2nd ed., pp. 155–170). Alexandria, VA: American Counseling Association.

Rimmer, J. H. (1999). Health promotion for people with disabilities: The emerging paradigm shift from disability prevention to prevention of secondary conditions. *Physical Therapy, 79,* 495–502.

Ring, K. (1984). *Heading towards omega.* New York: Quill/William Morrow.

Roach, L. F. (2005). *The influence of counselor education programs on counselor wellness.* Unpublished doctoral dissertation, University of Central Florida.

Roberts, B. W., & Chapman, C. N. (2000). Change in dispositional well-being and its relation to role quality: A 30-year longitudinal study. *Journal of Research in Personality, 34,* 26–41.

Roberts, D. (1983). Counseling and organization development: Another view. *International Journal of Human Resource Development, 4,* 23–28.

Roberts, G., & Stuifbergen, A. (1998). Models of health appraisal in multiple sclerosis. *Social Science & Medicine, 47,* 243–253.

Rogers, C. R. (1961). *On becoming a person.* Boston: Houghton Mifflin.

Rosenberg, M. (1985). Self-concept and psychological well-being in adolescence. In R. L. Leahy (Ed.), *The development of self* (pp. 205–246). Toronto, Ontario, Canada: Academic Press.

Rosenberg, M., & McCullough, B. C. (1981). Mattering: Inferred significance and mental health among adolescents. *Research in Community Mental Health, 2,* 163–182.

Rosen-Grandon, J. R. (2001). *The Characteristics of Marriage Inventory.* Greensboro, NC: Rosen-Grandon Associates.

Rotheram, M. J., & Phinney, J. S. (1987). Introduction: Definitions and perspectives in the study of children's ethnic socialization. In J. S. Phinney & M. J. Rotheram (Eds.), *Children's ethnic socialization* (pp. 10–31). Newbury Park, CA: Sage.

Rudolph, K. D. (2002). Gender differences in emotional responses to interpersonal stress during adolescence. *Journal of Adolescent Health, 30,* 3–13.

Rugel, R. P. (1991). Addictions treatment in groups: A review of therapeutic factors. *Small Group Research, 22,* 475–491.

Ryff, C. D. (1989). Happiness is everything, or is it? Explorations on the meaning of psychological well-being. *Journal of Personality and Social Psychology, 57,* 1069–1081.

Ryff, C. D., & Keyes, C. L. (1995). The structure of psychological well-being revisited. *Journal of Personality and Social Psychology, 69,* 719–727.

Santor, D. A., Messervey, D., & Kusumakar, V. (2000). Measuring peer pressure, popularity, and conformity in adolescent boys and girls: Predicting school performance, sexual attitudes, and substance abuse. *Journal of Youth and Adolescence, 29,* 163–182.

Schoenbaum, M., & Waidmann, T. (1997). Race, socioeconomic status and health: Accounting for race differences in health. *Journal of Gerontology, 52B,* 61–73.

Seligman, M. (1998). *Learned optimism.* New York: Pocket Books.

Seligman, M., & Csikszentmihalyi, M. (2000). Positive psychology: An introduction. *The American Psychologist, 55,* 5–14.

Selye, H. (1976). *The stress of life.* New York: McGraw-Hill.

September, A. N., McCarrey, M., Baranowsky, A., Parent, C., & Schindler, D. (2001). The relation between well being, imposter feelings, and gender role orientation among Canadian university students. *Journal of Social Psychology, 141,* 218–232.

Settle, J. E. (2002). Diet and essential fatty acids. In S. Shannon (Ed.), *Complementary and alternative therapies in mental health* (pp. 93–103). New York: Academic Press.

Sexton, T. (2001). Evidence-based counseling intervention programs: Practicing "best practices." In D. C. Locke, J. E. Myers, & E. H. Herr (Eds.), *The handbook of counseling* (pp. 499–512). Thousand Oaks, CA: Sage.

Shannon, G. W., & Pyle, G. F. (1993). *Disease and medical care in the United States: A medical atlas of the twentieth century.* New York: Macmillan.

Shannon, S. (Ed.). (2002). *Complementary and alternative therapies in mental health.* New York: Academic Press.

Shapiro, F. (2002). EMDR treatment: Overview and integration. In F. Shapiro (Ed.), *EMDR as an integrative psychotherapy approach: Experts of diverse orientations explore the paradigm prism* (pp. 27–55). Washington, DC: American Psychological Association.

Sharpe, M. J., & Heppner, P. P. (1991). Gender role, gender-role conflict, and psychological well-being in men. *Journal of Counseling Psychology, 38,* 323–330.

Shek, D. T. (1995). Marital quality and psychological well-being of married adults in a Chinese context. *Journal of Genetic Psychology, 156,* 45–56.

Sheldon, K., Frederickson, K. R., Rathunde, K., Csikszentmihalyi, M., & Haidt, J. (2000). *Positive psychology manifesto.* Retrieved May 17, 2004, from http://www.psych.upenn.edu/seligman/akumalmanifesto.htm

Sheldon, K. M., & King, L. (2001). Why positive psychology is necessary. *American Psychologist, 56,* 216–217.

Shurts, M. (2004). *The relationships among marital messages received, marital attitudes, relationship self-efficacy, and wellness among never-married traditional-aged undergraduate students.* Unpublished doctoral dissertation, University of North Carolina at Greensboro.

Shurts, M., & Myers, J. E. (2005). *The relationships among liking, love, and wellness: Implications for college student romances.* Manuscript submitted for publication.

Siegenthaler, K. L. (1996). Leisure and the elderly. *Parks and Recreation, 311,* 1–18.

Simon, H. (2003). *About stress.* Retrieved December 20, 2003, from http://www.reducestress.com/stressInformation.htm

Sinclair, S. (2001). *Objectification experiences, sociocultural attitudes toward appearance, objectified body consciousness, and wellness in heterosexual Caucasian women.* Unpublished doctoral dissertation, University of North Carolina at Greensboro.

Sinclair, S. L., & Myers, J. E. (2004). Weighty issues: The relationship between objectified body consciousness and wellness in a group of college women. *Journal of College Counseling, 7,* 151–160.

Smith, J. P., & Kington, R. (1997). Demographic and economic correlates of health in old age. *Demography, 34,* 159–170.

Smith, S. L., Myers, J. E., & Hensley, L. G. (2002). Putting more life into life career courses: The benefits of a holistic wellness model. *Journal of College Counseling, 5,* 90–96.

Snyder, C., & Lopez, A. (2001). *Handbook of positive psychology.* Oxford, England: Oxford University Press.

Spence, J. T., Helmreich, R. L., & Holahan, C. K. (1979). Negative and positive components of psychological masculinity and femininity and their relationships to self-reports of neurotic and acting our behaviors. *Journal of Personality and Social Psychology, 37,* 1673–1682.

SPSS Inc. (2003). *Amos (Version 5).* Chicago: Author.

Spurgeon, S. (2002). *The relationship among ethnic identity, self-esteem, and wellness in African American males.* Unpublished doctoral dissertation, University of North Carolina at Greensboro.

Spurgeon, S. L., & Myers, J. E. (2004). *Racial identity, self-esteem, and wellness in African American male college students.* Manuscript submitted for publication.

Squires, D. D., & Hester, R. K. (2002). Development of a computer-based, brief intervention for drinkers: The increasing role for computers in the assessment and treatment of addictive behaviors. *The Behavior Therapist, 25,* 59–65.

Steigerwald, F. (2000). *The relationship of family-of-origin structure and family conflict resolution tactics to holistic wellness in college-age offspring.* Unpublished doctoral dissertation, Ohio University.

Steiner, H., Pavelski, R., Pitts, T., & McQuivey, R. (1998). The Juvenile Wellness and Health Survey (JWHS-76): A school based screening instrument for general and mental health in high school students. *Child Psychiatry and Human Development, 29,* 141–154.

Steptoe, S. (2003, October 27). Ready, set, relax! *Time, 162,* 38–41.

Strawbridge, W. J., Wallhagen, M. I., & Cohen, R. D. (2002). Successful aging and well-being: Self-rated compared with Rowe and Kahn. *Gerontologist, 42,* 727–733.

Stuifbergen, A. K., & Rogers, S. (1997). Health promotion: An essential component of rehabilitation for persons with chronic disabling conditions. *Advances in Nursing Science, 19,* 1.

Sultanoff, B. A. (2002). The environment. In S. Shannon (Ed.), *Complementary and alternative therapies in mental health* (pp. 497–516). New York: Academic Press.

Sussman, S., Dent, C. W., Stacy, A. W., Burton, D., & Flay, B. R. (1995). Psychosocial predictors of health risk factors in adolescents. *Journal of Pediatric Psychology, 20,* 91–108.

Sweeney, T. J. (1995a). Accreditation, credentialing, professionalization: The role of specialties. *Journal of Counseling & Development, 74,* 117–125.

Sweeney, T. (1995b). Adlerian theory. In D. Cappuzi & D. Gross (Eds.), *Counseling and psychotherapy* (pp. 113–150). Columbus, OH: Merrill.

Sweeney, T. J. (1998). *Adlerian counseling: A practitioners approach* (4th ed.). Philadelphia, PA: Taylor & Francis.

Sweeney, T. J. (2001). Counseling: Historical origins and philosophical roots. In D. C. Locke, J. E. Myers, & E. H. Herr (Eds.), *The handbook of counseling* (pp. 3–27). Thousand Oaks, CA: Sage.

Sweeney, T. J., & Myers, J. E. (2005). Optimizing human development: A new paradigm for helping . In A. Ivey, M. B. Ivey, J. E. Myers, & T. J. Sweeney (Eds.), *Developmental strategies for helpers* (2nd ed., pp. 39–68). Amherst, MA: Microtraining.

Sweeney, T. J., & Witmer, J. M. (1991). Beyond social interest: Striving toward optimum health and wellness. *Individual Psychology, 47,* 527–540.

Tanigoshi, H. (2004). *The effectiveness of individual counseling on the wellness of police officers.* Unpublished doctoral dissertation, University of New Orleans, Louisiana.

Tatar, M., & Myers, J. E. (2004). *Wellness of children in Israel and the United States: A preliminary examination of culture and well-being.* Manuscript submitted for publication.

Taylor, J. R., & Turner, R. J. (2001). A longitudinal study of the role and significance of mattering to others for depressive symptoms. *Journal of Health and Social Behavior, 42,* 310–325.

Terenzini, P. T., Rendon, L. I., Upcraft, M. L., Millar, S. B., Allison, K. W., Gregg, P. L., & Jalomo, R. (1994). The transition to college: Diverse students, diverse stories. *Research in Higher Education, 35,* 57–73.

Thompson, C. L., & Rudolph, L. B. (1999). *Counseling children.* New York: Wadsworth.

Thompson, T. G. (2003). *Innovation in Prevention Awards Gala.* Retrieved August 31, 2004, from http://www.hhs.gov/news/speech/2003/031210.html

Tjaden, P., & Thoennes, N. (2000). *Findings from the national violence against women survey.* Washington, DC: U.S. Department of Justice.

Towey, K., & Fleming, M. (2003). *Healthy Youth 2010.* Washington DC: American Medical Association.

Travis J. W. (1972). *The wellness/illness continuum.* Mill Valley, CA: Author.

Travis, J. W., & Ryan, R. (1981). *The wellness workbook.* Berkeley, CA: Ten Speed Press.

Travis, J. W., & Ryan, R. (1988). *The wellness workbook* (2nd ed.). Berkeley, CA: Ten Speed Press.

Turner, R. J., & Noh, S. (1988). Physical disability and depression: A longitudinal analysis. *Journal of Health and Social Behavior, 29*, 23–37.

Tyre, P. (2003, November 3). Reading, writing, recess. *Newsweek, 66*.

United Nations International Children's Fund. (1989). *UNICEF convention on the rights of the child*. New York: Author.

United Nations International Children's Fund. (1996). *UNICEF mission statement*. New York: Author.

U.S. Census Bureau. (2000a). *2000 Census counts of adolescents*. Washington, DC: Author.

U.S. Census Bureau. (2000b). *National population estimates: Characteristics*. Washington, DC: Government Printing Office.

U.S. Census Bureau. (2000c). *Total population by race, Hispanic origin, and nativity*. Retrieved October 25, 2003, from http://www.census.gov/population/www/projections/natsum-T5.html

U.S. Census Bureau. (2001). *Age 2000*. Washington, DC: U.S. Government Printing Office.

U.S. Department of Commerce. (1996). *Current population reports: Population projections of the United States by age, sex, race, and Hispanic origin: 1995–2050*. Retrieved October 25, 2003, from http://www.census.gov/prod/1/pop/p25-1130/p251130.pdf

U.S. Department of Education. (2002). National Center for Education Statistics. *Profile of undergraduates in U.S. postsecondary institutions: 1999–2000* (NCES 2002-168). Washington, DC: U.S. Government Printing Office.

U.S. Department of Health and Human Services. (2000). *Healthy People 2010* (2nd ed.). Washington, DC: U.S. Government Printing Office.

U.S. Department of Health and Human Services. (2003). *Prevention makes common "cents."* Washington, DC: U.S. Government Printing Office. Retrieved September 1, 2004 from http://aspe.hhs.gov/health/prevention/

U.S. Department of Health and Human Services, Centers for Disease Control and Prevention, National Center for Chronic Disease Prevention and Health Promotion. (2004). *Fact sheet: Actual causes of death in the United States, 2000*. Retrieved May 13, 2004, from http://www.cdc.gov/nccdphp/factsheets/death_causes2000.htm

U.S. Department of Health and Human Services, National Institutes of Health. (2003). *Statistics related to overweight and obesity* (NIH Publication NO. 03-41.58). Retrieved May 13, 2004, from http://www.niddk.nih.gov/statistics/index.htm

U.S. Department of Health and Human Services, Substance Abuse and Mental Health Services Administration. (1999). *Prevention research: Worksite health care costs/claims*. Retrieved May 13, 2004, from http://workplace.samhsa.gov/WPResearch/Costs/HCcosts.html

Vandell, D. L., & Hembree, S. E. (1994). Peer social status and friendship: Independent contributors to children's social and academic adjustment. *Merrill-Palmer Quarterly, 40*, 461–477.

Van de Vijver, F. J. R., & Hambleton, R. K. (1996). Translating tests: Some practical guidelines. *European Psychologist, 1*, 89–99.

Vanderbleek, L. (2005). *Couple play as a predictor of couple bonding, physical health, and emotional health.* Unpublished doctoral dissertation, University of Central Florida.

Vecchione, T. (1999). *An examination of the relationship between career development and holistic wellness among college students.* Unpublished doctoral dissertation, Ohio University.

Velicer, W. F., Prochaska, J. O., Fava, J. L., Norman, G. J., & Redding, C. A. (1998). *Detailed overview of the transtheoretical model.* Retrieved May 17, 2004, from http://www.uri.edu/research/cprc/TTM/detailedoverview.htm/

Vickio, C. J., Mangili, L., Keller, B. Y., & Colvin, C. C. (1994). Promoting wellness: An enrichment day for faculty and staff. *Journal of College Student Development, 35,* 226–227.

Villalba, J. A. (2003). A psychoeducational group for limited-English proficient Latino/Latina children. *Journal for Specialists in Group Work, 28,* 261–276.

Vontress, C. E., Johnson, J. A., & Epp, L. R. (1999). *Cross-cultural counseling: A casebook.* Alexandria, VA: American Counseling Association.

Walker, E. A. (2000). Spiritual support in relation to community violence exposure, aggressive outcomes, and psychological adjustment among inner-city adolescents. *Dissertation Abstracts International, 61*(6-B), 3295.

Walters, S. T. (2000). In praise of feedback: An effective intervention for college students who are heavy drinkers. *Journal of American College Health, 48,* 235–238.

Walters, S. T., Bennett, M. E., & Miller, J. H. (2000). Reducing alcohol use in college students: A controlled trial of two brief interventions. *Journal of Drug Education, 30,* 361–372.

Ware, J. W., & Sherborne, C. D. (1992). The MOS 36-item short-form health survey (SF-36): I. Conceptual framework and item selection. *Medical Care, 80,* 473–483.

Waterman, A. S. (1993). Two conceptions of happiness: Contrasts of personal expressiveness (eudaimonia) and hedonic enjoyment. *Journal of Personality and Social Psychology, 64,* 678–691.

Watts, R. E. (2004, Spring). Are we in danger of losing the identity that we never clearly defined? *The CACREP Connection, 1,* 7.

Webster, S. (2005). *Toward a lexicon for holistic health: An empirical analysis of theories of health, wellness, and spirituality.* Unpublished doctoral dissertation, University of Florida.

Weil, A. (1999). *Breathing: The master key to self-healing.* Tucson, AZ: Author.

Weil, E., Wachterman, M., McCarthy, E. P., Davis, R. B., O'Day, B., Jezzoni, L. I., & Wee, C. C. (2002). Obesity among adults with disabling conditions. *Journal of the American Medical Association, 288,* 1265–1268.

Werner, E. E. (1989, April). Children of the garden island. *Scientific American,* 106–111.

Wilber, K. (1999). *The collected works of Ken Wilber: Vol. 3.* Boston: Shambhala.

Wilber, K. (2000, May). A spirituality that transforms. *Tools for transformation newsletter.* Retrieved May 30, 2004, from http://www.trans4mind.com/counterpoint/Wilber.shtml

Wilbur, N., Mitra, M., Walker, D. K., Allen, D., Meyers, A. R., & Tupper, P. (2002). Disability as a public health issue: Findings and reflections from the Massachusetts Survey of Secondary Conditions. *The Milbank Quarterly, 81,* 393–421.

Wilkinson, D. (1993). Family ethnicity in America. In H. P. McAdoo (Ed.), *Family ethnicity: Strength in diversity* (pp. 15–59). Newbury Park, CA: Sage.

Williams, D. (2005). *The relationship among athletic identity, sport commitment, time in sport participation, social support, and wellness in college student athletes.* Unpublished doctoral dissertation, University of North Carolina at Greensboro.

Williams, D. R. (1990). Socioeconomic differentials in health: A review and redirection. *Social Psychology Quarterly, 53,* 81–99.

Williams, D. R., Lavizzo-Mourey, R., & Warren, R. (1994). The concept of race and health status in America. *Public Health Reports, 109,* 26–41.

Williamson, I. R. (2000). Internalized homophobia and health issues affecting lesbians and gay men. *Health Education Research, 15,* 97–107.

Wilson, K. (2004). *Wellness as an outcome measure in counseling university students with identified problem behaviors.* Unpublished doctoral dissertation, University of Technology, Sydney, Australia.

Witmer, J. M. (1985). *Pathways to personal growth.* Muncie, IN: Accelerated Development.

Witmer, J. M., & Sweeney, T. J. (1992). A holistic model for wellness and prevention over the lifespan. *Journal of Counseling & Development, 71,* 140–148.

Witmer, J. M., & Sweeney, T. J. (1998). Toward wellness: The goal of counseling. In T. J. Sweeney (Ed.), *Adlerian counseling: A practitioner's approach* (4th ed.). Muncie, IN: Accelerated Development.

Witmer, J. M., Sweeney, T. J., & Myers, J. E. (1993). *The Wellness Evaluation of Lifestyle, Form O (Original).* Greensboro, NC: Authors.

Witmer, J. M., Sweeney, T. J., & Myers, J. E. (1998). *The Wheel of Wellness.* Greensboro, NC: Authors.

Witmer, J. M., & Young, M. E. (1996). Preventing counselor impairment: A wellness approach. *Journal of Humanistic Education and Development, 34,* 141–155.

Wolinsky, F. D., Wyrwich, K. W., Babu, A. N., Kroenke, K., & Tierney, W. M. (2003). Age, aging, and the sense of control among older adults: A longitudinal reconsideration. *Journals of Gerontology: Series B, Psychological Sciences and Social Sciences, 58B*(4), S212–S220.

Woodard, D. B., & Komives, S. R. (2003). Shaping the future. In S. R. Komives, D. B. Woodard, & Associates (Eds.), *Student services: A handbook for the profession* (pp. 637–655). San Francisco: Jossey-Bass.

Woodhill, B. M., & Samuels, C. A. (2003). Positive and negative androgyny and their relationship with psychological health and well-being. *Sex Roles, 48,* 555–565.

World Health Organization. (1958). *Constitution of the World Health Organization.* Geneva, Switzerland: Author.

World Health Organization. (1964). *Basic documents* (15th ed.). Geneva, Switzerland: Author.

Wright, A. (1998). Counseling skills: Part I. Can you live without them? *Industrial and Commercial Training, 30,* 107–109.

Wyker, J. (2002). Spiritual psychotherapy. In S. Shannon (Ed.), *Complementary and alternative therapies in mental health* (pp. 287–309). New York: Academic Press.

Wyman, P. A., Sandler, I. N., Wolchik, S. A., & Nelson, K. (2000). Resilience as cumulative competence promotion and stress protection: Theory and intervention. In D. Cicchetti, J. Rappaport, I. Sandler, & R. Weissberg (Eds.), *The promotion of wellness in children and adolescents* (pp. 133–184). Washington, DC: Child Welfare League of America Press.

Yelland, C., & Tiggemann, M. (2003). Muscularity and the gay ideal: Body dissatisfaction and disordered eating in homosexual men. *Eating Behaviors, 4,* 107–116.

Yen, W. M., & Henderson, D. L. (2002). Professional standards related to using large-scale state assessments in decisions for individual students. *Measurement and Evaluation in Counseling and Development, 35,* 132–143.

Yeung, A., & Chow, E. (2002). Correlates of subjective well-being of Chinese elderly in Hong Kong. *Journal of Social Work Research and Evaluation, 1,* 165–184.

Young, J. S., Cashwell, C. S., & Shcherbakova, J. (2000). The moderating relationship of spirituality on negative life events and psychological adjustment. *Counseling and Values, 45,* 49–57.

Young, M. E. (2004). *Learning the art of helping* (3rd ed.). Upper Saddle River, NJ: Prentice Hall.

Author Index

A

AARP, 99, 100
Abrams, L. S., 131
Adams, K., 61
Adams, T. B., 79, 84, 102
Adelman, J. U., 47, 93
Adler, A., 11, 15, 17, 18, 26, 34, 255, 256
Ainslie, R. C., 227
Akos, P., 231
Alexander, T. M., 185
Allison, N., 204
Alves-Martins, M., 227
Amaral, V., 227
Amato, P. R., 61
American College Personnel Association, 246
American Counseling Association, 167, 190
American Educational Research Association, 118
American Heritage Dictionary of the English Language, 8
American Medical Association, 67
American Psychiatric Association, 127, 151, 210, 217
American Psychological Association, 101
Amery, S., 45
Amrein, A. T., 227
Andersen, A. E., 133
Andresen, J., 201
Ansbacher, H. L., 11, 16, 17, 34
Ansbacher, R. R., 11, 17, 34
Ansuini, C. G., 68, 70, 71
Antonovsky, A., 79
Archer, J., 9, 78, 79

Tables are indicated by t following page numbers.

Ardell, D., 11
Armstrong, K. L., 111
Association for Assessment in Counseling, 118
August, D., 233
Austin, J. T., 117

B

Babu, A. N., 101
Bachman, J. G., 77
Bagley, C., 132
Baker, S. B., 227
Baltes, M. M., 89
Baltes, P. B., 89
Balzer, W. K., 257
Baranowsky, A., 128, 130, 131, 132
Barba, B. E., 239
Barbarin, O. A., 61
Bates, J. M., 248
Bechtel, A., 51, 80, 81, 85
Bell, I., 154
Bellino, L. E., 85
Bem, S., 127
Bender, F. L., 165
Benjamin, S., 182
Bennett, M. E., 85
Berger, E., 63
Bergin, A. E., 213
Berliner, D. C., 227
Berry, J., 255, 257, 258
Bezner, J. R., 79, 84, 102
Bockting, W. O., 127
Bollwark, J., 118
Booth, A., 61
Booth, C. S., 45, 52, 129
Borders, L. D., 228
Bowling, A., 101

Subject Index

Names of researchers and research organizations are in
a separate index. Tables and figures are indicated by t
and f following page numbers.

J

K

L

M